What's It All About?

I would like to thank all my family and friends for their wonderful support and help with the book. I would also like to thank Barbara Nash and Paul Forty for helping me get it all just right; and Jake Lingwood, Hannah Macdonald, Hannah Telfer, Di Riley and Sarah Bennie at Ebury Press. Finally, thanks to my special fans Tracey Fairweather, Sarah Evans and Stephen Munns.

cillablack

What's It All About?

EBURY
PRESS

First published in Great Britain in 2003

10 9 8 7 6 5 4 3 2 1

First published by Ebury Press
Random House, 20 Vauxhall Bridge Road, London SW1V 2SA

Random House Australia (Pty) Limited
20 Alfred Street, Milsons Point, Sydney, New South Wales 2061, Australia

Random House New Zealand Limited
18 Poland Road, Glenfield, Auckland 10, New Zealand

Random House South Africa (Pty) Limited
Endulini, 5A Jubilee Road, Parktown 2193, South Africa

The Random House Group Limited Reg. No. 954009

www.randomhouse.co.uk

A CIP catalogue record for this book is available from the British Library.

Cover and endpaper design by Two Associates
Text and photo design by seagulls
Photographs © credited copyright holders

'Liverpool Lullaby'
Words by S. Kelly, © Logo Songs Ltd. All rights reserved. Used by permission.

ISBN 0 09189036 5

Papers used by Ebury Press are natural, recyclable products
made from wood grown in sustainable forests.

Printed and bound in Great Britain by Clays Ltd, St Ives plc

What's It All About? is also available on audio cassette, ISBN: 1 85686791 9

contents

For Bobby

partone

1

Left Footer

They branded us 'Left Footers'; we called them 'Proddy Dogs'. All us Irish Catholics lived on Scottie (that would be Scotland Road to anyone from out of Liverpool), and all the Protestants lived on Netherfield Road across to the east, with Great Homer Street running parallel down the middle. Inevitably there were street gangs, and it could get pretty rough. There was always a lot of posturing and name-calling and, if you were really unlucky, it could end in push-shoves, digs in the ribs and fisticuffs. The divisions between Catholic and Protestant were as strong as in Northern Ireland – the Protestants against the Catholics and *vice versa*. But on Saturdays everyone, whatever their religion, went to do their shopping at the butchers (we always went to Wood's), the grocers, the greengrocers and bakers on Great Homer Street, buying family favourites like boiled ham and pigs' feet – so once a week the two sides would come face to face. We kept a respectful distance from each other, but of course on significant dates, such as St Patrick's Day on 17 March and the Orange Parade on 12 July, which I loved watching, there was more friction than normal.

Fortunately I was a very sporty child, and I always thought if a gang did pick on me, I could easily outrun them. Once, though, on 12 July, after watching the Lodge parade down London Road, I had just left a busy main street and entered a quiet, deserted side road, when a gang of five eleven-year-old girls – the same age as me – fell in step behind me. I didn't need to look twice to realise they meant trouble.

'What d'you think?' the leader was saying as they came into earshot. '*Is* she? Is she one of them? I *bet* she's one of them!'

She was a big, brawny red-head, and the other four girls, all mousey-haired, were not exactly tiddlers. Sure I was in for a hiding, I glanced up and down the street, desperate for an adult – anyone who might intervene and say, 'Oi, you lot, get home – yer mam's got cake!' but there was nobody.

I decided this was a case of flight rather than fight, and made a run for it. But they'd got too close, and this time I knew my skinny long legs weren't going to save me.

'She *is* one of them!' the leader roared, egging the others on.

The chase ended moments later. Having wrenched me to a standstill by one of my sleeves, the gang circled me. I swivelled this way and that, giving one last desperate look up and down the street, then, seeing nobody, I clenched my fists into tight, defensive balls.

Their mutterings, 'Yeah – she's one of them!', were louder now.

They grabbed me, poked me in the ribs, shoved me backwards and pinned me against the wall. I had tried to stand up to them, but my fists felt like cotton wool.

'You *are* one of them, aren't you?' their leader kept taunting me, her hot breath drizzling on my cheeks. 'You *are* a Proddy Dog.'

But I wasn't – I was a Left Footer. Her question had implied that she was a Catholic, too – so what should I say? Maybe it was just a trick and I'd get a beating anyway. I decided to tell the truth, take the punishment, and try to give as good as I got. Better that, I reasoned, than tell a lie and be chastised and called a coward by our priest in confession the next day.

'I'm a *Catholic*,' I cried out, the bold note I had injected into my voice camouflaging my fear and trembling.

The finger-jabbing stopped. Suddenly. Just like that. They exchanged frowns with each other, then the uncertain grimaces on their faces underwent a dramatic change.

'Jesus, Mary and sweet Joseph!' one of them whispered. 'Let her go, Bernadette. She's one of us. Leave her alone.'

They unpinned me and I stood breathless and wobbling as they drifted off laughing, their arms flung around each other's shoulders. My heart was in my mouth. Slowly it began relocating to my chest. One of the gang – the smallest of the ruffians, the girl with the most freckles – had the cheek to turn and give me a friendly farewell wave. I was tempted to run after her and give her a right thump, but even then, as a skinny eleven-year-old, I knew when to get out. So instead I hurried onwards down the still-deserted street towards the safety of my home in Scottie Road.

~

Scotland Road, the main road out to East Lancs, was about a mile long. With its huge Irish-Catholic population and a pub on every street corner, it had a bad reputation as the roughest residential part of town, but I felt totally safe playing in the streets there as a child, and later as a teenage girl walking home on my own after dark. The Church and Family were the foundation of our life, and we all grew up aware of what it meant to be good neighbours, good Samaritans, and a help to other people. Family priests had a great influence on adults' as well as children's behaviour. We all went to confession, said our rosary as a penance for venial sins, and lived in fear of committing a mortal sin and being damned or excommunicated. People in our area either went off the rails in a major way or stuck to them.

Thousands of Liverpool children were evacuated to the countryside during the Second World War, but many families, including ours, decided to stay together in the city. Fortunately, by the time I was born on Thursday, 27 May 1943, the worst of Liverpool's bombing was over. I was too young to be aware of D Day in 1944, or VE (Victory in Europe) Day in 1945, but, like most kids born during the war, I was very aware of rationing and ration books. The coupons we got only allowed us two ounces of sweets and were gone in a flash, usually at Saturday morning pictures. In between I used to eat the squares of gelatine that our mams used for making jellies. I loved stretching them until they became about a foot long.

Home was our flat at 380 Scottie Road, above George Murray's barber's shop, behind a branch of Midland Bank and next door to Mrs Lee's Chinese laundry. The bank was the landlord, and we rented the flat from Mr Murray. Despite the semi-derelict state of some of the bomb-damaged buildings around us, the flat was not short of space. I lived there with me mam, dad and two older brothers, George and John. When I was born, George was seven and John was three. When I was about five, little Allan joined us – he was actually a cousin, my Auntie Ann's baby, and me mam and dad adopted him at nine months old. Allan was an angel baby with perfect blond curls; he got a lot of attention, and I was definitely put out at losing my cherished 'baby of the family' position. Auntie Ann always came round at ours at weekends (she used to do my nails for me) and although it was meant to be a secret that she was Allan's mam, I found out quite early on.

Our kitchen-cum-living room was on the first floor, and the bedrooms were above that, along with another very large room which we used as a living room. This room, the best, was actually as large as the lounge of the house I live in now. It was certainly big enough for the piano that my father bought from the North End Music Store (NEMS), the Epstein family's furniture store in Everton, and spacious enough for all our family, friends and neighbours to get together on special occasions and Saturday nights. Making your own music was the norm in the fifties for people like us who couldn't afford television sets.

Not only were the rooms of our flat really large – but on the upper floor there were other rooms that we didn't even occupy. These were always left empty, though, because we were not allowed to rent them out. I loved singing up there, because there was an echo that amplified my voice!

Our home was full of music when I was a kid. We listened to records, and always had the radio on – I remember listening to Victor Sylvester on Monday mornings if I was ill and kept at home from school. Me mam, bless her, was named Priscilla, but she was known as 'big Cilla' after I was born, and I was dubbed 'little Cilla'. She was always singing, especially on Monday mornings, which was washday in our home; and me dad, whose name was John, was forever playing his mouth organ when he wasn't tending his budgerigars. Me mam had an amazingly high voice and she loved opera, especially 'One Fine Day' from *Madama Butterfly*. Arias from that, and her renderings of 'Chirri Chirri Bee', were second to none.

Irish, with thick jet-black hair on which he used Brylcreem, me dad had a strong, guttural Liverpool accent. Handsome and a bit of a stoic, he was nine years older than me mam, and before becoming a docker he'd worked in construction for eight years in London and helped to build the Dorchester Hotel in Park Lane. Even though he was a docker, he was a very dapper man who loved his waistcoats, and he never missed going to London for the Derby every year. Down at the docks, his workmates called him 'Shiner', because his boots were always so beautifully polished you could see your face in them.

He was a very quiet, shy man until he was in the company of men. He was very old-fashioned in that respect, but, like many Scousers, he could be a bit of a lad at his favourite pub, Fitzie's, on Bostock Street. Women never went to the pubs with the fellers in those days. It was very much a man's thing. Once inside, Dad and his mates would buy a round, then it was time for blokeish digs in the ribs, leg-pulls, and risqué jokes, most of which were considered too filthy, unfit for women's ears!

After the men had all had a few jars on a Saturday night, it was often back to our place for a 'jars out and a singsong' when the pubs turned out. They'd bring home shandy for me mam and Guinness for themselves. They'd also bring in pigs' feet and fish 'n' chips. Dad would then play his mouth organ and everybody would do a turn. My mam was very into

Country and Western as well as opera, and her party piece was 'T For Texas And T For Tennessee'.

I was always in bed when they came home, but I used to get up and sit on the back stairs while all the furniture, including the kitchen table, was being moved to make space for the Irish jigs, knees-up and group renderings of 'Danny Boy' and 'When Irish Eyes Are Smiling'. I loved crouching there, watching and listening and, from the age of three onwards, I could not wait to do my turn. Then, when I was five (it may have been around the time that Allan joined our family), on one magical night that I've never forgotten, everything changed. Instead of the usual: 'Get back to bed, girl', and being tucked back into bed with 'Off to sleep – church in the morning', somebody took me downstairs, stood me on the kitchen table, and said, 'All right, Queen, *you* do something.'

Standing on that table, in my creased winceyette nightie, looking down instead of up for once at the expectant faces of all those grown-ups, was the most marvellous feeling in the whole world. I was in my element. Then, after I'd done my turn – an Al Jolson number because our Georgie loved Al Jolson and Frank Sinatra – I basked in the adulation and applause. From then on, I never looked back. I'd be up there on every occasion singing songs such as 'My Old Man Said "Follow The Van" ' and loving every moment of it. I'd also do anything I could to make them laugh.

From then onwards that table was my stage, and the grown-ups squashed up together on the settee and armchairs, sipping their shandies and Guinness, were my audience. Even now, forty years on, I relive those moments.

~

The first present little girls were given in those days was a doll, followed by a doll's pram. The madonna or 'mother' thing was instilled in us almost as soon as we could toddle, so I was always walking aimlessly up and down Scottie Road with my dolly in her pram. One Saturday, when I was about six or seven, I was bored with all this and took myself off for a much longer walk. I must have got at least a mile, a long way at that age, before a neighbour spotted me.

'What are *you* doing here, little Cilla?' she said. 'Where's your mam?'

'I'm taking my dolly for a walk,' I muttered innocently.

She took me home.

I will never forget the look of relief on me mam's face when she saw us coming. She'd obviously been frantic and thought she'd lost me for ever.

None of us kids had gardens to play in, but we didn't feel deprived because we didn't know any different. The streets were our playground and, apart from the occasional fret when one of us – usually me! – wandered off and got lost, nobody seemed to worry about us being abducted. On sunny days babies were parked outside their houses in prams and, as the real thing was so much more interesting than any doll, I was forever kidnapping baby and pram and taking them for a walk. Today, if a mother found a baby missing from its pram, she would go into instant panic mode and ring the police, but not then. The mothers just used to say, 'Who's taken the baby for a walk?' and invariably it was me.

~

My school, which my brothers also attended, was St Anthony's, a Roman Catholic school run by nuns in Newsham Street, just off Scottie Road. I remember my first day at school very clearly. I hated it. As the only girl in a family full of boys I was a spoiled and rather clingy child, and I couldn't understand why my mother was abandoning me in this strange building. A pint-sized drama-queen, I kept clinging to me mam's skirts and crying pitifully, 'Please don't leave me. I don't want to go!' Then, when Mam did manage to wrestle free and disappear, worse was to follow. One of my plaits came undone and I burst into tears all over again because I was too frightened to ask the teacher to re-plait it for me. I couldn't wait to get out of there and get back to messing about on the streets.

Mam's best friend was a lady called Vera Davis, and her son Billy was my best friend in those days. Billy was fair-haired and a great looker. He was always very close to his mother and never minded holding her hand out in the street. Whenever we played our favourite dressing-up games he insisted on being the bride, and always wanted me to be the bridesmaid! I didn't think this was strange. I thought he was terrific. If anybody had ever tried to hint that his behaviour was odd for a boy – then or later – I would not have had any of it. I didn't know anything about what it meant to be 'a bit of a soft quilt', and I totally loved him for how he was and cherished him as my best friend.

'Let's play brides and bridesmaids,' he'd say. 'Oh, *yes*,' I'd always reply, nipping indoors for pieces of old curtain for his dress and mine, and old beads, and some discarded netting for his veil. 'You look *luvvvvely*, Billy,' I'd coo when he was all dressed up and staggering around in a pair of me mam's old high-heeled shoes.

'Just like the brides we see at the church?' he'd ask anxiously.

'Just like them,' I'd reassure him, lovingly straightening his veil.

~

St Anthony's was a very working-class school, with only one teacher and a music tutor for forty-eight pupils, and our parents had to give donations for the privilege of sending us there. They also had to pay for our books and pencils, but there was no school uniform. The only stipulation was that we had to wear navy-blue knickers for PE, which had a pocket in them for your handkerchief, and elasticated legs that came down to our knees. I hated them! We also wore liberty bodices that buttoned all the way down the front and then looped on to our skirts to prevent them riding up.

Although Sister Marie Julie, our headmistress and teacher, was a tiny woman who looked like a baby penguin in spectacles, she terrorised us into behaving ourselves. Girls and boys were taught together until the age of eleven, and then they were separated and even had different playgrounds.

Once I'd settled in, I adored school, especially the music class. I was popular with the other kids because I was a natural show-off who was always playing the fool, thinking up practical jokes and making them laugh.

A Protestant school in nearby Penrhyn Street used to run a play centre after school, which Catholic children were encouraged to attend, and I loved going there while our tea was being made because they had talent competitions – singing contests – every week, at which the prize was sixpence. I could hardly reach the microphone, one of those big, heavy jobs, but I used to get up there and say, 'My name's Priscilla Maria Veronica White and I'm going to sing …'

When I was about seven all the other kids were still warbling 'On the Good Ship Lollipop', but not me. I was doing Dean Martin songs which I had learned from the wireless. I particularly remember (although this must have been later, when I was about ten) singing 'When the moon hits your eye like a big piece of pie …' This was from the Dean Martin hit, 'That's *Amore*' – the real words were 'pizza pie', but I thought they were 'piece of pie' because we never had pizzas in Scottie Road and hadn't a clue what they were!

I won the sixpence prize-money so often at these singing contests that the headmaster, obviously thinking that all my friends were voting for me, decided to change the rules. He put the kids who were performing in his office out of sight, and rigged up the microphone in there. From then on, we were no longer allowed to say our names, which was a blessing in disguise for me. In the area I grew up, having a posh name like Priscilla was always an embarrassment! After the change of rules, we had to remain anonymous and say, 'I'm number six and I'm going to sing …' It didn't make any difference, though. I still won the competition and the sixpence every week!

My family never pushed me to enter anything, but I was always the first in the queue to get up on the stage. Eager for any opportunity to be in the spotlight and be the star of the evening, I also sang at the Dockers' Christmas Party shows, where kids were allowed to do a turn. But after I won three times in a row, I was banned so as to give someone else a chance. For me it was one of those rare occasions when it didn't pay to be first, and I was mortified.

When I was about twelve, my only thought when I was coming home from school was the echo in our new bathroom! This new echo was sheer joy for me, because when my father first rented our flat, it didn't have a bathroom. The only washing facility for bath nights, always a very steamy Friday-night event, was a tin bath in front of the kitchen fire which me mam filled with buckets of hot water heated on the stove. When my brothers and I were about seven or eight, we went once a week to the 'wash-all-overs', the public baths in Burroughs Gardens. That was bliss – and there was an echo there too! You could lock the door on your own bath-room, stretch out full length, bask in the steaming hot water, and linger for hours. I loved singing in there, with the echo amplifying my voice.

Then came the wonderful and unforgettable day when our flat was upgraded and we became the proud possessors of *our own bathroom*. It took me all of twenty seconds to discover that the echo in there worked wonders on my voice. From then on, I lived for the moments when I could belt out my favourite numbers in there.

Once inside our flat, I'd drop my things and head for the mirror placed over the hand-basin. Picking up my toothbrush as a pretend mike, I'd throw my head back and sing at the top of my voice. Renderings of 'Why Do Fools Fall In Love' would be followed the next instant by 'I'm Not A Juvenile Delinquent'. My poor dad, who worked mostly nights as a docker and was just waking up, would call down to my mother, 'For God's sake, Cilla, can't you keep that child *quiet*?'

'Cilla, keep it down, luv,' me mam would say, coming upstairs and putting her head around the door. 'Leave it off until your da's on days again.'

By this time, I was already convinced I had a talent that one day would be recognised. Neither me mam nor me dad ever pooh-poohed me when I announced 'I'm going to be a star.' It was more a matter of waiting patiently than of wishing and hoping. It may have been naive for me to think like that, but that's just how I was. I didn't confide in my brothers, though. George wouldn't have mocked, but John would have been more difficult. I cramped his style, and he might have taken the mickey if I'd given him the chance.

But it was very small wonder that I wanted to be a singer from such an early age. Although nobody in our family was a professional musician, my father played the mouth organ, John could read music and played the saxophone and clarinet, Allan played the guitar a bit, George provided all the records, and my mother was always singing in her fab soprano voice.

I was very close to my brother Georgie, but not quite so close to John and Allan. There was only three years between John and me, but that's a lot when you're a child. John was always being told to look after me, which he hated because I cramped his style. He didn't want me hanging around him, and when we did go out together, he was forever saying, 'Get home, your mam wants you.' I'd trot all the way back to the flat and say, 'What do you want me for, Mam?'

'I don't want you,' she'd say. 'Go out and play.'

I soon twigged that John was just saying that to get rid of me, but it was no big deal. Unlike some of my girlfriends, I was never bullied or punched by any of my brothers. Mind you, woe betide them if they had tried. I'd have told me dad and, as I was very much 'Daddy's girl', he'd have soon sorted them out.

Looking back, I can see I was a lucky little girl who had a very happy childhood. We never had much money left over from essentials, and we didn't have one of the highly prized two-up, two-down terraced houses. Me mam would have killed to have one of those, because living in the flat meant that we didn't have our own front door. We either had to come in through the barber's shop, which me mam hated doing, or when the shop was closed we came in through the back entry on William Moult Street. One day when I came home from school, I'd found her crouched on the stairs crying with frustration.

'What's the matter, Mam?' I asked, alarmed, as I squeezed in beside her and wrapped my arms around her neck.

'A man from the council has just called round and said our flat is going to be upgraded – *done up*,' she replied, disgusted.

I thought that was good news and, for a moment, I was puzzled by her tears.

'Don't you see?' she added, blowing her nose. 'That lick of paint means we're not going to get a council house.'

I had understood then that this was the end of me mam's dream to have her own front door. And although the 'doing up' meant us getting our new bathroom, which was wonderful and unforgettable for me, it was small consolation for her.

Mam's crying incident aside, what I remember most about her was her laughter, even on Monday mornings when she was doing the washing for the six of us in the big sink in the passageway that was our kitchen. She used to do all the sheets by hand and put them through the mangle, but she'd still be chuckling and singing away in her incredible soprano voice. She was a very glamorous, strikingly attractive woman, and a very strong character. I remember seeing a photograph of her and her sister Mary when she was only sixteen. Her hair was cut in the then-fashionable Eton-crop style, and she looked absolutely stunning. She was a very demonstrative, warm, touchy-feely person, so none of us ever lacked for hugs and cuddles. Our family has always been like that – and I can't get my head around people who are not.

In her own way me mam was a women's libber, and a great admirer of the suffragettes who'd won women the right to vote. She ran her own business selling second-hand clothes in St Martin's Market and was very good at doing deals. When I was fifteen, I remember her taking me to Nanette's, the posh clothes shop on London Road, to get my first grown-up coat. It was royal blue and very adult, and I thought, 'Gosh, this is great.' But when Mam said to the assistant, 'What's the lowest price you'll take for this?' I nearly died of shame and wanted to run away! But Mam was never embarrassed by doing that sort of thing. She was an incredible business-woman who always wanted her business to be the best. She was one of the very special breed of market people who are strong, funny, quick-witted and fazed by nothing. She had great charm and was brilliant at the banter needed to encourage people who are slow to buy or a bit too pushy when rummaging through the goods. The market was really her stage. I loved helping her after school and during the holidays. For me it was another classroom where I learned the art of riposte.

Mam used to buy the clothes she sold from private houses and I used to go collecting with her. Whenever I catch the scent of roses now, it takes me back to those days when we'd go over the ferry to New Brighton and visit posh places in Waterloo and Birkenhead. I loved walking down those roads with their lovely semi-detached and detached houses, with their lush front gardens full of red, pink and yellow ramblers and standard roses.

'Smell *this* one, Mam,' I'd say, nicking a red rose here or a yellow one there.

'Behave yourself,' she'd tell me, pocketing the trophy and smelling its crushed petals later.

Me mam had her regular clients back at her stall, and later, in the sixties, when thirties gear became the rage, she decided to specialise in these clothes which ranged from the romantic-looking, high-fashion cock-tail dresses to the practical styles of padded, broad-shoulder jackets that made waistlines look much smaller, trousers that were suitable for bike rides and tailored suits and hats that were strongly influenced by military uniforms. She was very successful at this, and became known locally as a vintage clothes dealer.

No matter how busy she was, though, Mam was always there for the four of us. My brothers and I were never 'latchkey' kids, left to fend for ourselves when we came home from school. I was pretty spoilt, being the only girl, an absolute cow if I didn't get my own way, and always an attention-seeker, but she never tired of my carryings-on, never told me to shut up. And when I said, 'I'm going to be a star', she never put me down. 'I know you are,' she'd say, making me feel I could do anything.

What's It All About?

I was lucky with me dad, too. He never had a lot to say for himself at home and had his own set ways of doing things, but when he did speak ('Bed – *now*', 'Do what your Mam says', 'Put that away') or discipline us with a sudden frown or leap from his armchair, we listened and did what we were told. He never raised his voice, and never smacked us even when we were pushing the limits and asking for trouble. My brothers and I always knew when he was really upset, though, and we used to nudge each other, saying, 'Watch it – Dad's got a cob on.'

Thanks to me dad, I learned that you can win the day with quiet determination rather than making a scene.

I wasn't all that close to Dad's mother, Dorothy, or to Dad's brothers and sisters, perhaps because I was so close to me mam's mother Ellen and all her sisters. We did visit Grandma Dorothy occasionally, though, in her house on Stanley Road. She was a fabulous baker and confectioner, and after she turned her front room into a shop, all the factory workers at British American Tobacco used to go to her for their pies, cakes and pastries. I never knew Dad's father, because he died before I was born.

My mother had one brother and six sisters: my Uncle Tom and (starting with the eldest) Auntie Mary, Auntie Nellie, Auntie Lottie (Charlotte), Auntie Jean (Georgina), Auntie Ann (Allan's mother) and Auntie Vera (my godmother). There was also Auntie Marina, who was strangely much younger than all the others and who I called Marie. I always thought she was another of Mam's sisters, but eventually we found out she wasn't. She was Auntie Nellie's daughter, born 'out of wedlock' as they used to say. What a horrible expression! Marina wasn't told until much later in her life that Auntie Nellie was her mother and not her sister.

Every Sunday we went round to me mam's parents' house in Bond Street, off Limekiln Lane, and, because my mother had so many sisters, there were always loads of grandchildren there. It was the same routine every week. I'd skip into the room, where there was always a wonderful comforting smell of a stockpot on the fire and delicious home-made bread, and me granddad, who seemed to sit permanently by the black-leaded fire-place smoking his pipe, would tease me by saying, 'Which one are you?'

'I'm little Cilla, big Cilla's girl,' I'd reply, and he'd give me a whiskery kiss.

Me nan was a very placid woman, an absolute saint who lived for her family. When I was going through a phase of wanting to do people's hair, she'd always sit there and let me make a mess of hers. 'Oh, that looks luvely, Queen,' she'd say when I was done, looking in a hand mirror at hair that now resembled a Maori's hut.

Kids were always very careful about how they talked or behaved when their parents or elders were around. Even when my brothers were grown men and George was doing his National Service, if they went into a pub and saw me dad in there they'd walk straight out; and once when I went to the pictures with me mam and she saw *her* parents there, she immediately stubbed out her cigarette.

~

Religion always dominated the weekly routine in our school and house. Me dad was an Irish Catholic and me mam was half-Welsh, with a Protestant father and an Irish-Catholic mother. Dad was a good Catholic, but he never went to Mass other than at Christmas and to do his Easter duty, which requires you to go to confession once a year and then Holy Communion. Mam was very religious. They used to say, 'she eats at the altar rail', because she was always in church taking communion. She was the treasurer of the Mothers' Union and eventually, because of her business acumen, its president.

I realise now that perhaps my dad was protesting at all this zeal of hers, and that maybe he was a wee bit jealous of how much time Mam spent in the church. If so, he never let these feelings filter down to us, but I suspect that he only did his Easter duty because he feared going to Hell. I know it sounds extraordinary today, but you were automatically excommunicated in those days if you didn't do this.

What's It All About?

As cradle-born Catholics, my brothers and I were raised to believe in the Church's teaching and to apply its values to our daily life. We always went to Mass on Sunday mornings, and we totally accepted that it was a mortal sin to eat meat on Fridays, the day that Christ was crucified. I used to love cutting an orange in half and rubbing an Oxo cube over the two sections. It created a fabulous sweet and salty taste. Once I was halfway through eating this delicious treat when I suddenly realised what day it was.

'Oh, my God!' I exclaimed, silently. 'It's *Friday* ...'

I should have thrown the remaining bits away, but temptation got the better of me. After I'd finished licking my lips, I was so overcome by guilt I grabbed my coat and went straight to confession.

'Forgive me, Father, for I have sinned,' I said to Father Biery. 'I was eating this orange with some Oxo rubbed on it when I remembered today was Friday.'

'What did you do when you realised that?' he asked.

I cast a desperate glance at his shadowy head-and-shoulder outline on the other side of the wrought iron grille, but I was too terrified to tell the truth.

'I ... I stopped,' I lied.

Back outside the church, I stood rooted to the spot, mortified by what I had done.

'Oh, my God,' I thought, petrified; 'I've lied in confession. I've now committed two sins instead of one. What if I die tonight? I'll go to Hell for sure.'

Somehow I found the inner resources to go back in and this time, having burst into tears as I got back on to my knees, I told Father Biery the truth.

The penance – ten Hail Marys – was sweet that night. It saved my soul.

~

Much of the earliest pop and jazz music I heard at home came out of a great big radiogram, which was more the centrepiece of the living room than a mere record player. Throughout the early fifties, before I was a teenager, me mam and dad and my brothers George and Allan remained ever-loyal to crooners such as Al Jolson, Nat King Cole, Dean Martin and Frank Sinatra, and to Country and Western; while John was very into traditional and modern jazz. The radiogram took ten records at a time, ten-inch or twelve-inch 78s or 33s which it slapped down on to a turntable one by one. A heavy pick-up arm would swing across in a slow-motion, hit-or-miss fashion, then drop on to a groove, often missing the opening bars. In the groove it definitely was not!

In 1953 we got our first TV set – but before that, Lil who lived just across the road, used to let me watch hers in return for scrubbing her lobby and steps. Our set arrived just in time for us to watch Elizabeth II's coronation, which totally captivated me. Our family were ardent royalists and we were always thrilled when the Queen visited Liverpool. On one occasion, her limousine came down Scottie Road. The pavement was knee-deep in people, waving flags and bunting, and I'd never seen it so colourful and busy.

'She looked at me, Mam,' I gasped. 'Right *at* me!'

I wasn't lying. The Queen had looked directly at me – and smiled and waved!

~

Music and singing aside, I was a tomboy who really wanted to be one of the boys, but apart from my Billy they wouldn't have anything to do with me. Because we lived on a main road, I had a choice of side streets to play in. If I came out of the barber's shop, for instance, and turned left there was Bostock Street, where lots of my mates lived. Around the corner from Bostock Street was William Moult Street, where there were quite a few factories, and heavily loaded lorries often came past on their way to or from Greenberg's Glass, the paperworks, or one of the others. (Also in William Moult Street was the rag and bone yard, where me mam bought me my first bike.) One of my favourite pursuits was to lie in wait for the lorries as they slowed down, then jump on to their back steps or bumpers to steal a freebie ride.

I came a cropper one day, though, when one particular driver, who obviously thought he was Stirling Moss, gave me the fright of my life. His vehicle, a big 'un, which had been going comparatively slowly when I managed to board it, suddenly gathered speed at a terrifying pace. I realised I was in serious trouble. I knew the driver would have to stop at the junction at the bottom of the hill, and that his tail lights would warn me when this was about to happen, but I hadn't got a secure enough hold travelling at that speed and I knew I couldn't keep my grip for much longer. I panicked, and decided to leap off before I was bounced off.

Having succeeded in hitting the road without slipping sideways and going under the lorry's huge wheels, I rolled over and over down the street. By the time I finished rolling and came to a stop in a crumpled heap, there was no breath left in my body, my hands and knees were lacerated and the rest of me was black and blue.

Stunned, I checked to make sure there was no other vehicle about to run me over and finish the job, then struggled into a sitting position. As I did so, I noticed to my horror that the lorry had pulled over to the side of the road and the driver was jumping down from his cab. Convinced he was going to come after me and give me a wallop, I somehow managed to get to my feet. Ignoring the blood dripping from the cuts on my hands and knees, I ran for my life, home to me mam.

'Jesus, Mary and sweet Joseph, what have you done to yourself?' she yelled as I crashed in.

Almost blind from shock and pain and hardly able to breathe from my sprint, I couldn't get any words out. Instead I just stood there panting, praying that Mam would never find out how I'd managed to get into such a state.

'Have you been fighting?' she rapped as she grabbed a tea towel and started to dab at the messiest gash on my knee – the one that was forming a bloody puddle.

Sobs – not difficult in the circumstances – were my best bet. If she learned the truth before I had time to manufacture a suitable explanation, it might well be a case of one injury deserves another. Just as my pathetic snuffles seemed to have gained some sympathy, there was a loud, urgent knocking at the door.

'Oh, God!' I thought. 'It's the driver. He's followed me.'

'Don't open it, Mam,' I pleaded. 'Don't open it – he'll go away.'

Silly me! The note of desperation in my voice had only aroused Mam's suspicion. Her expression changed – sympathy dissolved into a glower.

'Stay there, you,' she instructed. 'Don't you dare move.'

Those were words I always dreaded. They meant trouble and I was in enough of that already, trying to cope with the pain of my bruised limbs and aching bones. If Mam didn't give me a pasting, the driver surely would!

'Is she all right, Missus?' I could hear the feller saying.

Mam must have nodded and added something I couldn't hear, because the next moment the tone of his voice changed.

'I didn't even know she was on the back of me lorry until she fell off.'

'She's all right,' Mam was apologising. 'You've had a bit of a shock, lad. D'you wanna cup of tea?'

'Oh, no,' I groaned, sucking blood from my right hand. 'Don't ask him in!'

'No – I'm OK,' he was now muttering. 'I'd better get back to me load.'

I thanked God silently.

'She'll have a few bruises and a shiner,' were his parting words.

'Not one shiner – two if I have anything to do with it,' was Mam's reply as she closed the door.

Back with me, Mam was in no mood to sympathise with my tears.

'What were you doing to make a show of me like that?' she said, locating an unbruised, unbloodied section of my left leg and giving me the slap I deserved.

Was that the last time I stole a freebie ride on the back of a lorry?

What's It All About?

I cannot lie. The answer's No. And not long afterwards I actually nicked a lorry for a short ride, again in William Moult Street. The driver must have left it unattended for just a few minutes, and I jumped in, somehow got the brake off and put it into gear. The engine didn't start, but the lorry rolled down the hill, quickly gathering speed. I thought it was fantastic, but had no idea how to stop. The problem was solved when we smashed into a lamppost and came to a halt. I jumped down and legged it, and no one ever found out what I'd done. Luckily for me my guardian angel, which all Catholics believe in, was in its traditional resting place on my shoulder.

~

My other childhood speciality was breaking and entering. Behind our back wall there was a factory that supplied bathroom equipment and I used to belly-wriggle myself over the wall and then over the sills of broken windows. Don't get the wrong idea though: I never stole anything. It was the echo I was after! I always did this when I was on my own and it never once occurred to me that I could cut myself and lie there bleeding to death on the broken glass.

I had several near misses with nasty accidents. We used to make steering carts from wooden boxes and old pram wheels, so that we could lie on our tummies and steer with our feet, or sit back and steer them with a piece of old rope tied on the front. We'd set off from a slope on William Moult Street and career away at a breathtaking speed. I can't tell you how many times we crash-landed.

On another occasion, when I was about eleven and on roller skates, I launched myself off on the usual slope. As I whizzed out of control along Great Homer Street, I shot past the back of the Homer cinema. It had some iron girders around it, and I grabbed one to slow myself down, but I was going too fast. I swung around the girder, lost my balance and came crashing down and smashed my elbow. It's still out of shape today. I ran home to Mam, knowing that I would get a good hiding and that she would say, as all mothers do, 'How many times have I told you ...' Once indoors,

I collapsed on to the sofa. The pain in my elbow was unbearable and it had already swollen to twice its normal size.

'What *have* you done?' my mother asked, panicked, and then, having given me a good telling-off, she took me to Stanley Road Hospital, where I was kept in overnight.

Mam and Dad came to visit me the next afternoon. There was no colour in my father's face, and I knew he was really shaken because he had brought me chocolates – a real treat in my childhood. But I was in for a disappointment. They were dark chocolates and I only liked milk ones. After they'd gone, I gave the boy in the next bed some of my chocolates. I would not have been so generous, though, if they'd been milk rather than plain!

~

I never lacked for entertainment as a twelve-year-old schoolgirl. My mother was crazy about the movies and she used to take me every week. The moment we walked into the body-laden darkness of our picture house and sank down into the sagging springs of the bum-worn, red velour-covered seats, we would snuggle up, open our bag of sweets, and forget everything amid the striking of Swan Vesta matches and the glow of ciggies being lit up as the local lads ogled the girls and set out to impress them by producing perfect smoke rings. Then, the moment the film started, we'd be carried off in the instant silence that descended and be transported to a world of glitz, glamour and romance.

I totally believed in all the Hollywood spin and happy-ever-after endings, and I was always hugging myself and thinking, 'When will *my* life be like that? When will *my* Fairy Godmother come along?' I so wanted my life to be like Doris Day's and Natalie Wood's.

In the movies, when the leading lady breaks a leg or gets laryngitis or an attack of the vapours just as she's about to go on stage, something magical always happens. Some suave, cashmere-coated, cigar-smoking producer or director comes along and, towering over the would-be star waiting in the wings, says, 'Okay, kid. This is your big chance – you're on.'

What's It All About?

I was always waiting for – expecting – something like that to happen to me. I was only twelve, but I was in a helluva hurry. I wanted the lucky break. I wanted to make a fortune. I wanted the big car, the grand house, the fabulous jewellery. I wanted to be the one who was signing the autographs. I wanted everyone to adore me!

2

Forbidden Fruits

When I was thirteen, I dyed my hair with a Camilla-tone sevenpenny rinse from Woolworth's. I loved my Auntie Vera's auburn hair and I wanted mine to be just like hers. I crept into the bathroom, mixed it to a gooey paste, painted it on with my toothbrush and left it on for hours. When me mam first saw it, she was shocked to her very core.

'What have you done to your hair?' she asked, aghast.

'Don't you like it?' I giggled nervously. 'It's just like Auntie Vera's.'

'It's a good deal brighter than hers!'

But Mam must have seen the yearning look in my eyes because she didn't make that much fuss. 'I don't know what your da will say,' were her last words on the matter. I knew she'd sort it with Dad, and she obviously did, because when he next clapped eyes on me, he just let out a long sigh, shook his head a couple of times, and said not a word.

At school the next day it was a different matter. News soon spread that something weird had happened to Priscilla Maria Veronica White's hair. It had turned bright red – well, orange really – and there were outpourings of 'The state of you and the price of fish!' and 'Jesus, Mary and Joseph!' that only fizzled out when Sister Marie Julie rustled in.

'What–? How–? When–?' she spluttered, her right hand clutching instinctively at the crucifix that always hung on her chest.

As far as she was concerned I was always up to some mischief, and she had tried to warn me many times against allowing myself to be goaded on by the other girls. Once, after giving me a well-deserved wallop on the back of the legs, she had added sternly, 'Don't you see, child – they're the gun and you're the bullet.'

~

Unabashed after my attention-grabbing debut, I never reverted to my former mousey-coloured hair. I just went on topping up the dye!

Sister Marie Julie may have decided by then that I was a lost cause, but I idolised her. In fact, I admired all the nuns. They had such serenity. Once, after a religious convention that involved a lot of silent reflection, I decided I wanted to be one, but I soon realised that what I was most attracted to was the black-and-white uniform and being on the receiving end of other people's reverence.

It was at about this time that I was playing a game in the school playground called chainy-ainy, in which the leader ran after the other girls, and kicked them when she caught them, and then they had to join the chain. I was at the end of a very long line of girls when the leader suddenly stopped dead in her tracks. The chain skidded to a halt and everybody fell backwards like a pack of cards, except me who fell on my nose. I can still remember the eerie sound of it fracturing as I hit the ground.

When I got up, my nose was bleeding so profusely that Sister Marie Julie, who had come running over, ordered me sit down again. To my distress she then dropped a bunch of heavy, cold keys down the back of my blouse. I had no idea that this was an old-fashioned remedy to stop nose-bleeds, and when she made me lie down on my back with the keys still in place, I couldn't understand what I had done to deserve such a cruel punishment. 'They're hurting me!' I wailed, but she was having none of it.

When I was taken home by two bigger girls, my father took one look at me and said, 'Oh my God, what have you done?' I was in so much pain I couldn't answer, but I saw the colour drain from his face and I knew he was out of his mind with worry. He paced up and down until my mother came home. Although Mam was a drama-queen, Dad always relied on her to take control of situations.

'Why on earth didn't you take her to hospital?' Mam exploded when she saw me. 'Her nose is smashed.'

So we went to hospital, but they couldn't do anything, because in those days they didn't have the techniques. Meanwhile my nose was so swollen I couldn't speak, but at least I could just about breathe. When it eventually healed, my nose was left with a permanent bump on the top.

~

When Bill Haley and The Comets had first arrived on our music scene I was still only eleven or twelve, and I couldn't believe my ears. From then on I'd spent every penny I could on rock 'n' roll. Bill's record, 'Rock Around The Clock', the one that's now hailed by pop buffs as 'the birth of rock 'n' roll' – and of all the sexual gyrations that followed – didn't become a number one hit here until late 1955, but even before that we were aware of the number-one fans of rock 'n' roll, the teddy boys, with their slicked-back hair, long velvet-collared jackets and drainpipe trousers.

By then the craze for rock 'n' roll was sweeping from its UK birthplace in London's Soho coffee bars, such as the Two I's and Heaven and Hell, and was spreading throughout Britain. As 'skiffle', a variant of rock 'n' roll, burst forth from former jazzman Lonnie Donegan, cheap guitars and washboards became the rage and hundreds of kids formed their own rock 'n' roll and skiffle groups.

Throughout the late fifties and early sixties, we kids listened to our favourite pop music on the newly arrived jukeboxes that took pride of place in the newfangled coffee bars which were sprouting up everywhere. These bars had easy-wipe, plastic-coated tables and rigid bentwood chairs, which tipped over if you leant back too far. The jukeboxes – usually American imports modified to take British coins – were wondrous. I loved their tight-lipped metal pay slots, large bulbous glass fronts and their hard-to-read, often handwritten, song titles from which you selected your current favourite by inserting a sixpence, and pressing a square-shaped push-button.

Our other sources of listening were Dansette record players, Nanny's old Bakelite wireless for 'Family Favourites' on Sunday, or little tinny transistor radios hidden in our duffel bags or handbags on which we could hear Radio Luxembourg.

But now, in May 1956, my first teenage year, when the radio was belting out 78s from Tennessee Ernie Ford, Dean Martin (whose autograph I wrote off for), Kay Starr, Ronnie Hilton and Pat Boone, I only had ears for Frankie Lymon, who fronted a group called The Teenagers. A sort of Michael Jackson at that age, Frankie was only a year older than me and I was absolutely crazy about him. Alone with my echo in the bathroom, I imitated his way of singing. His voice hadn't broken and I could sing in his key. From July onwards, I drove my family round the bend playing his hit record of that year, 'Why Do Fools Fall In Love', over and over again. Me mam, dad and brothers loved that song, but they hated the B side, 'I'm Not A Juvenile Delinquent', which I also played incessantly. I can still do a fair impression of Frankie Lymon.

One day my friend Chris Riley borrowed her mam's mail-order catalogue and, buzzing with excitement, we snuggled up in an armchair in the living room of my home and started leafing through the pages until we came upon what we were looking for.

'What are you two up to?' Mam asked, sensing a conspiracy.

'Blue jeans, Mam,' I said, breathlessly. 'They've got blue jeans – and they only cost one and threepence a week on the "never-never".'

Mam sighed, stopped ironing, and came over to look at the catalogue. 'They're boys' jeans,' she said. 'They've got a zip down the front.'

'We know that, Mam. That's how *all* the kids wear them now.'

With a shrug of her shoulders, she went back to her ironing. But she'd been young once and I knew it was a 'Yes, all right, if it'll make you happy.' And Chris's mam didn't take much persuading either.

When they arrived by parcel post, they weren't proper denim, but otherwise they were exactly like the ones Frankie Lymon and his group wore. Those jeans became our uniform. We couldn't wait to put them on and could hardly bear to take them off. For us, it was like a rite of passage.

You can't begin to imagine our excitement when, thus be-jeaned, we heard that Frankie and The Teenagers were coming to Liverpool to appear in person at the Empire Theatre, Lime Street. We couldn't afford tickets, so there was no question of getting in to see them play, but I remember bolting my tea down and haring off to hang out for hours every night by the stage door. I was desperate to catch a glimpse of Frankie, but I was always disappointed. Then, one night, I struck lucky.

'They're staying at the Lord Nelson Hotel,' a dancer whispered, taking pity on me. 'You might be luckier there.'

'I dare you – go up to their room,' Chris exclaimed, when I told her. 'Go on, Cil, I *dare* you.'

That proved impossible: the security was too good. But I ingratiated myself with the twenty-something maid who was responsible for cleaning Frankie's bedroom. 'The next time you're emptying his wastepaper basket,' I pleaded, 'just empty it into this carrier bag. Nobody'll be any the wiser and you'll help me win a dare.'

Sure enough, the next day she came to the hotel's tradesmen's entrance and emptied the contents of Frankie's wastepaper basket into my carrier bag. I was so excited, I scuttled off without even thanking her. But, disappointingly, the only thing of any importance was the US equivalent of an Equity card, the union membership card that all actors and performers had to have in those days. Still, at least it had belonged to Frankie, and I squirrelled it into my bedroom and treasured it for years.

~

I was a teenager now, but when me mam thought it was the right moment for me to learn the facts of life, she gave me a Roman Catholic booklet and that, as far as she was concerned, was that! So, like most of the girls I knew, who were far too embarrassed to ask their parents for more information, I gleaned whatever I could from my mates' big sisters.

I was a good Catholic, not in the sense of being a holier-than-thou goody-two-shoes, but simply because I accepted our Church's teaching that the delights of sexual intercourse were for married couples who wished to procreate and that, for that reason, Catholics were forbidden to use condoms or any other kind of birth control, except for the hit-and-miss, time-of-the-month 'rhythm method'. A couple of my friends at school had risked this, been caught out, and had to get married for the baby's sake, and I certainly didn't want that.

Having known from the age of three that I wanted to be a singer – and hopefully a big star – I was very wary of doing anything that might jeopardise my dreams. Even Frankie Lymon couldn't have persuaded me otherwise! I was always a terrible flirt who gave the impression I was much more confident than I really was, but I'd have run a four-minute mile if anybody had really come on to me.

The first available boy I fell for was another Frankie – Frankie Wynn – who had jet-black hair and attended St Anthony's. We bonded when the two of us, having taken serious tumbles in two separate incidents, ended up having our wounds cleaned at the same time by a school attendant; and our 'love' blossomed as we sat on a bench comparing the raw grazes on our knees.

'You're going to have a helluva scab,' I said, admiringly.

'So are you,' he agreed.

This mutual admiration lasted only about as long as our knees took to heal.

I then had a terrific crush on Vincent Austin. Vincent had the obligatory dark hair and was a very handsome, tall young feller who lived on the opposite side of Scottie Road, in the same block of flats as my Auntie May and Uncle Tom. He never knew I was crazy about him. I was much too shy to let him know – and I was secretly relieved he never found out.

I was getting wiser to what can go on between boys and girls than I had been a year or two before. For instance, I remember that on Sundays, after we'd attended Mass and had our roast dinner, Dad and Mam always disappeared upstairs for an hour and locked their bedroom door. When I was a bit younger, I thought it was because they wanted some peace and quiet!

But I was still very naive, half believing that what we called 'French kissing' – kissing with tongues – was how you got pregnant; and I was very wary of the 'one thing leads to another' syndrome and the game, 'Catch the girl, kiss the girl'. Most of my girlfriends and I were still at the stage of practising passionate kisses on the backs of our hands. Experimenting with sex doesn't come safer than that!

~

Jerry Lee Lewis's 'Great Balls Of Fire' and Elvis Presley's 'Jailhouse Rock' was our soundtrack at the start of 1958, but my own dreamed-for singing career showed no sign of coming true. Real life, I was discovering, is not quite like it is in the movies. Despite the fact that for the last four or five years I'd never stopped singing for family and friends, and never ceased searching for echoes to amplify my voice, my best subject at school was English. Doubtless this was why my last school report read 'Priscilla is suitable for office work.'

Me mam and dad were very proud of this report, considered it a great compliment, but I didn't. Having won a singing talent contest and made my stage debut as Julius Caesar in a school play, I was downcast. I'd wanted the report to read 'suitable for stardom'!

A couple of weeks later, when our school's career adviser asked what I wanted to do when I left school, I was not backward in coming forward. 'Oh, I don't want a career,' I laughed. 'I'm going to be a star.'

There was a polite pause, after which she replied, not unkindly, 'In the *meantime*, Cilla, you have to think about getting a job.'

What's It All About?

I don't remember ever missing a day at St Anthony's, and one of my proudest moments was winning a copy of *Aesop's Fables* for 'extremely good attendance'. When the time came for me to leave in July 1958, I knuckled down to reality and went to Anfield Commercial College to do a year's secretarial and shorthand course. I was just a couple of months past my fifteenth birthday, and at this point, I would have much preferred to be with me mates and working at Tate & Lyle's packing sugar, but Mam and Dad always wanted me to do well.

The only reason I managed to get one of the handful of places at Anfield College was not because I did particularly well in the written entry test, but because I'd been to see James Dean in the film *Rebel Without a Cause*. Thanks to this movie, I gave such a good performance at my first face-to-face interview that I got in. Inspired by James Dean's bravado, I Americanised myself by wearing flat shoes, short white socks, a sticky-out skirt and pony tail, and a shirt and sweater borrowed from one of my brothers – my outfit was just like Olivia Newton-John's in *Grease*. Then, standing up to my full height (which is pretty impressive for a girl) and adopting a deep voice that the headmaster could not fail to hear, I said, 'If I get one of the places, I promise I will be a dedicated and sincere student.'

My Method acting worked, and I landed the place.

When I look back now on my schooldays at St Anthony's and Anfield, I sometimes feel very cheated of a good education. If I'd been in a class of twenty or so, I know I could have done so much better. I was always very keen to make progress and shine – and I loved reading. Blessed with a vivid imagination – almost too vivid at times – I'm sure I could have excelled if I'd been given half a chance, but I was always losing marks for writing like I spoke. We never studied things like grammar and science in depth, and we were never expected to do any homework.

The local library was a godsend. The only books we had at home – and there weren't many – were used to prop up one of our chimney breasts, and Dad had even papered over them to make things more secure. When

I was about fourteen I remember going through a phase of trying to teach myself Spanish. I really fancied dark-haired boys, with a smouldering Latin look, and I wanted to go on a package holiday where there were thousands of them! The only word I remember now is *burro* for donkey. 'Wouldn't it be good,' I used to think, 'to speak Spanish really well and impress the locals when I go on my package tour?'

~

I never did go on that holiday to Spain. The only trip I ever made outside Liverpool was a couple of years later when I and my girlfriend Pat Davies and some other mates persuaded our parents to let us go to Pwllheli in Wales during our summer holiday to see one of our local groups, Rory Storm and The Hurricanes, perform at a Butlin's holiday camp. We knew we could bunk in for the concert and, as we also knew the boys in the band by then, we thought I'd stand a pretty good chance of winning that day's talent competition, which was going to be held in the camp's dance hall.

It was while we were on the train to Pwllheli, the biggest and busiest seaside town on the Lleyn peninsula, that I saw my first live sheep and cows. Before then, I'd only ever seen them in the movies.

On the day, Rory and The Hurricanes, all dressed in teddy boy suits with black velvet collars, fluorescent socks and shoes called 'creepers', gave an absolutely deafening performance, which sent all the adults present diving for cover and whipped up a frenzy of dancing in the hall. When it came to my turn in the talent contest, I sang my heart out and won the prize, a pink cuddly dog.

Richie Starkey, the group's drummer, came over to me afterwards. 'Great,' he said, 'but even if you'd blown it, we'd have given you the prize anyway!'

By that time I already knew Richie well. Everyone called him 'Ringo' because of his rings, but he was Richie at home, and that was what I liked to call him – it made him feel like a special friend. He really went for it, with his Elvis hairdo and sideboards, which his friends called 'sidies', but I also thought he was very funny, disarmingly so. He was a good mate.

~

By 1959 I liked all the American rhythm and blues groups, but, with the exception of our local group, Rory Storm and The Hurricanes, and Cliff Richard, I wasn't really into British rock 'n' roll. I thought it was too sanitised. In those days, generally we liked either Elvis Presley or Cliff Richard – not both.

Cliff was two and a half years older than me, and when I was sixteen I *really* fancied him. It wasn't so much his singing, it was my hormones – just raw sexuality. He was the object of my teenage fantasies, my pin-up boy, and much more accessible than Elvis, who I somehow knew would never come over here.

Once, in the months after I'd left Anfield, Cliff did a show at the Philharmonic Hall in Liverpool. I still couldn't afford a ticket to get in, but I was desperate for a chance to meet him, and scuttled to the stage door with my friend Pattie Singleton after the show.

'You're too late,' the doorman informed us, waving a hand in the direction of a taxi that was just pulling away.

It seemed Cliff had done a quick getaway, still in his stage clothes, fleeing the moment the show ended.

'Oh, no!' we groaned.

Then, without a moment's hesitation, I stuck two fingers in my mouth and, using the deafening whistle that my brothers had taught me, I hailed a taxi for us.

'Follow that cab!' I instructed the driver as we fell into our seats.

'*Cilla*,' Pattie whispered. 'Have we got enough money?'

'Don't worry,' I replied. 'I've got plenty in my bag.'

I had my wages from my Saturday job at Nanette's, the posh dress shop in Bold Street, and my pocket money as well, but what I didn't tell Pattie was that all my money was accounted for. In and out of the streets we wove, our gaze fixed on the rear lights and back window of the taxi ahead of us. As we left the city centre, raced through the outskirts and suburbs and began to hit more countrified bits, my eyes were watering from the strain of trying to make out the shadowy outlines of the figures in the cab in front.

'There are some guys with Cliff,' I kept saying to Pattie, who was focusing just as hard as me.

'They must be The Shadows,' she kept replying.

When the cab's rear brake lights came on and the taxi at last stopped outside a house on the edge of Liverpool, our excitement knew no bounds.

'Just wait a mo,' I instructed our driver as we tumbled out and sprinted to the other cab.

But when we skidded to a halt beside the emerging figures, we were in for a huge disappointment. There was no Cliff, only two members of his backing group, The Shadows – Hank Marvin and Jet Harris – plus the young Liverpool comedian, Jimmy Tarbuck.

'Where's Cliff?' I gulped to Hank Marvin.

Startled by our sudden appearance, he replied: 'He came earlier in his sports car.'

I spun round and looked at the drive of the house. There, parked right outside the front door, was a bottle-green sports car. But no sign of Cliff.

'Oh, no,' Pattie and I groaned for the second time that night.

'Couldn't he just come out for a second?' I said, blocking Hank's path.

'No – sorry. We're here for a party in Jim's parents' house.'

When the two lads yanked themselves away from us and followed Jimmy up to the house, we caught a glimpse of Cliff in the hall and nearly died from delirium.

'Cliff! *Cliff!*' we yelled in unison.

But Jimmy blocked the doorway. 'Piss off!' he said in a tone that brooked no argument, as he slammed the door.

Forlorn – feeling so near and yet so far – we trooped back to our taxi.

What's It All About?

The Tarbucks' house was miles from where we had hailed the cab, and by now I knew the fare would cost me a week's wages. I was gutted.

~

The first snog I remember really enjoying was with a boy called Delia. I'd started going to dances at the Rialto with two girlfriends, Jackie Summers and Pattie Singleton. The Rialto was on Upper Parliament Street, a 'forbidden' area for us, but it was irresistible. It played the most marvellous music, not only rock 'n' roll, but spine-tingling black blues music that wasn't in the shops then; and all we wanted to do was m-o-v-e our bodies to it. The atmosphere was great. A seductive, heady aroma of Players, Senior Service and Craven A cigarette smoke and rum and Cokes and whisky macs pervaded the place, intermingled with a sultry tang of human sweat, the fellers' lashings of Old Spice aftershave and hair tonics, and the girls' syrupy sweet hair lacquers and eau-de-colognes.

There were also a lot of *very* good-looking black boys there and, my, could they move their pelvises! One of them was Delia. I thought his name was very exotic, and the first time I met him we jived the night away – then again the next Saturday night, and the next. Soon, he and his friends started to walk us to the bus stop when the dances ended. There was no way they could have taken us all the way home, just as there was no way that boys from Scottie Road could go into the area around Upper Parliament Street. It was all so territorial. If you were a white Protestant boy who lived in 'Upper Parly', that was okay; but a white boy from Scottie Road was the enemy. If you were a white Catholic girl who happened to dance well, that was different, but it was still very bad news if your neighbours in Scottie Road twigged where you were going. Then you'd be branded a slut.

I guess for youngsters, such as Jackie, Pattie and me, this was the beginning of not giving into prejudice, of not seeing 'colour' or 'religion'. When *we* looked at a person, it was a case of 'if I like you, I like you'. But our problem wasn't a black-versus-white one; it was the possibility of being found out in a forbidden area. In fact, in our circles, if you were black and Catholic, you were much more acceptable than if you were white and Protestant. A black Protestant, though, was the absolute end.

I certainly had crushes on boys during my early teenage years, but my singing was still the most important thing in my life. I also thought I was a very sophisticated girl who really preferred older men – meaning that when I was seventeen, they might be all of twenty-one!

In these early teenage years we couldn't afford tickets for the Empire, but my friends and I did manage the occasional night out at other dance halls on Sundays: the Locarno or Grafton Ballroom, and sometimes Orwell Park. The big romantic record of the day was The Platters' 'My Prayer', and if a handsome feller asked you to dance during this, usually the last one of the evening, you knew you were on for a good thing. Halfway through the smoochy record, he'd get around to asking you where you lived, and if it wasn't somewhere daft on the other side of the Mersey, like Birkenhead, he'd see you home and you'd have a snog. If you said you lived in Scottie Road, that usually scared the boys off, but I used to get round it by saying 'Scotland Boulevard' – and they usually didn't realise what was going on until we were there!

~

This period was a key one for making new friends. I had met a lovely, bubbly, dark-haired girl called Pauline Behan at college, who became a really good mate; and then, soon after, a girl called Pat Davies. Pat lived a bus ride or two from me in Medlock Street, and she worked as a clerk at Littlewood's in Church Street. In no time at all, we were best friends and always travelled together on the number 3 bus.

Both Pauline and Pat became very important people in my social life, and Pat is still my best friend today. We were a happy-go-lucky threesome, forever going to the popular Merseyside clubs together. Pat was absolutely brilliant at needlework, which meant we could create our own fashions from materials we bought from Lewis's department store. My favourite combination was green frocks worn with orange accessories, and Pat's was orange frocks worn with green accessories. It may sound awful, but we actually looked very smart, and we certainly helped to cheer up 1959 when the whole world seemed to function in black and white – black-and-white films, black-and-white television, black-and-white photos, black-and-white newspapers.

We were a colourful gang, and we began to discover places that were more and more colourful too. While I was still at Anfield College, Pauline and I had started to go the clubs along with a gang of other girls from the college. One morning Pauline suggested we go to a club called the Iron Door. 'Rory Storm and The Hurricanes are playing,' she said. 'You've got to come, Cilla, it'll be a real laugh.'

3

Stepping Out

If ever a place should have been raided and closed down for inflicting grievous bodily harm on the senses, it was the Iron Door! It was the sort of coffee-cum-music cellar that you entered with normal hearing, vocal cords and eyesight, only to be immediately rendered deaf, dumb and blind. But once your eyes stopped smarting from the smoke and grew accustomed to the dark, and your ears adjusted to the thunderclaps of sound, you were blown away, and you never wanted to be anywhere other than this ever again.

Perhaps the most incredible thing about all our jazz and rock dives in those days was that they were alcohol-free zones. All that was on offer to wet our whistles was coffee and soft drinks, mainly Coca-Cola. Occasionally you would trip over an empty beer, whisky, gin or brandy bottle that had been smuggled in, but this was a very rare occurrence.

I could tell from the moment we entered the Iron Door that night that Pauline, who loved my rendering of Peggy Lee's 'Fever', had her own agenda; and, as instructed by her, I kept a very firm grip on the back pocket of her jeans as she led me, follow-the-leader style, to where Rory Storm and The Hurricanes were making one helluva din. Once in pole position right under the feet of the group, I could see that Pauline's lips were moving, but I couldn't make head or tail of what she was trying to tell me, so I stopped trying and gave myself up to the music.

Between sets – not quite the right word for those wild, manic assaults on battered instruments, but never mind! – it was fractionally easier to hear and I soon discovered that what Pauline said carried some weight with the band, and when she kept repeating, 'Oh, gaw on, fellers, she really *can* sing. *Give* Cilla a chance. Oh, *gaw* on, give Cilla a *go*', they did. Wally, the bass player who looked just like Buddy Holly, shoved a mike in my face and said, 'Okay, gal, this is your moment. Show us what you're made of.'

Believe it or not, I wouldn't have done it if I hadn't been pushed, but with Pauline and all the other girls egging me on to have a go, there was no backing out! And once I was up there, I didn't hesitate. Head thrown back, I was belting out 'F-e-v-e-r' before anybody could change their mind. Pauline was determined that everybody else should shut up and listen. 'Shush!' she kept saying during the opening bars, and then, the moment I finished, she whipped them all up to a frenzy of cheers. I could not believe it. For the first time, I'd been singing with a microphone – and with a real band!

I must have done OK because after that night word got around all the clubs in no time. It was like *Boys from the Black Stuff*, with all the kids calling out, 'Let Cilla have a *go* … We wanna *hear* her. Give Cilla a *go*.'

Soon there was no need to ask. After singing quite a few times over the next couple of months, I became a bit of a performer in my own right. 'Cilla!' someone on stage would bellow, beckoning me over, 'it's your turn, girl.' Then one of the guys would say, 'OK, boys and gals. Here's what you've been waiting for – *our Cilla*.'

~

'D'you fancy going to the Iron Door again?' Pauline said as we sat on the number 3 bus.

'Great,' I said; 'who's on?'

'The Beatles,' replied Pauline, 'and my boyfriend's going to be there – you should come and meet him.'

When we got to the club after school that day, The Beatles were indeed on. But what Pauline hadn't mentioned was that her boyfriend was one of them – he was George Harrison. His guitar playing was just exceptional that day. The band were playing a bluesy kind of rock 'n' roll, and they all sang, except for Pete. Our gang cheered them on.

'Fancy doing a song?' Pauline asked me.

'Do I ever?'

'I *could* ask John.'

'Don't be soft, luv,' I said. 'They're much too popular now to let anybody get up and sing with them.'

But Pauline always had the cheek of the devil. As each set ended, she, and then my other mates too, called out to 'give Cilla a go'. They did it so often that John, suddenly getting thoroughly fed up with the lot of them and pretending not to know my real name, said wearily, 'Okay, *Cyril*, what song d'you wanna do?'

Amazed that he'd capitulated, but not slow to let him take my hand and haul me up on to the stage, I said: 'Summertime'.

That number from *Porgy and Bess* was a favourite of mine. I particularly loved the version sung by the great R&B singer Sam Cooke. Although it was written for a male voice and not in my key I thought the melody and words were beautiful. It was the kind of song you could put your body, heart and soul into and, as the boys began to play it, that's exactly what I did.

'S-u-m-m-e-r-t-i-m-e when the livin' is e-a-s-y ...'

I could hardly believe I was up there, being backed by The Beatles, and that, instead of dancing, everybody was now just standing there listening to me. When I finished there was a moment's silence, then the kids erupted into claps, wolf whistles and cheers and cries for more. I was so elated, I could hardly breathe.

'OK, Cyril, you've had your turn – now gerroff!' John said, pretending he was peeved.

'Our Cyril, folks,' he added to the audience, then, giving me one of his broad winks, he took me by the hand and led me off stage.

Needless to say, it was always a bit of a come-down the mornings after the nights before. Anfield was no match for looking down on upturned faces and knocking 'em all for six.

Lunchtimes were fun, though. A club called the Cavern, an incredibly popular local hang-out in Mathew Street, was just around the corner from my office, and Ray McFall, the Cavern's manager, had come up with the brilliant idea of offering lunchtime as well as evening group sessions.

'People will be able to come in,' he told Pat and me one evening, 'have a bowl of soup with bread, plus a cheese or ham roll, and listen to some music before going back to work.'

We were thrilled. By this time it was 1959 and I'd left Anfield and started working, at British Insulated Calendar Cables Limited, or BICC, in Stanley Street. Forever broke, but never ones to sit at our desks eating sarnies between twelve and one, Pat and I began to meet up at the Cavern every day. Although we were both very conscientious about earning our living – me at BICC and Pat at Littlewoods – we lived for the off-duty moments we shared together.

Ray was quite smartly dressed, sort of like a businessman, but he seemed happy to chat to us when we came in. He didn't crowd us, but he wasn't distant either, and he'd tell us about the club and how it started. Apparently Alan Sytner, a doctor's son who used to run traditional jazz nights at the Temple restaurant, opened it in 1956 after he'd fallen in love with a club in Paris called Le Caveau. Before that it had been a wartime air-raid shelter, then a wine cellar, and then an electrical store. On the opening night about six hundred kids managed to squeeze in, and fifteen hundred were left queuing outside.

Pat and I couldn't bear the thought of missing a night in clubs like the

Cavern or the Blue Angel – or the Downbeat which, by way of contrast, was a very high-tech, modern jazz club, full of stainless-steel fittings – a forerunner of the minimalist bars we see today. Obsessed was the word! All I lived for was the next chance to scramble up on to a stage and sing my heart out.

There were loads of fab clubs in Merseyside and there was nothing I liked better than doing the rounds, but the Cavern was one of my favourites. It was always traditional jazz at the Cavern until Ray decided to devote one night a week, usually a Thursday, to rock 'n' roll. And, even then, it wasn't until John Lennon, Paul McCartney, George Harrison and Pete Best started doing the Thursday-night gigs there in 1961 that rock 'n' roll really began to take off.

Later, many people claimed that the birthplace of The Beatles was the Cavern Club. But it wasn't. In fact, that group might never have come into being if Pete Best's family had not lived in a huge, sprawling Victorian house at 8 Hayman's Green, West Derby. The first time I saw that place I thought it was a palace!

'Look,' Pete's mam Mona said one day, when she was obviously being driven round the bend by the volume of noise that Pete and his gang of schoolfriends were generating, 'there's a huge basement cellar under this house. Why don't you clean that up and make it into a den for yourself? Then you and the lads can make as much noise as you like without disturb-ing anyone else.'

That was the kind of suggestion any teenager would die for – and Pete and his gang immediately set about sweeping and washing out the cellar, sticking up some cork tiles on its ceiling and walls and making fake fire-places out of chipboard. In no time at all, they'd created the kind of space they never wanted to leave and every other kid in the area wanted to be in. Before long, word was out on the streets that there was a club at the house, and Pete's mum was now being driven up the wall by kids knocking at the door and asking, 'Is the club open yet?'

What's It All About?

Most mothers would have called a halt at that moment and sealed up the cellar door, but Mo was no ordinary mum. A very astute woman, who was only too aware that coffee bars such as the Studio, the Jacaranda, El Cabala and the Zodiac were the 'hip' places at that moment, said: 'OK. Let's make it into a coffee-bar-cum-music club, issue membership cards and book some groups to play in here.'

From that moment on it was, as Pete was fond of saying, 'all systems go', and the Casbah Coffee Club came into being in August 1959. That basement was the birthplace of The Quarry Men, who then changed their name to The Silver Beatles, then to The Beatles. But John, Paul, George and Pete were not the only ones to benefit from Mo's brainwave. The Casbah also provided a venue for the likes of Gerry and The Pacemakers, Rory Storm and The Hurricanes, Derry and The Seniors, and The Searchers.

As for me, I'd found a second home where Pat and I could hob-nob with John, Paul, George and Pete and other musicians – and with all the other kids who were soon travelling in from all over Liverpool and even from across the water. There we'd be, all jiving the night away, hour upon hour, oblivious to the cigarette smoke forever hovering in the air.

When we were not at the Casbah, or one of the other clubs, we'd all somehow end up at NEMS, the local music store, and continue rubbing shoulders there.

'Ai ya, how ya doin'?' you would say, recognising other kindred spirits, then we'd all amble over to the record counter to look at the list of new releases and make a choice, such as Little Richard, Jerry Lee Lewis or Fats Domino.

Actually buying a record, though, was a rare occurrence in those days – we were all in the same boat, all skint.

~

There was always a scrum around the cloakroom at the Cavern at lunchtime. People just used to toss their coats in when they arrived and were never able to find them when they were ready to leave. One day the chaos seemed worse than usual.

'It's a right barny in here, we're all going to be late back to work,' I said to Ray McFall. 'Why don't yer get someone to hang the coats up?'

'OK,' he said, 'you do it.'

'How much are yer gonna pay me?' I said jokingly.

'Five bob a day,' was the answer.

Little did he know I'd have done it for free, just to listen to the groups. Instead I'd be getting £1 5s a week! I was only earning £3 11s a week as a typist so the extra money would be welcome. I could stop having to wear the same dress back to front – and free lunches at the club would help to satisfy my healthy appetite.

My office colleagues knew what I was up to between noon and one, but they didn't mind. It was no secret that my heart was set on becoming a singer, and everybody was happy as long as I pulled my weight and got through my work.

My only disappointment was that I never got a chance to sing at the Cavern during the lunchtime sessions, a) because I was much too busy hanging up and handing out coats, and b) because most of the kids who dropped in were only interested in listening to John, Paul, George and Pete. In those days the four were just a scruffy group of urchins who dressed in stiff black leather jackets, and torn jeans that had seen far better days. I loved rock 'n' roll, but although I'd heard them play a number of times at the Casbah, the Cavern and the Jacaranda, it was their boyish good looks as much as their music that appealed to me.

Once I was into my lunchtime swing at the Cavern, I also proved my flair for topping up my wages by getting an evening job as a waitress at the Zodiac Club in Duke Street. I was every bit as lazy as the next teenager, but I could always find the energy for things I wanted to do – and holding down three jobs in order to be where it was all happening was no trouble at all!

I was very popular with my gang of friends during this time. Having got to know the doorman at the Zodiac, I could get them in free at night.

What's It All About?

This was just as well, because none of us had any money then, not even for bus fares, and we often had to walk home at the end of the evening.

I particularly loved being at the Zodiac when the various groups and musicians were returning from their out-of-town gigs. 'Ai ya,' they'd say as they came in, scattering their instruments by the bar as they ordered mugs of coffee and then slouched around in dark corners, earnestly discussing where they'd just been, what they'd been doing, and whether or not they'd succeeded in getting any advance bookings.

Although I was only sixteen, I never had any trouble from me mam and dad about staying out so late. They trusted me to behave myself and, having always been into music themselves, they just accepted that I was one of two hundred or so local kids who loved dressing up in all-black clothes in order to look like a beatnik and be one of the 'with its'.

Me mam kept a discreet eye on me, though. Once, at an all-night session at the Iron Door, Richie Starkey stopped me in a frenetic jive and said, 'Just look at those two old women over there. They can't 'alf dance.'

When I glanced over my shoulder, I saw me mam and her friend, Vera Davis – Billy's mam – having a jive!

'*That's me mam!*' I shrieked, horrified.

By now they had an audience, and they loved it. I was dead embarrassed. Was she going to get a right volley from me in the morning! For now, though, I did what anyone would have done – I ignored her and Vera and tried to steer well clear of them until eventually they called it a night and went home.

When it came to me hanging around *really* late in the hope of doing a song at one of the all-night sessions, Mam and Dad put their foot down and insisted on me having a chaperon. But, being the person I am, I came up with the perfect solution!

'My brother, George, is a very strong, good-looking guy,' I said to the manager of the Iron Door. 'Loads of kids keep trying to get in here without paying and our George would make a *great* bouncer.'

I knew damn well that George, who was married by then, wouldn't hang around the club until the early hours of the morning, but I also guessed that me mam wouldn't call in much later than eleven to check up on us. Being in the market, she also knew most of the kids and their families, and she was pretty confident I'd be okay. Liverpool was – and still is – a massive place, but it's always been very much like a village in which word spreads like wildfire the moment anybody goes off the rails and misbehaves.

George *did* become the Iron Door's bouncer. He was paid £3 for the job and, as I'd anticipated, he always went home to his wife at about eleven-thirty!

~

Richie Starkey and I, who'd become the best of friends since we met at the Iron Door when I sang with Rory Storm and The Hurricanes, were brilliant at reducing each other to hysterics about absolutely nothing, but sometimes he was an awful embarrassment in my life. Part of my job at BICC was covering for the receptionist while she had her lunch break and, to my horror, Richie was always sauntering round to the offices during this time and totally freaking me out. With his side-whiskers, he looked every inch the teddy-boy rock 'n' roller and I was trying *so* hard to be the respectable 'butter-wouldn't-melt-in-my-mouth' office girl. My mum and dad had been thrilled that I'd got an office job. Most of my friends worked in factories, so a white collar job was considered a real step up. Not that Richie cared. The reception bell would ring and, when I slid open the window, there he'd be.

'Fancy coming to the pictures this afternoon?' he'd grunt, chewing on his Wrigley's.

'I *can't*,' I'd hiss. 'I'm *working*.'

'Working?' he'd query, as if he'd never heard the word!

'Richie,' I'd say, 'you'll get me the sack.'

'Oh, good,' he'd reply. 'You'll be free to come to the pictures with me, then.'

He was generous to a fault – and very lovable – but never an easy guy to get rid of!

Sometimes, though, because I was allowed nine half-days off annually in addition to my summer holidays, I *would* take the afternoon off and go to the pictures with him. And later, after Richie had replaced Pete as The Beatles' drummer, I also used to go round to his house to do his mam Elsie's hair for her. I always reckoned that if I wasn't going to be a singer, I'd be a hairdresser. Elsie was a real character, a surrogate mum to Pat and me and to the other Beatles, and we were forever bumping into each other there. She would cook us all delicious Spam, home-made chips and beans for tea and she never seemed to mind how often we came round for more or how loud we played the latest records. We thought we did Elsie's hair really well, but, some thirty years later, Richie's stepdad Harry told me otherwise: 'We didn't say anything at the time,' he muttered, 'but you used to make a right bloody mess of poor Elsie's hair!'

~

It was at the Zodiac Club in early 1961, when I was still seventeen and working as a waitress there after work, that I spotted an incredibly good-looking, sun-tanned guy with white-blond hair. As Liverpool was a port, I thought he was Swedish, off one of the ships. The last thing on my mind was romance, and I certainly wasn't looking for the kind of trouble that came with the 'one enchanted evening' scenario, but certain guys were always worth a few chat-up lines, especially if they looked as if they were in the money and good for a soft touch!

'Hey, take a butcher's at that one,' I said, giving Pat a nudge as I carried a tray of empty coffee mugs back to the bar. 'He looks a bit of all right, doesn't he? And his friend's not bad either!'

'He's not your usual type,' she replied dubiously. 'I thought you liked 'em dark, Cil.'

'I know,' I said, 'but he's the most promising one here tonight – and he and his mate might be good for a laugh.'

I decided to make the first move and sidle up to him, waitress-style, saying, 'Can I take that?' His name, I discovered, was Bobby Willis.

He was about as Swedish as I was, and he and his friend Alan weren't off the ships. That was disappointing. Gone was the hope of Pat and me helping them to spend all their lovely dosh before sending them on their way. How callous can you be! But, hey, we were young. We weren't looking for engagement rings and church bells. We were just broke, hoping for two nice fellers who'd be happy to take us out and pay for the fun.

Just back from a holiday in Lloret de Mar, which had cost him £48 all-in for a fortnight, Bobby was as brown as a nutmeg, and even though he was from Liverpool, there was something about him that made me neglect my crock-collecting duties that night to keep returning to him.

Over a cup of coffee by the bar, he told me all about himself. He said he was twenty-one and that he owned a car that was conveniently parked just outside, and that his dad had a bakery chain. Impressed, and thinking he might prove to be a soft touch after all, I made absolutely sure we'd have the last dance – always a slow, smoochy one, which determined who would take who home that night – and then I accepted gracefully when he offered to give me a lift in his car. There was no goodnight kiss, though, when he parked the vehicle in William Moult Street outside the back entrance to our flat. I may have been a terrible flirt, but I wasn't fast!

During the next couple of days – days when Bobby always seemed to be popping up like a Jack-in-a-box wherever I happened to be – I started asking around about him. He had, I soon discovered, told me a pack of lies. He was only a year and a half older than me (nineteen, not twenty-one), he worked at Woolworth's in the bakery and confectionery department; his father and brothers had jobs in a local engineering works; and the car he was driving was hired.

'Some enchanted evening' should have become 'Some disenchanted evening', but, to my own surprise, I didn't send him packing.

'He's dead good-looking, Pat,' I kept saying. 'Have you seen his suits? Italian mohair – really smart. And he makes me *laugh*.'

'Well, where's the harm?' she replied, her usual pragmatic self.

Meeting Bobby had certainly not been love at first sight for me, but I was very flattered by how quickly *he* had made up his mind and become besotted with me. He also had a really lovely smile and a great sense of humour, and he made me feel really special every time he looked at me or stood nearby, listening to me sing.

'Why did you tell me such fibs?' I asked one night.

'To make you think I was worth the time of day,' he replied.

'But you must have known I'd find out.'

'Ah – but by then I hoped you'd be smitten,' he replied.

'How do I know you won't tell me any more lies?'

'Because you're here and I don't have to any more,' he replied.

'I'm only *seventeen*,' I said, giving him a long searching look, 'and my heart's set on being a singer. I'm not looking for marriage, Bobby.' He knew the right thing to say.

'Neither am I,' he said, and he meant it! He was ambitious and wanted to earn a fortune first.

Although Bobby Willis was the complete opposite in looks and character to any other guy who had set my heart racing, he won me over and we started to knock around together on a regular basis. There's a saying: 'Some people come into your life for a reason; some for a season; some never go away – and stay forever.' At seventeen, I had absolutely no idea which of these would apply to Bobby Willis. But I was so glad that he'd singled me out and was hanging around waiting for me most nights.

4

We Can Work It Out

Bobby was only too happy, once I became his 'girl', to ferry me around Liverpool in an absolutely gi-normous old Crawford's Biscuits van. I don't think he paid more than a couple of quid for it.

'Well,' I thought, 'all fellers have to start somewhere – and wheels of any sort are better than walking or waiting at bus stops.'

There was the rub. I'd only known Bobby a couple of months and, despite the very rocky beginning when he'd tried to lead me up the garden path with all kinds of brags and blag, it seemed he couldn't do any wrong in my eyes. Somehow it was only too easy to forgive him anything, and that's how it was when well-meaning friends began to sidle up to me and say: 'Watch yourself, Cilla. He's a real ladies' man, you know, and he's broken a few hearts.' But even when I knew he was a terrible flirt and he'd had loads of girlfriends, it didn't seem to worry me.

Bobby had no such warnings about me. My reputation was unsullied: 'Cilla's OK', 'Cilla's a good kid', 'Cilla's *luvvely*', was apparently the only kind of gossip he picked up about me.

In truth, though, I wasn't as prim and proper as some people believed me to be – and I certainly wasn't a prude! I also knew I was as capable as any girl of getting 'into trouble' with boys, but I was lucky. I had a focus in my life other than fancying or pulling fellers, and somehow my head always managed to rule my heart. The last thing I wanted was to fall head over heels in love and settle down before I'd proved myself. My heart really was set on becoming a singer – and, hopefully, a star – and this, combined with my Catholic upbringing, genuinely helped me to stay 'pure'.

To be honest, I was also terrified of bringing shame on me mam, dad and brothers. With no older sister to confide in, I was stuck with my closest girlfriends, and they were no more clued up about safe sex than I was. The fact that a few of them had already 'given in to lust', 'been caught out', 'got a bun in the oven' and 'had to get married', was not reassuring – and I didn't want to be the next one in that line!

What soon became evident, however, was that Bobby was no ordinary guy who I could just enjoy flirting with and send on his way, and that the feelings he had for me – and I had for him – were very special. Like it or not, resist it or not, we both sensed, young as we were, that whatever else was going to happen in our lives we were meant for each other, and we'd only ever be truly happy when we were together.

A very independent feller, who was just as close to his friend Alan Dewar as I was to Pat Davies, Bobby was not always the easiest of guys to be around. He was very jealous and he had some very old-fashioned, dogmatic ideas about how girls – as opposed to boys – should behave. Surprisingly, perhaps, I didn't mind. I just felt flattered that he thought enough of me to care – and to put down a few ground rules!

The actual 'rules' of our relationship were never written in blood, but they might as well have been. Bottom line, it was a case of: 'If you're my girl, that's a commitment. *I* can go out with Alan, but on the nights when you and I are not doing things together, I don't want to see *you* out on the town.'

I could, apparently, go round to Pat's house and spend a girlie evening playing the quiet bird, leafing through magazines, doing our nails or watching TV or listening to records, but I couldn't go out to the movies or clubs without him. That was definitely not on – not even if I stuck to Pat like glue and never looked at another feller all night.

Sometimes I rebelled. 'What's the harm?' I'd think. 'It's gonna be a lovely sunny evening and who wants to be stuck indoors?' On these occasions – and there were a fair few of them! – I'd tell a white lie, pretend I was staying in to wash my hair or only going round to Pat's. In truth, though, I'd already made plans with Pat to do something else – and, whenever we were plotting one of these secret trips in the Cavern at lunchtime, our conversations would always go like this:

Me: 'What are you gonna wear tonight, Pat?'
Pat: 'Mmmm? The emerald-green jacket, I think.'
Me: 'OK – I'll wear my tangerine coat.'

Having a chance to get dressed up was half the fun and, by the time we left the table, we'd have had endless second thoughts and worked our way through our entire wardrobe. We were always very smart, always trying to look like Audrey Hepburn or another favourite movie star.

One night – inevitably – our luck ran out. I'd just finished looking at a canary-yellow sundress in a shop window in Bold Street when I saw Bobby and Alan walking towards us down the opposite side.

'Oh, no!' I groaned as Bobby's eyes locked on to mine.

Too late to dive for cover, Pat and I stayed rooted to the spot, waiting for him and Alan to cross the road. My mind was in overdrive, anticipating a showdown and sifting through excuses, but Bobby totally blanked me, stuck his nose up in the air, and, best foot forward, strode on, without even acknowledging me.

'Oh, God! I've mucked it up,' I muttered to Pat.

'He'll be all right, Cilla,' she said, in her most reassuring voice.

'No, he *won't*, Pat. He'll be absolutely *furious*. I'm supposed to be at home, washing my hair.'

'So?'

Pat liked Bobby, knew how important he was to me, but she was always a feisty gal.

'So?' she repeated, trying to nudge some fight into me. 'You're out with me – window-shopping. Where's the harm? For goodness sake, Cilla, he's out with Alan – why shouldn't *you* be out with *me*?'

I knew she was right, and part of me wanted to run after him and say: 'For God's sake, Bobby, I'm only window-shopping', but I also knew I was in the wrong. I'd led him on, let him believe that I'd accepted his 'one rule for the goose, one for the gander', and I'd told him a lie to keep the peace. That's one for confession.

'Oh, God, what can I do?' I thought, distraught. 'He's never gonna speak to me again and I don't want him out of my life.' And my next thought was, 'He'll drop me if I don't sort this.'

My one comfort was that I knew where he lived. But I'd never been to his house or met any of his family. Would I dare swallow my pride and go round there uninvited after work the next night? I knew it wasn't the done thing for girls to chase after boys but, if I didn't, he'd go on feeling betrayed and thinking the worst of me, and we'd never sort things out.

We Liverpool kids, by the way, had our own way of expressing things. We never said, 'I'm embarrassed.' Instead we said, 'I feel destroyed', which then often got shortened to just the one word, 'destroyed'; and if someone crept up to you and said, 'So-and-so really fancies you, you know', we'd reply, '*P-l-e-a-s-e* release me!'

That night, take it from me, I lay tossing and turning in bed feeling totally destroyed – the last thing I wanted was to be released!

~

The next day, leaden-legged and all of a quiver, I found myself standing outside Bobby's house at 80 Granton Road, Anfield, close to Liverpool's football ground. It was exactly as I'd imagined it – a neat little terraced house, fronted by a spick-and-span garden and a newly cut privet hedge, in a much more upmarket area than Scottie Road. The type of house where the front parlour was only used for special occasions like funerals.

When his dad, who looked like a crumpled carbon copy of his son, responded to my timid knocks at the door, he was lovely to me.

'Is Bobby in?' I asked in a choked voice.

'No, girl,' he said. 'But come in. He'll be home soon. I'm just having a cuppa – and there's plenty more in the pot.'

A maintenance manager at a local engineering works on Dock Road, his name was also Bobby, and he chatted to me for half an hour as I sat there, unusually lost for words, sipping tea in his neat little kitchen.

Just as he'd finished telling me how Bobby's mam had died when Bobby was eleven, we heard the sound of the front door being opened. Bobby was home.

Getting up to call out that I was there, his father only lingered a moment. As Bobby came into the kitchen and we stood, shifting from one foot to the other, exchanging mute destroyed glances, Mr Willis picked up his cup and saucer, and said: 'I'll leave you to it. I'm just going out in garden for a smoke.' Bobby took me to the parlour. It must have been a special occasion …

'I'm so sorry, Bobby,' I whispered when we were alone.

'So am I,' Bobby replied.

Ten minutes later, between my sobs and Bobby's tender reassurances, we sorted things out and kissed and made up. Moments afterwards we waved goodbye to his dad and, arms encircling each other's waists, headed up the road to where Bobby had parked the biscuit van. A kiss and cuddle later we drove off for a happy-go-lucky night out at the Iron Door.

~

'Me best mate Billy Davis is havin' a party. Will you come with me?' I asked Bobby a couple of weeks later.

'*Billy Davis*? I don't remember you mentioning a Billy Davis. Who's he?' Bobby asked, his suspicious nature once again to the fore. 'What's he look like?'

'Oh, I've known him since I was knee high,' I replied, adding as a wind-up, 'but he's six foot two now – white-blond like you, Bobby – and a really gorgeous looking guy.'

Bobby was always very jealous in those days, easy to get going, and I knew he was beginning to fester and think, 'Hello – have I got competition here? I'm a bit on the short side myself, nowhere near six foot two, and I might have to give this guy a pasting.'

Sometime after midnight on that Saturday, with Bobby not looking forward to meeting my best mate, we stood outside the door at 48 Lewis Street. Billy, wearing the latest faded blue jeans and matching denim shirt with some embroidery on its pockets, flung it open.

'Come in, come in – you're fuckin' late, you naughty girl,' Billy said (he swore like a trooper), sweeping me into his arms and giving me a big hug. 'Who the fuckin' 'ell 'ave yer brought with yer?' he went on, laughing his head off. Bobby wasn't laughing; he didn't approve of fellers swearing in front of girls.

'Billy – this is Bobby,' I said.

The two shook hands – one, I noticed, with a very *gentle* grip, the other with a very *firm* one!

'Well, the state of you and the price of fish!' Billy said, nudging me in the ribs as he gave his seal of approval to Bobby.

'You never said he was a bit of a soft quilt!' Bobby whispered in my ear as we made our way down the steps to the cellar.

'What's a soft quilt?' I asked, mystified.

'S-o-f-t,' Bobby replied curtly.

'Billy's *lovely*,' I hissed. 'I've got a very soft spot in my heart for him! It takes all sorts, Bobby, to make a world.'

'Sorry – sorry,' Bobby said, backing off.

At various times that night, as we took a breather from jiving and treading on everybody's toes and catching up with the other livewires there, I kept noticing a certain look in Bobby's eyes. At first I thought he was still being a bit off about Billy, but then I realised that this particular look was wistful and only seemed to put in an appearance whenever Billy was dancing with his mam.

'What are you thinking?' I asked eventually.

'Oh, nothing,' Bobby replied, defensively.

'Oh, go on – tell me.'

'All right,' he said, still reluctant. 'I was just being a bit soft myself – thinking that I'd have given anything to be able to dance with *my* mam like Billy does with his.'

It was the first time I really appreciated what it must have been like for Bobby to lose his mother – and suddenly I so wanted him to be able to share everything he'd felt then – and was feeling now – with me.

There was a pause, and then Bobby suddenly went on, 'I was the only one in our family who had white-blond hair, and her friends were forever patting me on the head and stroking it and saying, "Oh, what lovely hair he has. That hair should be on a girl!" But Mam would have none of it. She used to sort them all out, and say, "Well, it isn't on a girl and it looks just fine on our Robert, thank you very much."

I'd never seen Bobby like this before. He went on to tell me that his mam had suffered from rheumatic fever as a child, which had left her with a heart condition in later life. She was in her mid-forties when she fell pregnant with him.

'I think I was a bit of a shock,' he said sadly, 'one of life's little accidents.'

Young as I was, I sensed that he felt guilty about that – blamed himself for sapping her strength and causing her premature death.

'I also think I was a big disappointment,' he added a moment later. 'She'd already had three boys and I'm sure she'd have loved to have a girl that time.'

'Maybe,' I replied, feeling a little out of my depth. 'But not necessarily, Bobby. If she could see you as you are now, I think she'd be very proud of you.'

'D'you reckon?' he asked.

'I reckon,' I replied, stroking his face. 'Now gizza a kiss cos you've got me to dance with now.'

~

Taking a boy home for the first time is never easy, and even less so when everybody present senses it's someone you're really serious about. How, I wondered, would me mam react when she learned Bobby was a 'Proddy Dog' and not a 'Left Footer'?

I needn't have worried. Having given Bobby the once up and down, me mam turned to me and, right there in front of him, said, 'Ooh, very nice, luv. He looks as if he'll make a good Catholic.' And she was deadly serious!

By then I'd also made another unexpected discovery about the guy in my life. Bobby had an absolutely lovely, smooth-as-butter singing voice – just like Johnny Mathis – and, shortly before I met him, some talent scout on the prowl in the Jacaranda had tried to interest him in a record deal, which he'd turned down.

'Why?' I asked, astonished. 'I'd have *died* to be asked!'

'I've never really felt comfortable being up front,' he replied. 'And maybe I just didn't have the balls – and maybe he was a crap talent scout anyway.'

'Is there anything else you've not told me?' I asked.

'I like writing songs,' he replied.

'Really? That's great, Bobby. Show me one.'

'Not yet,' he mumbled. 'I've seen what other guys can write and mine are nowhere near good enough yet.'

The expression 'hide your light under a bushel' was tailor-made for Bobby. He was the kind of guy who never minded letting anyone know he thought the world of me and would do anything for me. He also made it abundantly clear whenever I shared a hope and dream with him, that if they came true, he'd wanna be around, backing me up in any way I wanted him to.

'Every successful woman needs a good man behind her,' he was fond of joking.

'Oh? I thought it was the other way around – "Every good *man* ... " '

'So? Why shouldn't we break the mould?'

I honestly hadn't been looking for love or romance, or dreaming of being showered with confetti, when I first met Bobby, but I was beginning to realise that I'd struck gold.

5

Wishing and Hoping

The Beatles had been missing from Merseyside's jive-hive-rock scene for some time, but we all knew where they were. The managers of the clubs in Hamburg's Reeperbahn, a really seedy red-light district, were always booking our lads to go over on the Harwich ferry and spend a few weeks playing there. The bands had to cram themselves into minivans for the journey and were only paid a pittance, but the boys were young and adventurous, and being skint in Hamburg was a darned sight more exciting than living at home with your parents!

When Rory Storm and The Hurricanes were booked to go over and play at the Star Club in Hamburg, it was agreed they should take a girl singer, so Richie came along to BICC one day to ask me to go with them. I said no without any hesitation. Me dad would never have let me go even if I'd asked him, but more than that I didn't want to anyway – I wasn't going to throw over my job for a short-term gig with no future to it, however much fun it might be while it lasted.

At the Cavern, where news always spread fast, we knew that John, Paul, George, Pete and Stuart Sutcliffe had built up quite a fan base in Hamburg and had even cut a couple of records, so there was a real buzz when word reached us on 18 December 1960 that they were back in Liverpool and had done a gig at the Casbah the night before. Not only this, but the band, now cheekily billed as The Beatles from Hamburg, were booked to play at a dance at the Litherland town hall on Boxing Day.

I didn't need to hear any more.

'Great! Let's all go dancing,' was my rallying cry.

Pat and I and the rest of our gang had often been to the Thursday night dances at the Litherland town hall, but we'd never seen the kind of crowd that was queuing for tickets that night. By the time we got in, The Beatles, dressed in the soft, skin-tight black leather jackets and trousers that Hamburg was so famous for – and wearing pink leather caps just like 'Be-Bop-A-Lula' Gene Vincent – had already kicked off their act with 'Red Sails In The Sunset'.

The buzz at the Cavern had been right! I couldn't believe my eyes, let alone my ears. They looked so sexy, so cool, exactly like Gene Vincent had looked on the night when he appeared at the Liverpool Stadium.

The most extraordinary thing, however, about the Litherland town hall occasion was that, although kids usually went there to pull girls or fellers and to jive or rock 'n' roll rather than to listen to the bands, tonight no one was dancing! The sound The Beatles were generating was so electric, so dynamic, it had physically drawn everybody to the front of the stage; and a huge mass of boys and girls were now gathered there, totally sent. But none of my gang was prepared for the kind of noise that suddenly erupted. There were ear-splitting shrieks and screams of 'More! More!'

I knew I'd witnessed an amazing breakthrough moment for The Beatles that night.

~

Around this time a guy called Johnny Hutchinson, the drummer for The Big Three – John Lennon's favourite band – sidled up to me one day as I was leaving a lunchtime stint at the Cavern and said: 'Ai ya, Cilla. Fancy doing a gig with us at the Zodiac?'

'Are you for *real*?' I laughed, thinking he was pulling my leg.

'Couldn't be more serious,' he replied, 'and, what's more, we'll pay you one pound ten.'

I was too gobsmacked to say anything other than, 'Right – okay, Johnny – thanks – just let me know when you need me.'

As he sauntered off to get a bowl of soup and a coffee, I stood where he'd left me, half wondering if I'd been overdoing the late nights and nodded off and dreamt what had just happened.

I was only earning £3 11s as a typist, plus another pound or two as a cloakroom girl and waitress, so £1 10s represented a lotta money. But it wasn't the pounds, shillings and pence that had set my heart on fire. I'd have sung with them for nothing! What mattered was that Johnny had just offered me my first professional booking.

Walking back to my office in a daze, my head was buzzing with The Big Three – Johnny Hutchinson, known as Hutch, on drums, Johnny Gustafsen on bass and Adrian Barber on guitar. Many Liverpudlians regarded them as much better than The Beatles – by far the best group Merseyside had to offer. They were very much into Ray Charles songs like 'What'd I Say', which I *loved*, and they used to come in with so much amp that local wits would say: 'Just listen! They make three musicians sound like an army!'

But I hadn't been dreaming. A couple of days later, as Johnny dropped his coat into the cloakroom at the Cavern, he said, 'I've brought you a copy of the *Liverpool Echo*. See the ad for our next gig on page nine? You're listed as "Swinging Priscilla".'

It was the first time I'd seen my name in print and I sat there looking at it for ages. I knew the 'Priscilla' bit would cost me a few blushes, but nothing could really spoil that moment and I couldn't wait to show it to me mam and dad and Bobby.

Me dad was dead proud, and me mam just said, 'I told yer, didn't I, Queen?'

'Swinging *Priscilla*, eh!' was Bobby's jibe.

Wishing and Hoping

'I don't want you to come and see me,' I warned Mam and Dad. 'You're much too old for the Zodiac – and I'm nervous enough already. I'll let you know how I get on.'

It was a different matter, though, when it came to Bobby.

'You will come, won't you? You won't forget – won't agree to work overtime – won't let me down on my big night?'

'Would I miss it?' he replied, pretending to cover his ears.

The Zodiac wasn't a big venue. It was just a softly lit coffee club with no stage to speak of and a small space in the corner, but it was a favourite haunt of the local kids and was always packed with twice the numbers the rules allowed.

On the Saturday of my launch as 'Swinging Priscilla', I was in such a state I got through at least three boxes of Fisherman's Friend throat lozenges. For the first time in my life I was utterly convinced I would lose my voice or miss all the high notes and let everybody down. I'd have been in an even worse state if Bobby hadn't promised to be there to literally hold my hand.

Johnny had made it clear that it was a rock 'n' roll style of singing that he wanted from me and I'd decided to do 'I'll Be Loving You, Always', Dinah Washington-style, and 'Autumn Leaves' in a rock style. I was trembling like a leaf myself when he beckoned me to the mike and I continued to hang on to Bobby's hand all the time I was singing. But I didn't miss a note, and there were more than enough wolf whistles and calls for more to keep me afloat.

Later that night, when we were all relaxing over post-gig cuppas, Johnny, who swore like a trooper but always modified his curses to 'Oh, puck!' and 'Puck this, puck that' when 'ladies' were present, made it clear that he would like me to sing with The Big Three regularly.

There was nothing in the world I would have liked better, but The Big Three – like most full-time musicians – lived hand-to-mouth between one booking and the next, and I knew, much as I wanted to, I couldn't just drop everything and do that.

'I'd love to, Johnny,' I said, 'but I can't afford to give up my job at BICC. I need the money.'

That was language Johnny understood.

'Life's a pucking bitch,' he muttered.

That night, however, did change my life in two respects. After my first pro gig at the Zodiac, a number of guys who liked to think of themselves as managers and promoters started to hover around me and buy me coffees; and requests started to come in from other local groups for me to sing with them. One of these, Kingsize Taylor and The Dominoes, worked particularly well for me because they, too, had day jobs and only ever took on bookings they could do in their spare time.

Ted 'Kingsize' Taylor, the group's leader, was a butcher. Six and a half feet tall and weighing twenty-two stone, the name 'Kingsize' couldn't have been more apt; and this time I was hugely relieved when I saw the advertising cards, which read *Presenting Kingsize Taylor and The Dominoes with Swinging Cilla*. Ted, bless him, developed a huge passion for me, and rumours began to fly around the clubs that I was 'Ted's girl', but that was nonsense. Ted was a great musician, a fantastic singer and a lovely guy – and that's all!

During this time I also sang with other local groups like Gerry and The Pacemakers and The Fourmost; and on another memorable night I went across the Mersey with The Big Three to perform at a Birkenhead YMCA dance organised by a guy called Charles Tranter, who must have been some kind of youth worker. Charles only had sufficient funds in the kitty to pay the boys, but after I gave a really heart-rending performance of 'Summertime', he obviously decided I deserved a reward.

'Hold on, Cilla,' he said, dashing past me when the boys were packing up.

I had no idea what he was up to, but he must have run back home to his garden. When he came back, he gave me an enormous bunch of sweet-peas that he'd picked. I was very touched. I still think of it as one of the most charming payments I ever received.

~

One of me mam's favourite sayings was, 'God works in mysterious ways His wonders to perform.' And sure enough, He finally worked a wonder for me.

Brian Epstein, who sold records by the thousand at NEMS, his family's music shop, visited the Cavern one lunchtime to hear The Beatles after they came back from Germany.

Sometimes life moves fast – and this was one of those moments. In no time at all, it seemed, news was flying around that Brian had drawn up a management deal and John, Paul, George and Pete had 'autographed' it. Their manager was now the man who used to come out of his office at NEMS to take one look at the scruffy foursome holding up the queue for the record booth, before calling down to an assistant: 'D'you think Liverpool's youth might be encouraged to while away their time *somewhere else?*'

It's extraordinary to think that, although Brian obviously already knew that a lot of local boys had taken up the guitar because of the influence of Elvis Presley and Tommy Steele and The Shadows, he had never considered managing anybody before that first visit to the Cavern.

Amazingly, within a few months of signing The Beatles, this fledgling manager, who was much more at home with Judy Garland than any R&B or rock group, had also signed up Gerry and The Pacemakers (who alternated with The Beatles at the Cavern lunchtime sessions); Billy J. Kramer and The Dakotas (Brian actually put Billy together with The Dakotas, a Manchester-based band); The Big Three, who changed their membership so often that half of Liverpool's hopefuls had played with them; The Fourmost; and a freckle-faced solo artiste called Tom Quigley, who changed his name to Quickly. It was hardly surprising, then, that in a few months Brian had earned himself the reputation of being a brilliant entrepreneur, and had become such a constant fixture on the Merseyside club scene that he was nicknamed 'Eppydemic'.

A gorgeous, shy, charismatic man who could turn on incredible charm when he wanted to, Brian was much more at home in his new role than he'd ever been as a record shop manager. Public school educated, he was a typical English gentleman who always wore elegant, expensive suits with an immaculate white shirt and a navy-blue spotted Hermès cravat, topped with a navy-blue cashmere overcoat.

In those days we young Merseysiders thought anybody who wore a suit had to have money and when I first saw him in the Cavern, I thought he looked like a film star with 'expensive' written all over him. The next moment I nearly swooned when I realised that John was bringing him over to meet me.

'This is Cyril,' John said to Brian. 'She's one to watch. You should sign her up, too.'

I couldn't believe I was chatting to the man who, in no time at all, was to put our Merseyside beat groups – and the clubs they loved to play in – on the international map.

One evening, soon after this, our paths crossed again at the Cavern.

'Ai ya, Brian,' I said. 'D'you want me to take your overcoat?'

He seemed very preoccupied, and I thought his mind was on John, Paul, George and Pete who were setting up their things for that night's act, but he suddenly turned to me and said: 'Would you like to do an audition for me at the Majestic in Birkenhead? The Beatles are doing a gig there.'

Would I? Is the Pope Catholic? I was so thrilled I could have jumped off me doll's house. It was the moment I'd been living for since early childhood and it had happened – just like that. And the guy who had asked me was even wearing a cashmere overcoat! Five minutes later, I was still standing there stunned, clutching his coat to my chest.

'This could be *it*,' I was thinking. 'This could be the best thing that's ever happened to you.'

My audition for Brian was to take the form of joining The Beatles for one number during their show. On the night of the audition I was so incredibly nervous as I climbed on to the stage of the Majestic Ballroom in Birkenhead that I just knew I was going to blow it. Moments before, back-stage, The Beatles had done their best to jolly me along but, realising I was half dead with fright, they'd all given up. Planting a few pecks on my cheek, they'd threatened me with a 'Liverpool kiss' if I didn't get a move on, then, having encircled me, 'dead man walking' style, they'd led me to the stage.

'Don't you dare do a runner,' John said as he stood me in front of the shabby old mike, and then back-tracked to where the others were tuning up.

I looked around me. I could see Brian out there among the audience. I wanted to go over, warm my hands on his overcoat, and break the ice, but he indicated with a wave of his hand that he was ready if we were.

'Okay, Cyril – ready when you are.'

'I'm ready.' But I was far from it.

Clearing my throat, I started to fiddle with the mike which was positioned a fraction too low for me, but to my horror, the moment I touched it the theatre filled with one of those horrendous high-pitched whistles that are guaranteed to make everybody cover their ears.

'Oh, God! Sorry!' I called out, mortified.

I'd chosen to do 'Summertime', but at the very last moment I wished I hadn't. I adored this song, and had sung it when I came to Birkenhead with The Big Three, but I hadn't rehearsed it with The Beatles and it had just occurred me that they would play it in the wrong key.

It was too late for second thoughts, though. With one last wicked wink at me, John set the group off playing.

'S-u-m-m-e-r-t-i-m-e ...'

I'd been right to worry. The music was not in my key and any adjustments that the boys were now trying to make were too late to save me. My voice sounded awful. Destroyed – and wanting to die – I struggled on to the end.

As the last notes of the music faded away, I risked a peep over towards Brian. He was clearly not impressed. It would have been a miracle if he had been.

'Thank you, Cilla,' he called to me politely as he stood up and left.

~

What's It All About?

In the months that followed, The Beatles continued to go from strength to strength in our Merseyside clubs and dance halls, but none of us saw much of Brian. News that we might soon be losing John, Paul, George and Pete to London was leaking out. It was rumoured that Brian had met someone called George Martin, who ran the Parlophone label for EMI. Then we heard that George Martin was giving them an audition.

Everybody held their breath.

'They've got it! They've got a recording contract,' was the next news, flashing from mouth to mouth around the clubs.

Soon after that, John sat down at a table in the Iron Door and told us that all Brian's footwork, telephoning and networking had paid off. Having found his way to George Martin, he'd got them a contract, and they were cutting their first record with this guy in September.

We'd barely got over celebrating this excitement when, hot on its heels in August 1962, there came a phenomenal shock. A shock so great that it rumbled through the clubs like an earthquake – and threatened to bury many a friendship. Pete Best, our Pete, who we all admired and fancied like mad, had been called into Brian's office at NEMS in Whitechapel Street and had been given the sack!

Nobody could take it in at first – there was silent disbelief everywhere. Gangs of Beatles fans, looking pale and shaken, moved from one coffee bar to another and sat there in a trance, mugs of coffee untouched, heads in their hands. It was as if one of us had died. But as reports continued to dribble out and we got the full gist of what Brian had said to Pete, the mourning turned to anger.

'Pete, I'm really sorry,' Brian had said, 'but I have some bad news for you. The boys want you out and it's already been arranged that Ringo will be their drummer and join the band on Saturday.'

'Why? What have I done wrong?' Pete had gasped.

'George Martin felt you weren't good enough. I'm not saying I agree with him, but there's nothing I can do. The boys have already made their decision and Ringo's already been asked to join the band.'

And that was that. Ringo – my mate Richie – had already agreed to take over Pete's drumseat.

It was not an easy time for The Beatles' fans. They still loved John, Paul and George, but Pete had always been their great favourite. Before long, anger turned to fury and, needing a scapegoat, they ganged up on Brian. Overnight he became the most unpopular man in Liverpool and he hardly dared put his nose outside the door. Banner-carrying gangs lay in wait for him, chanting: 'Pete for ever, Ringo never!' outside the Cavern, and even inside when The Beatles were playing.

The band still had three more gigs to play before their new drummer joined them, but as Pete, for obvious reasons, didn't want to do them, Brian had to hire Johnny Hutchinson of The Big Three to cover for him. Later Hutch told a group of us that Brian had actually offered *him* the permanent job with The Beatles before he had asked Ringo, but Hutch had laughed like a drain and said: 'Why on earth would I wanna leave The Big Three for The Beatles? The Big Three's far and away the best group in Liverpool.'

The next time The Beatles were booked to play at the Cavern, Brian decided he couldn't stay in hiding forever, banners or no banners, chants or no chants. Ray McFall, the club's manager, sent along one of his door-men, who was the size of a bus, to help Brian and the boys get in safely, but even this guy couldn't save them from Pete's fans. They had to run a gauntlet of fists and jeers and, by the time they got inside the club, it wasn't only verbals that had been traded. One of the punches had caught George off guard and he'd ended up with a very impressive black eye.

I loved John, Paul, George and Pete, and before I'd met Bobby I'd had a crush on each of them at one time or another. As for Ringo, he'd been one of my best mates ever since we met at the Iron Door. I wasn't happy about what happened to Pete, and didn't think he deserved it, but I wasn't going to take sides and risk falling out with any of them.

In the end, I kept quiet and took a leaf out of Pete's book. Once he was over the shock, he put the disappointment behind him. He never held a grudge, never once gave in to sour grapes. Eventually he got on with his life and formed his own band, The Pete Best Four. Later on still, he was always happy to talk about how much he had enjoyed the camaraderie that had existed between himself and the other Beatles, and whenever he bumped into anybody in the know he'd ask: 'What's happening with the band? How are they doing?'

One of my favourite memories from the time shortly after Pete left the band was of doing the Ouija board with The Beatles one evening at Rory Storm's house after a gig. The Beatles already had their first record out, 'Love Me Do'. Paul wanted to know if their next record would be a number one – and the board said yes, it would be an *NME* number one. The message was supposedly from his mam, who'd died eight years before, but then Paul said, 'Hang on – how would my mother know about the *NME*?' He soon tumbled that it was George who'd been moving the glass all the time!

~

In October 1962, by which time John, Paul, George – and Ringo – were squeaky-clean, dressed at Brian's insistence in suits, white shirts and black knitted ties, 'Love Me Do', with 'PS I Love You' on the flip side, had reached number seventeen in the Top Twenty charts. From then on they shot up the charts. When 'Please Please Me' was recorded just a couple of months later, it went to number one (just like the Ouija board said!), and by January 1963 they were billed as a star attraction on a UK tour with Helen Shapiro.

Until then our other groups remained relatively unknown outside Merseyside, but as Brian's reputation grew, more and more of them started to make demo records. By March 1963, Gerry and The Pacemakers had released 'How Do You Do It?', which was an instant number one hit for them; Billy J. Kramer and The Dakotas had recorded John and Paul's 'Do

You Want To Know A Secret?', and The Beatles themselves had had two more number one hits with 'From Me To You' and 'She Loves You'.

Brian's management business had now outgrown his Whitechapel office and had been moved to a suite in Moorfields, a charming street near the Exchange Station in Liverpool, and just a few yards away from the Wizard's Den, the most famous magic shop in the North of England. But it was Brian, aged only twenty-eight, who was being called 'wizard' and 'magic'.

The so-called 'Liverpool Sound' was soon being heard all over the UK, but because of my disastrous audition with Mr Eppydemic, I wasn't a part of it. By now nineteen going on twenty, I was still hanging up coats at the Cavern, waiting on tables at the Zodiac, and singing my heart out whenever I was asked.

Disappointed though I was, I was still high on life, and still wishin' and hopin' there'd be another chance. Then, like so many good things that happen to us in life, it came when I was least expecting it.

I was on the dance floor at the Blue Angel coffee club in Seel Street, doing a spot with John Reuben's modern jazz group. The songs I had chosen to sing that night were mainly non-rock 'n' roll numbers like Della Reece's 'Bye Bye Blackbird', because the clientele there was supposed to be a bit more upmarket. Feeling totally relaxed, having thoroughly enjoyed singing to them, I came off stage after my last number and, to my astonishment, saw Brian weaving his way towards me.

'Ai ya,' I said, completely taken aback. 'I didn't know you were in.'

'Why, oh why,' he replied, ignoring me, 'didn't you sing like that at Birkenhead?'

For a moment I was too gobsmacked by the intensity in his eyes and voice to reply – and, before I had a chance to recover, he added: 'That was absolutely wonderful. Have you ever thought of turning professional?'

'Who'd have me?' I laughed.

'*I* would,' Brian said. 'Come and see me in my office tomorrow.'

6

The Blackbird Has Landed

Ever since I was sixteen years old and first started singing around the Liverpool clubs, dressed in a tight black skirt and cardigan, would-be managers whom we jokingly called the 'Cockney fellers' had made the trip to our house for Sunday tea, usually left-over slices of meat from the Sunday roast with Dad's home-baked bread pudding to follow.

'Hey, Dad,' I'd say, indicating the latest chap in a shabby suit, 'he wants to be my manager.'

'No,' Dad would say later when we were alone, 'I don't like the look of that one', or 'No, he speaks funny.'

When Brian came round one Sunday in 1963, he was the only one to make a good first impression. He was a local lad, and he was obviously in the money because his family owned the store from which we had bought our piano. Dad said he could draw up a contract to manage me, and Brian brought it back to our house the same day.

As I was under twenty-one, Dad had to sign on my behalf. He read through the document very carefully, then, looking up from the papers spread out on our kitchen table, he exclaimed, 'There's a glaring error here.'

'Oh?' Brian replied, surprised. 'What? Where, Mr White?'

'My daughter's name is Cilla White – you've got it here as Cilla Black.'

I didn't dare say anything at that moment, but I kind of knew what had happened. In the Liverpool clubs I was known as 'Swinging Priscilla' or 'Swinging Cilla', and my surname was never listed on the publicity flyers or advertising cards. But once in *Mersey Beat* my name had been given as Cilla Black. Even if Brian realised this was a misprint, I suspect he thought Black was a much sexier name than White!

I wasn't bothered. The change didn't seem that important to me, but Dad *did* mind. Every time Brian repeated 'Black is a much better name than White for a singer', Dad kept shaking his head and replying, 'No, Mr Epstein, it's an unnecessary complication.'

Dad, I could see, was getting very hot under the collar. He was totally convinced that if my name was changed, his mates down on the docks would never believe him when he pointed to a record sleeve or a paper and said proudly, 'See there – that's Cilla White, my daughter.'

'Oh, yes, Mr *Black*,' they'd say, 'pull the other one!'

Brian, however, despite his obvious discomfort, stood his ground. Twenty minutes later, after much huffin' and puffin', Dad gave in to my 'Please, *please*, dad' appeals and signed the contract. But he was not a happy man! After Brian left, he sat there scowling, making it very clear to all of us that the change of surname had really upset him. It made him feel as if he was losing his daughter – giving her away to a strange new family named show business.

I didn't care. At last, I had a manager. I was so excited I didn't sleep a wink that night.

The news that Brian had signed a management agreement with me spread fast through the tight-knit world of the Merseyside clubs. It seemed that not everyone was pleased for me, though. Brian told me that he had received an anonymous telephone call in the early hours one morning. 'Keep off Cilla, Epstein,' a gruff voice had muttered. 'She doesn't need your management. She's signed with a friend of mine.' When Brian asked me about this, he was really rattled. I wasn't surprised – he was a gentleman, the last kind of person who would do the dirty and poach me from another agent.

'It's not true,' I told him. 'It's total nonsense, Brian. I've never signed with anybody.' Reassured, Brian said we should put the matter behind us.

~

That August, there was huge excitement at Scottie Road. The Fourmost, another of Brian's acts, were supposed to be performing with The Beatles in a show just along the coast in Southport, but Brian had to pull them at the eleventh hour so that they could do a spot on the TV show *Ready, Steady, Go!* in London.

'This is the perfect opportunity for you to make your debut appearance, Cilla,' Brian told me.

I was incredibly nervous on the day – so nervous I couldn't understand why I'd ever wanted to be a singer. Who in their right mind would want such a thing? But then, I'd never really been in my right mind since the night I first stood up on the kitchen table in Scottie Road.

Bobby took me to Woolworth's, where the manager was one of his old workmates, for fish 'n' chips beforehand. He'd bought me a French navy V-backed dress for the occasion. I'd been told the Southport show was a complete sell-out, which did nothing to help my nerves. Nor did the fact that Brian had booked a Country & Western band to back me – they only knew Country & Western, and I wanted to do rock 'n' roll. With some frantic last-minute rehearsal, though, we managed to get three songs ready. The very worst moment came when I was standing alone in the wings, knowing that as the next drum roll reached its climax, I would have to step out there into the spotlight and tread real boards on a real stage, without even being able to hold Bobby's hand for support.

At least I was among friends. Half an hour earlier, John, Paul, George and Ringo had put their heads around my shabby dressing-room door and had said: 'Go knock 'em out, girl – failing that, just show 'em your knickers.'

At last the drumroll peaked, and as I found myself on the stage, all my nervousness fell away. This was my moment at last. This was what I'd been waiting for since I was three years old.

As the Country & Western band struck up, I looked down at the row upon row of upturned faces, moistened my dry lips, closed my eyes, and opened my mouth to sing the opening number, 'Get A Shot Of Rhythm 'N' Blues'.

Nothing was going to stop me now – I was in the right key, hitting all the high and the low notes, and if necessary I could have held any one of them until I turned blue! It was the first time I'd been able to hear myself on the PA system, too, and it felt good – really good.

Afterwards, all aglow, my cheeks flaming, I walked back into the wings and fell straight into Bobby's arms. Brian had been watching from out front, and moments later he came rushing to my dressing room to join us.

'They *loved* you!' he told me. 'Just listen to the applause!'

I'd loved it too. I'd loved being out there, and I hadn't wanted to come off stage at the end.

Brian's smile engulfed me.

'This,' he said, 'is only the beginning!'

~

In September, amid cheeky cries of 'Don't do anything we wouldn't do!' and 'If you do, be careful!', I tidied my desk and waved tarrah to my office workmates. The chief clerk asked me what the problem was, and I simply said 'I'm gonna be a star!', at which he looked up to heaven and gave a faint smile. After three years at BICC I was on £7 a week by then, and he must have thought I was mad to be throwing it all away. My leaving present from the girls was the business, though – a vanity case in cream leather, full of compartments. Just the sort of thing a real star would have, I thought.

I hadn't told them the whole truth, though – hadn't said: 'Guess what, girls! I've turned professional and I'm off to London to audition for George Martin.' The future, as Brian had explained, was still very uncertain, and getting even this far had not been easy. When Brian first told me dad that he wanted to take me to London for a couple of weeks, every hair on Dad's head stood on end.

'Can't you do it in a day – get the night train back?'

'No,' Brian had replied gently. 'These things take time to set up, Mr White.'

'She's only *twenty*!'

Northern to his core, Dad wasn't at all keen on setting me free to go to the Big Smoke. He liked Brian and trusted him, but there were limits!

'Where will she stay?'

'A hotel in Bloomsbury.'

'Bloomsbury? Is that anywhere near Soho?'

'No. It's a very respectable area in Central London.'

'There's been a lot in the papers – white slave traffic operates in Soho.'

'Bobby will be there to look after me,' I kept interrupting at every opportunity. 'It's only two weeks, Dad.'

'Bobby's a good lad, John,' Mam said. 'He's already promised me he won't leave her side, so do stop ranting on about white slave traffic. This is a biggie for our Cilla.'

Much to our relief, Dad did eventually stop hummin' and ha'in' and, having taken Bobby to a pub down the road for a 'good talking to', he changed his tune from 'thinking about it' and gave Brian his permission.

'What did Dad say to you?' I asked Bobby later when we were sitting chatting in his biscuit van.

'He said I'd have more than a fluke's gob if anything happened to you,' Bobby replied.

~

I couldn't wait to get on the train and get started in the wicked city. Never having travelled far from Liverpool, this trip, just a few hundred miles up the track, was the equivalent of somebody else setting off to darkest Peru!

The very first thing I noticed when I arrived in my posh room at the very smart Kenilworth Hotel in Bloomsbury was the white phone beside the bed.

'Great!' I thought, 'I can call everyone I know.'

A moment later, though, I realised that nobody I knew had a telephone. That really upset me. It was so frustrating. There I was, staying in the kind of luxurious surroundings that I had only ever seen in movies starring Doris Day, Debbie Reynolds or Natalie Wood, but I was unable to tell anybody about it. There was only one thing to do. I rang Bobby in his room, No. 51, and asked him to ring me. That was fun! Every few minutes after that I kept ringing him, just for the hell of it.

'Are you all right? Have you locked your door?' he kept asking.

'I'm fine,' I kept replying. 'I'm going to have a shower.'

'But you've already had three!'

'I know, but there's still some hot water left.'

Although that hotel was very different from what I was used to at home, I took to the luxury and indulgence that came with room service at once. I'd spent so much of my life up to then living in an imaginary world of Hollywood dream magic that it all felt strangely familiar. The luxurious surroundings included, of course, a grand en suite bathroom, tiled from floor to ceiling. The echo, though, was nowhere near as good as the one I had left behind me in Scottie Road.

Brian was lovely – a real confidence-booster who made it clear from Day One that he was very proud of me. But Bobby, bless him, was a nervous wreck.

My first meeting with EMI record producer George Martin was on a Sunday evening at the Abbey Road Studios in St John's Wood. Brian, Bobby and I all went to the pub first – Brian had a brandy and Bobby had a beer – and then went to the studios to meet the man the press were soon to call 'the fifth Beatle'. He had made The Beatles' first hit, 'Love Me Do', and had then helped Gerry and The Pacemakers to be the first act ever to have three consecutive number ones in the UK chart – 'How Do You Do It', 'I Like It' and 'You'll Never Walk Alone'.

George's office was littered with record sleeves, brown box files and piles of sheet music, and nowhere near as grand as I'd expected. I was very impressed with George, though. He was a tall, thin, elegant beanpole of a man, and Brian had told me in the taxi that he had a magnificent ear for music, a great sense of style, and a brilliant reputation as an arranger, composer and oboist.

After just a few minutes breaking the ice, I could tell that George had a really sincere attitude towards Merseysound music and, over a cup of coffee and some tasty ginger biscuits, I also discovered that he produced the Goons for the radio, as well as the great Peter Sellers.

'Cilla was one of the girls who was always in the Cavern,' explained Brian. 'I knew she was an excellent singer, but to start with I had no idea she took her music so seriously and was willing to throw in her office job to become a professional. She's the first female artiste I've signed up – and probably the last person from Liverpool I'll be taking on. I'm delighted to be presenting her to you today. Her style and natural ease make her a joy to manage, and since she signed with me, she's never given me a moment's anxiety.'

As he paused for breath, I thought, 'Well! That was better than any school report I ever received from Sister Marie Julie!'

At one point in the meeting, I was asked to go and sit in a nearby waiting room while George and Brian continued to chat, but moments later I found Brian had worked his usual magic. George wanted me to go along to Studio No. 2 and sing for him. Brian's excitement was positively contagious.

Thrilled to have overcome the first hurdle, I set off down the corridors and climbed God knows how many stairs to what was called the producer's control box. By the time I got there I was out of breath and overcome by nerves, but no sooner had I started singing that old favourite, 'Get A Shot Of Rhythm 'N' Blues', than the nerves went and I was fine. The musicians who were there for my audition were top-class.

The Blackbird Has Landed

George didn't say much during that audition, but I couldn't help noticing that his attitude was becoming reassuringly different – much more smiley, relaxed and open. He also walked Brian and me to the lift, and, young though I was, I realised this was significant. Managers at BICC in Liverpool only did that for people they respected or considered important.

'I liked him,' I said to Brian, as we left the building. 'How do you think I did?'

'You were fine – just fine. I was really proud of you.'

Pausing to scrutinise his face, I knew that he meant what he'd said.

'So will I get the recording contract?'

'I'm pretty sure it's in the bag,' Brian replied.

Two days later, a bottle of champagne was delivered to my hotel room.

'What's this?' I asked suspiciously, ready to send it back. 'I didn't order any wine.'

'Somebody did, Miss.'

Attached to the bottle's neck, there was a card from Brian. 'Congratulations,' it said; 'The Blackbird has landed!'

7

Ready, Steady, Go!

By the time of my first recording session with George Martin, Bobby and I had long got past all that nonsense about his songs not being good enough. I'd realised that he was truly talented songwriter, and he'd already given me several wonderful songs. The way it worked was that he'd sing his new song to me, and I'd sing it back to him. It didn't matter where we were, but it usually seemed to happen at bus stops. We didn't have a tape recorder: I'd just go through it with him, line by line, and if I didn't get it right, he'd keep on at me until it was. We had a few rows in the process, but that's because he wanted it perfect, and so did I.

One of the songs we'd already done this way was 'Shy Of Love'. I thought it was wonderful, and on the day of the recording at Abbey Road George Martin needed no persuasion to put it on the B side of my debut single, 'Love Of The Loved', written by Lennon and McCartney.

This was only the second time I'd been in a recording studio and there seemed to be one thing after another to throw me. Recording a song wasn't a bit like singing in a club, dance hall or theatre. There was no audience, no other performer to help get me into the swing of things, and the atmosphere felt totally clinical. Everywhere I looked there was something I hadn't seen before: a glass booth, referred to as an 'iso' (short, I was told, for 'isolation unit'), a 'control box' containing a huge silver-grey console deck with lots of black levers, behind which George and the engineers were seated, and all around me a large studio space where the backing musicians were tuning up behind a screen that was used to partition off a large empty area.

Like a lamb before the slaughter, I was led up to a mike in the 'iso', while the musicians continued their tuning up.

It was the first time I'd faced 'real' musicians, playing from real sheet music, and I was so disappointed! What I wanted from the backing group was a really good club band sound – a Cavern sound – but it seemed I could whistle for it. George had his own ideas. Feeling very small and more jittery than I'd ever felt before, I didn't enjoy a single moment of that session. Every time I sang 'thurr' instead of 'there', George kept pulling me up.

'That word sounds much too Liverpudlian,' he kept saying.

'Right, George,' I kept replying. 'I'll try it again.'

I did. Again – and again – and *again*! In all, we did fifteen takes instead of the usual four or five.

Now, when I listen to my early records, I can see what he was on about. 'Where' and 'there' were the two words I had *not* lost my Scouse pronunciation on. I might have thought I had total accent control on 'Love Of The Loved', but I hadn't. I still said 'thurr'.

Having finished the recording, I was dreading the result – fully expecting Paul's 'Love Of The Loved' and Bobby's 'Shy Of Love' to sound absolutely unlovable. But when I sat listening with George, they sounded absolutely smashing. OK, 'Love Of the Loved' didn't have the group sound that I'd wanted, but it didn't half sound professional. Nobody could have been more surprised than I was.

~

After cutting the record, everything speeded up so fast I hardly had a minute to take in what was happening. I always seemed to be hopping into black cabs and crossing from one part of London to another.

What's It All About?

When 'Love Of The Loved' was released, the NEMS publicity team let it appear that the song had been custom-tailored for me. 'I've realised one of my biggest ambitions already!' I gushed during my first press interviews. 'I have a song specially written for me by John and Paul – of *The Beatles*!' But of course it was cobblers. I'd heard the lads doing the number themselves during lunchtime sessions at the Cavern, so I knew it wasn't a new song. But even if the song was off the peg, it suited my voice, and the recording had come out good. It was what I needed to get my foot on the first rung of the ladder, and that was all that mattered to me.

The pop music world of the early sixties was full of little white lies and cover-ups – and this was especially true when it came to a pop singer's life. Sales could drop to rock bottom overnight if the girl fans discovered their favourite pin-up boy was going steady, or getting engaged, or even married. Brian was protective to the point of paranoia about The Beatles and all his other stars, and he couldn't bear even minute details of our personal life becoming public knowledge. We were all expected to play along with this and keep anybody we developed a passion for out of the limelight. Bobby was the only feller in my uncomplicated love life, so I was no trouble to Brian. In answer to any prying questions about my feller's constant presence, Brian simply explained that Bobby was my road manager.

Bobby took this new job seriously, though. Very eager to learn, he never missed an opportunity to teach himself the ropes of the music business, and in no time at all he became a first-class roadie who was always there with the right information at the right time.

I would always say to him, 'You could be a singer yourself. You've got a great voice – you write wonderful songs.'

'That's not what I'm after,' he would reply. 'You're the really talented one. Being your roadie and looking after you suits me just fine.'

I still think about those words. It wasn't just me who thought Bobby could have gone places. Dick James, Bobby's music publisher, offered him a recording contract, but Bobby's answer was blunt: 'One star in the family's enough.' Giving up the possibility of his own singing career to enable me to pursue mine was the most romantic thing he could have done.

~

Dad was right to be worried about my change of name from White to Black. Once my record was given air time and I made my TV debut on *Discs A Go Go*, Mam told us that his workmates never stopped ribbing him. Their new nickname for him was the 'Frustrated Minstrel', because he didn't know if he was Black or White!

On my second TV appearance, this time for Southern Television in Southampton, Bobby asked the director what he would like me to do during an eight-bar instrumental break in the song.

'Oh,' he said, 'she can just dance around – and the camera will follow her.'

It was a live programme, and when the break came along, dance I did – right past the camera and out of sight, and they were left with a blank screen for about ten seconds!

Up in the gallery, where Bobby was sitting, the TV production people sat with their heads in their hands – they could not believe their eyes.

'What's she doing?' somebody asked frantically.

'You said she could dance anywhere,' Bobby replied defensively.

'Yes, lovey,' they said, treating him like a three-year-old, 'anywhere in front of the camera!'

Some people thought my disappearing act had something to do with my Liverpudlian sense of humour, but no, I was just being dead thick!

~

'Love Of The Loved' was released on 27 September 1963, and the very next day I appeared in the 'hot seat' on *Juke Box Jury*, which was compered by the silky-tongued David Jacobs and recorded at the BBC studios in Shepherd's Bush. On this show, which was watched by around twelve million viewers every week, the panellists voted songs 'hits' or 'misses'. I was excited to be on, but somehow it never occurred to me to be nervous.

Afterwards, the press claimed that my loud infectious laugh on the show had instantly won me millions of fans. I hoped that was true.

There were so many professional and personal firsts for me during those early visits to London – and I just loved leaning out of cab windows spotting the sights. 'Look at that', 'Oh, look at that', I kept crying out to Bobby as we whizzed past the Houses of Parliament, Westminster Abbey or Buckingham Palace. There was no spare time for more than that, but I was aware that in future, when I was off the leash, there would be plenty of nightclubs for Bobby and me to explore. And it was also on one of these visits that Bobby and I found the fast-food restaurant that was to become our favourite, the Golden Egg in Leicester Square.

Throughout this period I was still making the transition from being someone who had only sung at parties and in clubs to being a professional solo singer who performed on stage, radio and TV. It didn't always go smoothly. Once I went down to London to do *Saturday Club* on radio with Brian Mathew. Bobby and I arrived at the Playhouse in Charing Cross Road, where the show was to be recorded, and I was introduced to Bob Miller and The Millermen, the programme's resident band.

'What are you going to do for the show?' Bob asked me.

'"Love Of The Loved",' I replied.

'Fine,' he said. 'Where are your parts?'

'Parts?' I answered blankly, thinking, 'What on earth is he on about?'

'Parts,' he repeated. 'Your music.'

'Surely you know the song,' I said, peeved. 'It's being played on radio every five minutes.'

Perhaps I could be forgiven for not understanding what Bob meant. When I performed with the Merseyside rock 'n' roll bands, they just picked up a new tune in minutes and then we'd do it. But suddenly I was in a BBC studio and they wanted it all written out.

Bobby tried to come to my rescue.

'Look,' he said to Bob, 'I've got a copy of the record here and a portable record player.'

He opened the lid, played 'Love Of The Love', and said cheerfully, 'There you are.'

Bob Miller was very patient. Just as well. If he hadn't been, I might have gone straight back to Liverpool.

'Listening to the record is one thing,' he said gently. 'But I still need parts for all the guys in the band.'

'Well, where am I supposed to get those?' Bobby asked, starting to panic.

'Ring the publisher,' Bob suggested.

The publisher was Dick James. Bobby got on the phone to him.

'I'm with Bob Miller at the BBC,' Bobby said to him, 'and he says he wants parts for his band!'

'Haven't you got them?' Dick asked, surprised.

'No, I haven't!' Bobby almost yelled.

'Oh dear,' said Dick and immediately arranged for a set to be rushed over to the theatre. You live and learn!

~

I was also thrilled to appear on ITV's *Ready, Steady, Go!*. This show meant so much to all of us. It portrayed 'fab' London, where everything was all now happening, and the nation's music and fashion tastes. The original show, hosted by Keith Fordyce, used Manfred Mann's '5, 4, 3, 2, 1' as its theme and had the Friday-night, feelgood slogan, 'The weekend starts here'. Cathy McGowan, who presented the programme, was one of the first friends I made in London. I met her when we did the show. She was the only girl on it and a Catholic like me – not just that, but she was as normal as I was, too, and we got on straight away.

In early October we set off on my first UK concert tour, a month-long series of one-nighters with Gerry and The Pacemakers in cinemas and theatres around the country, thirty-two dates in all, ending back on our own turf at the Liverpool Empire. If me mam and dad were anxious, they didn't say. They needn't have worried anyway. The band was all one big, happy family, the work was exciting but demanding, and it was definitely back to my hotel room on my own every night for me!

Gerry was a really big hit in our neck of the woods and I, for one, was not surprised that he became such a big crowd-puller on stage, TV, cabaret and film. As Brian once said, Gerry had 'a smile as wide as he was short, a very generous personality and a great voice, full of melody and feeling'.

I loved watching Gerry working an audience. In just minutes, he'd have everybody in the palm of his hand. On stage, he was so humorous, always winking and nodding, and giving the impression that butter would not melt in his mouth. He had a good, clean-living 'boy next door' image – was every mother's ideal son who'd never dream of using a swear word. But, off stage, it was a very different kettle of fish. He was an earthy hell-raiser and a practical joker.

On one occasion as our tour bus entered Sheffield, I remember jumping up and down with glee, saying: 'Oh, my God – look! There's Woollies and, I don't believe it, a Marks & Spencer – just like back 'ome!' Gerry looked stunned by my enthusiasm. I was so inexperienced then that sightings such as these were still a really big thrill.

The day after the tour began, I appeared on another TV show, *Thank Your Lucky Stars*. This programme, recorded in Birmingham, had a panel of youngsters who gave their views and awarded points to the new records. I was on the show with The Beatles, Billy J. Kramer and The Dakotas, and The Searchers. Tough competition, but I held my own!

Brian always described Billy J. Kramer, a tall, well-made ex-railway lad, as 'the best-looking pop-singer in the world'. He was, believe me, very dishy. But – and I will never understand why – he was one of the most insecure guys I've ever met. He had very little self-confidence, and was always wandering around and asking everybody's opinion.

One day when he came round to Scottie Road for a cup of tea with me and me mam, he said to her: 'Can I ask you a favour, Mrs White? Would you mind listening to a record I've just recorded and tell me what you think?'

'Of course – I'd love to, sunshine,' Mam replied.

As we all sat there listening, Billy was full of tension, hunched up and wracked with self-doubt, but after just a few bars Mam's eyes and mine were full of tears. It was such a beautiful, touching number, and he sang it with such tenderness. We knew at once that it would be a big hit for him.

'Mark my words, Billy,' Mam said, dabbing her eyes, 'that song is going to be a big hit. The world's your oyster, lad.'

The song was 'Little Children'. It went straight to the top of the UK charts and very nearly to the top of the US charts too.

~

In October 1963, very suddenly and dramatically, catching even Brian on the hop, something huge hit the UK: Beatlemania.

The Beatles, who were by now the biggest music phenomenon since Frank Sinatra in the forties, were still performing for small fees, and their fans could get into their shows without queuing up for hours. Once in, though, they couldn't hear a single note of the boys' performance above the mass hysteria. The mind-blowing screeches, screams and shouts blotted everything else out.

All of us who knew the band from their Cavern days were very proud of them, but somewhat nonplussed by what was happening. They were home-grown lads. We'd known them since they were kids, but even we had to admit they'd scrubbed up really well – they were truly worthy of being called the Fab Four.

We'd always kind of known that John, with his hooded eyes and poetic nature, was destined to be a talented *something*; that Paul, who was an expert at making his face an impassive mask when he was rubbed up the wrong way, had sex appeal and charm; that George, with his slow, wide crooked smile, had a musical ear second to none; and that Ringo – my little bearded mate from Dingle – with his wonderful, haunted, wistful eyes was a lovable cutie who could reduce us all to hysterics without even trying. But 'Beatlemania'? You've got to be kidding!

For me, the frenzy of Beatlemania was followed by a concert tour with Billy J. Kramer and The Dakotas; and then in December, less than four months after I'd made my first professional steps, I rounded off the year by appearing for three weeks in *The Beatles Christmas Show* at the Astoria Theatre in Finsbury Park, London. Also on the bill were Gerry and The Pacemakers, Billy J. Kramer, The Fourmost and Tommy Quickly. Rolf Harris was the MC. On the opening night, when The Beatles' fans were causing pandemonium inside and outside the theatre, everybody was getting really twitchy about risking lives and limbs on stage:

'Just *listen* to them!'

'They're running amok – out of control!'

'They'll tear us apart!'

Once on stage, just as we'd anticipated we couldn't hear ourselves think, talk or sing. Nobody was there to appreciate our art. It was bedlam, and to this day I don't know how we got through the show. The rest of the run was grim, too, but it was nothing compared to that first night.

~

Not surprisingly, given The Beatles' success, Brian was soon to outgrow his Moorfields offices in Liverpool. Later the following year, and with his usual sense of style, he moved to new offices in London, in Argyll Street, right next door to the Palladium.

Brian was kept very busy with John, Paul, George and Ringo during my first year as a professional singer, but he never neglected me. Every time we met up, he made it clear that he had very ambitious plans for me to be a solo singer and was determined I would be the next Judy Garland! At the time, I often wondered why I couldn't be a lead singer with my own band, but he didn't see me as part of a group. In the end, I just went along with the solo singer idea and accepted Sounds Incorporated as my backing group. Baz was the arranger and keyboard player, Dave 'The Major' and

Alan 'Boots' both played saxophone, Tony was on drums, and John and Dick played guitar and bass. All Londoners, they were incredible musicians, who could also read music – which neither I nor The Beatles could do.

~

At Scottie Road again to celebrate the New Year as it rolled in to the usual peals of bells and midnight chimes, I paused in the middle of a 'Knees Up Mother Brown' and grabbed hold of Bobby's hand for 'Auld Lang Syne'. It had been a good year to say the least! I'd got myself a dynamic manager, said fond farewells to my boss and workmates at BICC, made it to London, cut a single that had made it into the charts, and also recorded a second song, Dionne Warwick's 'Anyone Who Had A Heart'. And I was still only twenty! That wasn't bad for starters, but what would happen now? The onset of the New Year was giving me the heebie-jeebies!

My New Year wish was to prove, whatever the odds, that I was *not* a one-record singer – a mere flash in the pan!

'Will I make it?' I asked Bobby.

'You already have, Cil,' he replied.

'No – really make it. To the very top – with a number one record in the charts.'

'That's a tall order, chuck.'

'I know! But I don't want to settle for anything less.'

'Then we won't,' he replied, resolutely. 'Not now – not ever.'

8

An Untutored Girl

'Sorry, it's a really bad line – run that past me again, Brian.'

I was standing in a red telephone box that smelled of pee at the end of Scottie Road, speaking to Brian in his Moorfields office. In truth, I'd heard what he'd just said, but I'd always had a vivid imagination and I thought it just might have got the better of me on this occasion.

'Run that past me again, Brian,' I said for the second time.

'OK – I've just got the latest retail figures. "Anyone Who Had A Heart" is selling nearly a hundred thousand copies a day, and you're the first girl since Helen Shapiro to be number one in the British charts.'

'You wouldn't kid me, Brian – not about something as important to me as this.'

'I'm not kidding, Cilla.'

'It's a *number one?*'

'It is!'

Brian must have thought I'd fainted or been cut off. The next moment there was only dead air at my end of the phone. I was outta there, flying down the road to our flat above the barber's.

'*Mam!*' I yelled, mounting the stairs three at a time, nearly giving her a heart attack as I burst through the door, 'I've done it! I've done it! I've got a number one!'

Her smile, as I wrapped my arms around her neck and began to jig around the room, was wide enough to swallow Liverpool.

''Ave yer? Well, they won't be callin' yer "Big 'ead, no bread in the 'ouse" after this!'

'Anyone Who Had A Heart' had been released on 31 January 1964. To have reached number one by the end of February was an unbelievable beginning to the year. It really was the stuff that dreams are made of. Brian's news had me positively tingling with excitement – I was deliriously happy. What made my achievement even more amazing was that the UK was still in the grip of Beatlemania, and that the pop scene was dominated by groups, almost to the total exclusion of solo singers like me.

Brian had first heard 'Anyone Who Had A Heart', by Burt Bacharach and Hal David, being sung by Dionne Warwick while he was on a trip to New York. On his return to London, he took a copy of it to George Martin.

'It's a really lovely song,' George had said, pleased. 'Thanks, Brian. It's absolutely ideal for Shirley.'

'I wasn't thinking of it for Shirley Bassey,' Eppy replied coolly. 'I was thinking of Cilla.'

Bassey, as all her mates called her, had already scored twenty hit singles, including two number ones, since she started recording in 1957, and she was now being described as 'the UK's greatest singing star'.

Brian told me later that George had said, 'I very much doubt that Cilla's ready for an emotional piece like this.' But Eppy stood firm and it was me, not Shirley, who recorded the song.

When I first heard the song I liked it a lot and wanted to record it, but I didn't rate it as a chart-topper. Recording it was a piece of cake. We had what must have been a forty-eight-piece orchestra, the biggest I'd ever worked with, and during the recording, I did feel there was some 'magic' for me in the song. Johnny Pearson scored it, using a string section and piano and a distinctive French horn. George was convinced that, from the orchestral point of view, Johnny had created a much better sound than Dionne Warwick's original recording, but I like to believe that it was my vocal treatment that turned it into a smash hit!

Dionne Warwick's version had only got to number forty-two in the UK charts, but mine soared to number one. When this happened, there was some bitterness among her fans. The Crystals, a US female vocal group who were in London for a tour at that time, criticised me in the press.

'It would be different,' Dee Dee Kenniebrew said, 'if Cilla had done the song her way, but she just took it from Dionne and copied her every move. It seems a strain for her to reach the high notes, whereas Dionne does that with ease.'

Much to the dismay of the music journalists, who love a bit of rivalry, I refused to get caught up in the controversy; and, unbelievably in an era that was dominated by male groups, I remained in the number one spot for three weeks, and in the charts for seventeen weeks.

Just doing their job, no doubt, the press tried to stir things up between Shirley Bassey and me because of the argument over which of us should have recorded the song. But there was never any bitchiness or huge rivalry, then or later, between Shirley and me. I really admired and *loved* her, and I never found her the difficult person she was sometimes portrayed to be.

~

Brian was so thrilled with my success in the charts that he bought me the first expensive present I'd ever had, a gold bracelet watch with diamond chippings from Boodle & Dunthorne, then a small Liverpool jeweller's; and at a press conference, he didn't spare my blushes.

'Cilla,' he said, 'is going to be the next Judy Garland – one of the biggest stars in this country for thirty or forty years.'

I was also cock-a-hoop when I was told that, during a press interview, John Lennon had said, 'I always said Cilla's the one to watch.'

As if this wasn't head-turning enough, Sir Joseph Lockwood, the president of EMI, rewarded me on 22 March with my first silver disc for sales in excess of a quarter of a million; and the next day the *NME* announced that I was heading the list of the first 'All British Top Ten in Pop History'. Below me on that list were The Dave Clark Five, The Bachelors, The Merseybeats, The Searchers, The Rolling Stones, Billy J. Kramer and The Dakotas, Gerry and The Pacemakers, Brian Poole and The Tremeloes and Eden Kane.

These were extraordinary moments for a girl who, until recently, had been hanging up coats in the Cavern!

When I received the silver disc for 'Anyone Who Had A Heart', I had to sit up front listening to Brian giving a speech in his own inimitable way to a bunch of reporters and photographers.

'I first heard Cilla sing with The Beatles in Birkenhead,' Brian began, 'but I wasn't greatly impressed because the acoustics were all wrong for her voice. On the next occasion, however, in the Blue Angel Club, she looked magnificent – a slender, graceful creature with the ability to shed her mood of dignified repose when she was singing a fast number. I watched her move, watched her stand, then I half-closed my eyes and imagined her on a vast stage with real lighting. I was convinced from that moment that she could become a wonderful artiste – and I was right.

'She's a beautiful lady from whom we can all draw something. She is what she is – an untutored girl from a large, happy, working-class family in a lowly part of Liverpool. She's not easily intimidated by anything or anyone. She's warm, natural and frank, which I consider far more important than protocol. I wouldn't dream of attempting to dragoon any of my artistes into unnatural postures, for the very reason that I engage performers in whom I see a quality of stardom which, if warped or altered, would be lost. I've never actually made a star. The material is woven when I buy it over a sixpenny stamp on a contract.'

Honestly, I didn't know where to look!

~

The moment I first absorbed that I really had achieved my ambition and become a star was when I was walking down a busy London street, near a building site in Leicester Square, and a dozen lusty workmen wolf-whistled me and began to sing the chorus of 'Anyone Who Had A Heart'. That really was a turning point. Having been recognised by strangers in public, I stopped thinking of myself as Priscilla White and started to think of myself as Cilla Black, the pop star!

A second seminal moment for me came on 26 April at the *NME* poll-winners' show at the Empire Pool, Wembley, when I collected my first award for being voted 'Top Female Vocalist in the UK' and 'Third in the World'. Was there anywhere else to go!

But I was soon brought down to earth during a *really* daft encounter in Liberty's, the smart London store. Having chosen several items, I placed them on the counter.

'Oh! Can I have your autograph?' the till assistant asked.

'Of course,' I replied, writing it on the piece of paper she gave me and passing it back to her.

When it came to paying, I wrote out a cheque from the first cheque book I had ever owned, which had Cilla Black printed on it, and handed it to her. Without even looking at it, she said: 'Have you any form of identification?'

'You've just recognised me and asked me for my autograph,' I said, nonplussed.

'Oh, no,' she said, 'that won't do. I have to have some official identification.'

'But you know who I am – and the cheque has my name on it.'

'I'm afraid I can't accept this,' she said, 'unless you can prove you're Cilla Black.'

By now a crowd of people had gathered around me at the pay desk and were clamouring for my autograph.

In no time at all, I was signing my name for a line of people who, like the assistant, knew I was Cilla Black, but, unlike the assistant, didn't need proof of identity. It was crazy! The actual goods were only worth about £40, and I had enough money in the bank by then to go down the road and buy a diamond bracelet for a thousand pounds. At last a supervisor was called and the problem was solved.

~

When I went on a concert tour of England in February 1964 with Billy J. Kramer, Gene Pitney, The Swinging Blue Jeans, and The Remo Four, I often used to come back to the hotels after a show to find that the boys had scattered a carpet of flowers for me all over the hotel lifts. I should have felt very touched, but I was always worried sick because I knew they hadn't bought them. They'd raided the hotels' flower displays on their way in!

That tour, thirty-six action-packed dates in all, criss-crossed north, east, south and west England, and finally came to an end at the Queen's Theatre, Blackpool, after which another tour of nine dates began.

In fact, after I signed with Brian, I did four hundred live performances in eight months. I couldn't do that now, not without some serious SAS training, but I took it all in my stride then. I never gave a thought to how lucky I was to be young, with good health and phenomenal stamina to back me up. But God knows why I *was* so healthy. We were living on chip butties, frozen hamburgers and fish fingers, but I never put on weight. Later, I did try to eat properly, but it wasn't always possible when I was in a show. Inevitably, Bobby and I often ended up snacking, and we sometimes missed meals altogether.

During those months on the road, I learned a lot about travelling from one venue to another. This was the age of the tour coach, when everyone, including the headline star, travelled that way. It wasn't until visiting Americans insisted on having their own limos that all the British performers insisted on that, too. But the old days of the coach were great and I wouldn't have missed them for the world. As snug as bugs, we were like kids on a school outing, all up for a laugh and telling sick jokes, and there were loads of pranks and frolics behind windows which were steamed up more often than not. It wasn't so funny, though, when we stopped for lunch. The loos were always full and we had to gobble our food and drink. If we didn't get the meals down fast enough, the coach would be off without us!

'I've got chronic indigestion', 'I feel as sick as a parrot', 'I can't stop blowin' off', 'I wanna go to the loo again', one or other of the fellers would moan as the coach sped off.

'Well, don't sit near me,' I'd say.

It was boys behavin' badly. Totally unsexy. Farts, belches, five o'clock shadows, smelly socks and vests – and Bobby was as bad as the rest of them.

~

With Bobby's help I soon got living out of a suitcase down to a fine art and, although I wasn't the world's best ironer, I never trusted the hotel staff to press my minidresses. I was forever crouched on the floor doing this myself.

Unlike with today's girl groups, there was only one of me, which was a bit lonesome at times, but at least I had Bobby with me. Being on tour was a strange amalgam of fairytale and nightmare. But I could do it because I was young, because I wanted to learn everything there was to learn. Nothing else – being constantly on the move, packing and unpacking – mattered. Once the slap and the stage dress was on, and the spotlight shone down on me, *that* was what it was all about – *that* was home for me in every town and city.

That moment before you step into the spotlight affects different people in different ways. Cliff Richard says sometimes he's very nervous before he goes on stage, but once I'd passed my auditions with Brian and George, I was like Red Rum, the racehorse, pawing the ground in his starting box – 'Let me out', 'Let me on.' Once there behind the mike, listening to the opening bars of the music, it was as if I'd been lifted to another planet. I *was* nervous. Of course I was. And I was glad I was. I knew that if I ever lost that completely, I would have lost a vital edge. But I knew it wouldn't happen.

Everything that happened during those early months was a learning curve. As a girl singer I was never subjected to the same screamin' and shoutin' and physical hassle as the boys, but as the only girl to come out of the Merseybeat explosion, I still attracted a huge amount of attention from fans and autograph-hunters. As my reputation grew and my air time and stage exposure increased, everybody in my group, including Bobby, became fair game. Kids were forever mobbing him, waving their books and pens and shouting, 'Are you anybody?'

'No!' Bobby would say firmly. 'I'm nobody, honest.'

But that didn't save him the day we were leaving the studios of Southern Television after another broadcast there. Suddenly a mob of Southampton girls rushed him and, catching him unawares, succeeded in dragging him to the ground. They were like tigresses, had completely lost it, and poor Bobby had only left the building first to clear the way for me!

When I followed him out, the fact that I was a girl counted for nothing. They abandoned him and rushed at me. All my squawks of 'Gerroff!' did nothing to deter them.

I was wearing a shiny black plastic mac designed by Mary Quant. It had cost a small fortune, but its buttons were ripped off and it was torn to shreds in five seconds. I was in shock – really upset. I loved that mac, and you can't repair plastic. Bobby didn't enjoy nursing his bumps and bruises either.

'We ought to be paid danger money,' he snorted.

~

Success, I was discovering, could be every bit as scary as failure. My number one hit with 'Anyone Who Had A Heart' had been great, had taken us all by surprise – and had made me rich. But what now? No British girl had ever had two successive number one hits. That was unthinkable. But, unbelievably, the unthinkable was what happened when 'You're My World' was released and reached number one in the charts on 1 May 1964.

I could hardly contain myself. I'd been on edge all week, wondering if it could happen, but when the record reached the number two spot I thought it might just stick there. It was agony – like watching a race in slow motion.

A big plus, when I heard it had reached number one, was knowing that the hurtful remarks dished out by Dionne Warwick's fans at the time of 'Anyone Who Had A Heart' couldn't stick now that I'd made such a swift return to the top of the charts.

A couple of weeks later, when The Beatles returned from America, Ringo told me at the Ad-Lib Club that 'You're My World' was also a big hit there – and, what's more, he had some other riveting news for me. 'You'll never believe this,' he said, 'but when we went to visit Elvis, your record was number twenty-one on Elvis's own jukebox.'

'Are you saying Elvis's finger has zapped *my* record in his own home?' I asked.

'That's what I'm saying, luv.'

'That's even better than being number one!'

~

Some of the things I was asked to do to promote 'You're My World' were just ridiculous. One PR at a photo-shoot had me standing on a narrow wall, just a ledge really, on the roof of the President Hotel off Russell Square, where there was nothing between me and the ground below but certain death.

'Just step up there, Cilla,' he said, 'face the camera and throw your arms out to the wind.'

Oh, yeah! I had no head for heights at the best of times – vertigo was *me*! – but, young, stupid and obliging as I was then, I took a deep breath, convinced it was my last, and did what I was told. Brian had inspired me with so much confidence early on, he had somehow convinced me that I was invincible and could do anything.

~

That spring, less than eight months after my launch as a professional, Brian told me I had been booked to appear at the London Palladium. I didn't realise at the time just how big a deal this was, but I probably should have done. In the fifties and sixties, the Palladium was considered the world's top variety theatre, and performers – singers, dancers, comics, jugglers and magicians alike – spent half their careers dreaming of getting a booking there. Even the biggest names in American entertainment queued up to top the bill, and *Sunday Night at the London Palladium*, ITV's star-studded, hour-long TV spectacular, was televised live from this famous West End venue each weekend. I'd gleaned, of course, that the Palladium was regarded with great awe and reverence in London but Liverpudlians looked upon it as just another theatre, and I didn't really appreciate until later that appearing there was very special, a landmark in anybody's career.

The show I was to appear in at the Palladium was called *Startime,* and its headline stars were Frankie Vaughan and Tommy Cooper, two of the biggest names in British showbusiness; and among the supporting acts were The Fourmost, home-grown Liverpudlians. The show was actually planned as a short season, but its run was extended because the box office bookings were so good. Between May and December I did thirteen shows a week at the Palladium, a total of over four hundred performances.

While I was there, I never sneaked out of the side entrances or used a getaway car to avoid the waiting fans. Having been such an ardent fan myself, who'd hung around stage doors in my teenage years, I thought that would be really cheating.

On Saturdays I'd go in at eleven in the morning, do three shows and finish at eleven at night. Then Bobby would drive me straight home to Liverpool so I could have me mam's Sunday dinner. He'd bought a brand new car – a Humber Sceptre – from his songwriting royalties, so we did the journey in comfort. Everyone at home was always pleased to see me, but there was no way I could get above myself in that family.

One weekend we'd driven through the night as usual. When I arrived, obviously feeling a bit full of myself and thinking, 'I'm a star now – I can do anything', I made the near-fatal mistake of parking myself in Dad's armchair. When he came in, this was the first thing he noticed.

'Hey, you! What do you think you're doing?' he said, real menace in his voice. 'Get out of my chair.'

Some changes he might accept, but that, bless him, was not one of them. In a few words he'd made it clear that there was no way I could ever become a prima donna around him. He was obviously still smarting about my change of name, too, and he never let me or my mam and brothers forget that he was still my father and that he hadn't signed away his authority over me.

The family never let my comings and goings interfere with their plans, either. If one of them wanted to go out, they went – never mind the fact that their daughter or sister – 'the star' – had just driven six or seven hours along the old A-roads to see them.

'Tarrah, chuck,' they'd say. 'See you later.'

One Sunday I was left in the flat with only Lassie, our dog, for company!

~

When I was at the Palladium I sang with the pit orchestra. That was a new and not very happy experience for me. Their music never seemed to come from their guts, they appeared to do everything by the dots on the page, and I thought they totally lacked soul and spontaneity. It was so different from being on tour when I always had Sounds Incorporated as my backing group. They were great, always understood where I was coming from, and were prepared to take risks.

While I was in *Startime* I very nearly came a cropper. I'd got into a bad habit of missing the finales, the final curtain calls when the entire cast makes their bows on stage while the audience goes wild wolf-whistling, clapping and foot banging. I was young, naive and a bit arrogant, and I just couldn't see the point of walking back down a load of steps when I'd already been on and sung my heart out. My attitude was, 'I've done my bit. I'd like to go back to the hotel now.'

On one occasion, I was in my dressing room when I heard the usual announcement over the Tannoy of 'Ten minutes, please. This is your final call', but I was so engrossed in washing my tights, it slipped my mind.

Management was not pleased. Finales were considered an important part of the show and it was, I soon learned, an unwritten law for performers to turn up for them. Ted Matthews, the stage manager, was so angry that he threatened me with a fine.

'If you miss one more finale, Miss Black,' he said, 'I'm going to fine you five pounds.'

'Five pounds for missing a finale?' I thought, horrified. Five pounds was a lot of money then – nearly a week's wage when I left BICC.

His threat cured me. From then on, I accepted that I had a responsibility towards the audience, the paying public, and to those who paid me, the management, and I never missed a finale again.

Frankie Vaughan, who also came from Liverpool, was like a god to me. I stood in the wings and watched him and Tommy Cooper every night. By the end of the run, I felt I'd learned everything there was to know about stage presence and how to make a good entrance and exit.

Frankie, who'd been a high-kicking, heart-throb singer since the fifties, was just great. He was so natural, never put on any airs and graces and would sit down and chat with anybody. He used to play cards with the band and smoke a cigar, even though he was a singer and shouldn't have smoked at all. He was so patient with me, never tired of me coming up and asking him questions.

'Frankie,' I'd groan. 'I've got a sore throat. What can I do for it?'

'Come with me. Saltwater gargle,' he'd reply.

Both of us suffered from catarrh and talking through our noses, and Frankie was forever advising me about this or that remedy.

Every time I watched him from the wings and listened to him singing 'Give Me The Moonlight' I thought, 'This guy's the tops. He's so experienced, so suave, so sophisticated – and I want some of that.'

Was I, in spite of all I'd achieved, in too much of a hurry? Perhaps. But success can easily disappear – and I was as nervous as the next person about that. It could all be over tomorrow.

9

The Weekend Starts Here

With two number one hits under my belt, sacks of mail were arriving at the London Palladium for me, but this didn't prepare me for what Audrey Jeans, a terribly glamorous singer and comedy actress, told me in my dressing room at the theatre one afternoon. When Audrey said, 'You know it's *you* who's drawing the people in and making *Startime* the big success it is,' I was speechless.

I could hardly take in what she was saying. By then I was used to going out and doing my act, but I'd thought the full houses were due to Frankie and Tommy.

'Trust me,' Audrey said, reading my thoughts. 'Frankie and Tommy are the greatest, but you're the one who's pulling them in.'

Click-click-click went my brain.

'You'd never believe it, though, to see your dressing room,' Audrey sniffed, disgusted. 'It's just awful!'

I glanced around me. The room was enormous, but it was pretty dreadful. The paint on the door and skirting boards was pockmarked, the walls looked like baby's sick, the sofas were too unsavoury to sit on, and there was only a tattered, none-too-clean curtain to separate the dressing area from the sitting area. The pull cord for this had snapped long ago and

I had to keep tugging the curtain across whenever I was changing or doing my make-up. Guys don't mind undressing in front of other people, but I wasn't that liberated. I liked my privacy.

'You're a *star*,' Audrey was rattling on. 'You deserve better. This dressing room needs a revamp. Why don't you go to the stage manager and tell him what you think of it?'

The stage manager was Ted Matthews, the feller who had threatened to fine me five pounds for missing finales, but, spurred on by Audrey, I went to find him.

'Mr Matthews,' I began, pinning him down backstage and repeating word for word what Audrey had said, 'my dressing room's a disgrace.'

'What's wrong with it?' he asked cautiously.

'*Everything*. It's absolutely awful. I deserve better.' I couldn't believe it was me talking!

'So? What do you want to happen?'

I could hardly believe he was such a pushover – and suddenly I felt very empowered, confident.

'I want it redecorated, please; and, if you can't get new sofas in time, at least get the existing ones re-covered – and I need the curtains to work!'

There was a short silence while he seemed to be studying his shoes. 'He's gonna put the boot in,' I thought. 'And, if he doesn't do that, he'll certainly fine me for being so cheeky.' But he did neither of these things. Having weighed things up, he said, 'OK. It'll all be done before you come in on Monday.'

I could hardly conceal my delight. In a few minutes, I'd discovered I was valuable enough to call the shots, but I would never have dreamed of doing it if Audrey hadn't spurred me on. I hadn't even told Bobby what I was planning. If I had, he might have said, 'Let sleeping dogs lie. We'll be outta here soon enough.'

Having spoken to Mr Matthews, I went straight back to my dressing room where Audrey was waiting.

'It's gonna be done – it's gonna be done!' I announced, triumphantly. And, sure enough, it was – by Monday.

~

On 27 May 1964, my twenty-first birthday, I faced a barrage of flash-bulbs at the Palladium. 'Oh, God,' I joked with the journalists during the photo-shoot and interviews, 'now you lot will always remember my age – and I'll never be able to lie about it in the future!'

Having done my duty, Bobby and I then went out for a fantastic lunch with Brian and George Harrison at the glamorous restaurant that is now called Le Caprice. It had a brilliant Belgian chef and was one of London's top three places to eat at that time. I felt so happy and so grown up, sitting there with my three handsome escorts. When it came to dessert I was feeling pretty full, but Eppy was determined that I should try the wild straw-berries and cream.

'Oh, go on,' he said, 'they're absolutely gorgeous. I'd have them myself if I weren't on a diet.'

So I gave in, but I didn't like them at all. Unsophisticated as I was, I thought there was much too much alcohol sprinkled over the strawberries.

'Oh well,' said Eppy, 'in that case I'll help you out' – and he polished off the lot.

As if that was not indulgence enough for one day, the birthday cele-brations continued at a swish cocktail party on the stage of the Palladium, and then, after that night's show, Bobby and I went on to a party that Brian had organised for me at his Knightsbridge flat. Up in Liverpool, me mam and dad were having a do for my birthday as well at Scottie Road – I could not be there as I was working at the Palladium, but I phoned them from Brian's flat, and I could tell they were having a right knees-up. All my rela-tives and friends were there, my Aunt Nellie, my Aunt Ann, and Pat, and truth be told, I really did miss my family that night. I would much rather have been at Scottie Road with all of them than standing around at a posh cocktail party in London.

Brian's present was a magnificent Austrian luggage set, which was just *perfect* when I had to go Paris soon after. *Fab 208* magazine wanted to photograph me in loads of different outfits, and we had to do it all on a Sunday, my day off from the Palladium. This was my first trip abroad and I had to get a passport. It was boiling hot on the day, but we had a fabulous time going up and down the Seine, and we finished off going to a club in the evening.

'Oh, Bobby,' I kept sighing whenever there was a spare moment to stop and look around us.

The French seemed to live most of their life out of doors and everywhere there were chic people of all ages out for a stroll or sitting watching the world go by in pavement cafés or bistros and tea salons.

Paris has always been renowned as *the* city for romance and for lovers – and it was lovely for Bobby and me to be able to snatch half an hour to walk hand-in-hand along the River Seine and steal a kiss or two under those famous bridges where I knew Edith Piaf had once busked for centimes, singing 'Sur Le Pont De Paris'.

We were whisked around the sights by the French lady who'd found the locations for the fashion shoot and, by the time the day was over, I'd got the bug and could hardly wait to go travelling again.

'Where d'you wanna go next?' Bobby asked me during a blissful dinner at Les Deux Magots, the street-corner café in St-Germain-des-Prés once frequented by writers like Jean-Paul Sartre and Ernest Hemingway.

'To see the whole world,' I replied.

That shows how easily I'd taken to my new-found wealth and stardom: I had no problems adapting to them, because they were what I'd wanted all my life. I was young and naive, but I took to success and money like a duck takes to water.

~

Back in London, I soon found myself nursing a bad throat and had to miss some of my *Startime* shows at the Palladium, so I went home to Liverpool to have a rest and get some sea air. I was so looking forward to going cockling at Moreton with Bobby, and to spending time on the beach at New Brighton, just like we used to do, but that was impossible. Everywhere we went, we were swamped by people. '*Cilla!*' they'd call out before rushing me for an autograph. And this continued the entire time we were up there.

Strangely enough, it was easier to hide in the West End of London. People did occasionally approach me in Oxford Street or Leicester Square, but it was mostly just to say a friendly 'hello'.

In 1964 I still thought I could go around town unmolested. So if I wanted to go to the pictures I'd just turn up with Bobby and queue with everyone else. On one occasion, after I'd finished a show at the Palladium, Bobby and I went to a late-night film in Leicester Square. Fortunately, on that particular evening there weren't that many people around. I signed a few autographs, then we went in and sat down. We hadn't been watching the film for long when, exhausted from the performance, I began to nod off. Bobby waited till I was fast asleep, then crept off to sit about four rows behind me where he could see better.

When the lights came up, I was still asleep; and a feller sitting in the same row as me suddenly realised who I was and plonked himself alongside me, pen and paper poised.

'Can I have your autograph?' he asked as my eyes flickered open. I almost took leave of my skin! I didn't know where I was, where Bobby had got to, and what I was doing waking up beside a complete stranger!

~

On most nights after the Palladium show, Bobby and I hadn't a clue what to do with ourselves. We didn't know any clubs or restaurants, and didn't want to go straight back to the President Hotel, so most evenings we just finished up at the Golden Egg in Leicester Square, sitting under the bright neon lights while everyone stared at us.

I'd always assumed that if I became successful it would be like winning the pools and that a magic 'they' would take care of everything for me.

'They' would tell me where to eat, what shops to go to, where to have my hair done. But of course for the most part it wasn't like that.

Tommy Cooper took us out for dinner once or twice, but on the whole things were pretty quiet.

~

Cathy McGowan was a different kind of friend, and very special – it was like being as close to home as I could really get. Here was an ordinary girl just like myself, of the same age, to hook up with, talk about fashion and go shopping with. I wasn't exactly lonely, but it was very good to have her as a friend. Once I'd met her, London seemed a whole new place.

'Kids want clothes to look fab,' Cathy announced one day. 'They don't want to wear them for very long so it doesn't matter if they fall to bits.'

I was *so* lucky. There I was, one of London's dolly-birds, with sufficient time off between working sessions to respond to spontaneous calls from the girl they called 'the queen of mod'.

Bobby, like most guys, didn't dig shopping, so I loved going off on these sprees with Cathy. I was *so* pleased we'd hit it off so well when I first appeared on *Ready, Steady, Go!*, and that she'd taken me under her wing. She always seemed to know what was 'in', what was 'out', where it could be bought and where everything else was happening. She was exactly the walkin' talkin' London-scene doll-guide I needed, and so modest about her own talents.

Intelligent, charming, witty and pretty, she never took herself too seriously – and her long, dark, fringed hair hung so perfectly straight some of us thought it was ironed! When the press first started dubbing her 'queen of mod' she always laughed it off, saying, 'Fab – smashing – but what's all the hype about?'

There was more to it than that. She wasn't just a star-stuck, pretty face, she really knew her stuff on-screen; and off-screen she was a mine of information about how to make the most of living in a fab place where it was all happening. And all this was at a time when 'youth' was the key word, and the capital was positively sagging under the weight of bright young things and new designers who were intent upon kicking aside all traces of middle-agedom and making new, exciting things happen.

Cathy introduced me to her boyfriend, Leslie Russell, who took my Vidal Sassoon geometric, boyish bob and cut it even shorter. I loved my new look.

Where fashion was concerned, Mary Quant was the first to start a revolution in fashion by opening a boutique called Bazaar, where groovy, dedicated followers of fashion, like Cathy and me, could happily roam along a rail and spend an absolute fortune on miniskirts and dresses in ten minutes!

There was nothing I liked better than a wake-up call from Cathy, followed by a jaunt on foot or a joyride cruise in her Mini around the week's newly sprouted boutiques in the King's Road, Fulham Road and Carnaby Street, which then eclipsed into girlie gossips of the 'Have you heard?' and 'He/she *never* did' variety. Being her friend was magic – and, where fashion was concerned, London was *the* place.

There seemed to be literally hundreds of boutiques with a flamboyant ear-rending ambience, specialising in eye-knocking, original clothes, usually at low prices! There was the designer Barbara Hulanicki, whose boutique, Biba, named after her sister, became *the* classic, and had three thousand of us dolly birds sorting through her Aladdin's cave of clothes, jewellery and sunglasses every week. The skinny sleeves of some of her dresses were so tight they hindered our circulation, but as well as Cathy and me, her customers included celebrities, like Brigitte Bardot, Julie Christie, Françoise Hardy and Mia Farrow. So we didn't care!

There was the rag trade's Carnaby Street, a frenzied alleyway at the back of Regent Street, where pop music blended with psychedelic colours and fashions that became a must for swinging Londoners and all those who travelled in from far and near in search of the super clothes, such as those designed by Sally Tuffin and Marion Foale, so they, too, could create a riot back home wearing what Cathy and I called 'Tuffy Fluffies'.

There was Top Gear and Count Down, a pair of adjacent boutiques run by the designer James Wedge and his fashion-model girlfriend Pat Booth, who became a great friend of Cathy's and mine. (Pat was a true East Ender – she'd started her working life on eel and whelk stalls – and she was later to become the author of several bestselling books, including her blockbuster, *Palm Beach*.) And there was the very camp and theatrical Granny Takes A Trip, in the King's Road, Chelsea, a match-box-size building, painted bright purple, with its slogan above the door, 'One should either be a work of art or wear a work of art', whose customers included among others The Beatles, The Rolling Stones and The Who.

Another must for us was Michael Rainey's Hung On You, in Chelsea's Cale Street. Filled with second-hand garments of a bygone age, this boutique, run by eccentrics for eccentrics, was considered the most extravagantly way out shop for guys' fashions, and The Beatles once ordered twelve floral-patterned shirts there. Many other pop stars, like Donovan, The Who and The Action, also found their way to it.

Bobby – and all the boys – *had* to go to John Stephen. The son of a Glasgow sweetshop owner, who'd become the 'King of Carnaby Street', John expanded his business into ten shops that attracted The Rolling Stones, The Yardbirds, The Dave Clark Five and many others. I don't think T-shirts were ever a fashion item before he came along with his, especially the pop-art versions. 'I've conquered London, now I'm conquering America, *next* it's the world,' he told us all, modestly!

Posh names proliferated, too. Cathy and I found our way to shops called Lord John, Lady Jane and Annacat – where we could buy simple miniskirts made in Thai silk – and Blades in Mayfair, started by a young Old Etonian named Rupert Lycett-Green, whose customers ranged from Mick Jagger to the Marquess of Hartington.

So, from the moment Mary Quant breached the citadels of middle-age fashion, the revolution in dress lapped over into trendier, must-go-see restaurants and nightclubs – and Cathy and I, and all the other groovy boys and girls, were not slow in making the most of it.

~

Brian, of course, helped Bobby and me whenever he could. A man of phenomenal style, who came from a posh, well-off family, he automatically knew things that were completely foreign to us. He was marvellous and I adored him.

He was also very busy. While Bobby and I were getting to grips with this new world, he was learning about management. As well as turning himself into a successful manager, he had to teach himself all the technical side of the music business; and what he achieved for the people he managed was absolutely amazing. In those days the biggest and most sought-after managers were Lew and Leslie Grade and Bernard Delfont. When Brian began, he was just a young Northern executive trying to get a foot on the first rung of the ladder. Most out-of-town agents would have found it too daunting even to consider breaking into the London scene; most would have been more cautious and maybe gone in with the Grades while they found their feet. Not Brian. He waded straight in and soon set up his own London office. This was not only a bold move, it was a very successful one. His style of management was different in days when most agents were just 'bookers' who handed their clients a list of dates and left them to sort out their own hotels and find their way from A to B. It didn't occur to them to do more than this because they thought pop groups and pop singers were mere flashes in the pan who wouldn't amount to much in terms of business interests and financial gains. With the exception of Helen Shapiro, Tommy Steele, Cliff Richard – and perhaps a couple of others – the life of a pop group or pop singer *was* usually very short. Top agents could reel off the names of dozens of people who, having had a couple of hits, had vanished from the scene.

Our Brian was the first to organise a complete management package, and those of us who signed with him benefited from a lot of extra services:

press agent, travel agent, secretarial help with fan letters, etc., and a general feeling that he would take care of us.

There was always a very special bond between Brian and us, and the secretarial people he lined up for us, and we all had a great sense of pride in what we were doing – together. I know it sounds a cliché, but we really were a family. It was Liverpool versus The Rest, so if anyone – me, The Beatles, Billy J. Kramer and The Dakotas, Gerry and The Pacemakers – had a hit record, we all shared in the triumph. Typical NEMS publicity photos in those days often linked two of Brian's acts in one picture. For example, a Christmas photo might show 'Santa Cilla' giving presents to Gerry and The Pacemakers!

I was still very naive and learning how to adjust to sudden fame, to being a 'somebody', but I was never intimidated by anyone, no matter how grand they were – or thought they were. That must have stemmed from something inborn in me, and I'm very grateful that it did. When you're twenty-one, you don't stop to weigh up all the pros and cons, you just jump in feet first and go along with it all.

Even though there was no magic 'they' to put me on the right track, I did come across some kind people who helped me along the way. John Lyndon, a NEMS producer, taught me about art. He had a wonderful collection of theatre posters which he bought at markets, like the one in Portobello Road. I was only too happy to be guided by him, but no art expert in the world could have persuaded me to buy the pictures that were brought round to Brian's office one day. They were all of nude boys draped around a swimming pool, and the fact that they were painted by a young artist named David Hockney carried no weight with me.

'If I put one of those on our wall,' I said, horrified, 'me mam will go berserk!' Brian, of course, loved them.

John also put us right about drink. This was just as well because we really hadn't a clue about alcohol. In Liverpool most people only had booze in the house when there was a funeral or wedding! The rest of the time, the kettle was on the hob, 'cos we all loved our 'cup of scald'. If the men wanted something stronger, they went down the pub.

When Bobby and I first came down to London, we never had wine with our meals in restaurants. We'd order steak and chips and Coca-Cola! In fact I'd never touched alcohol until well past my twenty-first birthday. The person who got us into more sophisticated habits like ordering wine was Muriel Young, a gorgeous, sexy TV presenter who became a good friend after we met her in a TV studio. She told us about the Pickwick Club, a very lively venue just off Leicester Square where you could always get something to eat late at night, and Bobby and I often went there with her.

'Let's have a bottle of Mateus Rose,' she used to say.

Mateus, a Portuguese wine (it came in low, flask-shaped bottles that became very popular for use as candleholders in restaurants and people's homes) became a cult drink with the rock bands. The Rolling Stones, for instance, who we had recently met in another TV studio, would come into the Pickwick Club, and say, 'Mateus, please', 'Yeah, I'll have a Mateus', 'Same for me', 'Yeah – yeah', – and the club did a roaring trade in the stuff.

Muriel used to read the weather forecasts, but they had to take her off that because she was too sexy – that was before the days of weathergirls in bikinis! I loved her tales about when she was Auntie Mu on the *Five O'Clock Show*. One day she had two puppets, Olly Beak the Owl and Fred the Dog, as her guests. When they were getting to the end of the show, Muriel saw the floor manager signalling that she was coming in under time and needed to carry on talking.

'Well, that's OK when you have human guests,' Muriel explained, 'but how do you fill in three minutes when you're chatting to puppets?'

Giving it her best shot, Muriel turned to Olly Beak and said: 'Well, Olly, what have you been up to lately?'

'Well,' replied Olly, 'the other day I was invited to a ball.'

'Don't be silly, Olly,' Muriel said without thinking, 'owls don't have balls!'

Olly Beak and Fred the Dog shifted quickly out of shot – and Auntie Mu was left on her own to finish the programme.

~

One afternoon when I was in Brian's new office on Argyll Street, I heard Brian talking to George and Ringo about the Ad-Lib. Apparently Alma Cogan's little sister Sandra, who was a singer at the Establishment Club, had taken George there and he had loved it, and he had taken Ringo and Brian there a few nights later.

'What's the Ad-Lib?' I asked, always eager to learn something new.

'It's a club, Cilla,' Brian said. 'But I'm not going to take you there because, if I do, you'll start behaving just like the boys and I'll never get you out of it.'

He couldn't have made it sound more tempting.

'Oh, go on, Brian, please take me,' I begged.

So he did – and it turned out to be an amazing place.

A new nightclub on the fifth floor of a Soho penthouse, close to Leicester Square, the Ad-Lib had exotic fur-covered walls, a large fish tank filled with piranhas and a huge picture window that faced Soho, Piccadilly and Mayfair. With coloured recessed ceiling lights, banquette seating, low tables, lots of large mirrors and a tiny dance floor, it was one of the first places to have the booming new sound system. The resident DJ, who wore a dinner jacket, stored his equipment in the piano, and alcoholic drinks were served in little bottles like those you get on planes, with the ice, soda, tonic and Coke separate.

Brian Morris, the manager, had just the right touch with all the bright young things like The Beatles, The Rolling Stones, The Animals, The Hollies and The Moody Blues, and the hot actors, models, photographers and designers who went there.

'Hi – hello there,' he'd say with genuine warmth and affection, wrapping his arms around his regulars.

John was very shocked the first time Brian Morris greeted him by kissing him on both cheeks. Fellers only ever shook hands in Liverpool.

What's It All About?

Before the Ad-Lib opened, we all felt that we were grafted on to clubs that were catering for an older generation who liked to dance to an orchestra – but this one, with its resident band that played R & B and Soul, was the first nightclub to cater for our tastes, tolerate our wild, exuberant antics and allow us to party non-stop if we liked. People never asked for autographs there, and the fellers could get drunk, stoned and fall on their faces if they liked without getting into any bother. They didn't play our own records to us, either – it was strictly only heavy US rock 'n' roll. One of the American records that we all loved goin' mad to in the Ad-Lib was Derek Martin's 'Daddy Rollin' Stone'.

Within months of opening, the club had become *the* place for the young and famous to go to relax and dance and not be stared at after their shows, and to rub shoulders with other up-and-coming names like Mary Quant and her husband, Alexander Plunket Green, Barbara Hulanicki, Vidal Sassoon, the hairdresser to the stars and dolly birds, the photographers David Bailey, Terence Donovan and Terry O'Neill, and actors Terence Stamp and Michael Caine. Everybody would cram in, grab a toasted steak butty, twist to the music, enjoy listening to the booming sound – and anybody who was so inclined would have a joint and get stoned. One night I remember the celebrated transsexual April Ashley was there – not only did 'she' look stunning, but she was wearing a gobsmacking see-through black chiffon top that concealed absolutely nothing. Not realising the true situation at first, a whole load of red-blooded rock 'n' rollers who wouldn't normally step on to the dance floor were on it like a shot that night!

Meanwhile, the cult drink had moved on from Mateus – first it became whisky and Coke, then it was all change again when The Beatles came back from a trip to New York. 'You don't want that,' they said, disgusted. 'You want Bourbon and Seven-Up.' So then we all switched to that. I never drank much, though. I'd only recently started drinking alcohol and I didn't like spirits, and it was no trouble to make one glass last all night.

It was no wonder that, by the early hours of the morning, Bobby and I would drift back to the President Hotel exhausted and ready to hit the sack.

~

John and Paul wrote my next single, 'It's For You', and Paul introduced me to the song by sending a demo disc that he'd made of it round to the Palladium. Although Paul had sung it as a waltz, George Martin took a big hand in my recording of it and asked Johnny Spence to arrange it. Johnny was a famous big-band arranger, and he later went on to be Tom Jones's personal musical director. It was a fabulous arrangement, a sort of jazz waltz. I definitely wanted to do it à la Della Reece, with a Big Band sound.

On the day I was recording it, John and Paul, who had only arrived back that morning from Australia, came round to Abbey Road. It was great to see them. They were in awe of Johnny Spence, as well as of George Martin, so they didn't dare to interfere with the recording.

When it was released, 'It's For You' notched up advance orders of 200,000 copies and went straight into the Top Ten, but it failed to give me a third consecutive number one chart-topper. I was gutted, but I tried to console myself by thinking, 'I can't have a number one *every* time or people will think I'm a freak!'

When I was asked to perform the song live on TV at Granada Studios, Manchester, the set was entirely made from unfriendly iron scaffolding poles. I had to enter very high up, while below me a couple of male dancers were swinging decorously from parachute cords and turning somersaults on the scaffolding. I have absolutely no head for heights. I can walk *up* any number of steps, but I hate walking *down*. I was terrified. 'C'mon Cilla, you can do this,' I muttered. It was a good job I was only miming. Somehow I managed to get through the song, but there was still a bit more trouble in store for me.

John and Paul were on the lower set, where they were sitting waiting to do a shot of the three of us over canned applause (there was no audience), and as I came off the steep ramp, wearing a *very* mini dress, and sat down beside them, John whispered something in my ear. I reeled back-wards, hand to my mouth, giggling nervously. What he'd said was 'Great! Look – no knickers!' For a split second I was terrified that it was true, and I couldn't wait to get back to the dressing room to check. Although I was happy with being on show all the time, there were limits, and moments like that made me suddenly aware of just how little privacy I really had.

~

Soon after this, I was due to sing 'You're My World' in front of the Queen at the Royal Variety Show at the Palladium. The lovely Millicent Martin, who had come to fame as a singer in the satirical review *That Was The Week That Was*, was happy to teach me all she knew about royal etiquette.

'When you first meet the Queen, you have to call her "Your Majesty". Never *ever* call her "Your Royal Highness" – that would be totally out of order. But once you've addressed her as "Your Majesty", when you curtsy – just like this – then you have to call her "Ma'am" – to rhyme with Spam. Then, when it comes to Princess Margaret, you say "Your Royal Highness", then thereafter you address her as "Marm" to rhyme with arm, but Her Majesty is "Ma'am".'

'I call my mother "Mam",' I said, surprised, 'and back home mams call their daughters "Queen" and their sons "Sunshine".' It was all very confusing. But there was more to come.

'And remember, she's probably never heard of you.'

'Are you crazy, Millie? There's a huge, life-size, full-length picture of me outside this theatre. She'd have to be blind not to know who I am!'

'She won't have had time to look at your picture. So, it's up to you to give her all the information she needs. Whatever she first asks you, elabo-rate on it. This will give her something else to pick up on if she wants to. And, remember, you have to wear gloves when you shake hands.'

'Is this for real?' I kept asking myself as I practised my curtsies and my Ma'am to rhyme with Spam. 'Am I really going to sing to the Queen?'

My family and Bobby's were beside themselves with pride, and they all travelled down to London for this great occasion. They had a grand time staying at the posh Mayfair Hotel, and there was a first in store for them, too. Neither my dad and brothers, nor Bobby's brothers, had ever worn dinner suits, which Bobby and I hired for them from Moss Bros. They all thought they were James Bond, and they were so proud of how they looked, they wore them all day and didn't go to bed after the show until about four in the morning.

There I was, just twenty-one years old, singing 'You're My World' to the Queen. 'It just *can't* get better than this,' I thought.

When it came to the royal line-up, I was standing next to Tommy Cooper. The Queen thanked him for a great show, and he said: 'Ma'am – are you going to the Cup Final at Wembley this year?'

'No,' the Queen replied sadly. 'Unfortunately I can't go this year.'

'That's a great shame,' Tommy said, adding, 'Can I have your ticket?'

When it came to my turn, I shook hands with the Queen and did my curtsy, and then she said, 'What are you doing at the moment?'

'I'm doing a season here at the Palladium with Frankie Vaughan and Tommy Cooper, Ma'am, and I have had two number one hit records this year …'

I babbled on and on, and her eyes glazed over. Waiting until I paused for breath, she then moved on to the next person.

It was the most marvellous feeling in the world to come up so close to her and, daft thing that I am, I was utterly convinced that the Queen was going to say to me, 'Oh, you're that little girl I waved to when I went down Scottie Road in Liverpool!'

Later, I asked my dad what he had thought of my performance, and for a moment I couldn't understand why he looked so sheepish. Slowly it emerged that he and Mam – and the rest of family – had been so transfixed by the proximity of the Queen that they hadn't taken their eyes off her all evening and had missed me altogether.

While Mam, Dad and my Auntie Nellie were in London, we took

them to what was then another 'in' club – Danny La Rue's in Hanover Square. When we got there we had a very nice table and when Danny came on, he introduced me to the rest of the guests. That was a very special moment for my parents and Auntie Nellie, and I could see that they were brimming over with pride because my presence had been acknowledged in such a posh nightclub. Then, just towards the end of Danny's act, Dad leaned over and whispered something in Bobby's ear.

'Don't tell the girls,' he said. 'But that girl's a *feller*.' Bobby looked at my dad, and saw that he was perfectly serious. So he thought he'd better not say, 'Well, yes, we all know that.'

'*Is* he?' he said incredulously, raising his eyebrows.

Me dad nodded: 'I've been away to sea,' he said, 'and I know these things!'

~

'How d'you feel about appearing in a movie?' Brian asked me one morning on the phone. 'Great! Hollywood, here I come!' I replied. I couldn't have been more excited. It turned out my old friends Gerry and The Pacemakers, who by then had become huge crowd-pullers on television, stage and cabaret, were in a film, *Ferry Cross the Mersey*, and I'd been offered a part in it. When the time came, they gave me rooms at the Adelphi, Liverpool's poshest hotel. I scarcely had time to use them, but being in that grand building was magic – it brought my success home to me in an unexpected way.

To shoot my brief but very exciting guest appearance in Gerry's first feature-length film (for which he had written eight of the songs himself), I had to make a nostalgic day-return journey to one of my favourite teenage haunts – the Locarno Ballroom, where I sang a romantic ballad, 'Is It Love?', specially written for the film by Bobby. I was so proud of his songwriting talent and, once again, I couldn't help thinking that he should have stuck with his composing rather than road-managing me. Bobby had a small part in the film too, as my roadie, and he had one line

– but his Scouse accent was so thick he had to be dubbed by an actor. He was mortified!

It was fun shooting the film, but back in London I was starting to feel terribly homesick. Despite all the carrying on, London was still a foreign place to us in those days, and I went through misery trying to get used to its different culture. I was desperately missing my family and friends and me mam's cooking. Bobby and I were still living in the President Hotel and, although it was dead posh, I was still refusing to rent a place in the capital because I didn't want to put down roots and break the bond with Liverpool. A lot of my Merseyside friends couldn't understand this.

'We thought you'd love living in London,' they kept saying. 'Surely that's where it's all happening now?'

London was an exciting place to be in the sixties, and I might have enjoyed living there if I'd got to know a residential area. But I was always in the West End – theatreland – which was full of tourists and foreigners, with hardly anybody making their homes there. I didn't like it at all, but then I wasn't living in the real London; I was living in the heart of it like a tourist. It wasn't until Cathy McGowan took me under her wing that my attitude began to change. One Good Friday she invited me and Bobby to her home in Streatham. 'Oh,' I thought when I arrived there, 'so people do live in houses after all! This part of London's not so different from Liverpool.' We had a warm, happy, family afternoon.

10

New York, New York

With my next single, 'You've Lost That Lovin' Feelin'', on the verge of being released, everything should have been sunny-side-up and rosy. But, as our local priest was fond of warning us Scousers, 'No man's an island – and what one person does can have a devastating effect on the rest of us.'

I was on a three-week headline concert tour of the UK, co-starring with the American singer P.J. Proby. Notorious for wearing his trousers so tight that absolutely nothing was left to his fans' imagination, P.J. was instantly beset by newspaper headlines airing shock-horror complaints from the civic authorities. This was not surprising. His trousers were so weakly sewn at the seams that they actually used to split open during his act. To make matters worse, Mrs Mary Whitehouse was just coming on to the scene, saying she was going to launch a National Viewers' and Listeners' Association to 'clean things up' and to target 'the evils of our "permissive society" '.

Refusing at first to get caught up in all the fuss and bother, I kept my cool and simply said to reporters, 'I was one of the first people to meet P.J. when he came over from America with Jack Good to make [the TV spectacular], *Around The Beatles*, and we get on just fine.'

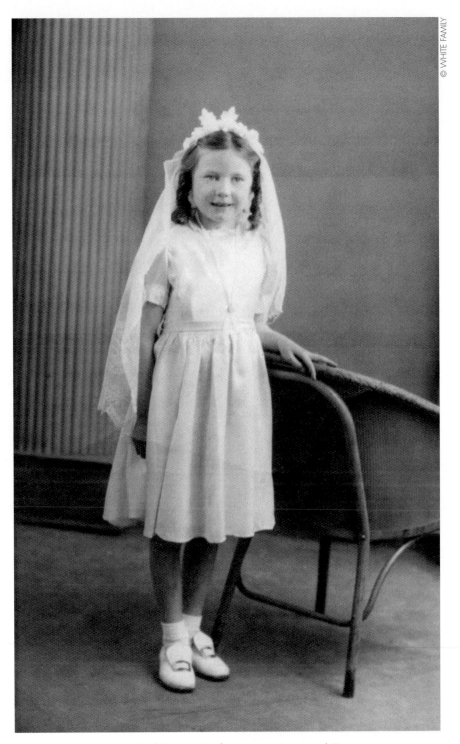

A real Left Footer. My first communion, aged 7.

Me mam (centre) and me dad (right) on a celebratory night out.

Our John (above right) hard at work at Lanson Parragon printers in Birkenhead. Factory work was what you went on to after school in 1950s Liverpool.

380 Scottie Road.

Me and my mate Christine Riley sporting the American High School look on a daytrip to Blackpool in the late 1950s.

Although Bobby Willis was the complete opposite in looks and character to any other guy who had set my heart racing, we started to knock around on a regular basis.

Me, our Alan and me mam on another daytrip – this time to visit Auntie Lottie near Manchester.

Me dad (right) and his mates, just back from the match.

Our George's wedding to Lily. I'm the reluctant bridesmaid (front row, third from left).
Mam and dad (far right), proudly look on.

Me and Bobby (centre back) on a Liverpool night out.

Me (middle row, right)
and Bobby (front row,
left) at the wedding of
Bobby's brother Kenny
to his wife Rose.

There was always a scrum around the cloakroom at the Cavern at lunchtime.

Me and Pat Davies couldn't get enough of the Cavern.

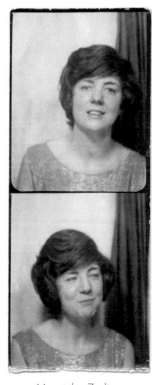

Me at the Zodiac.

© CILLA BLACK

Only twenty, but ready to conquer Britain.

1963. Cilla Black launched on to an unsuspecting world!

© CILLA BLACK

(left) Getting all excited – with Billy Fury and Gerry and the Pacemakers.

(below) 'Mam, I've got a number one! I've done it!' 'Ave yer? Well they won't be callin' yer "Big 'ead, no bread in the 'ouse" after this!'

(above) Brian Epstein was everything a posh feller and a gentleman should be.

(right) In answer to any prying questions about my feller's constant presence, Brian simply explained that Bobby was my road manager.

At Abbey Road for the recording of 'You're My World', with the whole Cilla Black company!

(right) My backing band Sounds Incorporated were full of soul and spontaneity.

(below) The wonderful George Martin, the other posh feller in my life.

At the Palladium 1964. I was
still very naive and learning
how to adjust to fame.

Relaxing in my publicist Tony Barrow's office in 1968.

Brian did everything for us and meant everything to us.

Our (second!) wedding was a good old Liverpool knees up. Auntie Nellie! Behave yourself!

(*left*) Me and Ringo.

(*below*) Recording 'Step Inside Love' with Paul in 1969. We'd all been mad kids together. And now he was in the biggest group in the world.

© EMI

Days later, however, when the theatre managements caved in and placed a ban on my co-star because his act was becoming too offensive, a young Welsh singer was whisked in at the eleventh hour as his temporary replacement. Tom Jones had just recorded his first single, 'It's Not Unusual'. As I stood in the wings and watched some of his pelvic thrusts on stage, I couldn't help wondering if we were out of the frying pan into the fire!

Besieged by the press again, this time I gave vent to my true feelings about P.J. 'He's a nice boy, but in my opinion he has let us and his fans down. I don't know *why* he feels compelled to behave like that.'

I was very worried, of course, that P.J.'s disgrace would have a serious impact on our bookings – and on our careers – but my fans continued to pour in, Tom Jones became an overnight success, and we still had a full house every night. Then, to the delight of us all, 'It's Not Unusual' soared to number one in the UK charts and, before we had a chance to take time off and celebrate this, Tom released two more numbers, 'These Hands' and 'What's New Pussycat?'

P.J. Proby's antics had given Tom his longed-for lucky break – and given Bobby and me a new friend. In fact, apart from his agent and close family, only we knew that Britain's latest sex symbol, who was driving women to throw their panties on the stage, was already married with a kid! Tom was just like us – he was dead normal, and he loved having a drink in the pub with his mates, despite all the girls throwing themselves at him. But he looked just like a real 'Tom Jones' (as in the film character played by Albert Finney) – a bit of a 'Lady Chatterley's Lover' type, complete with a rabbit's-foot charm dangling from his hip.

Meanwhile, I was back to holding my breath again. 'You've Lost That Lovin' Feelin'' had just been released. This song, which was also recorded in the US by The Righteous Brothers, had a vocal range of very high and very low notes and was really intended for two voices, but I sang it solo. Both versions sold extremely well and, at one stage, it looked as if The Righteous Brothers' single and mine would *both* reach number one. That would have been a unique event in the charts! But it was not to be. The Righteous Brothers were given an unsurpassed seven million US radio plays and remained number one in the UK's Top Ten for ten weeks; I reached number two in the UK and Australia, and stayed in the UK charts for six weeks.

Once again I was devastated not to make number one, but at least my first album, *Cilla*, turned into a long-term bestseller.

The pressures of my Speedy Gonzales success, which involved a constant round of telly spots, one-night stands and publicity sessions to promote the records, could well have taken their toll, and 1965 was proving my most frenetic year yet, but so far I seemed to be taking stardom in my stride. I was certainly putting plenty of bums on seats at the twenty-two venues on my UK concert tour.

By now I was a seasoned traveller throughout the UK, but I was still pretty green as far as 'abroad' was concerned. This was put right in March, when I set off for my first seven-date concert tour of New Zealand, to be followed by a five-date concert tour of Australia with Freddie and The Dreamers. To my delight, I was mobbed by fans seeking my autograph in both countries down under.

'Cillamania!' I said to Bobby, and I was very happy to be there and to be given such a good kick-off.

When we got to Australia, staying in the same Sydney hotel as me and Freddie and The Dreamers was Max Bygraves – half the time I felt as if I was back home in an English hotel!

Just prior to the shows at the Sydney Boxing Stadium, one of my supporting acts, the singer Mark Wynter, unwittingly let the cat out of the bag by revealing to news-hungry reporters that Bobby was the man in my life as well as my road manager. With the wrath of Brian in mind, I had to set to and deny this most emphatically. As guarded as ever about his clients' private lives, Brian would have hated the kind of love-life publicity I was attracting in Australia.

'Bobby Willis's role in my life,' I said, primly, 'is that of road manager. End of story.'

It was obviously only a matter of time before our secret would be out. But for the moment, it was a case of damage limitation. Bobby understandably didn't like the denials, but he put up with them because of my career. And he was just as scared as me of the religious situation anyway.

~

Although our tour vehicle down under was an all-black luxury coach with darkened windows, a big settee, a bar and a video, it left a lot to be desired. The coach was called 'The Bitch'. Anybody who wanted to hire it had to phone up the bus company and say, 'Can I have The Bitch?' That was bad enough, but in our case the company fixed a touring sign across the back of it that read 'You are following The Bitch on tour with Cilla Black'!

At first I thought the Aussies were obsessed with waving to everyone, but then I realised they were only brushing flies or flying cockroaches away from their faces. It would take more than a flapping hand to outwit Australia's amazing insect population, though – and I don't just mean in the outback. In Tamworth, in New South Wales, the mayor, the chief of police and other local bigwigs put on an open-air dinner for me and the crew. When someone placed a plate of salad in front of me there was a sudden 'whoosh', and a huge flying cockroach landed smack in the middle of it, scattering green stuff over everybody.

While we were in Australia, we often performed outdoors, which was absolutely fine until it started to rain, and then we were all terrified of the electrics. How we survived without being electrocuted, I will never know. We faced a different kind of water hazard when we were asked to perform at an Olympic-sized swimming pool in Perth. It didn't occur to us that the pool would not be boarded over or that it would remain open for 'business as usual' during our rehearsals! I had cheeky kids swimming past me, synchronising their strokes to the string orchestra; and as there was also a strong breeze on the day of the rehearsal, blowing the sheet music off the stands and into the water, it was sheer mayhem!

All in all, though, it was a great experience for a girl who had hardly left home soil before. The Aussies made it clear that they loved my miniskirts, long legs, cheeky humour and laid-back attitude. I was very chuffed when one lady said to me in Darwin, 'I know they call you "our Cilla" back home, but you're "our Cilla" here as well.'

~

I could hardly believe it myself, but New York, which I'd seen so often in movies like Audrey Hepburn's and George Peppard's *Breakfast at Tiffany's* and Frank Sinatra's and Gene Kelly's *On The Town*, was next on my schedule.

From the moment we touched down in 'the Big Apple' on a bright April day, I was bowled over by it. There I was in the city that never sleeps, where energy pumps day and night; and where just keeping up with the pace can be exhilarating – and exhausting. Skyscrapers are what New York's most famous for, and I couldn't stop gawping at the art deco Empire State Building and Radio City Music Hall, or the Rockefeller Center with its sunken plaza. I loved strolling around putting faces on places I'd only ever heard of before, like Wall Street, Broadway, Times Square and Grand Central Station.

As for Fifth Avenue, I couldn't wait to shimmy up and down this magnificent main street that runs through a wealth of eye-catching department stores and past buildings like the New York Public Library. Apart from the shops, I was fascinated by the gawky, fresh-faced young models who kept floating past us with their portfolios in one hand and subway maps in the other, and the drop-outs with hair tucked into pirate-style headbands and huge flared jeans. And I was breathless with excitement on the Sunday morning when Bobby and I caught the Staten Island Ferry, the commuter barge that gives its passengers such stunning panoramic views of Manhattan and the Statue of Liberty.

'There's so much to see and so little time to see it,' I said to Bobby, over a hamburger and milkshake at the end of a blissful day. 'I wish we could just go on and on exploring and sightseeing.'

But we weren't there as tourists. Brian had arranged a CBS TV debut for me on *The Ed Sullivan Show*, America's equivalent of *Sunday Night at the London Palladium*.

When I arrived in the studio, a great looking producer rushed up to me, saying: 'You're scheduled to come on after the chimpanzees.' This was Bob Prect, Ed Sullivan's very fanciable son-in-law. He was totally charming, and even sent me a dozen red roses after the show!

All afternoon in rehearsals the chimps were very well behaved. They had a circus ring in which they rode around on motorbikes and performed extraordinary feats. But, during a break, the director got the floor manager to remove some of the sections and make the circuit shorter. There was just one problem – the chimps had been trained in the full-sized ring.

When the chimps came on to do the live show, it was mayhem. They couldn't cope with the smaller ring, and were soon going every which way, and getting very frustrated each time they crashed into each other. Then the bikes were abandoned altogether and fighting broke out. All the chimps were wearing frilly boy and girl uniforms, and these were the first to go. Then it became even more physical, and lust crept in …

Ed Sullivan was horrified. Here on his show, which went out live to over eighty million God-fearing Americans, chimpanzees were doing unspeakable things which should never have been shown on TV. There was only one solution: 'Cut – and bring on Cilla Black!'

As I came on for my big moment on American TV, the chimpanzees were still at it. Ed Sullivan was very embarrassed, but, dimly recalling that I had said that my grandfather was Welsh, introduced me by saying: 'And now we have a great Welsh singer, from Wales in England – Cilla Black!'

Trying hard not to giggle, I launched into 'Dancing In The Street'. In the rehearsals I'd done this song as a solo act, but I was soon aware that I was not alone on the set. Something that was impossible to ignore was making passionate love to my leg. When I looked down, there was this chimp, pumping away! I couldn't think what to do except carry on singing until his trainer and the studio people finally grabbed the randy creature. Today I would stop the band until everything was sorted, but *The Ed Sullivan Show* had a strange effect on people as well as chimpanzees.

Next stop was on Hollywood's *Shindig* to sing 'I've Been Wrong Before', which would be my next UK single. When the song had first been played to me, I didn't think it had much commercial appeal, but my gang of musicians from Sounds Incorporated thought it was marvellous. To me, the voice on the demo sounded more hilarious than soulful. The singer was the composer, Randy Newman, who, as far as I was concerned, was sort of classical and wrote things like movie themes. But I was still very flattered when Brian told me that Randy had written the ballad especially for me.

'It does have a kind of haunting tune,' I thought. 'And other people like it – so perhaps it's just me.'

As I always placed a lot of store on what my family thought, I decided to ask their opinion. My mam really didn't like the song. 'What kind of a song do you call that?' she kept saying, her usually tentative self!

My eighteen-year-old brother Allan disagreed, however. '*I* think it's ace,' he kept repeating.

In the end, I told Mam I was sorry, but I didn't agree with her. 'I'll be the first British artiste ever to record one of Randy Newman's songs,' I added.

By then Brian had told me that Randy rarely allowed anybody to cover his songs. After I'd recorded it, Randy told the press he was 'knocked out' by my performance, which he considered his all-time favourite cover of any of his compositions.

It was really smashing walking down Fifth Avenue after I'd sung on *The Ed Sullivan Show* and *Shindig*. I loved hearing passers-by drawl, 'Hi Cilla, caught you on TV last night. Thought you were terriff!' I was also very amused when the American press kept referring back to my Cavern days and describing me as an 'ex-hat-check girl'. This really tickled me – people in Liverpool only wore hats for church, and nobody ever wore hats in the Cavern!

~

Three years had rushed past since The Beatles had first become famous, and ever since then the media had been busy trying to gauge whether their fame was still on the up or coming down. As a friend, I had no doubt which it was. Whenever a Rolls-Royce criss-crossed London, people either cried out, 'It's the Queen!' or 'It's The Beatles!' – and of the two, it was always the latter that created the biggest buzz!

Brian, who was usually very reluctant to use his management of the Fab Four as a bargaining tool on behalf of his other NEMS artistes, decided to bend his own rules that summer. In his passion to see me crack the American market, he asked The Beatles' New York agent to negotiate a cabaret season for me at a top Manhattan venue.

Beginning on 26 July, the agent booked me into the Persian Room of the very posh, five-star Plaza Hotel opposite Central Park for three weeks. So far, so good, but a midsummer heatwave had almost emptied New York City, so this booking did nothing for my career. And what little publicity the American public saw about me cast me as an offshoot of The Beatles, portraying me as a 'teenage phenomenon' rather than a cabaret performer.

In the Persian Room I opened with a rock 'n' roll act and sang all my hits, but when I realised that the room was full of millionaires, I changed my act to accommodate this unfamiliar audience. Perhaps unsurprisingly, my notices were very mixed, but I did get a glowing review in the *New York Times* from no less than Burt Bacharach's father, Burt Bacharach Sr.

Bobby and I took what steps we could to make the best of things, but I knew I was faced with my most dangerous professional challenge to date. By my side at the Plaza was London producer John Lyndon and musical director Johnny Pearson. With their help, I revamped my act and, by the end of the first week, I'd succeeded in commanding the attention of the million-dollar Persian Room clientele. They still greeted me with polite applause at each opening, but by my third song I had most of them in the palm of my hand. Certainly by the final week I was winning over new admirers every night and getting shouts for encores.

One night, after a show in which I had spontaneously sat on a guy's lap while I was singing 'On The Street Where You Live' from *My Fair Lady*, there was a tap on the door of my hotel suite. When I opened it, the same man, who looked like a typical all-American guy, was standing there. At first I didn't know what he was there for. Then, after a moment's awkward silence, he came clean.

'I just wanted to say "thank you" for singing my song,' he said, shyly. And when he said 'my song', he really meant it. I had sat crooning on the lap of Alan J. Lerner, the man who'd written most of the words for the songs in *My Fair Lady* – including 'On The Street Where You Live'!

I was destroyed! How embarrassing. Had I known he was in the Persian Room that night, I wouldn't have dared sing that number, let alone single him out and sit on his lap. How cheesy was that?

~

Just before I finished my three-week stint at the Persian Room, Brian's ex-PA Miss Johnson (or 'Johnny' as we always called her) rang. She was now living and working in Washington, DC, and not only that, but my childhood best friend Billy Davis had also moved to the States and was living in her house. I'd already been to visit them both in Washington on my day off. Johnny was calling now to say that she was coming to New York to see the last show, and could we all meet up. I was absolutely thrilled.

'Don't book a hotel,' I told her. 'I've got a huge suite at the Plaza. I've got a bedroom, Bobby's got his own quarters and there's also a huge lounge. You can share my room, Billy can share Bobby's, and we can all let our hair down after the show and have a party up here.'

Johnny was delighted with the suggestion. So was I – there couldn't have been a better way to mark the end of my appearances in the Persian Room. We were in for a shock, though.

The night was a scream, and in the early hours of the morning, long after our end-of-show party had ended, Johnny and I finished our girlie chatting and drifted into sleep. Bobby, meanwhile was watching one of the all-night movie channels in his room when Billy returned from wherever he had gone off to alone after the party. As Bobby looked up, said, 'Ai ya', and reached out to switch off the TV, Billy collapsed by the bed and burst into floods of tears.

'What on earth's the matter?' Bobby asked, shocked and confused – and suddenly realised that Billy's face was bruised and splattered with blood. It took a while, between sobs, but eventually Billy told Bobby that he was gay.

'Gay?' Bobby repeated, bewildered, only understanding one meaning of that word. 'We know you're good for a laugh, Billy.'

'No, Bobby, I mean I'm *homosexual*,' Billy said. 'And I've just been beaten up and robbed by a guy who picked me up in a bar and took me back to his place.'

Bobby was astonished by this revelation, and horrified at what had happened. It was a shock to get this insight into Billy's private life, but right then he was more concerned about Billy's welfare.

I know it will sound astonishing to people nowadays, but when Bobby told me about this the next morning, it was the first time I knew that homosexuals existed and that some men preferred to make love to other men and live in same-sex relationships. Before that, I'd only gleaned that some men liked to dress up in women's clothes, and that some men had no sexual interest in women, never got married, and remained 'confirmed bachelors'.

So Billy being a homosexual was a total shock and revelation for me. I knew he loved the company of women and was obsessed with platinum blondes like Doris Day, but once it had all clicked into place, I thought back fondly to all those times when we had played dressing-up games as kids, when he'd always wanted to be the bride and always expected me to be the bridesmaid. 'That should have told me something!' I thought.

As the sixties progressed, homosexuality ceased to be a criminal offence in the UK, and gays like Billy and others I met in my work were able to be themselves and talk much more freely about their sexuality. Times are so tolerant now, it's difficult to remember how in-the-closet things were back then, and how innocent we all were.

11

Do You Mind If I Turn On?

It's all very glamorous living in a hotel, and very convenient, but at the end of the day not as much fun as it sounds. And there's nothing like home. I'd been promising myself for months that I would ditch my hotel-room lifestyle and get a flat in London so I could indulge in an orgy of retail therapy and choose my own decor and furnishings. But I didn't actually get round to looking for a place until the beginning of November, when I finished touring in a show called *Star Scene* which was put on by Brian's new concert-promotion company, NEMS Presentations. Although I couldn't have known at the time, this was to be my last tour.

By this time I was absolutely sure that Bobby was the man for me. Although I'd continued to say from time to time that, as we had met so young, he must feel free to go out on dates if he wanted to and so must I, my heart wasn't really in this so-called 'open' arrangement. I had offers, of course, but I didn't seriously go out with anyone else. Bobby was just so right for me – and in any case I was so well protected by this time that I must have seemed pretty well untouchable.

Whenever I did go out without Bobby I always found myself wishing I was with him, and whenever we spent time apart he confessed he never stopped thinking about me. Neither of us had ever formed any other attachment since we first met, and it just became quietly accepted between us that we were in love and we both wanted to be together forever.

~

In the middle of the *Star Scene* tour, Brian hosted a fantastic party at the swish, trendy Scotch of St James Club in Mason's Yard, London – a club which had recently barred a millionaire member for asking for George Harrison's autograph! Having been away from home for so long it was great to have an opportunity to catch up with the old crowd – Ringo and his wife Maureen, Paul, Jimmy Tarbuck and Billy J. Kramer.

George brought his new girlfriend, the fashion model Pattie Boyd, along, and I immediately bonded with her. She had a very infectious giggle, and we knew at once where each of us was coming from. I particularly liked Pattie because she was kind enough to laugh at all my silly jokes. She was terribly posh and incredibly beautiful, with long, coltish legs and a great taste in clothes, but was totally unaware of her own beauty. She was also the first person (apart from the Aussies) to tell me I had great legs myself! She was just like a puppy who wanted to be loved by everybody. When she walked into a room, she lit it up – and of course we all fell in love with her at once.

By 1965 a lot of singers had made their own covers of Beatles songs and on 17 December some of them, including me, appeared with the guys on a TV special tribute, *The Music of Lennon and McCartney*, a showcase of stars singing John and Paul's songs. As well as me, Henry Mancini, who had first entered the charts with 'Moon River', was on the show, and Peter Sellers, who was by then a friend of Ringo's, did a hilarious impression of Laurence Olivier speaking the words of 'A Hard Day's Night'.

Ringo was hanging out with lots of entertainers by this time, and the rest of us enjoyed sending him up for having dinner with stars like Marlon Brando, Richard Burton and Elizabeth Taylor. 'Ah! But he can hold his own with all of them,' Paul used to say, to wind him up still more.

Do You Mind If I Turn On?

'I've known Ringo since I was a kid,' I told a reporter from *Melody Maker*. 'And then I became friends with George. But, funnily enough, it was John who used to push me and sing my praises. That was weird because he and I were never that close. John adores women, but he's a man's man who's never completely at home in female company. Paul's the one all the girls adore and I think John's always felt he's in his shadow. In order of popularity with the girls, it's Paul, John, George – and Ringo as the last resort!'

Sometimes I think it's a wonder that Ringo's still talking to me!

~

At long last, towards the end of 1965, the time came when Bobby and I could move out of our hotel rooms and into somewhere of our own – the first either of us had ever had apart from living with our families. And if it wasn't as good as being back in Liverpool, at least it was a start.

'F.A.B.!' I cried when Bobby and I spotted the cosy little cottage in Prince Albert Terrace Mews, just five minutes from Regent's Park and fifteen minutes from Piccadilly Circus. It was just the sort of place I'd been looking for and I didn't hesitate. In no time the rent was sorted out and we'd got the keys.

It was charming little house, fully furnished in stunning classic style, with lovely parquet flooring. It had a very large living/dining room, with French windows that opened out on to a little walled garden, and two bedrooms and a bathroom upstairs. It was just the right size and a marvellous little pad, much nicer than living in hotels, but it still didn't feel like home, and I always knew I'd move on quite soon.

Having somewhere of my own meant that Bobby and I could now entertain our friends in more privacy and style. Mind you, it was a bit of a shock not being able to pick up the phone for room service any more. I'm not the most brilliant of cooks now, and back then the only thing I could cook was cheese on toast. I remember Bobby cooking a leg of pork once, and I do like my pork, especially the crackling and the stuffing.

Unfortunately when it was cooked, the crackling didn't crackle, and worst of all, there was no stuffing. A row broke out, and I ended up by slinging the leg of pork out into the mews!

We had Tony Barrow, my NEMS press agent, round for dinner once. We did buy wine for the occasion, but we weren't that sophisticated then, and we didn't have a corkscrew – we didn't really drink wine, and we certainly didn't drink in the house, because of our upbringing. Bobby had to go out to the pub with Tony to buy new bottles of wine and ask for them to be opened there, because we didn't have the cheek to ask them to open the bottles we'd bought already.

I still used to phone home on an almost daily basis. I missed Mam and Dad so much, and I kept trying to persuade them to move south to be near me. By this time they'd moved from Scottie Road to Woolton, on the outskirts of the city. I offered to buy them a house in London, but they didn't want to leave Liverpool. I saw them as often as I could – about every two months – but I never wanted this to become 'an occasion'. If I'd arrived home to find out that me mam had made some fairy cakes especially for me, it would have spoiled everything – made me feel as if I'd really left Liverpool.

~

Having got the bit between my teeth, I decided that we'd celebrate my success, which Brian kept telling me was making me richer by the hour, by splashing out on a really posh Jag. But then I heard that all the fellers in Brian's stable were busy ordering themselves Rolls-Royces.

'Ey, Brian,' I said, when I next went to see him in Argyll Street, 'why can't I have a Rolls-Royce?'

'You can, if that's what you want,' he replied. 'But I think you should get a Bentley. That would be much more classy – the "Princess of the Road" for the "Queen of Pop"!'

The Jaguar I'd ordered never left the showroom. I lost £500 on it, which was a helluva lot of money in 1965, but it was more than worth it.

Do You Mind If I Turn On?

Bobby and I were now driving around in what Brian thought – and we now thought – was the car to end all cars. We couldn't wait to see the expression on me mam and dad's faces when we drove it up to Liverpool the day it arrived and parked it outside their new home in Woolton.

'Ohhhh, Cilla!' Mam exclaimed, clasping her hand to her mouth. 'Who'd *ever* have thought … ?'

'Well, I'll be damned!' Dad muttered quietly. 'I bet it cost you a few bob to hire that!'

'Hired be damned, dad. We *bought* it!'

~

Although I was now familiar with most of the London clubs and could reel off names like the Ad-Lib, the Bag O'Nails, the Speak Easy, the Club dell'Arethusa, and many others that were worth knowing, I'd never got into the heavier side of the club scene and was never tempted by the drugs that were so freely to hand. One afternoon, though, when I was trying to learn my lines at home for *Little Red Riding Hood* at the Wimbledon Theatre, a friend of ours named Tony King, who plugged records and who was renowned in our circle for his fabulous impersonation of Diana Ross, called in to see me at my new house. Standing in my sitting room, Tony reached into his pocket and started unravelling a small packet of cannabis.

'D'you mind if I turn on?' he asked.

'No, go ahead,' I giggled.

I didn't really mind. My attitude was 'You're grown up. If you wanna do it, do it. I'm not preachy. It's fine by me.'

'Why don't you try some?' Tony said. 'It'll help you relax – and you'll learn your lines in double-quick time.'

'No – I don't smoke,' I replied, primly.

'Chill out,' he urged. 'Relax.'

'No,' I protested. 'I've gotta be professional. I've got rehearsals tomorrow.'

'That script's making you paranoid. Go on – try this,' he said again.

I'm not sure why I weakened, but I did. Taking the newly rolled joint from him, I squirrelled it off to the bathroom, which was where I'd always noticed others going when they wanted to turn on. Why did they do that? I guessed they thought it was anti-social to smoke pot in front of others – especially non-users. Naive as I was, however, I also thought joints only worked in bathrooms!

I puffed away diligently and waited. Well, I can tell you it wasn't nice. I didn't feel the slightest bit 'turned on'! In fact, if this was turning on, I didn't like it at all. The joint did nothing for me, except turn me into a rather blue Red Riding Hood – blue in the sense of making me, a person who never swore, want to swear for some reason. On top of that I began to feel more and more queasy. Eventually I was very sick indeed.

The only other time I came close up to marijuana was in Brian's flat when The Beatles were lounging about there. Now, taking drugs with The Beatles – that is *very* rock 'n' roll, wouldn't you think? Not for me it wasn't! This 'thing', which was stuck on a pin, was passed around the group. It started out quite long, but by the time it reached me it was tiny and all soggy looking.

'Oh no,' I thought, 'this is not nice – and it's certainly not hygienic.' I politely declined.

The extraordinary thing was that when I smoked an ordinary cigarette on *Juke Box Jury*, Brian gave me a telling off. I didn't even like smoking, had never bought a packet in my life. I only did it because I wanted to look as sophisticated and cool as Lauren Bacall in the movies!

'Please don't do that again, Cilla,' he said, prissily. 'It's just not ladylike.'

~

My costume for *Little Red Riding Hood* was an absolutely fabulous red miniskirt and cloak designed by Barbara Hulanicki, of Biba fame. I knew Barbara, and I'd done a publicity stunt for her earlier in the year when she moved from Abingdon Road to her new shop in Kensington Church Street. She'd got a lorry for the move, and she had all the Biba girls on board to help, plus me and Cathy McGowan hanging off it too. It was a far cry from hanging on for dear life as I shot downhill on William Moult Street ten years before. This time we were posing for press photos – of which there were plenty – and I was being paid for it, too!

During the run of *Little Red Riding Hood* I was told Shirley Bassey was in the audience with her children.

'Oh no!' I thought.

I admired Bassey, but I was afraid that she didn't like me because of the disagreement between George Martin and Brian over who should record 'Anyone Who Had A Heart'. By the time I went on stage for that matinee I was really nervous knowing that she was there, and not surprisingly I soon found myself fluffing my lines. Never one to be defeated, though, I ad-libbed and said to the tall woodsman standing alongside me, 'I bet Shirley Bassey wouldn't have this trouble …'

'Oh, yes, she would,' came back a lone Welsh female cry from the auditorium.

'Oh, no, she wouldn't!' chanted the delighted audience.

Shirley brought her children round after the show. She looked every inch a star, but seeing her with her kids, she was also somehow every inch a mum. As always, she was very funny, very camp – in a nutshell, very true to how she comes across in that famous and hilarious appearance of hers in *The Morecambe and Wise Show*, wearing just one hobnailed boot. Scary as Shirley could be, I don't think she minded giving that impression at all – at least it meant she got the respect she deserved.

~

One morning I was sitting with Brian in his Argyll Street office. Like Brian himself, the room was stylish, chic but understated – definitely not flash, but you could see the money. It turned out he had something to say about my own money that day. 'You do realise you're well on your way to becoming a millionairess,' he told me. It came as a shock. I knew the offers kept coming, and my career was forging ahead, but I hadn't quite realised how much I'd earned already. I think Brian sometimes doubted that I had taken the level of my success on board at all, but I had, much more than he realised.

But then Brian went on. 'Theatre and TV producers are noticing your contributions to shows like *Juke Box Jury* and *The Eamonn Andrews Show*,' he was saying. 'They're beginning to realise that, as well as your superb singing voice, you've got the gift of the gab, and a flair for ad-lib on camera. They're starting to think of you as an all-round television and stage entertainer.'

'But I love singing, Brian,' I replied. 'That's my true vocation.' I was not being coy. I had no ambition to change tack and strike out as a TV presenter or game-show host. And anyway, for someone who had only turned professional three years earlier, it was considered pretty amazing that I'd already sung my heart out in the places I had – from a cinema in Southport to a long season at the London Palladium, to concert tours of New Zealand and Australia, and cabaret in New York.

As the sixties passed their halfway mark and 1966 kicked in, I had another hit, when 'Love's Just A Broken Heart' made number two, and it was in many ways a surprise to lots of people that I was still having hits. I was supposed to be a flash in the pan, after all. This was the number I would sing when I topped the bill on *Sunday Night at the London Palladium* in February.

I could hardly believe my ears when Brian told me that he was going to throw a party for me after the show, that The Beatles would be there – and that he had also invited Judy Garland, who was on a visit to London.

'Judy Garland?' I kept repeating. '*The* Judy Garland, Brian?'

'The one and only,' Brian replied, amused. He adored Judy Garland.

That night, my throat was lined with barbed wire and by the end of the show I could hardly speak. I couldn't bear to miss Judy Garland, though; she'd been an idol of mine ever since I'd seen her in *The Wizard of Oz*, *Meet Me In St Louis*, *Easter Parade* and *A Star is Born*, and Bobby and I drove straight over to Brian's fabulous penthouse apartment in Knightsbridge to meet her.

Do You Mind If I Turn On?

When Judy arrived, the first thing we all noticed was that both her wrists were covered in white bandages. We all knew that she had tried to commit suicide not long before, but we were still very shocked to see how pale and frail she was.

Brian had laid on a lavish spread, but at first everything felt rather tense. Gradually, though, everybody including Judy relaxed and thawed out. One by one or two by two, we all buzzed towards her like bees around a honeypot.

She and I talked perfectly happily, but Brian seemed very jumpy. What I didn't realise until I was on the verge of taking my sore throat home was that he was anxiously watching Judy's every move. Just as I was about to leave, he stopped me, hissing anxiously, 'Judy's been in the bathroom for at least fifteen minutes.'

'So? Women are not like guys, Brian,' I replied; 'they take a while in there.'

Five minutes later, as I was croaking goodnight to Ringo, Brian veered over to me again.

'She's still in there,' he muttered, distraught. 'We can't have her committing suicide here. Go in and get her, Cilla.'

'Oh, God!' I said. I was beginning to panic myself. 'You want me to go in there and see if she's slashed her wrists again?'

'*Please*, Cilla.'

The bathroom door was locked. I was standing there, trying to pluck up my courage and knock when the door opened and out stepped Judy.

Feeling a right Wilf, but pretending that I'd been waiting for the loo, I smiled, went in, waited for the appropriate amount of time, then returned to where Brian was still lurking behind a pot plant.

'Judy's absolutely fine,' I reported, gritting my teeth. 'I'm the one who feels like death warmed up – and I'm off!'

~

When Burt Bacharach first wrote to me from New York to tell me that he and Hal David, inspired by the film *Alfie*, had written another song especially for me, I was very excited and immediately ditched my plans to record an Italian ballad. When the demo disc arrived, however, I didn't like the song at all – and I hated the idea of singing about a guy called Alfie. That name, I thought, was really naff.

Because I really didn't want to record the song, but didn't want to say an outright 'no', I thought I'd be really difficult for a change and start putting up barriers. So first of all I said I'd only do it if Burt Bacharach himself did the arrangement, never thinking for one moment that he would. Unfortunately the reply came back from America that he'd be happy to. So then I said I would only do it if Burt came over to London for the recording sessions. 'Yes' came the reply. Next I said that as well as the arrangement and coming over, he had to play on the session. To my astonishment it was agreed that Burt would do all three – do the arrangement, fly in and play! So by this time, coward that I was, I really couldn't back out.

At the session itself, there was a big forty-eight-piece orchestra, plus my girl singers, The Breakaways, from Liverpool, and all my friends around me. Unknown to me at the time, Brian was having the session filmed. Burt, I swear, asked me to do at least eighteen takes, and he would have continued way beyond this number if George Martin hadn't become exasperated and said, kindly but firmly, and in front of everyone, 'Burt, what exactly are you looking for here?'

'That little bit of magic,' Burt, who was a total perfectionist, replied.

Quick as a flash (and this is on the film), George came back and said, 'I think we got that on take four.' He was right. There was something very special about that take.

12

Way Out in Piccadilly

'I heard Cilla before I saw her. I was rehearsing on stage and Miss Black was due to arrive at any minute. Suddenly there was this hyena-like shriek from the back of the stalls and I thought, "Well, anyone who can laugh at me like that can't be *all* bad. We're going to get along just fine!"'

That was the Frankie Howerd talking about me – and, because I was so slim at that time and had never sprouted much in the way of breasts, he went on to describe me as 'the girl with two backs'!

Frankie was talking to a journalist about my next big challenge, *Way Out in Piccadilly*, which was to open in November 1966 at the Prince of Wales Theatre. This West End revue was created by the TV comedy-writing team of Ray Galton and Alan Simpson in collaboration with everybody's favourite, Eric Sykes. I was to be Frankie's co-star.

Frankie was an extraordinary man. Thanks to our stage partnership, he became a very close lifetime friend, and once, after one of my many rows with Bobby, he invited me to stay in the South of France. We adored each other, even though he'd tell everybody I was 'common as muck', and we worked brilliantly well together during the rehearsals. Sometimes I think he taught me everything I know. I certainly owe my ability to time a joke or handle a heckle to him.

Bobby and I invested a good deal of our own hard-earned money in *Way Out in Piccadilly*. It was very different from anything I had done before and there's no two ways about it – I was scared. Getting on stage to sing involved acting of a sort, but this was a whole new ball game. 'I'm a singer – I don't think I'm really cut out for this,' I once told a reporter, 'but I'm enjoying it in a masochistic sort of way.'

Some time before working on this show, my skin had rebelled during the summer season at Blackpool and broken out into a multitude of spots. That's what you get for wearing heavy stage make-up for weeks on end. Desperate for some advice, I had phoned Cathy McGowan.

'Cathy, help! I'm *covered* in spots,' I said.

'Drink TCP mixed with water, Cilla,' she had advised. 'That'll do the trick.'

I did – and it *didn't*. (Thanks, Cathy!) So I went to see a local doctor in Blackpool, who prescribed some capsules for me. Usually I don't take pills, avoid them like the plague, but on this occasion, feeling very self-conscious about my skin, I took four of them. They brought zilch improvement, however, so I stopped taking them, but, being the hoarder that I am, I dropped the bottle into my vanity case. I then forgot all about it until the opening night of the revue with Frankie.

'What on earth's the matter, Frankie?' I asked, finding him in a terrible state in his dressing room.

'I need some more of these,' he wailed, holding aloft a bottle that only had two capsules left in it. 'But I haven't got time to go to my doctor for another prescription.'

I was surprised, because Frankie's skin looked fine to me. 'I've got loadsa them in my vanity case.'

'No, no,' Frankie replied. 'You won't have these.'

'But I *have*,' I protested. 'They're exactly the same shape and colour.'

When I went and got them and brought them back to Frankie, it was as if he had won the football pools.

'They *are* Valium,' he cried out, delighted.

'Valium?' I repeated, gobsmacked.

'Valium,' he said; 'to calm you down.'

I couldn't believe it. I'd only gone to the doctor for help with a few spots and he'd prescribed me an anti-depressant! What's more, so high and hyperactive was my normal state that the four capsules I'd taken hadn't had any effect on me at all!

~

To celebrate my twenty-fourth birthday in 1967, while I was still in *Way Out in Piccadilly*, Brian, bless him, arranged for my name to be put up in lights above Piccadilly Circus. HAPPY BIRTHDAY CILLA, they twinkled, Hollywood style. It's hard to express what moments like that felt like for a girl who'd grown up during really hard times in Scottie Road. Brian was always very romantic, and he'd make the most wonderful gestures. If we'd had a row, he'd get a handwritten letter of apology delivered to me by messenger – just as I was in the middle of a press call. I thought that kind of thing was irresistible.

While I was still in the show, I also made a film, directed by Sir Peter Hall. This little gem of a movie was called *Work Is a Four-Letter Word*, and my co-stars were David Warner of *Morgan* fame, and (until he walked out on the first day of rehearsals) the comedian Alfred Marks. Doing it meant arriving home at midnight after the show, going straight to bed, and getting up at four a.m. to drive up to Birmingham with Bobby for a day's location work on the film.

Work Is a Four-Letter Word was a very sixties fantasy film, a sort of cross between *Billy Liar* and *The Magic Roundabout*, but much madder! In one scene I was captured by a mad earth-moving machine which had a mind of its own. In the script I was supposed to have eaten a magic mushroom, naughtily shaped like a phallic symbol, which created a glorious euphoria in anyone who sampled it. I'd just fallen asleep on the grass when this digger came up alongside me and thumped its bucket down on the ground. I then had to be scooped up into the bucket and carried off. To give the film crew credit, they had rehearsed this scene several times without me, with a cross on the ground for the digger to aim at. I was to learn later that, although the digger always missed its mark, they decided to go ahead and film the scene anyway.

I did one take, and then Bobby, who was in much more of a panic than I was, called an instant halt.

'I'm very sorry,' he said, looking very hot under the collar, 'but that's all Cilla's doing. *Finish*. Cut! No more takes with the digger.'

So we moved on to the scene with the crane. Yeah, I had two *really* desirable looking co-stars in this film! I honestly don't know which was worse, the digger or the crane sequences. It was a case of either risking being decapitated by the digger's bucket, or being whisked seventy feet up in the air on a metal hook by a crane, with nothing to hold on to but a swinging chain.

I felt reasonably OK going up through the air, but not so happy when the crane driver put on the brake, and the hook, which was shaped like an anchor, started swinging manically from side to side. That was when the waves of panic first started to set in. I didn't actually go weak at the knees, but I thought, 'My God! What happens if I do?'

Peter Hall was a stickler for realism, and he'd asked me if I was all right to sit on this hook without a safety harness. I'd said 'Yeah', but now, perched on one side of this thing, I was rockin' and rollin' and swingin' – and prayin'. It was really very scary. Next to me was a tall building, where I could see a stunt man at a window. He looked at me, I looked at him and, doubtless able to see the whites of my eyes, he suddenly understood my situation.

'Get her down!' he started yelling, frantically. '*Get her down!*'

No one argued. Down I went on the hook, until I reached terra firma. This time the stunt man made sure I had a proper harness, and we shot the scene again.

In a way, I wasn't in the least surprised to find myself doing things for that film which were beyond the call of duty. Film was a whole new world to me and I wanted to prove myself. Although filming involved getting up at unearthly hours and some scary props, in the context of show business it seemed perfectly normal. You didn't work weekends; everything was done for you: they made you up, dressed you, looked after you, fed and watered you, and I loved the friendly, gossipy tea breaks.

The only problem was my embarrassment. I had to be made up to look like a plain Jane for that part, and I felt very self-conscious and uncomfortable. Being on stage and looking fabulous I loved, but this was different. Also, I've never liked people gawping at me, but I had to get used to all the technicians staring at me when we were on location. In the film studio there was a crew of ninety.

'I could never do a nude or a love scene,' I thought – not that they asked me to do one on *Work Is a Four-Letter Word*.

After completing the filming I became very screen-struck for a while. 'If I'm bombarded with good scripts,' I said to Bobby, 'I'll never sing again.' But I wasn't bombarded with good scripts.

~

In June 1967 (it was during the Six Day War) Bobby and I moved out of Prince Albert Terrace Mews. We moved to a large and classy flat in Wimpole Street, but by the end of 1967 I was on the move again. I was reading the newspaper and came across the incredible news that I was a millionairess! At least, that's what it said in the paper.

'Why didn't you tell me?' I said to Bobby, starting to leaf through the property pages, my head full of all sorts of ideas now. 'We could treat ourselves to a lovely new flat.'

'Why? Would it have made any difference?' Bobby asked. 'Haven't you got exactly what you want? Aren't you happy?'

'Of course I am,' I replied.

'So what's the problem?'

What's It All About?

'I'd have just like to have known *before* I read it in the paper,' I told him sulkily.

The truth, though, was that unless he had come in one day and tipped a million pounds in cash on to the floor, or thrown it up in the air like they do in the movies, it wouldn't have meant a thing. By then, I just took money – and buying nice things – for granted. Of course, money was never the most important thing in the equation.

'Bobby, I'm enjoying myself *so* much,' I exclaimed. 'I'd do it for nothing.'

'Don't ever let anyone hear you say that,' he said with a smile. 'So, shall we look for that new flat, then?'

So we left Wimpole Street and rented a really smart West End apartment in Portland Place, right opposite the Beeb's Broadcasting House. It was incredibly spacious, full of light and sunshine. The sitting room was a tasteful cream colour, and the bathrooms were en-suite. The dining table could seat ten, there were silk curtains, Regency cream striped wallpaper (no flock in sight!), under-floor heating and enormous built-in wardrobes. The windows were huge. There was even a wrought iron balcony leading off the large state-of-art kitchen. It had the lot! It felt like a movie star's flat and I adored it. This was definitely a move up the property ladder!

Frankie begged me to stay on in *Way Out in Piccadilly*, but although I felt guilty about leaving the show, the hectic schedule of combining it with filming had nearly killed me and I wanted to move on.

I'd also had a stressful time with Eppy during the Prince of Wales run. I fell out with him at that time, as did Bobby – and as I later learned, The Beatles weren't happy with what Brian was doing then either. Brian tried to make it up, of course. He asked me to his lovely home at Chapel Street, and we talked on the roof terrace. Peter Brown, his right-hand man, was there too. (Peter used to work in the record department at Lewis's, and he used to throw me out for listening to records again and again there when I was learning them to sing in the clubs. He was from Liverpool, but you'd never know it from his accent – he spoke real posh, much posher than

Brian.) Brian promised he would try to do better and pleaded with me not to leave him, because that's what I was going to do – leave him, leave NEMS, and let Bobby manage me full-time.

Fortunately Bobby and I had a holiday in the Algarve lined up which would give us some space to relax and calm down a bit. We'd had such a lovely time there the previous year that Bobby had booked it for us again. Our plan was to totally bomb out, take in the sea air, swim to our hearts' content, read our books, and meet up with Tom Jones, who had become a good friend of ours. Tom, now called 'the Welsh Wonder', had become a bit of a sex symbol and a huge star. Getting away from all the hustle and bustle would be bliss.

Bobby and I came back down from Liverpool where I'd been on a quick visit to see me mam and dad. We were met at Euston station by Brian with the great news of yet another first that he'd been working on – I was to host my very own BBC TV series. There was just one snag. The BBC wanted me to sing for Europe on the show. I said, 'No, Sandie Shaw won it last year – there's no chance another British girl will do it this year, and anyway, I don't wanna do a Eurovision song.' And that's where I left it with Brian. Bobby and I shared a taxi with him and dropped him off before going on to the airport.

While we were away, Brian got more news on the BBC deal. Excited but unable to reach me by phone at the hotel in Portugal, he dashed off a handwritten note for his secretary:

Joanne – Please send suitable cable to Cilla requesting she calls me where I am (Sussex or here) a.s.a.p. I've tried to contact her but impossible. Urgent matter. Brian.

But by the time Joanne saw this note, Brian was dead.

parttwo

13

Brian

As we sat in a dazzling white Moorish-style nightclub in a tranquil fishing village overlooking a white sandy beach and the Gulf of Cadiz, soaking up the Portuguese ambience, and laughing and joking over a bottle of champagne with Tom Jones, I noticed a waiter hurriedly approaching our table.

'Are you Cilla Black?' he asked in perfect English.

'Yes,' I replied.

'Your manager's dead,' he blurted out.

My stomach turned. I thought it was some kind of sick joke. I looked at Bobby, who also thought it was a prank, and he was furious, his voice rising to an unusually high pitch. He was all for putting one on the waiter there and then. Tom, who was not so emotionally charged, stood up.

'I'll ring somebody,' he muttered.

We sat there silently. I was scared, but I was sure it wasn't true. How could it be? After five minutes Tom returned to the table, having phoned the local Portuguese radio station in the Algarve. His face gave it away. 'I'm *so* sorry, Cilla,' he said. 'But it's true. Brian is dead.'

I couldn't take it in. I had spoken to Brian just two days before and he had been his usual self, saying that he would be in touch the moment he heard from the BBC about the TV series.

'Okay, Brian,' I'd said as I rang off. 'I'll wait to hear from you.'

To make matters worse Tom had only managed to get a garbled account from the radio station – yes, Brian was dead, he'd shot himself, he'd done this, he'd done that. We just didn't know what had happened and our isolated position made it all the more difficult. We sat in shock for what seemed like hours.

There had been no inkling of any kind of tragedy when we left England, and as I rose shakily from the table, unable to see for tears, I kept repeating to myself, 'There's been some mistake. He's fine. Brian's only thirty-three. He's fine. Somebody's got their wires crossed. It isn't true.'

But I was in denial – it was true.

As Bobby held on to my arm, Tom, only a young man of twenty-six then, didn't know what to say to console me.

I was crushed by the horror of it all. The thoughts pulsating inside my head, saying, 'Brian's dead, Brian's dead', were too overwhelming for me to hear anything else. I'd never lost anybody so close to me since my Nana and Granddad; had never even been to a funeral, because Nana and Granddad died while I was at the Plaza, and Mam hadn't told me until I got home, knowing I'd cancel the show if I heard.

The next day, Brian was global front-page news. He had died on 27 August, they were saying, alone in his bed at his Belgravia home, as a result of swallowing a lethal cocktail of booze, prescribed pills and other drugs. And the obituary columns were full of his astonishing, meteoric professional achievements.

I spent the next few days in shock. How could Brian have died? He was only thirty-three. I adored him and he was my greatest fan, who admired my work almost to the point of obsession, seeing me as 'the world's next Judy Garland'. For Brian, I was always 'my Cilla'. Whenever we had had a tiff over management affairs, he had confided in his close friend, producer Vivian Moynahan, that he was always so upset he was left on the verge of tears, which he held back until I was out of sight. Afterwards he would send me a touching gift to make up the quarrel.

I had always been so impressed by his sophistication and his gentle manner. He was everything a posh feller and a gentleman should be. He was a brilliant businessman, but full of creativity. I couldn't help remembering that at one of our first meetings he had promised to design a whole wardrobe of stage outfits in leather for me, but the vivid mental pictures he drew that day had never had a chance to come to fruition. In no time at all he had become too successful a management operator to take time out for fun things. I also remembered my first Christmas in London. I – and The Beatles – had assumed that we would have to remain in the Big Smoke in our hotels, but Brian had amazed us all by hiring a plane and flying us home to Liverpool.

He did everything for us and he meant everything to me. Now he was gone.

~

Within forty-eight hours of hearing the news of Brian's death, Bobby and I flew back to England. Once there, we were anguished by persistent newspaper stories that Brian had killed himself. But I never believed that. It simply was not true. Brian had been perfectly all right when Bobby and I set off to Portugal.

'I've just bought my mother a flat in Grosvenor Square,' he had told me. 'And she is moving down to London to be with my auntie.'

Life was *good* that August for Brian – and, when he died, the contract he had just negotiated for my first TV series, *Cilla*, was on his bed. His death could not have been suicide. It was so obviously a terrible, tragic accident.

The chilling thing was that the weekend he died none of his close friends or relatives was in London. Bobby and I were in Portugal; The Beatles, who had taken up meditation, were in Bangor with the Maharishi; Gerry Marsden was at his place in Wales; Brian's mother, Queenie, was still in Liverpool;

Peter Brown, his business associate, was in Sussex; and Vivian Moynahan was working in Russia. Even if Brian had wanted to get in touch with any of us, he'd have had a job doing it. All this, of course, was pure coincidence, but it also seemed uncanny to me that all his friends and close relatives were suddenly not there when he was going through that fatal crisis.

As for Bobby and me, Brian was 'family' and when he died it was a huge tragedy.

There is no doubt that Brian had a deeply unhappy, rocky private life. But, regardless of anything that others said or wrote about him being gay and his 'promiscuous lifestyle', I had always closed my ears to this and only knew him as a wonderful, caring and protective man. To him, I was 'my Cilla'; to me, he was 'my Eppy'.

He never discussed his personal life with me, but I had picked up on the gossip. In the early days when an acquaintance had come up to me in the Blue Angel Club in Liverpool and said: 'You do know he's queer?', I just thought he meant that Brian was an oddball.

'I like Brian – what's wrong with that?' I had replied defensively.

'Cilla! He buys mohair suits for young boys.'

I hadn't a clue what he was hinting at; I had no idea then that men had sex with other men and if somebody had tried to tell me how they managed this, or, for that matter, what a lesbian was, I would have been as amazed as Queen Victoria. Being me, though, I was perplexed by the mohair comment and I did challenge Brian about this one day.

'Is it true, Brian,' I said, 'that you buy mohair suits for young boys?'

'Of course not,' he replied, looking so haunted that I backed off immediately.

Since those days, I've often wondered if Brian found Bobby, who was so cherubic-looking, attractive. But neither Bobby nor any of The Beatles, nor any of the other guys in the groups, was ever uneasy in Brian's company; and if he had come on to any of them, I know he would have got a Liverpool kiss – otherwise known as a 'back-stitch' or head butt – in return.

Brian

I am aware that there was a much-publicised rumour that Brian had invited John to go on holiday with him to Torremolinos when Cynthia was pregnant, and that he and John had a relationship while they were in Spain, but I find that very difficult to believe. Brian was very professional and John was so heterosexual.

While Brian was still alive, I also picked up on the stories about his being discharged as 'mentally and emotionally unfit' when he was doing his National Service in 1952. Homosexuality was illegal then – it didn't become legal until 1967, ironically the year he died – and the description 'mentally and emotion-ally unfit' was often used then to describe practising homosexuals.

I'd also heard the gossip that when he first started mixing with other gay men in Liverpool, he told his parents, Harry and Queenie, and his brother, Clive, that he was gay and, although they were disappointed, they had stood by him. Then there was the incident with an undercover police-man at Swiss Cottage that had resulted in Brian leaving RADA and giving up his brief foray into acting; and the gossip of how he had been beaten up and robbed one night after a furtive sexual encounter with a construction worker in Derby; and how, after this macho guy had turned up at his family home threatening public exposure unless he was paid off, Brian's father had informed the police and the feller was arrested and put away for three years.

But none of this ever surfaced in my relationship with him. What mattered about Brian was his fabulous charisma. When I first came to London and went with him to premieres, he made me feel like a million dollars. I was a girl from a poor background with nothing to my name, while he seemed to have everything a person could wish for. I had such faith in him – and he gave me so much confidence. If he had said, 'Cilla, you can climb Mount Everest', I'd have replied, 'Where's me haversack?' I'm off!' and done it. He had that much influence over me.

~

When The Beatles received the news of Brian's death on their meditation retreat, they told the press that Brian had intended to join them on the very day that he died to be initiated as a member of the Maharishi's International Meditation Society. Gerry and The Pacemakers and Billy J. Kramer cancelled concerts to pay their respects. And Elvis Presley sent us a message of condolence.

When John, Paul, George and Ringo returned from Wales to Liverpool, they were absolutely distraught. 'It was such a shock,' George told the press, 'that I can't even remember who took the phone call in Bangor. I think it was John. Blood drained out of his face. "Brian's dead," he said.'

Like Bobby and me, The Beatles didn't believe Brian's death was suicide. 'I don't think Brian set out to die,' Ringo said. 'I think he took his downers, then woke up and took some more.'

George Martin, who was very fond of Brian, found out about his death in a very bizarre way. George had a country cottage, and after a busy day recording in London he'd gone down there for some rest and recuperation. 'Sorry about the news,' his local shopkeeper said, when he called in for some provisions.

'What news?' George asked.

'Your friend Brian Epstein has died,' the shopkeeper replied.

George hadn't heard a whisper before this. His wife, Judy, had just had their first baby, Lucie, and when George collected her from hospital and they returned to their London flat, there was a huge bouquet of flowers on their doorstep. It had been sent by Brian on the day that he died. The flowers were dead.

~

The Beatles were not even able to go to Brian's funeral for fear of turning it into a media-and-fan circus. Ringo was so gutted the night before that he asked me to come with him and the others to a seance to try to contact Brian. But I didn't want to do that. If my Eppy had come through, any words I could have spoken would have been inadequate, and it would only have made the loss of him worse. I'd always felt so touched that Brian, who always appeared uneasy in the company of young women, was so relaxed and happy with me.

In the end the Maharishi told Ringo not to hold on to Brian – to love him but let him go, because we were all powerful forces who could halt him on his natural progression to heaven.

'You have to grieve for him and love him,' the guru said, 'but you also have to send him on his way.'

That message helped all of us.

After the funeral service at the Jewish Cemetery at Long Lane, Aintree, Brian was buried near his father, Harry, who had died only one month before. In accordance with Jewish law, women were not allowed to attend the burial, and I was so distressed by the funeral service that his mother, Queenie, had to take me back into the synagogue and give me a Valium to calm me down. Perhaps it was just as well I couldn't attend the burial, because I heard later that Rabbi Dr Norman Solomon had upset the mourners who could attend by implying that Brian had been part of the 'decadence of the sixties'.

When I returned to the flat, I wept and wept. Anyone who was really close to Brian loved him. He was so much more than a manager to me. I couldn't imagine ever having had any success without him. It was a tragic waste that he should die so young.

'If only he had talked more to us and all his other friends,' I kept sobbing to Bobby. 'If only he'd opened up a little and taken us into his confidence, then we could have shared some of the pressures that were getting him down and causing his insomnia.'

Now he would never know the end of his – or our – story. He would never hear a new song. He would never truly appreciate the magnitude of just how much he had achieved in so little time. He would never know what a difference he'd made.

I was absolutely bereft.

14

Cilla, Lulu and Sandie

For months after Brian died, I felt fit for nothing, but Bobby helped me to try and take pleasure and comfort from my family and friends. I was also very reassured that he and I had got into the habit of discussing all Eppy's proposals before I agreed to anything, so Bobby was up to speed on what was supposed to be happening when and where.

By the closing months of 1967, Bobby, realising that my only way through this tragedy was for me to concentrate on work, was already well into his role of being my personal manager. He cut his teeth on *Cilla*, the BBC TV series which Brian had negotiated for me; and in October he geared me up to do a one-week cabaret at the Variety Club, Batley. The management there always booked big stars and paid huge sums of money for the privilege.

As part of my act, I was quite flirty on stage even though I could barely make out through the spotlights what anybody in the audience looked like. In the interval, the management used to wedge open the outer door to my dressing room and place a small table there so that people could queue up for my autograph. On one occasion, however, there was no table and when Bobby opened the door to a knock, there was a good-looking guy standing there.

'Cilla *wants* me,' he blurted out. 'I could tell by the eye contact when she was on stage.'

'No – *no*, mate,' Bobby replied. 'That's part of the act. Have you got an autograph book? She'll sign it for you.'

I was in my changing room, but I could hear this exchange going on, and then I heard the chap muttering something as he tried to push by Bobby. The next moment there was fisticuffs. Bobby was one of Liverpool's schoolboy boxing champions so he knew where to aim his punches, and I knew he was laying into the other feller.

When I opened the door there was blood splattered on the walls, on the carpet – everywhere.

'Look at this!' Bobby was saying. 'Look at my new shoes. They're ruined.'

'Bobby! What have you done?' I replied, horrified. 'This'll be headline news tomorrow.'

But it wasn't. The guy immediately backed off when the owner of the club said it was him who was out of order.

I was still anxious about going to the club the next night, though. The Scousers have a reputation for fighting – and getting their revenge – and I thought the guy might turn up with a gang of fellers to have another go at Bobby, or damage the Bentley in the car park.

But I was in for a surprise. A couple of his mates came round to my dressing room and said, 'Sorry, Cilla. He wants you to know he was out of order – a bit tanked up – and he's very embarrassed now.'

~

In November, my new single, 'I Only Live to Love You', was released and remained in the charts for eleven weeks. As I'd looked at Bobby when I was recording that song, my thoughts had slipped off to Brian – and I was so *very* glad I still had Bobby and that he was fit and healthy and still in my life.

When somebody close to you dies, memories float in and out of the mind at the most unexpected, inappropriate times. I could be singing a song on a live TV programme and suddenly I would see Brian's face as clear as day, and remember moments we had shared together – a laugh here, a giggle there. Or I would be sitting at home reading and suddenly I'd recall things that people had said about him, when for instance Ringo declared, 'Brian was great. You could trust Brian. He was a lot of fun and he really knew his records. We used to have a game with him where we'd say, "Okay – c'mon, Brian, what was the B side?" and he always knew the answer. Then we'd say, "OK – what number did it reach?" and he'd tell us. He was amazing. He had a mind like an encyclopedia.' Or when Paul said, 'Brian would have been really happy if he could have heard how much we all loved him.'

The first time I saw the mugshot of myself on the cover of the *Radio Times,* accompanied by the words 'Cilla Black in her own show on BBC1', was one of these Brian moments. Excited though I was, I just couldn't help thinking how thrilled he would have been to see that week's edition on the shelves of his local newsagent. 'Cilla!' he would have said when he phoned. 'Have you seen it yet? If not, don't worry, I've got a dozen copies here. Well done. Isn't it a great shot!'

When *Cilla* began in January 1968, I was still reeling from the loss of him, and I remember saying sadly to the press, 'Bobby's my talisman – my security blanket now.'

Some of my friends, ranging from Ringo to Cliff to Frankie Howerd, from Lulu to Sandie Shaw to Les Dawson and Spike Milligan, made guest appearances on that show, and I sang 'Moon River' with Henry Mancini. It was a very exciting time. Among the first-night telegrams I received was one from Gracie Fields, which I still treasure today.

Between January and the end of March that new, nine-week, prime-time, fifty-minute series attracted record viewing figures of over thirteen million for each show; and the way I interacted with the studio audiences before the transmissions caused an uproar at the BBC, although all I did was sing some raunchy pub songs to get a friendly ambience going!

In my mind, I was still on that kitchen table at home in Scottie Road, making eyes at the upturned faces and letting them know 'I'm *your* kid'. But, then, I never did see myself as playing to millions of anonymous viewers; I always performed to the five hundred people seated right there in the studio. That, I think, was half the reason why my TV shows were such a success. The real secret, though, lay in their length. I could never have done a twenty-five minute show, I'd have run out of time and had to be faded out on the screen while I was still talking!

The success of *Cilla* marked the beginning of a new phase in my professional life. I was now accepted as an all-round television entertainer and the series also provided me with another hit record, 'Step Inside Love'. This number, which was especially written by Paul for the show, wasn't released as a single until the series was almost over. This was because Paul's songs, although simple in essence, were often difficult to arrange and get the sound that was wanted, and he had left writing it until the last moment.

At the first key-setting session, in a recording studio in Bond Street, Paul played it on guitar, but the key wasn't right for me – and I had to have it taken up a few notes. Although Paul and I didn't talk about Brian that day, he was in my thoughts, and I know he'd have been over the moon that Paul came up with the idea for the song. Later on the song was banned from the radio in South Africa – they thought it sounded like a prostitute inviting her client into her house, which was totally out of character for me!

When I was photographed for the sleeve of my next album, *Sher-oo!*, released in April, I was sporting a hairstyle I had never had before. Created by Leslie for the photographs that were being taken by John Kelly, I was transformed by a perm that produced masses of big sausage-like curls. It lasted all of a week.

~

As a lead-up to the 1968 Eurovision Song Contest, Cliff sang a song for Europe in special segments on my *Cilla* shows. Whenever he was on the show, I'm not kidding, my skin came out in goosepimples. He was so pretty – still is. I could hardly believe he was there. I'd always idolised him and whenever I was alongside him I couldn't help recalling how I'd hung around the stage door in Liverpool, praying for a glimpse of him. Now, here he was, singing on *my* own show. Sometimes I thought I was dreaming!

'Cliff,' I said one night. 'There's a party at my flat in Portland Place after the show. D'you fancy coming?'

'My mum's in the audience tonight,' Cliff replied dubiously.

'Bring her along.'

'Bill, my manager, is with her.'

'Bring him, too.'

'Are you sure, Cilla?'

'Yes, I love your mam – she's a sweetheart – and I love Bill, too.'

Peter Brown was organising the party for me – and he'd invited fabulous people like the heart-throb *Dr Kildare* actor, Richard Chamberlain, who had not yet come out. But when Peter saw Cliff, plus his mam and his manager, enter my sitting room, he forgot all about the other guests – The Beatles, The Rolling Stones, The Mamas and the Papas.

'How good can things get?' he kept muttering, looking at Cliff and his entourage. 'That's *so* cool!'

'A party's a party,' I replied, pretending to be laid back, but hardly able to believe that all those beautiful people were huddled on my sofas in my sitting room.

When Cathy and I heard that Cliff was gonna be starring at the Talk of the Town, a swank theatre-cum-nightclub, cum white-linen restaurant in Leicester Square, we decided to book a table and go to see him.

'Fab' and 'smashing' were two of Cathy's most frequently used words, but they were never irritating when she said them. They just seemed to go with her trendy haircut and groovy Biba clothes. We were always very kittenish when we were together and, just before the show, Cathy sent Cliff a telegram asking him to dedicate a special song just for us.

And he did – announcing 'This song is especially for two ladies I love, Cilla and Cathy.' We swooned and squealed like teenagers while he sang it.

Adoring Cliff – as I did – didn't mean I was being disloyal to Bobby! My feller was a very jealous man, but he'd got me sussed by then, knew me like a bad penny. I was a terrible flirt – 'I luv you – take me, I'm yours,' I used to say breathlessly to Cliff, but Bobby always knew I'd break the record for the four-minute mile if anyone took me seriously and came on to me.

~

It was the last night of the first series of *Cilla*. I was feeling very down about it all coming to an end. Still young and very successful, I was looking straight into the camera saying goodbye to the viewers. What they couldn't see, however, was what I could see – the studio audience and the crew standing beyond the camera I was looking into. As I stood there gazing into the camera that night, I saw the huge frame of Jim Moir, now the Head of Radio Two, but my floor manager in those days. The last-night blues had got to him too, and he was crying his eyes out. 'Oh, my God!' I thought, and burst into tears myself in front of the millions who were watching the show.

The first person on the phone to me when I got back to Portland Place was me mam. 'I saw the show,' she said curtly, 'and it was great. But don't you *dare* ever make such a show of me again. You just don't do that – d'you hear?'

She was obviously upset at me being upset, but nevertheless she gave me a pull-yourself-together speech. I've tried very much to keep my feelings to myself ever since.

~

It was that spring, at the London premiere of *Work Is a Four-Letter Word*, that I first had to endure the horror of seeing the bump just below the bridge of my nose in panoramic Vista Vision. It had never looked that bad on the telly, but up there on the big screen it dominated my profile.

'Oh, God! Look at my nose. It's awful,' I kept muttering to Bobby. 'I *hate* it.'

'Shhhh. Watch the film,' Bobby said, squeezing my hand. But all I could do was watch my nose.

I loved acting – I still do. But I found it very frustrating having to wait so long for the film to be finished in the cutting and editing rooms before it was shown; and it was an absolute age before any of us knew how it was going down. I was used to knowing whether a record was a success or failure very quickly, but in the film business this process can take anything up to a year. Despite the drawbacks, I convinced myself for a time that I'd like a change of direction and a move into films. The offers that did come in, though, were usually for me to portray some typical 'Northern girl', whereas I wanted to do serious stuff and become a Dame and maybe win an Oscar or two.

Sadly, no Academy Awards or Oscars were won by the film or by me. It seemed the only Dame I was gonna be was Priscilla the Goose in pantomime!

In spite of what he'd said at the premiere, Bobby made me have a nose job soon after. I had it done on my twenty-fifth birthday at the Queen Victoria hospital in East Grinstead, because we thought it would be quieter there.

Bobby was his usual supportive self. 'It's a good move, Cil, for someone who's going to spend so much of her life in front of the cameras,' he said.

The nose job cost me £210, but I was in a private room and it didn't seem outrageously expensive. Immediately after the op, I felt a bit bashed about, but I began to feel better day by day. By the end of the week, the bandage was off and I was ready to return home. The press had got the story by then, but I didn't really mind, and in due course I was perfectly happy to show off my new nose. In fact, once I'd fully recovered from the operation, I was able to indulge once again in my fantasy that I looked just like Jean Shrimpton or Brigitte Bardot!

~

Soon after the premiere, the *TV Times* arranged to do a photo shoot with me and Gracie Fields at her home on Capri, a gem of an island on the Italian coast just off Naples, and overlooked by Vesuvius, a live volcano which still snorted flames up in the air from time to time. They flew me to Naples and then we took the ferry out to the island. The 'taxis' in the picturesque harbour enchanted me – they were little carts drawn by donkeys – and whenever the ferry arrived, laden with tourists, many of whom were Gracie's fans, the donkeys went on autopilot and started trotting off for her villa the moment they heard an English voice.

Unsurprisingly, I was too young to appreciate Gracie's kind of music, songs like 'Sally – Sally'. If I had, it would have been rather like one of today's popsingers being into Vera Lynn's 'I'll Be Seeing You' and 'The White Cliffs of Dover'. But I was very aware that Gracie had legendary status.

The reason for the shoot was that there was a plan for me to play Gracie in a film about her life, but I was shocked to the core when I read the script. I'd always assumed that she'd led a sunny-side-up life, but the story of her early years and her marriage to Monty, her manager, was very dark. Monty, for example, had his mistress living in the same house and Gracie had to put up with this *ménage à trois*! The film's producers, of course, thought this was a fabulous racy story.

'I'm too young to play this,' I kept saying to Bobby as I turned the pages. 'I've been blessed. I've never experienced this kind of life.'

'That's what acting's all about,' he kept trying to reassure me.

It also became apparent that, because Gracie was so unhappy, her life on stage was a form of escapism – and she literally used to do cartwheels in the wings before she went on. 'There's no way I can do these cartwheels,' I said. 'I'll break my back! You'll have to get a double for those scenes.' In the end, the film never got off the ground, which was perhaps just as well for me.

When we met Gracie, who was now thankfully happily married to an Italian called Boris and living on a breathtakingly beautiful, sun-splashed patch of the island, she was not happy about the film. This was nothing to do with the script. It was because she wanted me to mime all her songs, while the film's producers wanted me, not her, to sing them. I thought Gracie was right. Her fans would have gone ballistic if she didn't sing in the film. But it proved to be a total impasse. She put her dainty foot down and the film was never made.

I loved visiting her, though. It was at the time she was singing 'Lily The Pink' and she was exactly as I'd imagined her to be. She was full of Northern humour and grit – so down to earth – and her hillside homes (she had two) were absolute paradise. One of the houses was quite low down, within easy reach of the sea, where she swam every day. 'But when it gets cold,' she said, 'then we go up to my other house', and she pointed higher up the mountain to this other fabulous house. The lower house was a typical Italian villa with fabulous gardens and a patio. She wasn't an old lady at all. She was big-boned, as we'd say up North, with incredible skin and silver-grey hair. She swam in the sea every morning and was very fit, and she'd go to great lengths to get all the English newspapers and read them from cover to cover.

'Ey, Bobby,' she said, at one moment. 'You've done deals for Cilla at that Batley Variety Club. They want me to sing there. How much should I ask? What does Cilla get?'

We were taken aback. This was the great Gracie Fields comparing herself with me and asking Bobby for advice. For a moment Bobby was nonplussed, but rising to the occasion he replied, 'D'you really want to leave all this to go and sing there?'

'You bet,' Gracie replied.

It was the old ego thing that all artistes share. We're all so flattered when somebody's willing to pay us to perform.

'Well,' Bobby said, 'I'll tell you what, Gracie, Louis Armstrong performed there last month, so you ask for the same amount of money he got. You're in the same calibre as him.'

'Right, chuck,' she replied happily, 'I'll do that.'

Cilla, Lulu and Sandie

Having met the great lady and seen for myself how down-to-earth and straightforward she was, I felt I could understand why I was being compared with her. Of course, when I got back to London I went straight out and bought her records (about time too!). The one I played the most was 'The Biggest Aspidistra In The World'. It was great fun, and Gracie had a simply incredible voice.

We returned to the good news that the first series of *Cilla* was not to be the last. It was so successful in the ratings that I was booked to round off 1968 with a second, six-part *Cilla* series, the first to be shown in colour. I loved being spontaneous on this live show. I never worried about making mistakes. Sometimes I forgot people's names or the words of a song, but it all helped to make things seem more natural – and me more human – and the audience really liked that.

By then the music press was intimating that the real heyday of the British girl pop singers with star quality was over. This category apparently included the very shy Dusty Springfield, with her gorgeous blonde hair and panda eyes; Marianne Faithfull, with her captivating natural beauty, long eyelashes, groovy clothes and big hit single, 'As Tears Go By'; Petula Clark with her fresh, girl-next-door appeal; Sandie Shaw with her long legs and slender pair of bare feet pattering around splintered boards; the tiny, feisty Lulu with her amazing lungs; and me. We had, according to this theory, all peaked between 1964 and 1967!

The press were always making out that we were huge rivals who didn't get along, but because we were all so different we were actually all good mates; and, as my *Cilla* series progressed, each of the girls was only too happy to come on the show.

I really liked Dusty, who was an ex-convent girl like me, and I loved her 'white queen of soul' voice, especially her desperate sounding rendering of 'You Don't Have To Say You Love Me', which became her signature tune on stage and TV. She was a very pretty, wacky, fun-loving girl, but she had zilch self-confidence.

What's It All About?

Dusty was famous for her parties, and that summer she invited us to one at her house on Aubrey Walk in Kensington, which she was sharing at that time with her partner, Norma Tanega – a woman (I know, shocking!) with wonderfully high Mexican or Indian cheekbones and long, dark hair. As Dusty opened the front door the heavy scent of joss sticks wafted around us, and we saw that everything in the house was painted in her favourite colours – pink and purple. The walls and floors were reverberating with her guests' laughter and the music from two stadium-sized speakers turned up to full volume. She took Bobby and me aside to meet her mam, Catherine (or Kay), who was a very lively, sparky lady, and her dad, Gerard O'Brien, a quiet, pipe-smoking intellectual. I'm sure she did this to convince her parents that she had some sane, normal, non-gay friends! Bobby and I spent the whole evening sitting on a pink sofa talking to them while everybody else, including people like tennis champions Jimmy Connors and Billie-Jean King and her tennis partner, Rosie Casals, and the Motown trio The Vandellas, best known for 'Dancing In The Street', were going crazy.

I'd first met Dusty on a TV show. She sang fifties numbers and wore fifties-style clothes – sticky-out frocks and a beehive hairdo. She had originally been with a folk group, The Springfields, and was already a seasoned performer by the time I got to know her. I was very much the new kid on the block and singing sixties-style numbers, but I think she learned a few things from me – not vocally so much, more in terms of dress sense. We got to know her well, although I never really took much notice of Norma.

Having watched herself once too often on TV, Dusty had decided that the worst part of her body was her legs. After that she would never appear in anything other than long dresses or trousers. We discovered that she also had a range of back-combed wigs to balance her jawline, which she thought was much too heavy, and her nose, which she considered far from perfect. She named her wigs Cilla, Lulu and Sandie – and she was often seen picking one of these up in her dressing room and shaking it like a rat. 'Grrr, Cilla!' or 'Grrr, Lulu!' she'd say, before hurling the wig across the room!

The stories about her throwing – and smashing – dishes were all true. But she didn't do this out of anger – she did it out of devilment or boredom when she just didn't know what to do with herself. For me, a girl who was brought up in total thrift in the North, this was shocking. I could never have broken good china in the way Dusty did. I'd have thought, 'My God! What a waste – how much did that cost?'

~

Everybody was missing Brian's parties, which had always been such fab affairs, and it was decided by one of the lads that, as the only girl in Brian's stable, I should play Mother Hen and take on the party-giving mantle, largely because my flat was so central. As someone who loves to party, I didn't need too much persuasion.

'Okay,' I said, deciding to make that New Year's party a Liverpool 'do' and play all the Jimmy Shand Band records.

The usual crew was there – The Beatles, Vivian Moynahan, Peter Brown, Joe Brown and his wife, Vicki Wickham, my best friend, Pat Davies, and The Rolling Stones, plus wives or girlfriends. I was fond of all the Stones, and we knocked around a fair bit with them – they were always in the Ad-Lib, and I used to fancy Keith Richards on the quiet. He was just the kind of pretty boy that caught my fancy at that time.

At one point Ringo was sent out of the flat to knock at the door as the traditional 'dark stranger', holding the traditional piece of good-luck coal in his hand, but we all forgot about him – couldn't hear the constant ringing of the bell over the din. He was left outside for ages before we remembered him. Then, when he was let back in, blue with cold, he had four Americans, all dressed in plaid trousers, in tow. They'd been consoling him in Portland Place. It was strange that we sent Ringo out really – we should have sent Kenny Lynch out as he was much darker, but perhaps he was hiding somewhere.

What's It All About?

Cynthia Lennon hid herself at that party too. Georgie Fame came and told me she'd locked herself in one of my wardrobes. When I went to find her, she said she was waiting to see how long it would be before John noticed she was missing and came to find her. I told her not to waste her time and to get out and have a good time – just like John was doing!

The party eventually became pretty wild. Joe Brown suddenly said, 'It's shirt-ripping time' – and he decided that all the girls should rip the shirts off the boys' backs. Amid much chasing, screamin' and shoutin', one by one the fellers were cornered, tickled close to death and were left with only their collars and ties still intact on their upper bodies. They were a picture of hairy chests! That game only came to an end when Maureen returned from the loo, took one look at Ringo and got upset.

'That was a new Italian dress shirt – it cost a *fortune*,' she wailed, shocked, as Ringo stood there bare-chested with the rest of the boys, while we girls crept off shamefaced, heads hanging, into the nearest corner!

As that year came to an end and our guests trooped off home, neither Bobby nor I had a clue that, one month into the New Year, Peter Brown, Brian's old business associate and now our very good friend, would come up with a suggestion that would change our lives for ever.

15

Barefoot Days

Bobby was never what people would call a romantic man. Where presents were concerned, I would have been over the moon if, on impulse, he had bought me something that cost a couple of bob, like a pink poinsettia in a pot, or my favourite lilies or a small bunch of yellow roses. These really were things I adored that didn't cost a fortune. My girlfriends always knew how I felt and got it right!

'If Pat can do this,' I said to Bobby, 'why can't you? You don't have to buy me expensive jewellery. Little things really do mean a lot!'

Like so many fellers, though, he never quite believed this. Take the time he bought me a Cartier watch encrusted with diamonds. I know this will sound ungrateful, but the last thing I needed was yet another watch. On this occasion I tried to teach him a lesson, with the aid of that wonderful song, 'Little Things Mean A Lot'.

I was trying to make the point that he didn't need to make a big statement with his Cartier watch. It wasn't that I didn't like the watch, I loved it, adored it, but I didn't want him to think 'the more expensive the present, the better'.

It took two days, but then he suddenly said to me, 'You don't like that watch, do you?'

'I do,' I said. 'I love it.'

'But you've not worn it.'

'I never wear a watch when I'm at home over the holidays.'

'You don't like it.'

'Bobby, I *love* it.'

'No. Normally when I buy you something, you wear it all day.'

I played him along, making as many flippant excuses as I could dream up, then I said, 'OK, Bobby. I do like the watch but, you know, you didn't have to do that.'

'I know,' he said.

Then, playing me at my own game, he took the watch back to Cartier! When he got back, he picked a bunch of weeds and came in saying, 'Little things mean a lot – there you are!'

That taught me a lesson.

~

When I was doing *Cilla*, Eric Morecambe and Ernie Wise were said to be the highest paid artistes at the BBC, but Bobby told me that in fact *I* was getting paid more, because Eric and Ernie had to split their fee between the two of them!

We were finding out more and more about the TV world, and as we did, we found we could do things in our own way and add our own little touches. We had big stars on my show, but the budget never covered everything. So Bobby, not the BBC, used to make sure that every star who appeared on *Cilla* had a personal card from me, with a bottle of champagne, in their dressing room. He also used to invite all our guests out to dinner. We'd take them after the show to San Lorenzo in Beauchamp Place, Knightsbridge, which at that time was quite a small restaurant; we knew the owners, the tiny, indomitable Mara and Lorenzo, very well, and Bobby, not the Beeb, would pick up the tab for all these people. Our dear friend Peter Brown, his boyfriend Tommy Nutter, and Pat Davies were regular guests at these occasions.

One evening in San Lorenzo, when Peter was there as usual, one of our lady guests said something that set Bobby off.

'Oh, no. It wasn't like that. It was like this ...,' he began to explain.

'Oh, *no*, Bobby,' I said, contradicting him. 'She's right, you know. What happened was ...'

Bobby's expression changed, as if to say, 'What are you doing? Why are you taking her side?' Then, all of a sudden, things became quite heated and personal, and we were having a proper row, until Peter interrupted us. 'You sound just like an old married couple,' he said. 'Why on earth don't you get married?'

Bobby paused, looked at Peter, then at me, then back to Peter and said, 'OK, Peter. You fix it – and we will.'

I swear to God, that was it. No romantic, down-on-one-knee proposal from Bobby. It wasn't the first time marriage had occurred to me, of course – back when I was about nineteen, and most of my friends were getting married and having babies, it was something I'd thought about quite a lot – but by this time Bobby and I hadn't really discussed it for years. We were comfortable with how we were, and we always knew we'd get married eventually. It was a matter of when, not if, but we were in no hurry.

A couple of days later, when Bobby and I were in a meeting at the flat, Peter Brown called up on the entryphone from the street entrance. By then both Bobby and I had forgotten all about the marriage suggestion.

'I'm on my way to Marylebone Register Office,' Peter said to Bobby. 'Can you come with me?'

'Hang on,' Bobby said. 'I'm in the middle of a production meeting for next week's show.'

'OK. Is it all right, then,' Peter asked, 'if I put up the banns for forty-eight hours?' (That's how long it took in those days.)

'Well – yes, OK,' said Bobby.

When the meeting ended, Bobby came through to me and said, 'That was Peter Brown. Do you remember the dinner at San Lorenzo?'

'Yes?' I said warily. 'You're not going on about that argument?'

'No – what Peter said to us.'

'Yes?'

'Well, what d'you reckon? Do you want to do it or not?'

It wasn't quite the proposal I'd been hoping for, but, realising it was all I was going to get, I said, 'OK, Bobby – yes. I guess it's on.'

And that was that. Peter put up the banns; and Bobby and I never discussed the preliminaries further. But then I went all girlie and rang Cathy who was going out with the handsome young actor Hywel Bennett. Hywel hadn't popped the question yet.

'Guess what?' I said. 'I'm getting married.'

'Ohhhhh!' she exclaimed. 'When?'

'In forty-eight hours!'

With no time to find a wedding dress, I decided to wear a dress I'd bought for £8 two years earlier at Granny Takes A Trip, in Chelsea. It was a ruby-red, high-waisted velvet dress, and to make it look more fashionable I took up the hem. The addition of a new blue garter took care of the traditional 'new' and 'blue' items in one. I didn't have a wedding ring. I just had a friendship ring that Bobby had bought me. I knew exactly what flowers I wanted, though, to complement my ruby-red dress – a bouquet of purple and red anemones.

Then, on the Friday, the day before the wedding, me mam was on the phone, crying her eyes out. It turned out she'd just heard the news in the worst possible way – on the radio.

I'd wanted to surprise her with the news after it was all over, but now I felt awful when I realised just how stupid and thoughtless I'd been.

I'd given my real name, Priscilla Maria Veronica White, at the Register Office but this hadn't protected me. Somebody had sussed the name, Cilla Black, and now it was all over the TV and radio news. Me mam, of course, didn't want us to have a civil wedding in a Register Office. In her eyes that didn't count for anything. She wanted the full Catholic works – the cathedral job – Paddy's Wigwam, Liverpool, no less.

'Mam, I'm doing it in Marylebone tomorrow, on Bobby's twenty-seventh birthday,' I said, interrupting her in full flow. 'I don't want the showbiz thing. I don't want to go through all that. My *life* is show business. I don't want the wedding to be that as well. We don't want any fuss or hassle. We just want to get married quietly.'

The weeping continued, then Mam played her ace card: 'Whatever you say, I won't come, Cilla. I won't come because it won't be a proper wedding.'

I felt awful, but that was her last word on the subject. My dad, though, was great about it all. 'I'd love to come, Queen,' he said. 'But it's more than my life's worth to come without your mother.'

So we had to go ahead without my parents. Peter Brown arranged it all and invited the other guests: Gabrielle Crawford, who was married to the actor Michael Crawford; George and Judy Martin; Vivian Moynahan; and my dear hairdresser, Leslie.

That night, before the ceremony, Cathy came over to Portland Place for a girlie night. I will not be left out of a 'do', and as Bobby was having a stag night dinner with Peter Brown and Tommy Nutter at the posh Mirabelle restaurant, Cathy and I decided to gatecrash it. If Bobby minded, he didn't show it. That cheered me up and gave me confidence, but, oh God, could Cathy *talk*! When we two got back to the flat (Bobby was staying the night with Peter and Tommy at their Conduit Street home), she rabbited on and on, never drew breath, and we ended up sharing a bed, so that she could continue until I drifted off.

The next day, 25 January, Cathy was my maid of honour, Peter gave me away and Tommy was Bobby's best man. Everyone seemed to be nervous except me – including the registrar! One way and another it was quite a bizarre wedding, but apart from the heartache I'd caused me mam, a great day was had by all. The lunch was kept simple – even if it was at the Ritz! – although Peter had ordered caviar, which I hated but Bobby adored. Pat Davies was working abroad, but she made it back just in time for the Ritz. We all went back to the flat afterwards, and Tommy's brother David, a professional photographer, took our photos there. The newspaper reporters and cameramen also came out in force to cover the occasion, and whenever I look at the wedding pictures today, I can see the Cathy-induced bags under my eyes!

I was rehearsing the next day so we didn't go away – we stayed at the flat for our wedding night. On Sunday I was back at work, rehearsing a dance routine for *Cilla*.

A week later Mam was still moaning, and still determined to have the cathedral job on top of the civil ceremony. Surprisingly Bobby was also getting a lot of earache from his side of the family. His dad was no longer alive, but his aunties were furious. 'How could you do this?' they exploded. 'Your mother will be turning in her grave.'

There was a lot of pressure on both of us. You'd expect it from my mother, who never let up on the religious front, but curiously it was Bobby's lot, the Protestants, who were really going mental. I never thought he would give in. He only did now because he was being given such hell by his family.

'Just let's do it, then we can have a quiet life', was my new husband's view. We may have been wealthy, successful and fashionable, bright young things, but Bobby and I could have been any Liverpudlian couple of kids at that moment. We were so in trouble!

When I phoned me mam to capitulate and to let her know that we were after all thinking of having a church wedding as well, she was over the moon. Then, of course, it all began to get out of hand.

'You started this, Bobby,' I said. 'Now me mam's arranged an interview for us with the Monsignor at the cathedral!'

Bobby and I returned to Liverpool for the hour-long interview with the Monsignor. He was dignified and seemed genuinely saintly – I felt honoured to be in his presence, and, more surprisingly, Protestant-agnostic Bobby seemed to be awed by him too. After a courteous interview, he gave us his decision.

'I can't marry you in the cathedral,' he said in a voice that was intended to let us down gently. 'I mean what I am about to say in the nicest possible way, but it would set a very bad example to other young girls and women. In the eyes of the Church, you two have been living in sin since the civil ceremony and they, too, might believe that they could do this, then marry later in church.'

'He's hit the nail on the head!' I thought. Although I was married already in law, but as far as the Church was concerned I'd been living in sin with Bobby for a month already. I didn't see that the Monsignor could possibly have reached a different conclusion.

I was disappointed for our families, especially for me mam with her dreams of church and white veils. I knew she would take it hard. But after I'd thought about it, I was relieved that the cathedral thing was off. After all, the reason we got married in the Register Office was to avoid all the pomp and ceremony.

As a consolation, Mam's local parish church of St Mary's, Woolton, a very picturesque setting for photographs and only a few minutes' drive away from where me mam and dad lived, agreed to give us a lunchtime service of blessing. Clive Epstein, Brian's brother who had taken over Brian's company, had arranged to take Bobby and all the guys to the Rembrandt Club, Liverpool, the night before and I saw no reason why I should miss out.

'Remember you have to go to Mass tomorrow,' my mam warned me.

'Fine – OK,' I replied.

'It's at six in the morning.'

That was a shock, but I thought: 'I'm not missing out on Bobby's second stag night dinner – and I've never been to the Rembrandt Club.' The Rembrandt was a private club, not far from the Jacaranda where me and my mates used to go to watch The Silver Beatles when we were kids.

'Well,' I said to Mam, 'I'm still going out. I'd give my right arm to go to the Rembrandt. I stood outside it often enough watching others going in when I was a kid.'

So I went. Despite its discreet entrance, once you got upstairs to the club, the Rembrandt was as grand as I'd expected – very luxurious, quiet and comfortable, with thick carpets and deep sofas. It was a great evening, and I didn't get back home to my parents' house at Woolton until about one-thirty in the morning. True to her word, me mam got me up at five to go to Mass, and as a result I looked thoroughly hung-over on both my wedding days, and certainly much older than Bobby in the photographs!

For the blessing, I went to town on my clothes. I didn't go in for a traditional white wedding dress because in the eyes of the Church I was a scarlet woman anyway. Instead I wore a white jersey-wool dress, trimmed with ostrich feathers. This was from the wonderful London fashion house of Jean Varon, designed especially for me by John Bates. I'd met John when Jane Asher suggested him to me, and he'd laid on a fashion show, complete with models, just for Jane and me! He became a great friend. I still have that dress. The feathers kept getting up my nose and sticking to my lip gloss. I also wore long white boots. I felt great, which was just as well, because we were having the 'do' at the posh Adelphi Hotel where I'd had a room during filming for *Ferry Cross the Mersey*.

Bobby was in a grey suit by Nutter's of Savile Row – Tommy Nutter's tailoring firm, in which I had a small financial stake. My nieces Gina and Lesley, and Bobby's niece Jacqueline, all dressed in scarlet velvet, were my bridesmaids.

My parents and my brothers, George, John and Allan, were there for the blessing, of course, and Bobby's aunties and his brothers Bertie and Kenny, and their wives Ann and Rose too. Only close relatives and a hand-ful of personal friends attended the church. These included Clive Epstein, my agent Bernie Lee, George Martin, Tony Barrow my publicist, and my fan club secretaries Linda Thomas and Valerie Bettam, who travelled from Birmingham for the occasion. Dad gave me away, and Mam wore the kind of lovely hat that all brides' mothers wear. But hordes of other people turned up at St Mary's as well, which was actually a relief, because I'd feared that a lot of people, especially the Scousers, would have turned against me for getting married in London and disappointing my family.

The event didn't feel like a wedding to me. I wasn't doing it for me or Bobby, but for my family, the media and my fans. It was really just another showbiz occasion, and in the years to come, only me mam celebrated our wedding anniversary on that day, 6 March! Bobby and I never did – and I only ever gave him anniversary cards on 25 January, the day we were married at Marylebone Register Office.

The reception at the Adelphi Hotel afterwards was a riot. It was a typical Scouse do. We didn't care whether the hotel was posh or not, we were determined that it was going to be a good old knees-up. A lot of our London friends couldn't come because it was a Saturday night and they were working, but George and Judy Martin were there – and George gave a speech. George looked rather like a dashing version of the young Prince Philip, and he was, as always, very articulate. Bobby's brother Kenny, who was his best man, was supposed to follow George on the mike, but he was much too overawed to read the telegrams in front of what he called 'all your great showbiz people'. Bobby, realising that he was struggling, read out the telegrams for him.

As we were waiting for the toastmaster to come and take over the mike from Bobby, I could see my Uncle James weaving his way through the crowds of guests. 'Oh,' I thought, 'Uncle James is going to make a speech.' But once he was behind the mike, he threw back his head and started to sing 'Barefoot Days', a song about people who have no money. Lots of Liverpudlians – especially after they've had a few jars – sing songs like that. Fortunately, Uncle James had a good voice, and the wedding photographs show him singing the song like a professional crooner, with me and Bobby, looking the other way, convulsed with laughter. He was fab, but Auntie Vera thought he 'showed me up' and told him off!

The only shadow over the reception was that my dad was not feeling at all well. He had acute bronchitis and shouldn't have been a smoker, and was also suffering from heart problems. I didn't realise he'd slipped away until Bobby and I left the reception and stopped off at my parents' house to pick up our stuff at about nine in the evening. Dad was there, on his own, and it was really nice having a chance to sit down and talk to him for an hour or so. I was very worried about his health, though, and it was on that day that it first occurred to me that he might not be with us for much longer.

A bit before midnight, my frock a bit grubby and my feathers drooping, we set off back to London because once again I was working the next day. When people see today's young boy and girl bands ricocheting from one place to another, they say, 'I don't know how they do that', but *I* did it. And, as well as being a pop singer, I also had a TV career. To-ing and fro-ing was my life. Bobby and I spent our Merseyside 'wedding' night driving back to London, and we had no more time off for a honeymoon than we'd had after the first wedding.

By the next day, the news of my two marriages had reached showbiz circles. Michael Hurll, my director, who is still a dear friend, could not believe that we hadn't confided in him – and suddenly we were in hot water all over again.

'How come we weren't invited to the Register Office?' all our friends were saying.

'Peter made all the arrangements,' I kept replying.

'How come Gabrielle Crawford was invited? I'm much closer to you than Gabrielle.'

I had grief galore to cope with. If I could have turned the clock back, I'd have done it to put everything right. I'd had no idea that I would upset so many people. I'd only expected to have a problem with me mam.

They said in the sixties that if a young pop singer got married, it could affect their fan base. I couldn't be worrying about any of that! I was twenty-six, which was considered quite old then to get married, and I felt reasonably secure. Paul McCartney and Linda had also got married in March. 'I've had a good innings,' I thought, 'and I'm well established now.' Even if you were really good, people only expected you to last three years as a pop singer back then, and I'd already exceeded that.

There was no need to worry anyway. Within a week of the blessing, I was back on *Top of the Pops* promoting my latest single, 'Surround Yourself With Sorrow' – a record which had nothing to do with my marriage and absolutely nothing to do with any fans deserting me!

~

I had a wonderful present from Bobby for my birthday that year, my twenty-sixth. I'd seen a large and beautiful dog called Sophie on *Blue Peter* a while before – a Briard, part of the first Briard litter to be born in this country. I fell in love with her at first sight. Bobby phoned the breeder, Mrs Trueman, and bought her for my birthday present. One very lovable dog, who we knew would grow almost to donkey size, should have been sufficient for a couple of flat-dwellers, but when she let us know that she was feeling very lonesome and pining for company, we went back and bought her sister, Ada, who'd also won our hearts.

~

Bobby, who was usually a very easy-going person, could also be very territorial. The type of man who would always go out of his way to avoid trouble, he could suddenly snap over a trifle. It was usually something to do with me, and there were a few occasions when this happened, especially when we first came to London from Liverpool. He would get into such a paddy with me that he would take off home, but he always turned the car around halfway there and came back. Later in 1969, we went to see Sacha Distel, the French singer who'd become famous for singing 'Raindrops Keep Falling On My Head'. Sacha had oodles of Gallic charm. He would say stuff like 'Why are all the gorgeous girls married?' which I would think was so romantic and flattering – until I heard him use the same line on one of my backing singers!

Sacha had often appeared on my *Cilla* shows, and we had become very good mates. On this occasion he was co-starring with Olivia Newton-John in a show that was opening at the Prince of Wales Theatre, and we were invited as guests of Dickie Hurran, who had produced most of my shows, especially my summer season ones.

'Would you like to go to Sacha's opening and have dinner afterwards at the White Elephant Club in Mayfair?' Dickie said.

It seemed a very nice idea – or so we thought!

Having enjoyed Sacha's show, we went backstage afterwards and had photos taken with him and Olivia — then off we went to dinner. When we arrived at the club, I waited on the pavement as Bobby parked our car. As I stood there, I was groped by a tipsy old guy who was walking past. I was really narked!

'Do I *know* you?' I said, in a terribly English, affronted way. He shuffled off and made his way into the White Elephant.

I didn't mention it to Bobby because I knew he would be right in there. But when we were sat down having our meal with Dickie and his wife, I saw the groper, by now more drunk than before, approaching our table. I could see what was coming next.

'Oh, no,' I groaned inwardly.

'I'm from Liverpool, too, you know,' slurred the groper, giving me a lecherous leer.

Bobby, of course, didn't know what this was about and, as I leaned over to whisper a warning in his ear, he turned to me and said, 'Sshhh.'

The guy, thinking Bobby was talking to him, replied, 'Don't you shush me, young fellow.'

Suddenly, Bobby just flipped. In no time at all, he had stood up, schoolboy boxing champion-style, gone thwack-thwack-thwack – and suddenly blood was pouring from the guy's split nose. And Bobby didn't even know this guy had groped me!

A waiter came over, picked the feller up, and led him away from our table. Then, just as we were coming to the end of our meal and making moves to leave, the manager came over.

'You,' he said, pointing at Bobby 'are barred from this club.'

'*Barred?*' Bobby replied, livid. 'No – I'm bloody barring you. I'm not coming to this place again, not with you letting in a gob-shite like that.'

The 'gob-shite', who was still staggering around in his blood-drenched shirt, reeled over to Bobby, saying, 'I know who you are – and I'm going to get you.'

'Why wait?' Bobby retorted. 'Get me now!'

He didn't, of course, which was a relief, because we'd come out for a pleasant evening, not World War Three!

The story was headline news the next day – and a major publicity coup for Sacha and Olivia's show. There was the photograph of Bobby and me posing with them alongside the news item, with me all dolled up in my lovely first-night dress. Bernard Delfont, the show's producer, actually thanked us because the publicity had put tons of money on the box-office returns.

~

One day when Bobby came back to Portland Place after a TV contract meeting, he sank down in an armchair with a groan and said, 'Gosh, that was hard dealing there.'

I had my head in a book and wasn't really paying attention, but I caught the words 'hard dealing'.

'I have to tell you something,' Bobby said as I put the book down. 'You've become what they call "the product". You're just like a packet of Persil or Daz.'

'What are you on about?' I said, confused. 'What d'you mean, a packet of Persil?'

'They actually talk about you,' Bobby explained, 'as a product. You're not a person at those meetings.'

I was shocked. I'd always been Cilla to everybody and I'd got used to TV bosses and producers saying, 'Cilla's great', 'Cilla's a good friend', 'Cilla's nice to everybody.' That was my image, of course, but it was the real me too.

'I thought these people were my friends!' I exclaimed, mortified.

'Not around the business table,' Bobby replied, 'and I have to take that. You're my wife. I love you dearly and I'd die for you, but I have to sit there and talk about you as if you are a product.'

That was a real wake-up call for me – and I was so upset, it was a week before I could get used to the idea. Those people who were all over me like a rash, telling me I was 'the greatest thing since sliced bread' – I couldn't look at them in the same way again, not now that I knew some of them were talking about me like a packet of soap powder! But once Bobby had said it, I could see that it was true.

Naive as it may sound, it was an unbelievable shock and a proper eye-opener for me. From that moment, I never took anything – or anybody – for granted. I just started to see this world I was working in for what it was – a very tough, ruthless business, where you were only as good as your last record or TV show.

~

That was the year in which Neil Armstrong made history and left us all breathless when he became the first man to walk on the moon. It was my first year as Bobby's wife. And it was the year that closed the infamous, raw-kick, let's-do-it sixties. Bobby and I were there for all of it. I was one of the lucky ones who'd been in the sixties, the swingingest of parties that the UK had ever known. It was unforgettable, and it was magical – but as it came to an end I couldn't escape the feeling that things were changing. Nothing I could put my finger on, but it seemed as though there was a harder, tougher edge to things. Perhaps the party wasn't going to last forever.

But none of that seriously worried me. After all, things looked pretty good for me. In fact, I'd got it all now – my career *and* Bobby! There were only two more things I wanted. One that might seem trivial – and one that I felt would complete my life.

16

Child of Mine

As I teetered, stiletto-heeled, on the edge of the new decade, I seemed to be living life so fast I couldn't be sure I wasn't missing anything as it shot past. Every week and every month seemed packed with enough action and excitement to fill a year – ten years, even. But I was young and full of energy, and on a fantastic high – for years I'd felt as though there was always enough time and the future stretched out ahead of me forever.

But now there were moments when I was feeling quite thoughtful – moments when I was starting to realise that nothing could stay the same forever and that whatever the future had in store for us, we could only try to make the most of each day as it came along. And with my twenties seemingly gone in a flash, there were moments when things seemed too good to last. Off stage, I felt restless and vulnerable.

I guess for all of us the downside of being so happy and fulfilled is that we take a lot for granted, so we're hardly aware that time is nudging us into a new phase of our life which, along with the good moments, may have some really awful events in store that can knock us for six.

Perhaps these thoughts of mine were brought into even sharper focus in April 1970 when the papers found out what was happening with our Fab

Four friends. 'Sad-faced youngsters,' reporters told their readers, 'were dressed in mourning black in Liverpool after they'd heard the news that the city's favourite sons were splitting up and going their separate ways.' Paul, they said, was now at loggerheads with John, and had issued a High Court writ to end the partnership which had recently been under strain from squabbles within The Beatles' Apple Corporation.

I was devastated at the thought that there would be no more Beatles music, and even though I knew by now that money and legal wrangles can get in the way of old friendships, it made me sad to think that The Beatles' fantastic partnership could be under such strain that it was falling apart.

Meanwhile, with a new, long, swinging hairstyle, with peep-through fringe, and my fingernails painted silver, I was one of the few of us left from that first wave of kids from Liverpool still up there on stage and on TV. I had a lot to be grateful for, but for the first time I couldn't help wondering if there was more to be had from life.

~

People could certainly be forgiven for thinking that my life was all work and no play, but that wasn't the whole story. Between recordings and TV shows, Bobby and I had some really wonderful holidays, in Austria, for example, with George and Judy Martin, who were absolute ski fanatics. Judy is Roedean-educated and dead posh, and when I first met her I was a bit put off by her far-back, 'royal' way of speaking, but I was soon to find that she has a great sense of humour – kind of like a posh Scouse! By the time she and George introduced us to this caper, they'd tried out a lot of winter resorts, but the one they liked best was Lech in western Austria, where you didn't need to take a bus or a taxi ride to find good slopes. Within its one little valley there was a drag chair, two cable cars and three chair lifts which delivered you to different ski runs; and all of them were within walking distance of our hotel.

When Michael Hurll, my BBC producer, heard we were going skiing, he wasn't very happy about it.

'What'll happen to the *Cilla* series,' he said, 'if you go and break a leg?'

'Don't worry,' I said. 'I'll be all right.' As if I knew!

But he hadn't finished.

'While you're over there,' he said, 'you could utilise the time [typical BBC!] and Bobby could film some shots of you skiing, and we'll put them into the show.'

Lech was a wonderful place, but not exactly easy to get to. On our first trip there, we flew to Zurich, then took a train which wove in and out of the snow-covered mountains for hours. We shared a compartment with a man who, when he wasn't picking his nose, was breaking wind. The compartment was cramped and stifling, and he kept this up for hours. One experience like that was enough, and the next time we went, we hired a car instead.

Excited by another shopping opportunity, I bought a short bomber jacket, knickerbockers and lovely woollen socks at Lech. Once I'd got into them, I thought I looked the cat's whiskers, but I was soon disillusioned. On the first day out, I was learning to walk up the slope when I fell over and in no time at all I was soaked through.

'I've had enough of this!' I complained to the tall, blond, dishy instructor. 'I'm absolutely freezing and wringing wet.'

'Well,' he said, eyeing me up and down, 'look at the way you're dressed!'

He was right. When I bent over, the little bomber jacket rode right up my back and there I was, exposed to the elements. In minus temperatures on an Austrian mountain, that's no joke. What I should have worn was either one of those all-in-one suits that look like a Babygro or a really long, bum-hugging jacket. As for the knickerbockers, they were hopeless. Bobby, sensible feller, had bought a couple of pairs of proper ski trousers.

'Tomorrow,' I said to Bobby in a voice that brooked no argument, 'I'm going to wear your trousers.'

There was, however, a problem I hadn't foreseen. I had much longer legs than Bobby and when I pulled on the trousers, the crutch came halfway down to my knees. We found some braces from somewhere, and it was a case of stretch-stretch, with me ending up feeling like a sausage, but at least they stayed up and kept me dry.

It's amazing what you can learn in a couple of weeks. Once we'd found our feet, we got into a marvellous daily routine. Up at eight every morning, have breakfast, get our gear together and out on the slopes by ten. Having skied till lunchtime, we came back to the hotel and had a super lunch. Our hotel was like something out of *The Sound of Music* – the female staff even dressed like Julie Andrews in the film – and all the dishes on the menu were traditional, beautifully cooked ones like meatballs and noodles. We usually finished lunch at around two and went back out on the slopes until four-thirty; then, after a shower or relaxing soak in the bath, we'd change and go downstairs for a little *Sektorange* – a blood orange with champagne – and into dinner. After we'd eaten, we either went out to a disco or settled down with George and Judy and get childishly over-excited by board games, some of which got quite fierce.

Another night we went by sleigh up to one of the other hotels. The sleigh ride was magic – just like *Dr Zhivago*. All we could hear was the jing-jing-jing of the sleigh bells and the soft thudding of the horses' hooves in the snow. And, in the moonlight we could see deer coming down from among the trees.

We had a good laugh at the hotel and one or two glasses of *Glühwein*, then set off back to our own hotel. The sleigh set us down only a few yards from our door, but we had to go down a steep flight of steps which led to the main street. The snow had been falling and we couldn't see where the steps were. Bobby and I both slipped while we were feeling around for them and slid a fair way down on our bottoms. We weren't hurt, in fact we were shouting and laughing. As we picked ourselves up, a feller appeared and, without turning a hair at finding me at the bottom of a flight of steps in an Austrian ski resort, said: 'Ey, Cilla. How yer doing? Can I have yer autograph?'

Bobby had hired a cine camera to do the filming the BBC wanted, and one day we took it up to the top of one of the runs.

'Give me ten minutes to get down to where I can film you,' Bobby said. 'Then follow on.'

It's ever so cold standing about on a mountain, and I was freezing to death. As soon as I thought Bobby had had long enough to get ready, I set off.

I skied *beautifully*, never made any mistakes at all, and once I was down at the bottom I looked around for Bobby. I couldn't see him anywhere at first, but over to one side there was a group of people crowding around something and chattering away in German, so I went to have a look. They were pulling this figure out of a wall of snow. It had got embedded in there, with its arms stuck out sideways – a bit like the figure in a Crucifixion scene. Then I saw the beard, and I knew who it was.

Bobby, camera around his neck, had skied down the slope quickly in order to be ready to film me. The run had a lot of little bumps in it, and each time he came to one of these he'd done a turn and zigzagged away. Then a little French feller came up alongside, and started skiing exactly level with him. Each time Bobby turned, he thought: 'I'm going to get away from him, he's dangerous.' But he couldn't. They were going down the slope like Siamese twins. He started to lose his temper.

'Get lost!' Bobby shouted at the Frenchman.

All this looking sideways and shouting must have upset his sense of direction. He did another zigzag and went straight into a wall of snow. He must have gone in about four feet. To get him out, people were pulling on his ankles, which just pushed his head further in. When he was finally out he looked a terrible mess. The mad *Englander* – Willis of the Antarctic – with the camera still hanging from his neck.

Skiing is not always the most relaxing holiday you can have. And although Bobby was the most loyal husband and manager in the world, things had a way of sometimes just happening to him. When we were ready to return from Lech to London, the runway was frozen and all the airlines decided to stay on the ground. (I was terrified of flying at this time, incidentally.)

What's It All About?

We all stayed the night in Zurich, and as there was no improvement the next day, we decided to catch a train to Paris and get a flight from there. By then, I had no more time to spare. I had to get back to London for work.

At the station, I got on to the train with Judy and Bobby, but when we looked round there was no sign of George, who had gone off to change some money into francs.

'I'll go and look for him,' Bobby said.

Having got out of the train he walked up the platform towards the station buildings but, as he did so, the train started to move off.

'Bobby! *Bobby!*' I called frantically, leaning out of the window.

But although he heard me and saw what was happening, and began to run after the train, he was outpaced and was left further and further behind. Then he stopped, and my last sight of him was a forlorn figure standing helplessly on the platform as the train pulled out of the station with only me and Judy on board. Minutes later, we realised the guys had our passports and all the money.

Left on his own, Bobby thought he'd check into a hotel and do some phoning, but before he had the chance to do that he bumped into a very sheepish-looking George. Together they went along to the stationmaster's office and got a clerk to telephone down the line to get a message to me and Judy. Then they settled down to a four-hour wait for the next train.

Meanwhile Judy, who being very posh never flaps easily, was absolutely marvellous. While I was panicking and thinking, 'Oh, God! What's going to happen?' Judy had been spotting friends and making lunch dates.

'Hello there,' she called out to this feller. 'Don't I know you?'

'Judy, darling' he said. 'Where are you off to?'

'Paris,' she replied.

She might have lost her husband and mine, but it didn't stop her from arranging for all of us to have lunch in Paris.

'But my work!' I was thinking desperately.

'I won't be a minute,' Judy said as we got off the train at Basle; and, having parked me with all the luggage, she disappeared.

'Oh, God,' I thought, truly waif-like by then. 'Now *she's* gone.'

By the time she returned, she had found out that the local airport was open, and had booked all four of us on a flight to London.

How anyone can be that organised in a crisis beats me, but Judy took the whole thing in her stride. Rightly so, because everything turned out fine. Bobby and George arrived on the next train and were shown into the Lost-and-Found section of the left-luggage office, where they were reunited with their lost-and-found wives.

'Oh, hello, Poopie,' Judy said to George in a bright, matter-of-fact voice.

As for me, I took one look at Bobby and burst into tears.

~

There was something Bobby and I knew before the holiday that we hadn't told George or Judy, or anyone else, come to that. I was three months pregnant.

I'd realised what was happening from very early on, but when my doctor (a private GP in Harley Street, who Cathy had recommended) confirmed the news, it was still hard to take in. Bobby and I had taken ourselves back to the flat in Portland Place and sat down in a state of shock. I don't think either of us felt grown up enough to be parents. We were still kids ourselves.

When I finally got up, I couldn't resist doing what every mother-to-be does. I kept sneaking back into the bedroom to stand in front of a full-length mirror and gaze at my tummy from every angle.

The baby was not planned. That was something Bobby and I had always agreed we shouldn't try to do.

'If we wait until everything's right, it never will be,' we had said to each other. 'There'll always be a thousand reasons for putting it off.'

So, that settled, we had decided to let matters take their natural course – and they did. As a result I felt totally unprepared, but I somehow felt I could cope.

What's It All About?

'It's not the responsibility of bringing a baby into the world that's frightening me,' I said to Bobby. 'It's practical things. This flat is totally unsuitable for a baby. We can't go on living here. And if I don't even know what kind of cot to buy, I don't know anything.'

Bobby was far too freaked out to listen to me banging on.

'It's wonderful news, Cil, just wonderful,' he kept repeating in a dazed kind of way. When we sat down to a meal that evening, though, I couldn't help noticing that it was him, not me, who was eating for two!

I was astonished to find that I felt absolutely marvellous. The tiredness I'd felt dissolved as quickly as it had come and each time I looked in the mirror, I looked better! My hair was glossier, my skin was as smooth as a baby's bottom, and the only change I made to my beauty routine was to put oil on my tummy to avoid stretchmarks. There was no sign whatsoever of the dreaded morning sickness, I hardly put on any weight and, as the weeks turned into months and a tiny bump began to reveal itself at the front, nobody behind me would have known I was pregnant!

As soon as they were given the news, the press – mercenary lot! – immediately began telling their readers that the pregnancy would cost me £100,000. This sum represented the fees they reckoned I would lose from cancelled stage and television appearances and a planned tour abroad.

'Who cares?' I kept retorting, cheerfully. 'Having a baby is more important than all the money in the world.'

I really meant that. I could not have been happier. I was young, fit, healthy and radiantly pregnant; and still forging ahead professionally. Immediately after the Lech holiday, there was the *Cilla* series, followed by a tour of Europe including TV shows in Amsterdam, Stockholm, Helsinki, Madrid, Paris and Berlin, and then *The Royal TV Gala* recorded in the presence of the Queen.

It was while we were in Amsterdam that I first felt the baby move, late one night when we were in our hotel room. It totally freaked Bobby out, and he had to rush out into the night to buy some cigarettes from the nearest vending machine.

Bobby may have been jumpy, but I was high on happiness most of the time. There were still moments when I felt irrationally frightened, though; times when I'd hear mothers saying awful things about their kids – and kids being very rude about their mothers.

Luckily I had a husband I could talk to. At such moments, I'd curl up on the sofa beside Bobby.

'It's not so much the thought that the birth might be painful, although that does bother me sometimes,' I confided. 'It's more the fear that I'll make a mess of it all, that something might go wrong and I'll be responsible for letting the baby down.'

'You'll be a great mum,' he kept reassuring me. At least we realised the baby would have parents who loved each other. But the other dread that kept rearing up in quiet moments when I was resting or had nothing to distract me was that the baby would be imperfect in some way. Bobby's sister-in-law Rose, a lovely Irish nurse, assured me that many women felt this way during their pregnancy, and she was a great comfort. Judy Martin, too, was a wonderful help.

'It's easier said than done,' they kept saying to me, 'but just try to keep your mind focused on the millions of babies who are born perfect every year.' It was indeed easier said than done!

My expected delivery date was 14 July and my immediate plan after having the baby was to take six months off work.

In the area I came from in Liverpool, everybody had their babies at home rather than in hospital, but my Harley Street GP was desperate to do the delivery himself.

'Can I?' he said. 'I'd really love to.'

'Of course,' I replied. It never occurred to me that it might be better to have the baby delivered by someone who did this kind of thing the whole time. He was a friend by now as well as my doctor and I thought, 'Better the devil I know …'

I had no idea how much hassle this would cause, but as I became more clued up about maternity matters, I soon found out. Medical opinion now insisted that it was wiser and safer for first babies to be delivered in a maternity hospital. Desperate for everything to go right, I settled for that, but there was still a problem.

'GPs,' my doctor told me, 'are not allowed to deliver babies in maternity hospitals.' So, not wanting to disappoint him, I made further enquiries and then booked myself into the Avenue Clinic, St John's Wood, London, which was perfectly happy to allow him to do the honours!

~

When I was seven months' pregnant, Bobby and I geared ourselves up to go house-hunting. By then, even he was facing facts and saying, 'We can't squeeze a baby plus a nanny into this flat – not to mention Sophie and Ada.'

Our dilemma now was to find a home in the country that was large enough to accommodate us and the baby and a nanny and the by-now vast dogs, but close enough to London for me to avoid hours in traffic jams when I had television, recording or other commitments.

'What we need,' we kept saying, 'are healthy surroundings away from all the noise and pollution of London, but near enough to be practical for work.'

Then my sexy TV presenter friend Muriel Young telephoned to say that her best friend's husband was selling their house in Buckinghamshire, and I thought, 'Great! Let's go for that.'

I'd met this man, Lord Birkett, a couple of times at Mu's dinner parties and liked him a lot, and was sure we'd love his house. It turned out to be a vast pile, set in masses of green acres, and Bobby, nudged on by me, immediately made an offer for it. But all did not go well. Lord B, who proved to be every bit as stubborn as Bobby, would not come down a shilling on the asking price. Five pounds would have done it, but he was not in a giving vein and wouldn't budge, and that, as I knew only too well, was no way to deal with Bobby. I wanted the house, but no one was going to get the better of a Scouser, and the deal was off.

I was so disappointed. It was terrible to be foiled and I was desperate to move in to our new home. But having said that, I'm a great believer in fate and, once I'd got over the initial upset, I said: 'Okay, Bobby – it wasn't meant to be.' We would simply have to find somewhere else.

~

A few days after that non-purchase, Bobby had to go in to hospital to have his wisdom teeth out and I was left alone in the Portland Place flat with two dogs who were each now the size of a fireplace. Heavily pregnant, I needed help to take the dogs for a walk. I'm afraid I must admit that I could only think of one thing to do. I hired a chauffeur to drive them in our Rolls-Royce to Regent's Park! Oh God, how embarrassing. I promise you, I wasn't showing off, I was simply not prepared to be whisked off my feet, Mary Poppins style, at the waddling stage of my pregnancy.

Bobby had the constitution of an ox, so I wasn't overly worried about his operation. But his resilience, which was phenomenal, did have its downside. Doctors and dentists alike found it almost impossible to knock him out. Even when he went for dental check-ups, he could still feel the pain after he was given the injection. And it was no different on this occasion. Having plied him with the usual pre-med and the anaesthetic in the operating theatre, the medics thought he was dead to the world, but he wasn't!

'They thought I was out for the count,' he told me when I visited him after the op, 'but I was eavesdropping on their conversation. D'you know what one of the theatre nurses had the gall to say?'

'Go on,' I said.

' "I don't think he's nearly good-looking enough to be married to our Cilla, do you?" "No – it's a mystery," her friend said.'

I laughed like a hyena when he told me this. When Bobby just sat there with a fluke's gob on, feeling sorry for himself, it just made me laugh even more.

The next day when I went to visit him in the hospital, he was fast asleep, so I sat there reading the *Sunday Times* property pages. Halfway down one column, lo and behold, there was an ad for an eight-bedroomed house in rural Buckinghamshire, which sounded just perfect for us; and I was even more excited when I saw that the write-up stipulated that the asking price was not negotiable!

We went to see the house as soon as Bobby came out of hospital. By then time was running out. It was the last week in June and I was due to have the baby in two weeks' time.

The house stood in seventeen acres of landscaped garden, lawns, woodland and a green meadow sprinkled with wild flowers. It was a 1912 Edwardian mansion, originally built for the Gilbeys – the gin-distilling family – but now owned by the chairman of Bowaters, and it was only a stone's throw from Denham Golf Club and airfield. At one stage in its history, the owner told us, it had also been owned by the conductor Sir Malcolm Sargent, who had spent some years in charge of the Liverpool Philharmonic Orchestra when I was a child.

When we looked over it, we were like a couple of kids, cantering here, cantering there. It had huge windows with lovely views, was wonderfully light, spacious and airy – and, absolutely irresistible, there were *six* echoes in the *six* bathrooms!

'It's exactly what I wanted!' I exclaimed.

We both thought the house and its setting were perfect, and when we went back to see it again the next day, Bobby turned to me, put his arms around my shoulder, and said: 'What do you think, Cil? D'you want this one?'

'Oh, *yes*,' I replied.

So, two days after we first clapped eyes on the house, the deal was done. When I put down roots, I put them deep. I love that house, and I have lived in it now for more than thirty years.

~

Having got over the house-purchase excitement – and the release of my album *Sweet Inspiration* – I settled down to the last week of waiting for my baby. We didn't plan to move until after the birth, as there was a lotta work to be done on the house before we could move in – new kitchen, re-do the bathrooms, rewiring, you name it.

Ends of pregnancy are *never* comfortable times for mothers-to-be and mine was no easier than anybody else's. Just as the end was in sight, a really grotty, humid spell hit London, which made it almost impossible for me to get any sleep in our Portland Place flat. London felt dirty and noisy, I felt huge, and the baby seemed determined to put itself into every awkward position it could. I was restless and frustrated.

One miserable night as I lay tossing and turning at three o'clock in the morning, while Bobby lay blissfully snoring alongside me, I found myself being driven up the wall by loud music coming from the next-door apartment. All I could hear was Michael Jackson singing 'ABC, ABC' and the record, which kept promising to come to an end, was obviously on repeat. Normally I love his music, but that night, about to give birth and feeling horrendously uncomfortable, if I could have got my hands on Michael Jackson, I'd have cheerfully choked him!

Bobby, at the best of times, was very much the perfect 'live-and-let-live' kind of human being, a mellow, tolerant man who always thought twice about spoiling anybody's fun. Everybody, even those who feared his business acumen, respected and adored Bobby. On this occasion, having been rudely nudged awake by me, he was still very sleepy and therefore unresponsive, while I was very agitated and very pregnant.

'You've gotta go next door,' I repeated, nudging him again, 'and tell them to tone it down. It's three o'clock in the morning, for God's sake.'

'Come on, go to sleep, Cil,' he replied gently. I was furious.

'If *you're* not going to do it,' I snarled, sliding out of the bed and stomping across the room, '*I* will.'

From our kitchen, you could step out on to a balcony and make your way along to the next apartment which, at that time, had been let to some young guys from the American Embassy. So off I went, all set to wag my finger at the revellers and make it clear in no uncertain terms that I was 'nine months pregnant', blah-blah, and 'How could they do this to me?'

Things did not go according to plan.

When they saw me outside their window wagging my finger at them, they thought I was trying to get on down! Instead of thinking I was asking them to turn it down, they thought I was finger-dancing and waving my hand about in time to the music. Thrilled to have me on board, they threw open the door and welcomed me into the party.

'If you can't beat 'em, join 'em,' I thought and, before I had time to change my mind, I was whisked into the centre of the room where I had the time of my life jiving the night away. Bobby, who had gone straight back to sleep, didn't see me again until eight o'clock the next morning.

By then, I'd passed my expected delivery date and the clinic had made arrangements for me to be induced on Sunday 26 July. On the day, feeling somewhat tearful because I'd wanted the birth to start naturally, I phoned Pat Davies for a comforting chat.

'All being well,' I said at the end of this conversation, 'the baby will be born by teatime.'

Pat, for some extraordinary reason, always thinks I know what I'm talking about and never ever doubts anything I say. But when she told a male colleague, who was married with children, that I was going to have my baby at teatime, he dismissed this as a loada nonsense, saying, 'Pat, don't be daft. Cilla can't say that she will have the baby by teatime. It just doesn't happen like that!' 'If Cilla says it will be teatime,' Pat replied stubbornly, 'it *will* be teatime.'

A few minutes later a sizeable bet was placed on who would be proved right, and Pat, totally convinced that she was the surefire winner, dashed out to order some flowers to be in my room when I returned from delivery. As it turned out, I was not going to let my best friend down. Pat would win her bet later on when a BBC newsreader announced the birth of my baby at – yes – teatime!

Meanwhile, back at the clinic everything was going well. I'd been induced, I'd gone into labour, and at last I'd been given the blessed pain-killing epidural. I just wanted to bury my head in the pillows and go to sleep, but the nursing staff had other ideas.

'Come on, Mrs Willis,' they kept saying, prodding me awake, 'you have work to do!'

Bobby was in the clinic, but not in the delivery room. This wasn't because he was squeamish. 'I could do it for anyone else,' he kept saying to me and anyone else who was interested. 'But not for Cilla. I'm just too emotionally involved.'

Thankfully, one of my girlfriends, Janet, who was then married to Leslie, my hairdresser, had a great sense of humour and she obviously thought that the best approach to labour and birth was to laugh your way through it. To ensure this was the case, she'd given me a dirty joke book to read while I was waiting for things to happen.

While I was reading this in my beatific post-epidural state, a Turkish lady in the next room, who was already a mother of six, was moaning and groaning, making blood-curdling yelps and screams that I could hear through the wall. When the nursing sister went back to her, this lady, having heard me giggling and laughing, said, 'Can I have some of what that lady's on?'

You'd think labour would be easier after six children, but that didn't seem to be the case for her. I hung on to my dirty joke book, but things did quieten down when she, too, was given an epidural.

My labour did not last long, and I was not allowed to finish my book. Three jokes from the end, I was roused to action. With my doctor and the nurses exhorting me to '*Push*, Mrs Willis – *push*', and with a mounting sense of excitement and urgency, it seemed we were all desperately strain-ing together. And then, quite suddenly, it was over. My baby was born.

I was absolutely elated. There, amid all the white gowns and the excited clamour of the delivery room, I could see my GP smiling and holding aloft the brand new human being that had been created by Bobby and me. Our baby's first piercing cry was the best sound I'd ever heard.

'Well, Mrs Willis,' the nurse said, turning her attention to me, 'you have a fine baby boy.'

'But is he all right?' I gulped – I was laughing and crying all at once.

'Everything, I promise, is present and correct,' she replied. 'He's really bonny – at least eight pounds.'

There's no way I can do justice to how it felt to cradle him in my arms for the first time. He was a miracle, no other word for it, and I couldn't get my head around how he had tucked himself into such a small space. At 8 lb 12 oz he looked more like an eight-month-old than a newborn baby. He was so perfect, so surprisingly strong and yet so heart-touchingly fragile. And his ten fingers and ten toes, and twenty tiny nails were so amazingly translucent. The biggest surprise, though, was his really fine mop of jet-black hair. I'd expected any child of mine to be blond like Bobby, but this baby boy had my dad's hair.

When Bobby came into the room, he was wild eyed and flustered and only had eyes for me! He walked straight past the baby, who was now placed in a cot by the bed, saying: 'Are you all right, Cil?'

I was touched by his concern, but I couldn't wait for him to look at our baby.

'Look – *look*,' I kept saying, pointing at the cot. 'Oh, Bobby, *look*.'

When he did, he was astonished and sat there in complete silence for a few minutes.

'He's got jet-black hair,' he then kept repeating incredulously. 'Masses of jet-black hair.'

We were awestruck. How could this perfect little thing have been created by us?

'He's fantastic,' Bobby kept repeating. 'Just fantastic.'

The hospital staff must have heard what we were now saying hundreds upon hundreds of times, but for us it was a unique, miraculous and mind-blowing experience, and we just couldn't stop cuddling each other and billing and cooing.

As I sat there with my baby, my first child, I realised that I had never been happier in all my life.

17

What Is Life...?

'How about Luke?' I said when I was speaking to my mam on the phone.

Even before the baby had arrived, I'd thought up two names which I thought would be fabulous if we had a son.

'Luke?' There was a short silence. 'Oh, I don't know, Cil. I don't know about Luke.'

'All right. What about Oliver?'

The response was emphatic this time.

'Oh, *no*, Cilla, luv! Don't call him Oliver. That'll be tempting fate.'

'Why?' I replied baffled.

'Because he'll always be asking for more!'

In the event, we didn't call our son Luke or Oliver. We called him Robert John after his two grandfathers.

Have you ever looked at your life as if it's a TV drama unfolding? Have you ever wished you had a fast-forward or fast-rewind button to speed some things along or allow you to linger longer on certain memories? Well, becoming a mother had that effect on me. As I lay in the clinic cradling my first-born in my arms, I was so happy, so totally fulfilled, I could hardly bear the hands of the clock to move. It had taken the birth of our first son for us to appreciate how blessed we really were.

Those days in the clinic, free from the hurly-burly of my work diary, were just perfect for taking stock, and between all the baby feeds and burping moments I lay there relishing the thought that this girl dressing her son in designer baby clothes was the same girl who had once been bathed in a tin bath, warmed by coke that was collected from left-over spillages when the containers were unloaded in the dockyards; and this girl would soon be moving into a house that had *six* loos; and this child, unlike his mum who hadn't even had a tiny garden to play in, would have seventeen acres all of his own.

Yet – and I *so* wanted Robert to appreciate this when he was old enough – I'd never thought of my childhood as poverty-stricken or disadvantaged; and me mam and dad – now his nana and granddad – couldn't have been more wonderful parents. Thanks to them, I'd been rich in all the things that matter most – love, companionship and unstinting support. Whatever happened in his and my future, I wanted him to know that I hadn't forgotten my roots and my values hadn't changed. Stardom, having more happiness than we needed, was great, but I regarded winning Bobby's love and giving birth to a son as my two greatest achievements.

'I promise you won't be an only child,' I whispered. 'I'm broody already and longing to do it all over again!'

~

The day after the birth, flowers and telegrams were pouring into the clinic. Along with bouquets from our family, friends, fans and colleagues, there were messages from Dusty Springfield, Sandie Shaw and Clodagh Rogers, and Ringo and Maureen sent a huge bouquet shaped like a teddy bear. When I left the clinic, Avenue Road was knee-deep in press and fans.

I was lucky. I had no postnatal depression, and on the personal front, things couldn't have been better. A week after Robert was born, I only weighed eight stone four pounds and didn't even need to diet. That, my girlfriends kept telling me, was a huge bonus.

But some of my postnatal euphoria was intermingled with angst and fright. Those age-old questions every new mother asks herself ('How will I shape up to this?' 'Will I be a good mother?') didn't pass me by, and sometimes I felt very close to flipping with the pressure of it all. I wasn't even a normal mother. As well as being Mrs Willis and the mother of Robert, I was Cilla Black. I know many people think that success – and the wealth it brings – is a plus, but for me there were moments when it all seemed too much too soon, and I was momentarily panicked.

First-time motherhood is daunting, a constant learning curve even before you leave the clinic and have sole responsibility for your baby, and at times I wished I didn't live two hundred miles from me mam. Fortunately, I had a wonderful woman by the name of Nurse Bobby to help me. An absolute marvel, she'd been nanny to George and Judy Martin's children and, long before I was pregnant, I'd said to her: 'Even if you're retired by the time I become a mum, promise me you will come and help me.'

'I promise,' she had always said and, to my great relief, she had moved in just before Robert was born.

Even with Nurse Bobby to help, though, I was constantly on the phone to me mam about the slightest thing, and doubly so on Nurse Bobby's days off.

My Bobby, who in the normal course of events was a stickler for order – 'a place for everything and everything in its place' type of guy – proved to be the best support and the best father ever. He never seemed to fret, was always calm, and always seemed to know when and when not to pick the baby up. I was the hysterical one who was forever checking and re-checking while I tried to savvy out which gurgle was potentially a life-threatening choke and which hiccup was a blockage in the throat! But, slowly, I learned to take ten steps back and go into what became known as my 'Bobby mode'.

My other worry was that although I had Nurse Bobby to back me up, I knew she only ever looked after babies up to eight weeks old and I was dreading her leaving us at that point. She was such a comfort. If anything untoward happened and I panicked, which was usually about five times a day, she was always there to reassure me.

I know some people claim that if you have a nanny, your baby is confused about who is who in his or her life, but I never had that problem. Robert always seemed to know instinctively that there was something very special about his relationship with me – and with his dad. There was no doubt, though, that while Nurse Bobby was with us she called some of the shots. For example, when we brought Robert John home to the flat, she insisted that we should move without any further delay to the house at Denham. 'Fresh air's so important for babies,' she said, firmly, 'and we can manage with a makeshift kitchen while the other work's carried out.'

She was absolutely right.

While we were still living in the flat, though, the DJ Kenny Everett, who knew I lived just opposite his studio in Broadcasting House, used to enjoy larking about and sending me messages over the air on his late-night show.

'This one's for Cilla,' he would say as he put a record on the turntable. 'Are you *all right*, luv? She's probably Brillo-ing the baby's bum right now!'

Moments like that, especially when I was feeling tired and giving Robert his two a.m. feed, kept me going.

Before Robert was born, I'd planned to take six months off work, but only six weeks after the birth I was already going mental. I loved my baby – absolutely adored him and knew he was my greatest achievement ever – but I was also desperately missing my career and convinced I was shrivelling up. When I found myself dressing up in my sequined frocks to hoover carpets that didn't need hoovering, I knew it was time to get back to work. This was not an easy decision. Even before I began to reorganise my life I knew I'd be a jumble of conflicting emotions; that when I was away from home I'd be thinking of all the things I might be missing there.

With a first baby, there are so many 'firsts' – unforgettable moments when your offspring manages to situp for the first time without a helping hand or bottom-shuffles across a room, or says his first 'M-m-m's or 'D-d-d's, or takes his first uncertain steps. I loved Robert so much it was sheer agony to miss any of these things, yet I was also driven by something that was calling me back to performing.

For new mums, life's a hotchpotch of maternal feelings and personal yearnings. Likewise the world is no longer the safe place that you once took for granted. It's a commando course, a minefield, where even a lamp socket or two-inch puddle can snatch your baby from you. There are dangers everywhere. Whatever you do, however many precautions you take, you feel you can't really win. When you're there, you dream of being some-where else and when you're somewhere else you dream of being there.

Fortunately Nurse Bobby had met all these contradictory emotions before and, by the time she left us, she'd broken her own rules, had stayed with us for six months, and had even found her own successor – Jenny, the daughter of the couple who ran the bar at the Denham Golf Club. As far as Robert was concerned, Jenny was 'playtime' and I – now a more seasoned mum – was the 'heavy', the one who had to say: 'Come on, my lad, it's time for bed.' Jenny stayed with us for nearly a year but, having got the taste for travel after travelling around with us, she decided to become an air hostess. That was when I found my lovely Penny, who is still with me today as my housekeeper.

~

Me mam couldn't understand why I needed a nanny. In her view, it wasn't normal; after all, she'd managed to run a business and bring us all up with-out one, so why couldn't I? (She conveniently forgot about all those times when my godmother, Auntie Vera, looked after me, and the pre-school nursery I went to.) 'I'll come down and help,' she'd say, but she couldn't understand – I was in London now, I could afford the help, and above all I had a career. Why should I cut the umbilical cord on that?

I also didn't want to bring me mam down from Liverpool and away from me dad. Ever since that day of Bobby's and my blessing, I'd been fretting about him. I knew he was not at all well and both before and after Robert was born I'd done everything I could to persuade him and Mam to come south and live near us. That would have been bliss for me, but in the end I just had to accept that, much as they adored their new grandson, they didn't want to leave Liverpool, where my brothers and their children still lived, and Merseyside would always be home to them. Every time I saw me dad he seemed to have shrunk into himself and I knew he was only struggling on for the rest of us. Despite having serious heart problems, he had not stopped smoking and he was always in and out of hospital. Every time the phone rang I was on tenterhooks thinking it was the news I was dreading.

'Your dad has to go back into hospital today,' my mam said on the phone one Friday morning, 'but don't come up. He'll be fine – they're just going to drain some more fluid off his legs.'

'Are you sure?' I asked anxiously, not sure what to believe.

'Absolutely,' she replied.

She was always saying that, but Dad had had this procedure many times before. I was working, and despite my anxiety, I decided to believe her.

'Okay,' I said, keeping to our original plan, 'I'll come up tomorrow. I'll see you then.'

Later that day, Bobby took a phone call from one of the nursing sisters in the hospital. 'Cilla's mother,' she said, 'is in a really awful state.' This was worryingly different from the usual cheery tone of the hospital staff – on previous visits there I'd been asked for my autograph when I arrived. Immediately I rang my brothers to find out what was wrong.

'It's no different from any of the other times Dad's been in,' George reassured me. 'You don't need to come up today. Come up tomorrow as planned. Mam and Dad'll be fine.'

But just as Bobby and I were about to set off the following morning, Mam phoned with the news I had prayed would somehow never come.

'It's too late,' she said.

I was devastated. I couldn't believe he was gone, and I couldn't forgive myself for not going the day before. I was his little girl and now he would never be there for me, ever again. We didn't make a show of it, but I adored him and I knew he adored me without him telling me every five minutes – there was so much love there, I couldn't bear to think of him being dead. 'Why couldn't they have told me he wouldn't last the night?' I thought. But me dad had had other nights like that, so how could they have known? I was in turmoil, unable to work out what I thought or what I felt.

When I arrived at Mam's, she kept saying, 'I don't want him put in a chapel of rest – I want him here at home.'

'But that's the way it's done now,' we all kept telling her.

'Well, don't you dare do that to me,' she replied. 'I'll be frightened.'

The only way she would come round to the chapel of rest was when Bobby said, 'Look, Mrs White, there's going to be an awful lotta people wanting to come and pay their respects. Cilla's staying with you and you don't want them coming in and asking for autographs or whatever, do you?'

She thought for quite a long time. 'No,' she said at last. 'You're right. He was such a good man – and loads of people will want to see him.' After she'd been to the chapel of rest, she came home and said to me, 'Why don't you go down, Cil? He looks lovely.'

'I *can't*, Mam,' I said. 'Please don't ask me again. I just can't do it.'

I really couldn't, and Bobby understood. 'No,' he said, 'you don't want to do that.'

I loved me dad so much I couldn't bear to see him in a box. I kept having flashbacks to when I was a child of about eight playing out in Bostock Street, and this kid I barely knew came up to me and said, 'D'you wanna come and see my grandmother?'

'Why would I wanna come and see your grandmother?' I'd replied. 'I've got a grandmother of me own. Why would I wanna see yours?'

'Because she's laid out dead in our front room!'

Curiosity had got the better of me and I'd gone with her. It was a very hot day. Barefoot and wearing only my ruched swimsuit, I stood there gazing at the wizened old lady in the coffin. I didn't like it at all. The white shroud frightened me – and, when my dad died, I couldn't shake that memory.

His death was the cruellest of blows for Mam, my brothers and me. My faith was rocked for the first time, and I said over and over to God, '*Go away* – I've fallen out with you.'

Nobody, not man or priest, could console me for his loss. He really was the best of dads and, for me, the world has always been a lonelier place since then without him. Even today, more than thirty years later, I find myself thinking, 'Me dad would have sorted that out.' And then I remember how he would take me as a little girl to the pictures at the Tatler cinema on Church Street (they only showed cartoons), and then to tea at Woolworth's opposite. It is one of the happiest memories I have.

~

There were, I was soon to discover, some very odd ideas about mothers who had nannies. Many people genuinely believed that if you had one, you didn't do anything for your child except possibly give 'em a peck on their soft, downy cheeks when they were all pink and fresh and ready for bed. But, even as I retorted, 'That just isn't true! A nanny is for when you are *not* there, not for when you *are*', I was aware that if I'd never left Scottie Road to live the life I was now leading, I might have thought the same myself.

Nevertheless, I was very hurt when I suddenly found myself being attacked in the papers for accepting a 'Personality Mother of the Year' award. This particular poll named Her Majesty Queen Elizabeth in third place! But that was not the reason for the controversy. Some people simply thought that I should have refused the award because I was only a part-time mum who, in their view, relied on a nanny.

My definition of a mother, however, was not somebody who had to be with her baby every minute of the day, but somebody who loved and cared for her baby when she *was* with him. When I was with Robert I did everything for him, but I didn't think I was the only person who could.

Although I was back at work by then, the highlight of any day was seeing the way Robert's face lit up whenever he saw me or Bobby; and I knew, without checking in a mirror, that the same radiance was lighting up our faces whenever we saw him.

My philosophy was simple: good parenting is loving. If you have that, the rest will follow. I loved Robert, I loved Bobby, I loved my work. As I saw it, I had a duty to my baby and to Bobby – *and* to the people I entertained. But if I'd thought for one moment that Robert or Bobby was suffering because of my career, I'd have given it all up. Meanwhile, a nanny was essential. As long as he had us and wasn't being passed willy-nilly to different people every day, I always trusted that he would take life in his stride.

That certainly proved to be the case. From the moment he could toddle into a room, Robert proved he was capable of charming anyone, however resistant, out of their chairs. But he hadn't a clue about 'yours' and 'mine'. One day when we were walking past a bus stop, he saw a little boy with a bag of crisps; and, before I realised what was happening, he'd walked over, helped himself to the bag and walked on. The other little boy was too stunned to protest. Fortunately his mother thought it was very funny, but I was mortified and gave Robert a good telling off.

Thanks to my career, Robert was also a very sophisticated little boy who I could take anywhere, including restaurants. 'How do you do it?' girlfriends kept asking. 'My kid would have been climbing up the curtains by now.' But Robert was just used to it.

Although we had all those acres of land for him to play and let off steam in, I was very keen for him to meet lots of other children and I liked him to go to the swings at Gerrards Cross to socialise with other kids.

I was only too happy to focus on the qualities I most wanted to encourage in my boy: truthfulness, fairness, generosity of spirit, tolerance and determination. Tolerance is a marvellous quality and so is determination. If you believe you can strike a match on a jelly, you will.

These qualities were also the ones which my own mam and dad had placed a lot of emphasis on when I was a child. We may have lived in a very poor neighbourhood, but you shared what there was. If you had a party, for example, you didn't just invite your closest friends – the whole street had to have a bit of the fun. If you had a toy everybody played with it. Sharing, I knew, would be even more important for Robert than it was for me because he would have so much more to share, and I wanted to give him as many opportunities as possible to be generous with others. So when we gave a tea party, I always bought presents for the other kids and tried to get Robert to hand them out. He got it eventually, but at first it was not easy. He only ever wanted to give away things he was fed up with or had no use for. He was always happy to give a bunch of flowers to my mam, but handing over a toy car was another matter!

~

For me, that first year of the new decade ended in a flurry of work. On 4 December my next single, 'Child Of Mine' (and what could have been more appropriate?), was released, at the end of the month I played Aladdin in a pantomime, and on Christmas Day I hosted the BBC's *Christmas Night with the Stars*.

Unable to spend Christmas in Liverpool because I had two performances of *Aladdin* to do at the Palladium on Boxing Day, Bobby and I settled down to enjoying what we could of the festivities with Robert at Denham.

When I looked out of the window on Christmas Day morning, a pale sun was lighting up the garden and I was astonished to see one single red rose peeping through a blanket of snow. It was a very special moment for me. I was convinced my dad had paid us a call.

'I don't want you to miss this beautiful day,' I said to Robert when it was time for his nap. 'I'm going to tuck you up, snug as a bug in your pram and let you enjoy a sleep in the fresh air.'

Much later, when I was on the phone to my mam, exchanging Christmas greetings and family chit-chat, she said: 'How's Robert?'

'Oh, he's fine, Mam,' I replied cheerfully. 'I put him out in the garden about two hours ago and he hasn't even stirred. He's still fast asleep.'

There was a horrified gasp at the other end of the phone.

'Oh, sweet Jesus, Mary and Joseph!' my mother barked, obviously panic-stricken. 'Bring him in. Go and get him now – *at once!*'

Bewildered, but panicked by her panic, I flung down the phone, fled into the garden and scooped Robert from his pram.

As a new mother, I hadn't realised that breathing in cold air makes babies sleep and that they can die of hypothermia. All I can say is that when Robert, having been jerked so rudely from his sleep, let out a huge wail of protest, I nearly died from relief. 'I thought the fresh air was doing him good!' I kept sobbing to Mam and then to Bobby.

As a mother who was usually so careful that I called out a pediatrician even if Robert had a tiny spot on his cheek, I could hardly believe that my ignorance had placed him in such danger. His indignant wails were the best Christmas present I had that year. But I was still plagued with doubts over whether or not I could be a good mother. I wanted to be the perfect mum, but sometimes it was so hard. In my heart I knew, though, that Robert would not be on his own for long. I couldn't wait to have another child.

18

It's Different Now

Motherhood gave me a new lease of life and new sense of purpose. There I was in the new decade, doing and enjoying all the things I'd done before – putting on glamorous dresses and teetering off in my stilettos to walk the walk before the footlights and cameras, and tread the boards not only in the UK but also in Australia, New Zealand, South Africa, Kuala Lumpur and Singapore – then going home to cradle my baby in my arms and continue my first steps into motherhood.

Far from flagging during the seventies, my career as a singer and TV performer was on the up. My *Cilla* series and other star-studded specials were still winning the battle of the ratings for the Beeb; and between 1972 and 1974 readers of the *Sun* newspaper voted me 'Top TV Personality' continuously. On the music front, I was voted 'Top Female Vocalist' by *NME* and *Musical Echo*, and was presented with a gold disc by EMI to mark my first ten years in the business!

Despite all my feelings of insecurity as the sixties gave way to the seventies, I'd had no need to worry. Far from my showbiz days being numbered, I saw my workload increase quite dramatically. In many ways I couldn't believe my luck.

~

What's It All About?

I loved doing *The Cilla Black Show*. A really lavish £100,000, twice-nightly, eight-week Palladium production, it was directed by my friend Dickie Hurran, the creative genius who staged some of the UK's most spectacular shows during the heyday of variety. Roger Whittaker appeared with me on the show, and I have very fond memories of the absolutely stunning, satin-trimmed white trouser suit that Tommy Nutter made for me for the opening night.

During the lead-up to this extravaganza, little Robert must have thought his mam was crackers! I was forever walking around the room at breakfast time in the incredible sequined gowns I was going to wear on stage. But that was simply because I couldn't feel happy in them on stage until I got used to wearing them at home! I had to test how safe it was to throw myself around without a strap breaking or a seam going. Unlike some of my earliest performances when I stood with my arms absolutely riveted to my side, with no Bassey-type theatrical flourishes, I now liked to be able to free-wheel around the stage and do some twirls while holding a hand mike.

After seeing the preview of the Palladium show, the London journalist James Green wrote, 'She's a kind of northern Bisto Kid who gets a great deal of pleasure out of singing and doesn't give a thought to nerves on the big occasion, lucky girl!' And it was true. My knees no longer knocked, my hands no longer shook and my tummy no longer turned somersaults while I was standing in the wings. Ten years had passed since I first hit the boards and I was still as keen as I'd been in my Merseyside club days to get out there – be *loved* and earn some applause! Some stars might be overcome by stage fright however often they performed, but I just couldn't wait to walk the walk, talk the talk, and throw back my head and sing!

There are some things that can do more than shake your confidence, though. One Saturday morning during the run of *Aladdin*, also at the London Palladium, my press agent Tony Barrow called us at home. Bobby took the call in the kitchen. It seemed the *Daily Express* had given Tony a tip-off. An anonymous caller was threatening to kill me on stage during the show.

Bobby seemed totally unconcerned. 'It's just a hoax,' he said. 'They get threats like this all the time – you don't want to worry.'

It was easy for him to say. I was terrified. My imagination was immediately racing, conjuring up an array of lethal weapons that might be used against me.

'Are we going to cancel the show?'

'No – *no*,' Bobby replied. 'The police are drafting in Special Branch officers to keep an eye on things.'

I'd been in the business long enough to know how seriously managements took 'the show must go on' syndrome, but I didn't see how a few policemen could make it safe for me to go out on stage.

'Come on, Cil,' Bobby replied, putting what was meant to be a re-assuringly strong arm around my shoulders. 'I'm sure it's a hoax. We're not going to let a nutter scare us. You're not that scared, are you?'

'No,' I said quietly. 'I'm *terrified*.'

I couldn't finish my breakfast. My stomach was churning. I hoped Bobby was right about it being a hoax, but I had a very bad feeling he wasn't.

'Please, Bobby,' I said. 'What kind of protection am I going to get? Are you sure we have to do the show?'

But Bobby's mind wasn't really on the problem. He wasn't even going to be there himself for the matinee. Liverpool were playing at Wembley that afternoon, and Bobby had tickets for the match. Far from trying to cancel the performance, when the time came to leave for the Palladium he ignored my mounting panic and hustled me into the car. When we arrived at the theatre, I looked jumpily at the battalion of autograph-hunters waiting by the stage door. Bobby didn't even get out of the car.

'Off you go, Cil,' he said, patting the ticket in his top pocket. 'I'll be back before you've had time to miss me. You'll be all right.'

As I stared at the innocent-looking fans, I wondered which one had the knife, the poisoned needle, the hand grenade, the loaded pistol.

'You'll be *all right*, Cil.'

What's It All About?

Climbing with as much bravery as I could muster out of the car, I tossed my head back and said: 'Well, let's just hope you're right.'

'That's the spirit,' he said, pulling away.

It's always lovely to meet the fans. They come from all walks of life, all age groups, and they're always so warm and so generous with their praise. But that day's batch must have wondered why I kept looking over my shoulder and to my left and right before hurriedly signing their autograph books at arm's length. I couldn't wait to get through the stage door and into the temporary safety of my dressing room.

Nothing untoward happened before the curtain went up but, once I was on stage, I soon realised that my co-stars, Alfred Marks, Terry Scott, Leslie Crowther and Basil Brush, were behaving very oddly indeed. None of them was coming anywhere near me, and Alfred in particular spent the entire performance hanging about by the wings. When he did have to come centre stage, he adopted a curious bent posture that gave the impression he was walking backwards. Basil Brush wasn't much better. Behaving like a puppet on speed, he fast-tracked in and out, and avoided me like the plague whenever he could.

I felt lonely and very exposed out there, and the show seemed to drag on forever. By the time we got to the final scenes, my nerves were at breaking point. All we needed was a kid to burst a balloon or shriek out of turn, and there'd have been no genie or any other character on stage. They'd have all been back in their dressing rooms before anyone could have said abracadabra!

As it happened, the nutter never put in an appearance on that day or any other and, no thanks to Bobby or to my fellow thespians, I lived to write the tale.

~

The early seventies saw us spending a lot of time in sunny climates, trying out new holiday destinations and experimenting with new, continental eating habits. One of the first times we went to the South of France was when Ringo invited Bobby and me to join him and Maureen and some other friends – George Harrison, Pattie Boyd, Roger Shine and his fiancée Christine, and Marc Bolan and his wife June – on holiday in 1971. He'd chartered a yacht for the week of the Cannes Film Festival, and John, who'd taken to film very seriously, had two films showing at the festival, one called *Erection*, the other *Imagine*.

'Yeah, we'd love to come,' I said. 'But d'you mind if we check into a hotel? I get seasick just going over to New Brighton on the *Royal Iris*, never mind floating about in the Mediterranean.'

'Suit yourself,' replied Ringo.

Nurse Bobby told us firmly to go and have a holiday and leave Robert at home with her for the week, so Bobby and I did as we were told. We flew down to Nice, booked into our hotel in Cannes, then got into a taxi with some overnight things in case we decided we did want to stay on board, and went to the new marina to look for Ringo's yacht, the *Marala*. Having driven all along the quay without seeing the boat anywhere, we went to the Port Control office where a chap suggested that we try the old marina at the other end of town. So we drove down there. By then, we were beginning to wonder if perhaps we were having our legs pulled. Having reached the old port, we started asking again and at last we found someone who directed us to a very smart boat where a uniformed feller, with gold tassels on his shoulders, was standing on the quayside.

He saluted us, we gave him our bags, paid the taxi and got on the boat. On the deck there was no one else in sight.

'Where's Mr Starr?' Bobby asked, thinking the others must all be down below.

'He's on the yacht,' the feller said, and pointed out to sea at this great big three-decked liner. So we weren't on the proper boat at all. This was just a launch!

They took us out to the liner. In the dark you could see it twinkling for miles. Apparently it was owned by Princess Marie de Savoy and was the sixth largest private vessel in the world. It had a crew of twenty-two and five launches like the one which had collected us. I reckoned that a ship that size wouldn't be too uncomfortable, so we decided to risk sleeping on board after all!

It was more sumptuous than anything I'd ever seen. There were three dining rooms on board, one decked out in blue and yellow silk, which was arranged tent-fashion, and all the furniture, including the long dining table and chairs, was polished dark brown mahogany. Behind each chair stood a young man, all decked out in white plus white gloves, and it was his job to seat you, and to place and remove your plate. Nothing was passed up or down the table. The trouble was that our lot weren't royalty. We were a load of pop stars from very down-to-earth backgrounds and we were breaking the chef's heart. Ringo and Maureen were vegetarians and ate very little, even if it was vegetables, George was a very fussy, picky eater, and so were Marc Bolan and his wife. Roger Shine and his girlfriend and Bobby and I were the only meat-eating gannets there. Whenever the chef offered us something and we said, 'Yes, we'd love it', his eyes used to light up as if he'd won the pools. Every morning he used to go the market and buy beautiful fresh vegetables, fish and meat, but until we turned up, he'd had no one to cook it for. All Ringo ever seemed to want was chips.

'That's *pommes frites* to you,' he'd say to the chef, 'not chips, because if I'm not careful you'll be bringing me crisps.'

In fact, the chef and the bar staff were under strict orders to provide chips – *pommes frites* – with everything, and not just for Ringo. So, if you were lying on deck and you ordered a drink, it came with a big plate of chips. A lot of weight was put on during that week!

Given the titles, when we went to see John's films, *Erection* and *Imagine*, we were all of a buzz, expecting the obvious, but dream on! *Erection* was about a building site. There were no people in it – and not even a single frame of a builder's bum. It started with a close-up of an architectural plan of the site, then we watched the building grow, brick by brick, to the music of 'Imagine'!

We also went on a trip in the yacht to St Tropez where I bought a lovely denim jacket, very French, with studs on it, and a pair of blue jeans. We spent the day there, then we sailed back to Cannes. The weather on the return trip was dreadful! As we came round the headland, the yacht was heaving up and down and water was pouring over the deck. In the main saloon, where we were all sitting or lying about, the paintings – original masterpieces – were bouncing against the walls while our friends were gradually turning green and disappearing to their cabins, one by one, until only Bobby and I were left. Bobby was lying flat on his back on a sofa reading a book, so he didn't suffer so much from the pitch and roll, and I was fixing the hem on my new jeans, so I didn't notice much at all.

The next day, we compared notes. The others all admitted they'd been sick, then Bobby explained that lying on the sofa had probably saved him.

'But I'm surprised at Cilla,' he added. 'Usually, she doesn't last five minutes on a boat.'

Then we looked at the hems I'd been stitching on my jeans. Up here, down there, they went, like a load of hairpin bends on a mountain. At least they'd saved me from a nasty night.

We had a lot of fun on that trip, and we even got a song written. George was writing one for me called 'Photograph', and everyone on board was chipping in with words and lines for it. I was very pleased.

'This is lovely,' I thought. 'Here we all are working together, and when I get back home I'll have a new song to record.'

'That song's great,' I said to George when it was time for Bobby and me to leave. 'You will put it down on a demo and send it to me, won't you?'

'No,' Ringo said, 'it's too bloody good for you. I'm having it myself.'

And the bugger had a hit with it too!

~

We loved what we saw on that holiday, and couldn't wait to get back. Later that year, when Robert was about fourteen months old, we were staying at the Hotel du Cap, Eden Roc. This time we'd taken Robert with us. From the hotel a long driveway leads down to the restaurant and the pool area, which is built into the rock – that's where the hotel's name comes from. One day Bobby and I were pushing Robert in his pushchair down this driveway when we heard a sudden rustling in the bushes. We took no notice at first, but then, a few yards further on, there was more sinister rustling – and out jumped Ringo, roaring like a lion and waving his arms.

Quite by coincidence, he had taken a villa in the hotel grounds at the same time that we were staying in the main hotel. We had a wonderful time that week.

'It's our last night tonight, let's make it a good 'un,' Ringo said on our last day there. 'Come over an' have a bit dinner with us.'

So Bobby and I went over there, the Dom Perignon came out, and we all ordered our meal. Bobby and I had Dover sole and Maureen ordered some sort of fish as well. There we were in one of the best hotels in the South of France, and Ringo ordered double fried egg and chips.

The food was delivered to the villa from the main hotel, and the waiters rushed round serving us. Our fish was delicious. But Ringo was horrified when he saw his order. They'd brought crisps instead of chips with his double fried eggs. He's really a very gentle person, but he sat there fuming quietly. Bobby thought it was very funny and egged Ringo on, suggesting he ring up the manager. Ringo was taking it all deadly seriously, but by the end of the conversation the rest of us were in fits.

'Hello,' he began, 'this is Mr Starr here. Can I speak to the manager?'

There was a pause. Then: 'All right. Can I speak to the deputy manager?'

There was another pause. 'Right. Now this is Mr Starr here – in the villa. I want you to know that you have ruined my friends' last evening here. You've totally ruined it.'

Pause. 'Well, because I ordered a meal and only half of it turned up.'

Pause. 'Yeah. The *pommes frites* didn't arrive.'

Pause. 'No, no, no! It's no good sending the *pommes frites* now! The half that did turn up has gone cold.'

Pause. 'What half? The double fried eggs, of course!'

We could just imagine what the deputy manager must have said when he put the phone down: '*Sacre bleu*! Double fried eggs! 'Ow can you make an evening any worse after you 'ave ordered a dinner of double fried eggs!'

~

Our home in Denham was really starting to come together. And it was all so full of life. Our huge dogs, Sophie and Ada, had both become mums and we Willises were now sharing our seventeen acres of Buckinghamshire with ten Briards, a couple of horses and an aviary full of Bobby's budgerigars and cockatiels. But Pat Davies, my gorgeous Liverpool pal, who'd always had a heart of gold, was always happy to house-sit while we were away. In fact, she was such a frequent visitor to our home in Denham that I swear I was the first person to coin the phrase: 'There's three in our marriage'! She was such an integral part of our life that when people asked her, 'D'you have any children, Pat?' she'd nod and point to Robert! She did this so naturally and so often, I even began to think this was true myself!

Unlike Pat, some people thought my so-called 'normality' was odd and they just couldn't understand why, when I was doing so well and could so easily afford it, I didn't have any staff in the house at weekends. I was then, however, and am now, queen of the Marigold gloves; and my all-time favourite pair were the ones given to me by the other Pat, Pat Booth. These had the words 'Bitch' printed on their backs and diamonds outlined on their fronts! Daft as it may sound, I've always found washing-up, hoovering, dusting, cooking and looking after people very therapeutic.

Likewise, crazy though I know it is, I've always been one of those people who runs around the house, plumping up cushions and vacuuming carpets that don't need vacuuming, because I'm always expecting royalty or their equivalent to drop in: 'Sorry to disturb you, but our car's just broken down at the end of your drive' is a fantasy that's never left me!

What's It All About?

The first year of the seventies was a very special time – a period when all was well in my career. Every morning I got up to the best view in the world – my two Roberts. The little one wide awake in his cot in his room next to ours, his arms outstretched through the rails, the larger one still fast asleep in our bed. Life, for now, was relatively easy, happy and carefree. But it hadn't always been that way. I'd worked incredibly hard for a decade, I'd seen first Brian and then my poor dad die and then I'd had to cope with the challenges of being a mother for the first time. But it felt like we'd got it worked out, and we were settled at last.

~

The happiness of 1971 seemed all set to continue through the following year. That summer I was in Blackpool, breaking all box-office records in an extended run of an *International Spectacular* at the Opera House. By then Robert was nearly two years old, and we had an awful time when he suddenly developed gastroenteritis. I was doing two shows daily, and then rushing back to our rented house to take over from Penny and nurse him through the night. It was exhausting, but we desperately didn't want him to go into hospital. Thank goodness he got better and after a few days he recovered – we knew he was better when he sat up and ate a sausage!

I thought this episode might have been why I was feeling a little below par, but I was absolutely thrilled when I discovered that in fact I was three months pregnant.

'It's perfect timing,' I kept saying to Bobby. 'Robert will be three when the baby's born and he'll love playing big brother.'

As I was resting between performances of the show one afternoon, I realised I was bleeding. A local doctor checked me over and prescribed some pills to stop it, but they didn't work. The fear that I might be losing our longed-for second baby was bad enough, but I was also wearing an all-white dress on stage and having panic attacks about a red stain seeping through this while I was in full view of the audience.

I was going out of my mind with worry, fear and dread. Bobby was too, although he tried hard to reassure me that everything would be OK. In the end, as the bleeding was increasing rather than decreasing, I returned to London on my next free day, a Sunday, to consult my own doctor in Harley Street. The news was heartbreaking. The baby could not be saved and I had to go into hospital at once for an emergency D&C. Our hopes for a baby sister or brother for Robert were dashed.

Bobby and I didn't share our grief with anybody, not even our family or closest friends. Not even with Pat.

I was back at work the next day, and on the surface I erased the miscarriage from my mind and went through my usual paces, but in truth, I never got over the shock of losing that baby. And, however hard I've tried since then, I've never stopped tracking how he or she would have looked at this or that age, and what kind of person that child would have grown up to be. Like so many women before and after me, I knew that, even if I was blessed with more children in the future, I would still grieve for that lost child for the rest of my days.

19

You're My World

The miscarriage had been a terrible blow. I dragged myself back to work in Blackpool on the Monday, but however hard I worked, and however hard I tried, things never seemed to go right.

During the remainder of my time in Blackpool, rumours began to fly around that I was about to bring out a recording of 'I'll Still Love You', a song written and produced for me by George Harrison, with Ringo on drums. Like most rumours, it was partly true. I had travelled to London one Sunday to record the song at Apple Studios in Savile Row, but I'd been to the dentist in the morning and I was in pain, so I wasn't in a fit condition to sing and the session didn't come off. There was a second attempt later, with Dave Mackay as the producer, which luckily we recently found in the vaults at EMI and released for the first time. However, at the time the song sort of disappeared and never came out.

Probably as a way of trying to be positive and keep my life moving along we'd decided it was time for a new beginning on the musical front. George Martin was an enormous international artist himself, and it was getting more and more difficult for the two of us to find time when we were both free to work together. Bobby and I ended my collaboration with the Parlophone label and negotiated a five-year recording contract for me with another of EMI's labels.

My next album, the last on Parlophone, was called *Day By Day*, and featured the Andrew Lloyd Webber and Tim Rice number 'I Don't Know How To Love Him', taken from their hit musical *Jesus Christ Superstar*. I worked so hard to make this song, which I loved, one of my most inspirational and innovative recordings, but there was a problem. Although I'd finished recording the album the previous summer, its release was delayed until January 1973 because EMI was having industrial problems at its pressing plant. This meant that by the time my album reached the shops, its impact had been lost by other recordings of the songs coming out ahead of mine.

Disappointed though I was, there was at least a crumb of comfort for me when Tim Rice hailed my recording as '*the* definitive version'.

~

'I'm not preggers yet, because it just hasn't worked out that way,' I said chirpily to a journalist who was clamouring for my New Year resolutions and plans for 1973, 'but my most ardent wish this year is to have another baby.'

I could see her thinking, 'That'll cost you a bob or two', but I didn't care. Robert was the most wonderful thing that had ever happened to Bobby and me and, despite all the heartbreak of the miscarriage the previous year, I couldn't wait to do it all again. Every time I looked up and saw Bobby playing with Robert, I was overwhelmed with this desire – and the longing to throw my arms around them and hug them to bits. I simply couldn't believe that it wouldn't be possible for us to have another child.

Then, in December 1973, Bobby and I were able to announce to the world the good news that we'd been keeping secret for three months. We were expecting our second baby. What we didn't say, of course, was that my heart had been in my mouth for the last twelve weeks. When you've lost one baby, you never have quite the same trust in yourself – or in life – that all will be well again. I couldn't wait for the baby to be born in April.

~

Four days into 1974, we kick-started the New Year by releasing my new single, 'Baby We Can't Go Wrong' – a very apt title, I thought, for a singer who was pregnant!

Up until the release of this record, there'd been no plans afoot to replace the signature tune of my *Cilla* shows, but the record turned out to be such a strong number that my record producer David Mackay and TV executive producer Michael Hurll thought it would be an ideal replacement for 'Something Tells Me'.

By then, I'd given up predicting what would or would not be a hit record for me, but 'Baby We Can't Go Wrong' was more soft rock than anything I'd done before and it was certainly my personal favourite from the first four titles I recorded with Dave Mackay. Dave is Australian and was highly recommended by EMI. He took great pleasure in telling me that he'd had a number one in Australia with a cover version of 'You're My World', which I didn't mind at all – in fact, I was delighted. Despite the weekly plugs on my show, though, and a shoal of other TV spots, including *Top of the Pops*, that song was not one of my biggest hits, and it never rose any higher than the mid-thirties in the Top Forty chart.

It was a strange time for me. In the last eighteen months I'd had so many hopes and plans, and been through so many disappointments, some small, but others bitterly upsetting. Filming my new nine-week *Cilla* TV series was a fantastic diversion. I always enjoyed working on these programmes, and true to form we had lots of fun with them. We'd also decided to take a new tack for the latest series, as the producer, Colin Charman, who tragically died later in the year, announced at the press launch. 'We think it's time to get away from the regular run of variety turns,' he said, 'so we've included actors and other unusual entertainers on the show.' He then named Bernard Cribbins and Twiggy as my first guests. The comedy sketch in the first programme featured the indomitable Bernard and me as young Cub leaders in the bridal suite of a seaside hotel! That was a good indication of how that series was going to carry on.

~

Sadly, although I was pregnant, there was none of the usual retail therapy in store for me. This was because, when I was expecting Robert, I'd gone absolutely bonkers buying baby things, so there were now plenty of his hand-me-downs for my second child. Nothing but the best had been good enough for my first-born. I'd even flown to Paris to buy designer-label baby clothes.

I did hope, though, that our second offspring would like my singing a bit more than Robert did! He always made it very clear that he far preferred Marc Bolan and Sparks to any of my songs!

When the baby was due, I wasn't surprised that things were running late. The same thing had happened with Robert and that seemed to be my pattern. Two weeks after the due date, I remember sitting in a consulting room with my gynaecologist, Professor Geoffrey Chamberlain, and being told that if I hadn't delivered by the end of April it would be a good idea to induce me. I wasn't very happy about it, but if that was the case, I asked if it could be on 1 May.

'Oh, but it *can't* be the first of May,' Bobby interjected.

'Why not?' I asked, surprised.

'Because Liverpool's playing,' he said.

'Hang on,' I said, dead narked. 'I can't guarantee it, but I'll try and deliver the baby the week before!'

'That would be great,' Bobby replied. 'If you can do that, there'd be no problem, Cil!'

Our baby – a second son – was a buttocks-first, breech birth, which is never good news. He was, however, very obliging where his father was concerned. Born safely on 30 April 1974, at Queen Charlotte's Maternity Hospital in Hammersmith, London, he weighed in at 7 lb 11 oz. We named him Ben, but Bobby came over all posh when he registered him and gave his name as Benjamin. Needless to say, he has always been Ben.

When Liverpool won the Cup Final on 1 May, Bobby said: 'I *knew* we'd complete the double, Cil – it's been a wonderful week.'

What's It All About?

If Ben had been my first baby, I might never have had another child. He was so different from Robert! My first-born did everything by the book: he slept for four hours at a stretch, woke for feeds on time, and even slept through the night when he was a couple of months old. He was bliss. Trying to nurse Ben, though, was a total nightmare, though; he did none of these things. I'd been told that if he cried, I shouldn't pick him up at once; that if I let him cry awhile he would soon realise he didn't rule the world. But he just cried and cried. I was distraught. I couldn't understand *why* he was crying when he'd just been fed and changed. I bottle-fed him, as I did with Robert, every four hours, but he was always bringing the milk back up again. Then he'd bellow. I was totally demented!

One day, hollow-eyed and yawning nineteen to the dozen, I unburdened myself during an interview with a female journalist from a health magazine.

'Perhaps he's a demand-feed baby,' she said.

I'd never heard of such a thing.

'If he's a demand-feed baby,' she explained, 'he needs to be fed little and often, because by the time you're ready to do the four-hour thing, he's ravenous. He then takes too much food too quickly and brings it up again. Then you're back to square one half an hour later.'

I was astonished. Robert had been so straightforward to feed and nobody had ever mentioned any of this to me before, but lo and behold, when I did what she suggested, Ben was transformed!

However, Ben and Robert were like chalk and cheese. Ben was a very stubborn, challenging child. There was no way you could push him. If you said 'Ugh – *naughty*', he thought that was great; and you couldn't punish him by saying 'Right – off to your room with you', because he didn't mind! He was a fantastic character, a really lovable child, but so very different from his brother. I never had a favourite, but whenever I held Ben in my arms, I just knew that this handful was going to be famous for something one day. What for was another matter – I just hoped it wasn't for being stubborn!

Bobby fortunately had endless patience with Ben, but I had to learn that art. He was a lazy child and refused to walk. He was very plump and even had hard skin on one thigh where he would just shuffle across the floor. At least I was at home when he took his first steps at fourteen months, so I didn't miss that milestone.

~

One day, when Robert was about two, Judy Martin said, 'What schools have you put him down for?'

'What d'you mean?' I asked.

I hadn't given this a thought. In Scottie Road, kids simply went to St Anthony's when they were five.

'Oh, my dear,' Judy replied, 'you've got to put his name down for a school. You can't just send him to a local school. These things matter. What you must do is get in touch with an agency called Gabbitas-Thring and it will send you lists of good pre-prep schools in your area.'

As Judy had been so right about the wonderful Nurse Bobby, I arranged for the lists to be sent to us. There we were living in Denham, in the middle of seventeen acres, with no next-door parents to consult, and with little chance of getting to know local people because I was so often away. I needed all the help I could get. Sometimes I wished I was a mum in Liverpool, surrounded by family, swapping advice, sending the kids to an ordinary school. But I was in a different world now.

It's awful when your children go to school for the first time – they're no longer babies and that day marks the end of a very special time. I disgraced myself when I took Robert to his first day at pre-prep. I sat on one of the tiny chairs, so that I would be at his eye level while I was settling him in. He was fine and so was I until I noticed a little girl crying. My eyes filled up with tears and I started crying as well. Then Robert started crying and so did every other child in the room. The mothers and the helpers were all cursing me.

When it came to Ben's turn to go, we took a family decision not to repeat that episode. So Bobby delivered Ben for his first day – and I cried at home!

~

We'd known Jimmy Tarbuck and his wife Pauline for years. They'd become great friends of ours and, as we both had young children in those days, we went on holiday together whenever we could. I'd known Jimmy since the time when Pat and I used to go to the Blue Angel jazz club in Liverpool, and every time I saw him after that I giggled about the first time we had met him there one Friday night. It was very cold outside and Pat was wearing a pink woolly hat. As she was sneaking into the cloak-room to take it off and fluff up her hair, Jimmy outed her by shouting, 'Oh my God, *what a hat!*' Quick as a flash Pat called back, 'Who knitted your face and dropped a stitch?'

When we were all in Spain together, we were invited to have dinner with some very wealthy Texans who had once had political connections with John F. Kennedy. Also at the table were Bruce Forsyth, Sean Connery and Ronnie Corbett. Jimmy and Ronnie were in great form, cracking very classy jokes, when a beautiful Texan woman joined in and started telling a very risqué joke about a watermelon. It really was in very bad taste and, at the end of it, there was a short silence while all the fellers looked at me to see how I'd taken it and how they should respond. I was in shock, amazed that such a sophisticated woman should have told such a filthy joke, but out of nervousness I roared with laughter and everybody joined in.

I went back home from Spain to a new challenge. I would be doing a situation comedy series, entitled *Cilla's Comedy Six* for ITV. This was a big new departure – I'd never done anything like it before, but I was keen to prove I could act. I was excited at the prospect, but not scared. I'd been told both by my regular writer, Ronnie Taylor, and by Bobby that I could do it, and I believed them. I've always had complete faith in the people I love.

'The only trouble,' I said at the time, 'is that I'm a bit worried about sticking to my lines. I'm a notorious ad-libber who's always making things up on the spur of the moment, but I'm going to try *very* hard – for the sake of the professional actors – to keep to the script.'

~

My Bobby had a memory like a sieve, and unless I was there to remind him about personal things, he always forgot everybody's anniversaries and birthdays, including his own! While we were in Australia in the spring of 1975 for my fourth concert tour, though, he gave me a wonderful surprise. To my astonishment he nudged me awake with a huge bouquet of flowers and a jug of buck's fizz on my breakfast tray. I'm dead certain that the tour manager had told him to, but it was still lovely!

I'm pretty sure that it was on that very morning, when we were having a really lovey-dovey time, that my prayers were answered and I conceived another child. Certainly I was very pregnant during the sweltering summer of that year.

That autumn I was appearing in a stage show at the Coventry Theatre. I was seven months gone and desperately hoping for a baby daughter. On Friday 4 October, a really miserable, cold day, Bobby and I had lunch at the Leofric Hotel where we were staying, then went to see *Blazing Saddles* in the afternoon. During the film I had what felt like terrible indigestion: I thought it was because Bobby had made me rush my food so as not to be late. I went to the theatre and did the evening show, had ham and chips at the hotel afterwards, and went to bed.

~

That night, at about two or three in the morning, I had a showing of blood. Late as it was, Bobby phoned Professor Chamberlain in London. The professor insisted that I get to the nearest hospital immediately and promised to get there himself as soon as he could. There were no ambulances, so we went by taxi. When we arrived, I was having strong contractions, and I was told I was too far into my premature labour to be given an epidural. I refused gas and air because I can't bear having a mask coming down over my face, so I went through the full labour without pain relief. It was horrific.

In the early hours of Saturday morning, my longed-for baby daughter was born. Then a doctor came to my bedside. He looked worried and told me very gently that my baby was in intensive care. Her lungs were not fully formed when she was born, and the situation was critical. Two hours later, as I lay there, stunned by what I had been told, Professor Chamberlain came and broke the news to me that my tiny baby daughter had just given up her struggle for life and died.

I was someone who had always thought, 'I can do this', 'I can strike a match on a jelly.' Now I felt utterly powerless. Here was something I could do nothing about at all. I couldn't replay it and make it all come out different. The day before everything had been OK. I had been feeling marvellous and looking forward to my baby's birth. Now my life was in shreds. The little girl I had carried within me for seven months had died, and I felt as if my life had drained away with her. One moment I'd been full of a new life, the next I was empty. I couldn't even share the loss. I couldn't speak to anyone. I couldn't see the point.

My little daughter had only lived for two hours, but I knew that it was essential to name her. She was real. She had existed. My maternal grandmother's name was Ellen, and I named our baby daughter after her and my Auntie Nellie. In the future the press always got my daughter's name wrong and called her Helen, but they could be forgiven for that. When Bobby went to register the name, he got it wrong, too, and spelled it with an 'H'.

Only somebody who has lost a child can understand how you feel at such times. To go through pregnancy and labour only to find yourself arranging and attending a funeral is horrendous. Even if a baby lives for only a couple of minutes or hours, you can never, ever forget. There is not a day that goes by after such an experience when you do not confront something that reminds you of your grief. Even your existing children are a daily reminder of what you are missing, what you have lost, what will never be. '*Why* has this happened?' I kept asking myself. 'What did I do wrong? Was I too sure of myself? Should I have stopped work?'

I was inconsolable, riddled with guilt, enmeshed in a depression from which I was convinced there was no return. When I got home to Denham, I shut myself in the bedroom and never wanted to come out again. I'd always thought of myself as somebody who could cope, but not this time.

Bobby, of course, was also distraught. As well as coping with my grief and his own, he had to sort out matters at the Coventry Theatre where, ironically, I was appearing in *The Birthday Show*, a title which now had a very cruel ring to it. He had to find somebody to fill in for me, and he phoned Jimmy Tarbuck in Scarborough. Jimmy, lovely man, left the golf course, drove straight to the theatre, and went on stage in his golfing gear, complete with a hole in his sweater.

'What else can Pauline and I do to help?' Jimmy asked Bobby a week later when Val Doonican had taken over the show from him.

'We've somehow got to get Cilla out of the bedroom,' Bobby replied. 'Can you and Pauline ask us out to dinner?'

Bobby knew that Jimmy and Pauline were probably the only couple in the universe for whom I would make a supreme effort. A date was arranged for us to go out to a restaurant in London and I forced myself to get up, get dressed and go along. Jimmy and Pauline were wonderfully kind and supportive over dinner, and I got through it with their help. We even went on to Tramp for a while afterwards.

Although I knew I would never feel the same trust in life again, that evening was a breakthrough of sorts; and, after it, I also knew if I didn't plunge myself back into work I'd never sing again. Val Doonican was only free for a short time and, as usual, the show had to go on. After a fort-night's bed-rest, I resumed work at the Coventry Theatre.

It was Val who had first sung the number 'Liverpool Lullaby' and I had been singing this melody, with its marvellous words, during that autumn season. Back in my dressing room, I ran through the lines of the song for at least twenty minutes in my head while I was putting on my make-up. I managed the mental run-through from 'Oh, you are a mucky kid' right up to the last two lines, 'But there's no one can take your place / Go fast asleep for Mammy', but then I was reduced to a puddle. As I left the dressing room, I asked Bobby to take 'Liverpool Lullaby' off the show's running order. That song has remained one of my most popular hits, especially the line, 'Oh, you are a mucky kid, dirty as a dustbin lid', but there was a time after losing Ellen when I thought I'd never be able to sing it again.

For the first eighteen months after that, I saw Ellen's tiny face in every carrycot and pram, and I had to turn away. I scarcely dared look at a paper in case it included a story of a baby being abandoned on a doorstep or left in a dustbin, because that made me feel so angry, so violent.

My obstetrician told me that doctors, too, were always asking why – why, in one year, should as many as 10,000 babies in England and Wales die before they are seven days old? He told me that many doctors were so distressed they'd set up a charity to raise money for research into why babies were born with defects. The charity was called Birthright.

Like many celebrities, I was frequently asked to make appeals for charities, but this time I was personally involved. I so hoped that one day it would be possible to save other women from having to experience the same loss that I had been through. Still feeling very raw from our baby's death, I took a deep breath and did a television appeal for Birthright. The money that was raised went towards buying a heart monitor. It was great to see it and to know that the money raised by the appeal had been put to such good use.

When your baby dies you feel you are the only person in the world to know such sorrow, so realising that you are one of 10,000 parents who experience this grief each year does help you to cope with powerful feelings of guilt. Since its early days, Birthright has helped bring that annual figure down considerably, and it will always be my special charity. In fact, working with Birthright helped stop me being so self-absorbed, and showed me that I could at least do *something* to save other people from going through what I had experienced. Later on, I was even persuaded by Birthright to talk openly about my tragedy.

Diana Dors also lost a baby in that year and she helped me to deal with my grief. It was the first time I'd met anyone in the same circumstances and it was so good to talk. I think she coped much better than I did. For me it was a very dark period, perhaps the worst of my life. I felt trapped in a constant cycle of reminders of my loss, of guilt, of blaming myself – and it was useless to tell myself there was no reason for guilt or blame.

Bobby knew me inside out, always knew what was right for me, but now even he couldn't get through to me and I just couldn't listen to him. I shut him out, and was very private in my grief. The actual sadness takes forever to fade and in the beginning you are quite selfish about it. When you see babies everywhere, you keep looking at their mothers and saying, 'Why me?'

'Well, why *not* you?' Bobby finally snapped one day. 'What makes you so special? Why *not* you?'

And suddenly the truth of this hit home.

'Yes, why *not* me?' I thought.

Other well-meaning people kept saying 'Every day will be a better day' and gradually I did learn to live with the heartache and go on. But I only managed this because I somehow came to accept that I'd been blessed with two sons, and I should be grateful for the happiness they had brought me. I kept reminding myself of this, but the heartache never truly went away. It is still with me today.

At the end of November, I began the first of five UK concert dates. It was hard work, but it was the best work because it was also therapeutic. It offered some respite from my often overwhelming grief. On stage I can be a different person. From the moment the curtain goes up, I set about winning the audience until I'm sure I have them in the palm of my hand, and I don't leave the stage until they adore me. I have to get out there and make them love me. I don't know why this is, and maybe some people will think it's needy or sad. But this is the kind of work I do, and doing it at this time helped me through some of the darkest days of my life.

20

Easy in Your Company

Cilla's Comedy Six attracted ratings of around eleven million viewers which was a huge comfort professionally even if it couldn't completely light up some of the darkness of these years. The series, written by Ronnie Taylor and produced by Johnny Hamp for ATV, also featured actors like Keith Barron, Leslie Sands and Henry McGee.

The critics, true to the age-old tradition of building celebrities up only to pull them down, were relentless in their criticism. As far as they were concerned, I was a thirty-something who'd reached 'thirty-nothingdom'! After my critical pasting, nobody was more surprised than me when the UK Writers' Guild named me 'Britain's Top Female Comedy Star' for the series. I didn't even know I'd won the award until I read about it in the papers, but there was a bigger surprise for me on the day of the Pye Ladies of Television luncheon at the Grosvenor House Hotel.

Sitting alongside the actresses Polly James and Nerys Hughes, famous for their roles in the spectacularly successful sit-com *The Liver Birds*, who had previously won this title, I thought it was a lunch for everybody who was getting an award that year, and I was totally thrown when I learned that the lunch was just for me! The penny dropped only when I was sitting at a table, reading the menu, and I noticed that my name was included in all the dishes that were being served. (The dessert, for instance, was the 'Cilla Black Black Forest Gateau'.)

One of the organisers told me that Tommy Trinder (the comedian with the extraordinarily skinny legs), who I had never even met, was going to give a half-hour speech saying how wonderful I was. When I realised I would have to give an acceptance speech, I was terrified, shaking in my boots. I hate doing things like that. Fortunately, once I was up on the stage, the old magic worked, and I ad-libbed my way through it.

As well as the award, I was given a cheque for £500, a lot of money in those days. I was so overcome, so embarrassed. I'd never seen a wage cheque, let alone a cheque for that kind of money, and I had no idea what to do with it. To this day, I can't remember if I ever actually cashed it or paid it into a bank account! I may have been a wealthy woman by then, but Bobby always made all the financial arrangements and I never saw the money. A reporter once asked Bobby, 'What's it feel like being married to Cilla Black?' He had a one-word reply: 'Rich!'

~

Having stayed in hotels or friends' places in Portugal, the South of France and Spain for several years, Bobby and I now decided that, with two growing kids to amuse on holidays, we should have a villa of our own.

We were lucky, and found exactly what we were hoping for – a fresh development situated on a hillside that faced the sea on the coast between Marbella and Estepona in Spain. I'd never actually fancied Spain until we saw Jimmy Tarbuck's little villa there. I've always loved the sun, but Bobby hated it and always parked himself on the terrace in the shade when he wasn't playing a round of golf. The piece of land we chose, known at first as 'Plot 2', was large enough to accommodate a small whitewashed *casa*, a decent-sized garden and a kids' swimming pool. There was also a golf course attached to the development, which would cater for Bobby's holiday needs!

Having found the land we wanted, we built the villa from scratch. What began as a three-bedroomed villa, built in typical Andalusian style with a fine view of the Sierra Bermeja mountains on one side and the sparkling Mediterranean on the other, was then extended over the years to accommodate visiting relatives who joined us and the boys from time to time. I don't garden, but there were lovely yellow roses on the terrace. Nearby was the vast Atalaya Park Hotel and resort complex, and a little way along the coast there was Puerto Banus, Marbella's millionaires' marina, with its chic quayside shops and seafood restaurants. Although we kept a shortlist of our favourite places to eat out, I always stocked up the villa's fridge from the supermarket when we arrived. The British are the only people who frown upon babies and children in restaurants; the Spaniards are smashing and doted on children of all ages. Even so, I still took five pounds of bacon with me from Denham, and sometimes minced beef and frozen hamburgers, too. I'm sure they thought I was crackers at Heathrow Airport. To this day, I still pay regular visits to our villa, but it's against the rules to export bacon now!

~

To coincide with the launch of my eighth *Cilla* series in 1976, I made a new EMI single. For this I turned to one of my favourite golden oldies – the first time I'd ever done this in my twelve-year recording career – and I recorded 'Little Things Mean A Lot', Kitty Kallen's number one hit way back in 1954.

The first show of this eighth series took a hammering from the TV critics. I wasn't too surprised, as I'd never been the critics' darling, but this time they all attacked at once! It didn't matter, though. It turned out to be the most successful series in the entire eight years and the ratings were excellent.

After the reviews came out, I had a sweet telegram from Paul and Linda, who I hadn't seen for ages. I loved Paul and I loved Linda. She was the kinda New York girl who wore T-shirts, loafers and socks with blue gaberdine skirts, usually with one sock up and the other down. Here was a girl who could have anything, who could have pampered herself to death, yet she probably hadn't even had a manicure since she met Paul and she far preferred domestic simplicity to glamour. How often in this world, let alone the crazy world of rock 'n' roll, does anyone find their soul mate? But she and Paul had found each other.

Their telegram was simple and to the point: 'Don't listen to the critics, girl. We think it's a smashing show.' It did the trick, and reassured me that I wasn't losing my touch.

Chatting up strangers still came naturally to me, and strangers always felt they could be very up-front and friendly with me. One evening in a very crowded nightclub, a girl came up to Bobby and me and said, 'I think it's wonderful that you two are still together.'

I agreed! Bobby might not have been a lovey-dovey, romantic feller, but I always thought I was very lucky to have him in my life, and I would not have changed him for the world.

~

Given the hostile press reviews for the 1975 series of *Cilla's Comedy Six*, I was very relieved that it had notched up such healthy viewing figures. In fact it was so successful that the series was constantly listed among the top three shows of the week. ITV now commissioned six more episodes, re-titled *Cilla's World of Comedy*, for 1976, so I found myself in the enviable professional position of having two TV series on at the same time, one on BBC and the other on ITV.

That year turned out to be my busiest since my pop-star heyday in the mid-sixties. My two top-rated TV shows achieved an audience of more than thirteen million and proved that I was truly a fluent television performer. It seemed very apt that the theme song for *Cilla's World of Comedy* was titled 'Easy in Your Company'!

In 1977 Bobby and I decided to make a radical change, switching me over from the Beeb to ITV.

'Cilla Black,' said the official announcement, 'has been wooed over from the opposition for an undisclosed sum and is to make a one-hour spectacular for Thames Television next spring.'

Behind this courtship – and the irresistible deal which followed – was a guy called Philip Jones, ITV's Light Entertainment Controller. This was not the first time I had come across him. I'd made one of my earliest 1963 TV appearances, singing 'Love Of The Loved' on *Thank Your Lucky Stars* when he was an up-and-coming producer on that show and now, fourteen years later, long after we sixties high-flyers were supposed to have faded away, there we were together again!

~

I might have been doing it right on TV, but I didn't feel I was doing much right on the home front. After a visit from his Nana and Auntie Nellie, Robert said to me, 'Why aren't you as much fun as Nana and Auntie Nellie? I mean, we locked Nana in the airing cupboard last night and she didn't go mental or berserk.'

That really hurt, but then I thought, 'That's fine, but Nana and Auntie Nellie don't have you and Ben twenty-four hours a day, three hundred and sixty-five days a year!' At moments like that I really felt the stress of being a working mum. You can't be there all the time, and if you're not careful – or lucky – you can miss out on a lot of the fun. It's the same strain that every working mum is under, but I did feel that there was an added pressure from being in the public eye.

Nor was it always easy for the boys to understand my TV work. A year or so before, I'd been sitting on the sofa with Robert at Denham while one of my *Cilla* programmes was on. Robert was none too pleased – Basil Brush was on the other side and he was longing to switch over. I never wear make-up or false eyelashes when I'm at home, and I'm usually dressed in a shirt and jeans. Suddenly, Robert turned from the TV to me and said, 'Why don't you bring that pretty mummy home with you?'

~

When I was a kid the whole of Scottie Road went to a Christmas panto every year on Boxing Day, but we could never afford to go to the Empire; we were always taken to sit up in the gods at the old 'Shaky', the Shakespeare Theatre nearby. In the eyes of Merseysiders, particularly our struggling local performers, the prestigious Empire ranked as a sort of London Palladium of the North; and this was where I had queued up twenty-two years earlier, to see my favourite American singing group, Frankie Lymon and The Teenagers.

It had always been my ambition to work at the Empire, and in December 1978 I was appearing there in *Dick Whittington*. It was during that show that my life nearly came to a horribly messy end. One foul night when the roads were covered with black ice, Bobby and I were driving back to Denham for the weekend when the engine of our Rolls-Royce started making a loud knocking sound. Just at that moment, we saw lights flashing around a traffic incident up ahead.

'That's lucky,' Bobby said, 'there's an AA van coming our way.'

As I glanced ahead through the sleet and the glare of the lights, I realised to my horror that the AA van was actually in our lane and hurtling straight at us.

'My God!' I screamed. 'It's in a skid. Bobby, he can't stop! He's gonna hit us head on!'

Instinctively, I flung open the door and turned to throw myself out of the moving car.

'What are you doing?' Bobby yelled, leaning over to drag me back in and forcing my head down on to his lap.

As he did so, there was a sickening bang and we went into a giddy spin, bouncing on and off the verge. Slowly the car came to a stop and, very shaken, we managed to climb out on Bobby's side. It was bitterly cold and eerily quiet. Holding on to each other, we made our way slowly round to the other side of the car. The open door on my side was unrecognisable – it was just a mess of twisted metal. As we stared at it, I realised I was trembling uncontrollably.

'Oh, God!' Bobby said, holding me tight. 'If you'd jumped –'

There was no need for him to say any more. If he hadn't grabbed me, I wouldn't have stood a chance. As it was, I was very lucky to have escaped with only whiplash and bruised legs. We neither of us spoke, and Bobby held on to me like he would never let go of me again.

Despite my injuries, I was back on stage on Monday. We never told anybody at the theatre about our ordeal.

~

There was something about that run at the Empire. It was as if they were trying to have done with me! Some time after our crash, the police called Bobby to tell him there might be a bomb in the theatre.

'What would you like us to do?' Bobby asked.

'Well, strictly speaking, you should stop the show,' the police officer replied.

'Right,' Bobby said. But he wasn't keen, and went on to ask, 'Surely they wouldn't want to blow up a theatre?'

He wasn't being naive; he genuinely thought that no one in the IRA would want to alienate the public by bombing a 3,000-seat theatre. On the other hand, he wanted to do the right thing by the audience, especially as that night it included our sons, Robert and Ben, and Penny, their nanny.

When the anti-terrorist squad arrived with their sniffer dogs, they only had time to do a search of the foyer, the toilets and some areas backstage before the audience started to arrive in the auditorium. But they needn't have worried – Bobby was in charge and he had a really innovative idea to resolve the situation!

'All you've got to do, Cil,' he informed me, 'is go on stage, face the audience and say, "There's a special prize hidden somewhere in the theatre. Would everyone please look under their seats. But if there's anything there, *don't* touch it. Just put your hand up and call out like you do at bingo and an usherette will come and sort everything out." '

'But,' he added, reading my incredulous expression, 'before you go on and tell them, Cil, I promise I'll get Robert and Ben out.'

Not entirely convinced by this plan, I went on and, gazing out at row after row of bright eyes and shiny, upturned faces, asked everyone to look under their seat for the special parcel. No one called out or put their hand up. So I decided to come clean and told them what it was all about.

'We had to ask you to do that,' I explained, 'because we've had a bomb scare. And if any of you wanna leave, we understand. But if you wanna stay, you're very welcome – 'cos *we're* staying.'

'We're with you, Cilla!' one guy called out amid a big cheer from the rest of the audience. I didn't see anyone leave.

21

Imagine

After losing our baby daughter Ellen in 1975, Bobby and I had decided to take my gynaecologist Professor Chamberlain's advice and wait a couple of years before trying again. But when we did start trying, we had no success. Before Ellen I'd desperately wanted a girl, but afterwards I thought I'd like another boy. By then I'd become accustomed to having men around the house.

I worked hard at getting myself healthy, but nothing happened. Only those in our closest family circle knew just how desperate I was feeling, and as the new decade began, I was at my wits' end to know what we could do. But at last, in 1980, after all the waiting and the hoping, my prayers had been answered. I was pregnant again.

My initial joy, however, quickly gave way to angst. There was no warning last time that anything was wrong, and it had been so terrible to go through a pregnancy with all the expectation and excitement and not have a baby to cuddle at the end of it. I was terrified of the same thing happening again. I wanted to make sure this baby would be OK, but it was hard to know what to do.

In February, I was on my seventh (seventh!) concert tour of Australia, with bookings after that for concert tours in Kuala Lumpur and Bangkok in March. I felt good. Everything seemed perfect, but the first three months of pregnancy are a very vulnerable time, and every time I got on an aeroplane I had a showing of blood. Scared I was going to lose the baby, I telephoned Geoffrey Chamberlain.

'Rest as much as possible, but ultimately the outcome is up to nature,' he told me. 'Hard though this may sound, nature often knows what's best. If your body makes the decision to abort that's beyond your control – and mine. Provided you're not planning to go horse-riding or bungee-jumping down under, all you can do is be careful.'

Despite his reassurance, I still decided to go everywhere on that Australian trip by car rather than plane.

Like most people I work with, I enjoy the odd glass of champagne, but from the moment I knew I was expecting I couldn't bear to be in a room where people were drinking. This was all right by me – it was my reaction to the smell of wine that first let me know I was pregnant – but it was a bit of a challenge for Bobby when he, too, decided to go on the wagon. If I wasn't able to drink, he reckoned he might as well give it a rest too.

At one knees-up after a show, Dennis Smith, the tour promoter, noticed Bobby standing there with a glass of fizzy water in his hand.

'First Cilla, now you,' he exclaimed, shaking his head as if the whole world had suddenly gone mad. 'What's going on?'

'I'm on a diet,' Bobby replied.

Promoters always panic if anyone mentions pregnancy – they like their headliners reliably energetic – so it was probably just as well that Dennis didn't notice I'd also developed a craving for raw carrots. I had my little orange friends delivered under cover by the crate load, and I was eating them morning, noon and night. I even dreamed about them when my head touched the pillow.

'One thing's for sure,' I thought. 'If I can only get through this pregnancy, the baby will have perfect eyesight.'

The spots of blood were still there when we flew on to Kuala Lumpur, but I kept my worries bottled up and performed to sell-out shows. I can do the PR thing until the cows come home. That's my nature. I never want to upset anybody. But whatever I looked like on the outside, I was very frightened, and the fear stayed with me until we arrived back in England.

Although I took a break from my usual summer-season show, cancelled my autumn season at Nottingham's Theatre Royal and put off doing a pilot for an intriguing sounding 'brand-new television concept', I agreed to as many one-off seaside concerts as I felt I could manage. The first of these was at the Winter Gardens, Margate, at the end of June. Now that I didn't have to get on and off aeroplanes any more, I was feeling fabulous again, and it was just a matter of asking a seamstress to let out my frocks another inch or so as the weeks went by.

Because I was thirty-seven, Professor Chamberlain thought I should have an amniocentesis test to show whether or not the pregnancy might result in a special-needs baby. I'm not keen on tests anyway, and one that could potentially result in me having to decide whether or not to go ahead with the pregnancy was particularly unwelcome, but although I kept asking myself '*Why* am I doing this?' I went ahead and did as he said.

I had the test on a Friday and after it I went to do a recording at EMI. On the Sunday, Frankie Howerd came over to Denham for dinner. He and Bobby were in the kitchen, and as I walked in I couldn't believe what I was hearing. 'Well, Cilla is thirty-seven,' Bobby was saying, 'and if the test shows that the baby is damaged in any way, Geoffrey has said that he will go along with our wishes and take care of it.'

They hadn't noticed me coming into the room. Stopped in my tracks by the words 'take care of it', I banged the table and said, 'Hang on, Bobby. This is *my* body. Do I have any say in this?'

'Of course,' Bobby said, startled, realising he had really acted out of line. "We just want what's best for you, Cil.'

'Absolutely, love,' Frankie agreed.

'*Best?*' I repeated, still in shock. 'I'm desperate to have this baby. I don't know what I will do if anything's wrong. I can't make a decision just like that.'

'You do have to think about it very carefully,' Bobby said.

Bobby was the kind of feller who thought everything through; he wasn't just saying this because he was thinking about himself and the boys. He was thinking of me. Always meticulous, in his head he had laid out the future for us if the baby I was now carrying was imperfect in any way. He had done his homework and he knew that some of the possibilities could be very scary. He and Frankie were obviously in total agreement about what to do if the worst should happen.

For the first time in my life, though, I felt that people were making decisions for me that they had absolutely no right to make.

'Look, Bobby,' I said, flushed with anger, 'we don't know yet whether the baby is going to be well or not, and if all is not well, I don't know how I will feel – or what decision I will make. I only know that the decision should be up to me.'

'I know, Cil, but ...'

'I'm carrying this baby,' I went on, incensed. 'It may be yours, as well as mine, Bobby, but Frankie has nothing to do with it.'

Frankie looked at the floor.

Bobby was quiet for a moment while we all got our composure. At last he spoke up. 'You're right, Cil,' he said. 'It's *our* baby, but it's *your* body and you are the one who has the right to choose.'

Bobby and I had a hug, but what can I say? I was scared witless. My career was important, but Bobby and family always came first. In my heart I knew that if our baby needed special care, I would give up everything to care for him or her.

'Let's have a cuppa tea,' Frankie suggested, and as I nodded I said, 'I'm not really angry or upset with you, Frankie. I'd have to go around the world twice before I found a better friend than you. It's just that I'm so scared.'

Thankfully, the test showed nothing wrong. The baby continued to grow happily inside me as we set off for Margate where the end of the storm-damaged pier was marooned out at sea and men were sunbathing on the beach in vests and braces. Having smelled the tang of fish 'n' chips as the car wound its way along the coast to the Winter Gardens, I gave one of the stagehands a fiver to pop out for bag of cod and chips. As I ate them, I remember knowing that I was getting fatter and fatter.

~

Seeing as they'd stuck by me for so long, it seemed that it was about time we gave 'Cilla's Circle of Fans' – organised by Joan Organ, Sarah and Sue Evans, Donald Holgate and Alan Hardy – official recognition. The club had evolved from a London-based group and, after seventeen years, had branches in the UK, the USA, Australia and Germany. It was marvellous to know that so many people cared. A truly great gang, I don't know where I would be without them. With their help, we sold more than 60,000 copies of my new album, *Especially For You*, in two months and I was presented with a silver disc that found its place on the shelves among my other treasures.

Behind the scenes there were discussions for a new TV series, but most of the suggestions put forward were for variations on the *Cilla* format, which I'd done for nine years at the BBC, and none of them seemed quite right.

'Marriage isn't *The Dick Van Dyke Show*,' Bobby was fond of saying to me and anyone else who'd listen; 'you have to work at it twenty-four hours a day – and a career is just like a marriage. If you want to stay on top – or just in the race – it's essential to keep reinventing yourself and trying out new things.'

I'd been a mini-skirted dolly bird in the sixties. I was now a mum, a pregnant mum, a 'woman of a certain age', but I could still feel my wings flexing and I got a tingle of excitement each time I thought there might be a new TV show for me soon.

Negotiations take *forever*, though, and as the leaves on the trees started turning yellow and gold that autumn, I had more important things on my mind. It was time to pack my hospital bag once again, this time ready to go back to the maternity ward at Queen Charlotte's Hospital in Chiswick.

I'd felt the little creature within kicking away and I'd tried so hard not to think back to the last time when I'd been through this experience. To carry a baby, to give birth to it, and then to lose it, is just so awful. You try to take comfort in those around you, but nothing really dulls the pain. In those final days of my pregnancy, all I could do was let the world drift along without me. At last the day came to go to hospital.

Of course I had Bobby, but although he could sit happily in front of a TV watching a woman having a baby, he could never stay in the delivery room when I was giving birth. 'I'm too close to you for that,' he said, firmly. He couldn't bear to watch me suffer. But he was in for a shock this time!

One second I was lying there on the hospital bed, the next, the baby was primed like an Exocet missile and on its way out. Just as the nurse popped in to see how my dilation was going, Bobby glanced up from his newspaper, realised he was sitting at the wrong end of the bed, and – typical man – panicked and ran from the room. I was rushed to the delivery room, and in no time at all, it seemed, I was back in my own private room with baby Jack nestled in my arms. We'd decided on that name a long time ago because it couldn't be shortened. It hadn't occurred to us that Robert and Ben would lengthen it to Jacko, which I thought was horrible.

When the nurse eventually found Bobby, he was as white as a sheet and looked as if it was him who'd just given birth. The colour soon came back into his cheeks, however, when he saw me lying there with a contented baby in my arms.

'The Willis family is complete,' I said, proudly. 'We have our three boys.'

'Hang on a minute,' Bobby said, shocked. 'His hair's bright red!'

'It must have been all those carrots,' I giggled.

It was a bit of a shock, though! I couldn't think of anyone with red hair in my family, except me and Auntie Vera, both with a little help from

Woolworth's, and Bobby couldn't have been more blond. Jack must have siphoned off some of the Irish genes from my forgotten past.

I called my mam in Liverpool straight away.

'Hey, Mam, what do you think? Jack's a redhead!'

'It's all that dye you use, it must have got in your bloodstream,' she said. Then she went on, 'Hang on, your great uncle Jack had red hair.' After a pause, she added, 'Mind you, he only had one leg as well, but not to worry.' She hadn't changed much, me mam!

She was thrilled for me, though. It seemed as if after all the heartache and pain of the last few years, everything was at last all right.

When ten-year-old Robert and six-year-old Ben came into Queen Charlotte's to meet their new brother, I thought, 'I always wanted six kids, but I'll settle for four.' When people say to me, 'You had three children,' I don't correct them and say, 'No, four.' I don't want to embarrass anyone; and I don't really want to explain over and over about Ellen. But, for me, four it would always be.

~

Jack was born on 20 October 1980, and in less than a month I was back at work. I knew this was an important time for me. I'd had a successful innings as a recording artist, but it was television that had made me a household name, and I knew intuitively that if I was going to stay in the public eye, that was where my future lay.

I've been lucky in always getting my figure back again very quickly after giving birth, with no need to diet, which was just as well as I needed to look my best at the Thames Television pre-recording in November of the *London Night Out* show, to be broadcast on Christmas Eve. Thanks to my having been addicted to carrots rather than Mars bars or Wagon Wheels, I had no problem in shedding a few pounds in three weeks; and, even if I do say so myself, I stunned everyone as I stood in front of the cameras in my slinky, shimmering, black-sequined gown. Even the critics were kind, and one said I looked 'drop dead gorgeous'.

~

Imagine

My mam's birthday was on 8 December, but I couldn't celebrate it with her that year because I was in the Arab Emirates. We were staying in a posh hotel – they're all like palaces out there – and Bobby and I were stretched out on sun loungers by the pool getting a tan.

Just to the left of us were some members of an airline crew, gossiping and laughing among themselves. As I glanced up from my magazine, another air hostess joined them, still in her uniform. She was out of breath.

'Oh God. Have you heard? I can't believe it! I've just heard on the radio,' she said to her friends. 'John Lennon's been shot.'

They couldn't believe it. I couldn't believe it. Bobby and I reached for each other, suddenly shivering in the heat.

'It *has* to be a sick joke,' I said to him. 'Who'd want to shoot John?'

But then I'd thought it was a sick joke when the Portuguese waiter told me Brian had died – and what he said had eventually proved to be true. As I picked up my glass, my hand was shaking. I was still trying to comfort myself with the thought that the air hostess was just a rotten girl who'd deliberately said something awful within my earshot.

Bobby could see I was getting in a state. The colour had drained from my cheeks and I must have been as white as the beach towels.

'Some people are just so sick,' I said through my teeth, glaring angrily at the air hostess.

'Come on,' Bobby said. 'Let's go.'

Having gathered up our lotions and bags, we rushed back to the suite. The moment I switched on the radio, my stomach lurched and my heart sank. John was belting out 'Please Mr Postman'. I never thought I'd say it, but a Beatles song was the last thing I wanted to hear. I didn't have to wait for the newsflash. I suddenly knew it was true. I knew John was dead. I collapsed into a chair weeping.

John was dead. It was like saying the Martians had landed, something daft and impossible, totally unreal. John belonged to the world. He had just turned forty. How could he be dead?

'It's true, Bobby,' I gulped. 'They wouldn't be playing "Mr Postman", would they, if it wasn't?'

I was grateful for Bobby's arms around me, and as he sat there and held me I thought about John. It was a long time since I'd last seen him, but that didn't mean a thing. His voice on the radio had reminded me of the old days in Liverpool when we were all so young and struggling so hard to make it. John was a great rock 'n' roller, a poet, an extraordinary song-writer. I looked up at Bobby. I felt stunned and sick. And I couldn't understand what had happened, and why.

I couldn't stop crying. I cried for John, cried for Cynthia, cried for Yoko, cried for John's sons Julian and Sean. And I cried for me. It was as if a bright, shining light had been turned off. It was the end of an era. Part of my past had been taken away. There would have been no Mersey Beat without The Beatles – and no Beatles or Cilla Black without John. He was an international star, a spokesman for peace, and in many ways he was our conscience. But he was also just a man who'd once been a lovely boy who I'd hung out with in the old clubs and homely front rooms of Liverpool.

The song came to an end. I turned off the radio so I could try and get a grip on myself. I was on stage later and this was one of those rare moments when I felt I couldn't face it.

Bobby had read my thoughts.

'You don't have to go on tonight,' he said.

'We'll see,' I replied, sniffing back my tears.

I changed out of my swimming cozzie. In the mirror I looked dreadfully pale and drawn. I still couldn't believe it. John would never be there again. I kept getting flashbacks to when he was young and awkward. He liked women, but was always a bit uncomfortable, a bit nervous in their company – always a man's man. Paul was beautiful – still is – and I know John thought, 'God, with him around, I don't stand a chance.' It's one of those things young lads have to put up with. They're all dead worried about whether or not they're going to get the girls, and John, as a teenager, saw

Paul as his rival. That made him moody, but it was his moodiness that gave the songs they wrote together an edge. When he was four, John had been abandoned by his dad, deserted by his mum and brought up by his Auntie Mimi. He'd always felt rejected, but that gave his writing depth, a darkness. Paul was the counterbalance, the light. You could see this in Paul's eyes and the girls just tumbled in and were washed away. What John never really appreciated was that he, too, had charisma, and that women did think he was sexy.

It was an innocent time and had been over for years. But now it felt *really* over. The era of peace and love, it seemed, was at an end.

The sheer horror of what had happened to John reached us slowly throughout that long day in the Arab Emirates. The telephone just never stopped ringing. The papers all got hold of me, wanting me to do obituary notices – the *Liverpool Echo* was the first, and they seemed as distraught as me. Doing those notices was one of the worst things I've ever had to do.

John being shot was an act of pure evil, and that made his death all the harder to endure. His killer, Mark Chapman, didn't even run away. He just stood there reading *Catcher in the Rye* until he was arrested. The only thing he said was that he had done it because John had once said The Beatles were bigger than Jesus. But I knew – and everyone who knew John knew – that he didn't mean that The Beatles were really bigger than Jesus, simply that the fans treated them as if they were. 'We're bigger than Jesus' is what you *would* say in Liverpool to show that you thought Beatlemania was ridiculous.

With so many friends and reporters ringing from all over the world, we had to take the telephone off the hook. All the papers wanted me to make a comment, but what could I say? I'd lost a friend and life would never be the same without him.

Around teatime, some food was wheeled into our room on a trolley, but my stomach was so knotted up I couldn't eat a thing. I kept humming songs from John's new album, then my eyes would well up and I didn't know what to do with myself.

The sun was going down, silvering the sea outside the window. I kept hearing John's voice in my head – and the words from 'Imagine'.

'You don't have to go on tonight, Cil,' Bobby said again. 'People will understand.'

'Bobby,' I said. 'D'you remember what you said to me the last time you were feeling really sick?'

Bobby shrugged his broad shoulders. 'Just got to go on and do it?'

'And what would John say?'

'You don't have to ask, Cilla.'

We'd been trained the Epstein way. If you're lucky enough to have an audience, if you live a good life thanks to that audience, then you have a commitment – a job to do. I was in a state of shock, but shock is a kind of anaesthetic that can help carry you along. You may be hurting like hell, but you *can* march out with the mike and give a performance everything you've got. You might crawl off stage on all fours afterwards, but during the show you carry on.

I had a shower, did my make-up, slipped into a black sequined dress and matching stilettos, and stood there waiting for the show to start. I was no longer thinking, 'My mate John's been shot dead', I was changing my running order so I could finish the show that night singing 'Imagine'. God knows how I did it. There were tears cascading down my cheeks. Many in the audience were weeping along with me. I was a total wreck after the show. But it was my homage to John and somehow I got through it.

~

John was cremated just twenty-four hours after he'd been killed, and I felt cheated because I missed that opportunity to mourn him. It's a time when you want to be with your friends, when you want things to be how they always were. Yoko was very dignified through those dark days, and after we got back to the UK she did something that I thought was really nice. She chose a certain time and said that if everyone would go out at that particular time and look up at the sky, we would feel John and we'd all be one with his spirit.

Imagine

Bobby and I were two of the thousands – probably millions – of people who did that. We went out into our garden at Denham and looked up at the sky, at the shifting clouds, and I just felt so sad. A shiver ran through me. But then, as I stood gazing into the void, the clouds parted. There was a glimmer of light and, for a moment, I did sense John's presence and it made me feel warm inside. He was up there somewhere. He was safe. It was we who were the broken-hearted.

22

Now or Never?

After John was murdered, people kept asking me if his death had made me feel insecure, but it hadn't. At the time I thought of it as an American thing – and I still do. People close to me, though, who had always worried when I insisted on walking about London or taking taxis like everyone else, worried all the more.

'I want to be like everyone else,' I kept reminding them. 'I don't want to live my life in any other way.'

Back home in the UK, I had loads of things lined up for 1981 – cabaret, concert tours at home and abroad, a summer-season show in Blackpool, and recordings – but the funny thing is, the more you do, the more you *can* do. That old saying, 'If you want something done, give it to a busy person', is absolutely true!

It was always a real treat to spend more time at home but, as Bette Davis once said, 'Oscars on the mantelpiece don't keep you warm on a cold winter's night. You've got to keep working.' Nevertheless, the boys were doing well, Bobby was just great and I was contented. At thirty-eight, I felt healthier and sexier than ever before. The skinny girl might have gone the way of all skinny young things, but I was exuding a new mature confidence!

Now or Never?

Between working, I still had lots of time with the family, which was just as well because Ben, just coming up to seven, was troubled. He'd always been the baby of the family, but suddenly, after a long gap, there was Jack usurping his place – and Ben was now neither the youngest nor the eldest. Being a middle child can be tough.

'Why d'you keep kissing Jack and cuddling him all the time?' he asked me one day.

'Because he's a baby,' I said. 'And that's what you do with babies.'

'Well, be careful. You don't want to spoil him,' Ben replied and, from the way he said it I knew that he knew, and he knew that I knew, that he was jealous – and rattled.

It's the process siblings have to go through when a new baby comes along. First they're at the mercy of the green-eyed monster, then they start to get fond and protective of the little one, then they love it so much the monster disappears.

Jack was a sweetheart, but from the time he learned to walk we knew that he was going to be accident-prone just like me. I was always tripping, bumping into things and bruising myself, but at least I put my hands out to save me from the worst when I fell. When Jack fell, he didn't even bother to protect himself. He just fell flat on his face, his arms still at his sides. Once when Robert was pushing him around the garden in a wheelbarrow, he stood up, tumbled head over heels, and landed face down on the gravel. Penny was forever sitting him on the kitchen counter and covering him in plasters or tying knots in bandages.

One day when we were out for our Sunday lunch on holiday in Spain, a woman stopped at our restaurant table, looked at Jack who had a black eye, and said suspiciously, 'Oooh? What *has* your Mummy been doing to you?'

I was absolutely gobsmacked. I hadn't even heard of child abuse then, but I thought it was such an awful thing for her to think, let alone say. My mouth just dropped open and I was too shocked to speak. I mean, I'd hardly beat up my kid then take him out to lunch. If she'd been a bloke,

Bobby would have given her a volley, but as it was he just pretended to be deaf and got on with his lunch. Jack, meanwhile, was proud of his shiner.

The one thing I was always determined to do for our boys was to make sure they got a good education. Robert was already at Thorpe House at Gerrards Cross, where the poet John Betjeman had once been a master, and in 1981 it was Ben's time to join him there. Robert was preparing for his Common Entrance, and if he passed this exam we wanted him to go to Merchant Taylors' School in Northwood, Middlesex, when he was thirteen.

~

Maths was never one of my talents, but even I could work out that I'd now spent more of my life in show business than I had in dreaming about it. I never had to worry about booking hotels, parking the car, carrying my bags – everything was taken care of. Once you're the star – the headliner – you get treated like a totally dependent, helpless baby, or a Ming vase from China, something so rare and fragile you might shatter into a thousand pieces. But I was hardly fragile! So far that year I'd done six cabarets and twenty-four concert dates, including a month down under in Oz.

Every show has its own flavour, but the one that sticks in my mind for 1981 was in Manchester, when the fans showered the stage with about a million flowers. It was a bitter November night outside, but inside the theatre it looked like high summer. Half the audience wanted to climb up on the stage and give me their flowers; and, when I finished the perform-ance with 'Step Inside Love', they lined up at the front of the stage, some with tears in their eyes, and it took forever to shake everyone's hand.

Millions of people tuned in to watch Thames Television's *London Night Out* on 9 December that year, without knowing what we'd gone through to put that show together. This show was such a hassle it almost made you want to chuck it all in!

The recording date had been set for 12 October. I had had a brand new dress made – a stunning scarlet one that rustled like leaves and shim-mered like a jewel, and it had such a sexy slit in it that it made me shimmy the moment I put it on. The dress was topped by a scarlet, sequined bolero and, as I slid out of my dressing room looking my best ever, a stagehand with a lugubrious expression stopped me in my tracks.

'Blimey, you look great, Cilla,' said the stagehand.

'Oh thanks, luv. So? Why the long face?'

Before he could answer, Bobby was pressing towards me along the corridor, followed by a cluster of people – manager, agent and a publicity girl whose tears were turning her face a streaky black as mascara ran down her cheeks.

'We've been cancelled, Cil,' Bobby said.

'You're pulling my leg!'

'Industrial dispute. Nothing we can do about it.'

I felt like a bride left at the altar. I had to go back into the dressing room, take off my slap, peel off the red dress, and let Bobby drive me home.

Fifteen days later, once more clad in the red dress, red hair, red lips, I looked good enough to eat. I gave a last twirl in my dressing room. I was a vision in red in the mirror. I turned sideways and, glancing over my shoulder, said to myself, 'You'll do.'

As I stepped out into the corridor, there was the same stagehand, same lugubrious expression, same glassy look in his eyes, *same* words!

'You look great, Cilla.'

As my host, Tom O'Connor, finished his warm-up routine and introduced me as 'the sensational, the super, the sexy, the one-and-only Cilla Black', I wriggled out on stage. The lights went down and I took a deep breath. I was just getting into a fine rendering of 'Still', when Tom rushed back on, waving his arms. The music ground to a halt.

'We're off, Cilla.'

'Off? What d'you mean, off?' I demanded, hands on hips.

'Bomb scare!'

My jaw dropped. Bobby had followed Tom out on to the stage with the stagehand in tow and the four of us fled from the studio to the nearest pub, where the young producer (a Liverpool guy) passed his credit card across the bar and opened a tab. By the time the bomb scare proved to be a hoax, everyone was pleasantly sozzled, we'd run out of studio time and the audience had long gone home.

Two days later, when I had a late show in Caerphilly starting at 11.15 p.m., we were sitting down at breakfast. Jack was putting more cereal on the floor than in his mouth, and I nearly went head-over-heels on the mush as I rushed to answer the telephone. It was my producer.

'Can you do the *London Night Out* recording today?'

'Today? Have you lost your mind?'

'It's the only time available on the studio schedule.'

'I haven't even finished my egg yet.'

'*Please*, Cilla.'

'I don't know, chuck.'

'*Please. Please. Please.*'

It worked. Ask nicely, and I'll always pull out all stops.

We dashed off to the studio and went through the whole performance again – red dress, red hair, red lips, the same stagehand.

It was like one of those repetitive dreams when you keep running up spiral staircases that never end, or swimming towards a horizon that gets further away with each stroke.

Tom O'Connor was out on stage, doing the same warm-up in the same tone of voice, with exactly the same pauses. Bobby was standing at my side in the same navy-blue suit, both of us smiling as Tom's joke reached the punch line.

'It's now or never,' I said.

'Go break a leg,' Bobby whispered, patting me on me bum, and I strode out on stage.

As I went into the routine, I was wondering what could happen this time. I'd added the number 'It's A Miracle' to the set and I was thinking it would indeed be a miracle if we managed to get through this recording.

Now or Never?

Sure enough, my worst fears came to pass when, in the middle of my performance, my brother John phoned Bobby. Me mam had taken a tumble at home and broken her hip.

Breaking off from the recording, I wanted to dash up to Liverpool at once to be with Mam, but John assured me that she was comfortable and my visit could wait a day or two. I still had the show in Caerphilly to do. It was a case of out of the red dress, into a pair of blue jeans and a speedy drive west to Wales as the moon rose into a clear winter sky.

It was a while since dad had died, and me mam was now in her seventies and had been diagnosed with osteoporosis, but until the fall she had been coping pretty well. John and his wife Joan lived just around the corner from her, and their eldest daughter Janice went round every day after school and did her shopping for her. She'd had a nasty fall, but although she was in her seventies by now, she was made of strong stuff and by the time we arrived in Liverpool she was already limping around the hospital, treating the staff as if she was in a posh hotel, and generally laying down the law to all around her.

~

It's not often that I watch my own shows, but I made a point of watching *London Night Out* that December, just to make sure it hadn't all been a dream.

It hadn't. The scarlet dress had looked smashing.

In fact, the scarlet dress looked so smashing I didn't know how I'd ever manage to squeeze into it again. Here we were, just a few months on, and I couldn't fit into it. When your mam makes stuffed hearts even though she's balancing on one leg, heaven help you if you refuse a second helping. The enemy was back on my hips, climbing on to my waist and peeping out at me from the mirror, as I set out on another seventeen-date tour on the first day of 1982.

A wardrobe girl asked, 'Would you like me to let that dress out a bit?'

'No,' I replied, 'I would not.' And then I thought, 'Cow!'

What's It All About?

It was, I hoped, a temporary glitch, but it was just as well that *Woman's Own* called and asked me to join their Slimathon to raise money for the Save the Children Fund. I didn't need much persuading. I love doing things for children and … well, it was hardly going to do me any harm.

'How much do you want me to lose?' I asked the features editor.

'Five pounds?'

'Make it ten,' I replied, obligingly.

'No, Cilla, that's *too* much.'

'All right, let's split the difference. Make it seven and a half.'

I got the crispbread out of the back of the cupboard. That red dress would soon be hanging off me like a sloppy joe.

And I pulled it off!

The seven and a half pounds had slipped away by the time I did my next charity gig – this time for the Harefield Heart Transplant Trust. Just as well. I was terrified those heart specialists were going to be eyeing me up as a potential candidate!

~

As 1983 came in, I was shocked when I realised that I had now been at this game for twenty years. Where had they gone? Not only that, but my fortieth birthday was looming. That particular anniversary feels significant for many people, but even though I still felt about nineteen I had an extra reason to worry about hitting the big Four Oh. I'd done something really daft and secret in my youth – something that I'd never been able to get out of my mind.

Just after I'd appeared on *Top of the Pops* for the first time, I went to see a fortune teller in Liverpool. The lady in question proved to be straight out of central casting, an elderly woman with penetrating black eyes that seemed to look straight into the very core of me. Taking me into a spooky room where there were dusty veils placed over the light shades and candles lit as if for Mass – a black mass most likely! – I realised I'd made a terrible mistake by coming, but I'd gone too far to back out. I just knew somehow that she was going to say things I wouldn't want to hear and suddenly I was very frightened. As I held my breath, she took each of my hands in hers and gazed at my palms, tracing the lines on them with a sharp fingernail.

'You're a very successful young woman,' she began. 'But it won't last.'

'*What!*'

'Your career,' she said, pinning me with her black eyes, 'will end when you're forty.'

Forty seemed a long way off then, but I still felt very tearful and I couldn't wait to get outta there.

Now, come 1983, I was just a few months from forty, and her words were ringing in my head like a funeral knell.

It was a peculiar time – a time when I began to despair that the right TV format might never come along. I'd always believed in fate – *che serà serà*. As far as I was concerned, everything had always been mapped out by the Man Above, and nothing had happened to prove otherwise. Even so, Bobby and I were forever taking stock of what I'd done and what I might want to do in future. Show business is a very fickle affair. When it's going well, there's a tendency to think, 'look my name's still up there in lights, the reviews are good, I'm loved – I'm a star – I can fly.' But it's wise to remember that you can come down to earth with a bump! You might not want to change your act when everything's going well, but you can't keep doing the same old things forever. Even if it's not boring the audience, it will eventually bore you. It's a tricky balance – and one that's easy to get wrong.

I was still being offered loads of jobs, but many of these were requests for me to take over existing shows on the telly. I was offered, for example, *Family Fortunes*, which I absolutely adored watching and thought was a fab show.

'What do you think?' I asked Bobby.

'You're not a stand-in, Cilla.'

Bobby was right. While producers were still talking of finding a new, tailor-made television format for me, I would be wise to remain patient, but still, this seemed to have been going on for years. In the meantime, I was busily covering just about every inch of every highway and byway in the land.

'Have you dropped out, Cilla?' a woman about my age and with the same red hair as me asked across the cash desk in a supermarket one day. 'Have you retired?'

'No, luv,' I replied. 'I've no plans to shut up shop yet.'

'That's a relief,' she said, smiling broadly. 'Ta-rah for now, Cilla.'

It's nice when fans behave as if they own a part of you, and I suppose they do in a way: they buy your records, watch your shows, read the titbits in the papers. It's a strange sort of relationship, but a close one. Your fans, I discovered, always want to see more of you, but more is never enough. In 1983 I was on TV at least twenty times, which probably entailed me going into their sitting rooms more often than their sons and daughters!

But I kept thinking about the fortune teller.

'Am I finished?' I kept finding myself thinking. 'Is it all over? If so, what am I going to do with the rest of my life? To be forty and a has-been would be too awful!'

I wished I'd never been to see that bloody woman!

We are a superstitious lot, us performing types, and we know it's not what we've done, it's what we're doing now that counts. Success last year doesn't mean a thing if your new show's not getting full houses and good reviews. But what was I worried about? My shows still had full houses; the phone was still ringing; offers were still piling in. The old woman's words might be haunting me, but my career surely couldn't be doomed just a few months down the line. I was still everywhere! It didn't feel like the end of anything.

For all my come-forty fears, Bobby was still spending more time considering TV proposals and contracts than reading the newspapers. As far as producers were concerned, it was still Cillamania, but Bobby was being cautious. We both were. I did still seem to be on a high, although I was once again suffering a terrible bereavement. Ronnie Taylor, my lovely scriptwriter, had died of Legionnaire's disease and a part of me had gone with him.

Losing Ronnie was like losing my right arm. He was a wonderful guy, who totally understood television – he'd been the head of ATV at one time. He'd also been a professional singer in his youth, and sang like Bing Crosby. Ronnie had written everything I'd ever said on television, all the sitcoms, the sketches and the links. Whatever show I did and whatever channel I appeared on, it was Ronnie who'd given me all the words; he was like a ventriloquist with his arm up my back! He was one of the best – and I still miss him today.

With three children, now aged thirteen, nine and three, to consider, television work would be a lot easier to manage than traipsing around the country. After my stage shows, I always wanted to dash home to read Jack a story – and just be a good mum. But by the time I got home, I was dog-tired and only the Briards were awake to greet me. I didn't see my boys till breakfast time. Television work, then, would be ideal and, as I approached forty, that was the direction I hoped my career would now take me in.

With perfect timing, and as if destiny really was keeping an eye on me, I did a spot on the one-thousandth edition of *Top of the Pops*. At thirty-nine, dressed to kill and wearing a very short skirt, I swivelled my hips and – even though I didn't sing – proved I could still rock 'n' roll with the best of them. I was busily promoting my *Best of Cilla Black* album, and my last plug date was on *The Terry Wogan Show*. When my guest spot on *Wogan* ended, the phones were jumping with every TV producer in the land trying to reach me. The late, great David Bell, at that time the head of London Weekend Television's light entertainment said, 'Promise me you won't sign until I've spoken to you.' And a week later on 17 May, after years and years of waiting for the right format to come along, just ten days before my fortieth birthday, Bobby strolled into the room, waving a proposal.

'This looks promising, Cil,' he said, grinning from ear to ear. 'I think it's the one we've been waiting for.'

'Really?'

My heart soared.

A few weeks later I agreed to record a ninety-five minute pilot for what sounded like a promising new show. It had been created specially for me. And it was called *Surprise! Surprise!*.

23

Surprise! Surprise!

I've always hated surprises, so much so that I was deadly serious when I threatened Bobby with divorce if he ever allowed Eamonn Andrews and his *This Is Your Life* red book anywhere near me.

'I *mean* it, Bobby,' I used to say. 'If you ever do anything like that to me, I'll file for divorce. You won't see me for dust. You'll never see me again.'

I wasn't kidding. The thought of *This Is Your Life* – and any kind of surprise party – horrifies me. I honestly can't think of a worse nightmare.

Surprise! Surprise! was a brand new concept in variety entertainment, though, and it was the kind of show I'd been waiting for. Instead of just standing there and singing my heart out, this would enable me to do nutty things like Cillagrams and comedy sketches that could be fitted around a well-known song. There would also be weekly phone-ins and a serious slot where I could do things like reuniting families and highlighting the extraordinary achievements of ordinary men and women who did courageous things out of the goodness of their hearts.

As I would be switching between being in the studio and out on location for live broadcasts, I needed a co-host who could complement my style – whatever that is. No one has ever been quite able to define it!

What's It All About?

Showbiz types always tend to describe their fellow performers as 'gorgeous', 'a total professional', 'one of the nicest people you could ever hope to meet and work with' – at least in front of their faces! – but when Christopher Biggins was chosen as my 'roving reporter', this was all true for once. If I could have adopted a brother, it would have been Biggins. A great big, cuddly Briard of a friend, who always made it clear he loved me and who never tried to upstage me in all the time we worked together, he was just perfect for the job.

We got on like a house on fire from the moment we met – he was so warm and such a great wit, off and on the box. What you saw was what you got with Biggins. In a world of make-believe that can be pretentious at times, he was real. With a heart as big as himself, he could also be droll and entertaining with a caustic tongue and an acute sense of the absurd.

Biggins has done a lot of comedy in his time, but he is also a serious actor who lives, eats and breathes the theatre. If he's not working, he's usually to be found sitting in the stalls, watching a play. The press has not been kind to him, saying things like 'Christopher Biggins will turn up for the opening of a fridge door', but I've always thought he's a very subtle, underrated performer.

A TV pilot, I should point out, is only a try-out – loads get made and come to nothing; and after Biggins and I had done our thing, Alan Boyd, the executive producer, spent days locked in an editing suite with his team. As for Black and Biggins, they spent all those spare moments feeling like two teenagers waiting for their exam results. Had we passed the test? Would we do the series?

'Come on, chuck, this is killing us,' I said, when Alan next appeared in front of us.

'In a word, Cilla,' he replied, 'it's bloody marvellous.'

'That's *two* words,' Biggins muttered.

Surprise! Surprise!, then, was at the starting post – and Alan made it clear that he wanted to make this series one of LWT's major new entertainment ventures. He'd settled on a sixty-minute slot and, just as we'd done for the pilot, I was to be the host, with Christopher Biggins as a 'roving reporter'.

'There might be times,' Alan explained, 'when we will want you to sing in the show, but this will not be the staple ingredient. It's going to be very big,' he added. 'You have a magical touch with audiences, Cilla – and that's what came through on the tapes.'

I was really happy – and so relieved. He didn't know about the palmist's dreary prediction, but it now made a kind of sense. I wasn't about to quit the race at forty, I was just changing horses!

~

My birthday a few days later on 27 May was a media event. The *Daily Mirror* did a feature, Granada Television did a special greeting on the lunchtime news and, there were tributes from the Radio 2 DJs. Frankie Howerd turned up amid the chaos with a birthday cake *without* candles.

'I was going to wheel it in with a candle for every year of your life,' he said, 'but I was driven back by the heat.'

Then I had to dash off on a long drive to Scotland for a show at the Playhouse Theatre, Edinburgh, and when I shimmied out of the wings, the entire audience rose to their feet and sang 'Happy Birthday'.

To celebrate my twentieth anniversary we had arranged a special concert at Lewisham Concert Hall. But I was in for a shock. I had been warned that the show might be interrupted by protesters and, lo and behold, that's just what happened.

I was in the middle of singing 'Step Inside Love' when four young-sters, one a girl with what looked like blood poured all over her, rushed the stage, shouting at the tops of their voices, with placards held aloft. They were protesting against animals being killed for their fur. I'm the first to think everyone's got a right to their views, but it was terrifying. I wasn't wearing fur (although I did own fur coats) and it was hardly fair to use my anniversary concert to make their protest – not that it lasted very long. What they hadn't bargained for was facing a theatre full of Cilla fans. The blokes were soon on their feet, chasing the protestors out of the door, and I got on with the show.

When everything's going well, my life's a dream, but it does no harm to be woken up sometimes. Nina Myskow did that in the *Sunday People* during my anniversary festivities by nominating me as 'Wally of the Week'.

'Cilla Black, who with one wavery swoop of her voice wiped out her wonderful appearance on *Wogan* is this week's wally. Her warbling as the star turn on *Live From Her Majesty's* last Sunday was woeful. Wally of the Week. Cilla, dear, it's not that I don't have a heart. Anyone who had an ear – never mind two as I have – must have wondered what it was all about. You never did have much of a voice. But the remains have floated straight down the Mersey. Stick to your mad-as-a-hatter lovely chatter. Remember, Miss Black, it's best never to go back.'

I can't pretend that didn't hurt for a moment, but I was getting a bit long in the tooth to be too sensitive. I'd learned at an early age that if you can't stand the heat you should get out of the kitchen, but I also knew from past experience that, however many good reviews I got, it was the bad ones I tended to remember.

~

Back in London in early 1984 after a well-deserved rest in the Virgin Islands, I started dashing around doing location work for *Surprise! Surprise!*. The first episode was aired on Sunday 6 May and (no surprise) met with mixed reviews.

I too had had my doubts, not about the shows, but about some of the more daredevil sequences! When I aired these to Alan Boyd, however, he just shook his head in that wise, producer way and said: 'Just get out and do it, Cilla. It's going to be *very* big.'

And, as always, I did as I was told and followed the producer's instructions, however insane they were. I had complete trust in the people I was working with. I must have been daft, soft in the head, a complete loon, *certifiable*. You'd only have to look at the alligator episode, one of the first, to agree with me. My job – and I accepted it! – was to climb into an alligator's cage and clean its teeth.

It's not something you think about, but alligators in captivity have to have their teeth cleaned once a week. In the natural world, ticks and small birds slip in their mouths and pick out all the bits of rubbish for them. In the zoo, it's down to the keeper and loons like me who turn up from the telly.

It was, I was told, perfectly safe because the heat in the cages had been turned off for twenty-four hours and when it's cold, alligators go all sleepy.

The camera crew had arrived at the zoo, the electricians had set up the lights and everything was ready by the time I got there. Hair. Make-up. Then I was humming 'See You Later Alligator' and, armed with an eighteen-inch toothbrush, I approached the cage.

'Ready?' said the director.

I looked in at the alligator. He didn't look at all sleepy to me. In fact, he was a frisky old feller and when he yawned he could have swallowed a grand piano.

'He doesn't look tired,' I said nervously. 'He looks like he's just woken up after a kip.'

'Don't worry,' said the director, 'it'll be fine.'

By then, I'd learned that you have to have faith in people; now I had to extend this to animals. Keeping an eye on the plaque-infested reptile, I slipped my diamond ring off my finger. I might be able to put up with losing a digit in the name of entertainment, but I didn't want to lose that rock!

Crossing myself, just to be on the safe side, I set off – not through the gate, mind you. Oh, no. I had to crawl through a tunnel with the alligator handler and one of the young lads from props, a boy with red hair, green eyes and gritted teeth – a volunteer, I assumed. The rest of the team? They were outside the cage twiddling with lenses, reading meters, adjusting the lights, all those things that occupy camera crews and, I must admit, they looked more preoccupied than usual.

What's It All About?

As for the alligator, well, he wasn't exactly waiting for us, but – remember, this was *Surprise! Surprise!* – he didn't exactly look surprised either. Singing 'See You Later Alligator' somewhat more in earnest now, I got the scene going by scrubbing the beast's back with a scrubbing brush. It lay quite still like a giant handbag and seemed to enjoy that. Now for the *pièce de résistance*: the prop boy, looking a teeny bit bolder, passed me a giant-sized toothbrush. The alligator winked at me. 'Saucy,' I muttered, then it was my turn to wink as his mouth gaped open like the lid of an enormous box. This was turning out to be easier than I'd anticipated. I stuck the toothbrush in, but before I could even start to clean his teeth, those jaws slammed down with a mighty crack and, inches from my fingers, snapped the brush in two.

Two things occurred to me at the same time: one, that the only protection in the cage was the keeper's broom, which was no protection at all, and the other, which was more to the point, was that I wanted to get out – and fast. I actually surprised myself – as one sometimes does on such occasions – by not going into total panic mode and screaming the place down. Instead, with a presence of mind born of real fear, I turned to the camera and said calmly: 'I don't like this very much. In fact, I'd like to get outta here.'

The director did not demur!

'… and cut,' he said.

I could have killed him for using such a word at such a moment.

Slowly, like a crab, I edged my way towards the exit tunnel and crawled to safety, the boy from props hot on my trail, the handler bringing up the rear.

On the way, I passed a small pile of logs – only they weren't logs, they were baby alligators just waking up. Just like their dad, they had been duped into hibernation, but the lights put up by the camera crew had heated up the cage, and it was like the jungle in there. Nobody, of course, had thought about *that*. I wasn't sure who to blame, but I took comfort in the thought that, had the worst come to the worst, I would have had my revenge on the continuity lot – because if I wasn't there at the end of that sequence, they'd have had a real problem!

It was only later that I discovered that there had been no tranquilliser gun handy to subdue the beast if it had got its scaly thighs in a twist – *and* the production team had actually insured me for a fortune in case I lost a limb or two. On discovering that, I got quite carried away imagining my grisly end, and upsetting myself by picturing the bereft faces of my three young motherless sons.

But saying yes was a habit I had formed way back when I was first signed up by Brian.

'This business,' he'd said, 'is all about trust, Cilla. You have to have faith in people.'

If Brian said it, I thought it had to be true; and when producers said: 'It's all right, chuck, there's no danger,' I'd jump out of a helicopter. Which, of course, is what I did soon after for the *Surprise! Surprise!* feature on the Air-Sea Rescue Service.

We told the Air-Sea Rescue guys that we – and our viewers – wanted to know what it was like to be saved by one of their rescue helicopters. What we didn't tell them was that when they came on the show to see the film, we were going to surprise-surprise them by bringing on fifty people whom they had saved. This was how our show was designed, like Chinese boxes: true-life drama to get you in, a frothy middle played for laffs, and a core of human-interest stories that had audiences reaching for their hankies.

In order for me to be saved on the telly, I first had to be placed in danger. They dressed me in a flying suit with a pair of earphones, which gave some protection against the noise, and I carried a mike to catch my every reaction, my every heartbeat – and, boy, was my heart beating fast that day. We took off, rising into the sky, the blades spinning above us. It was exciting at first and I felt safe with all those young airmen grinning and giving me the thumbs-up.

What's It All About?

Before climbing on board, I'd been through an intense, thirty-minute briefing to learn what to do in case of an emergency; but there are so many things to remember, like if the helicopter goes down in the sea, you have to climb out of one particular window; if it turns upside down, you have to do something else – which I'd immediately forgotten. In no time, though, we were hovering over a tiny, isolated, desolate chunk of rock where I was to be marooned.

I'd been expecting something flat and friendly, a grassy hill, perhaps a few goats for a bit of a chin-wag. But it wasn't even a rock, it was a stalagmite pointing like an angry finger straight at heaven.

'What you have to do,' the instructor said, yelling over the noise, 'is follow me out of the helicopter.'

Swallowing hard, I nodded.

I could see the second camera crew on a distant cliff top. I knew Bobby was there with them and that gave me some comfort. If anything went wrong, I felt sure he'd rip off his clothes, dive six hundred feet from the cliff and swim the mile or so through those twenty-foot waves to get me. I looked back at the instructor and tried a smile.

'I'll be on the line just below the door. You sit on the edge with your legs over the side. When my colleague gives you the word, you jump …'

'Jump?'

'You jump out, put your legs around my waist and just hold on.'

'Don't worry, luv,' I said, 'I'll hold on all right.'

He grinned. This was fun – for him.

'We'll winch you down to the rock and leave you there for a few minutes before we come back and rescue you.'

This was definitely one of those times when I had to have faith in others. There was so much noise and so little time, I didn't really have a chance to think about anything. I closed my eyes and jumped. We were winched down in an ungainly way. It was incredible … and terrifying. I had my legs wrapped around the instructor like I'd been told. He was a redhead and gorgeous, and I tried to be brave by saying, 'Does this mean we're engaged now?'

I landed with a bump, then watched the helicopter and instructor whirring off, the trailing winch slowly rising, the machine getting smaller, the sound of the engine fading. And there I was. Nowhere to sit down. Nothing to eat. Nothing to read. And there I was, standing on the only square foot of flat surface. And what exactly did 'we'll leave you there for a few minutes' mean?

Time obviously flies for fliers. I only learned at the last possible moment that the first thing they had to do was go back to base and refuel. Then they had to load the camera crew on board so they could return to film the rescue and, if there's one thing I know about camera crews, it's that these guys are perfectionists. They take their jobs seriously – they take their time.

If there was a silver lining it was that flying suits have about a million pockets. I went through these and, to kill time, I got my make-up out to powder my nose and then searched through another six pockets to find my gloss. The wind was whistling by at about a hundred mph and my lips were as dry as the desert. I was talking to myself: there was no one else to talk to. I'd forgotten I was miked up and the soundmen miles away on that nice, safe, warm cliff could hear me muttering things like: 'What did Bobby say about the rock being completely covered at high water? No, it can't be. It's much too tall. If I look down from here … hang on a minute, I'd better not: vertigo. Oh, my God, *where are they?*'

I looked at my watch and discovered that if you look at the face long enough, the hands actually freeze.

I shook my wrist. The battery must have gone dead. Finally, I did look down. The tide was turning, lapping over the rock. The sea was grey and angry-looking. I gazed up into the sky. *Nothing.* Not even a nosy seagull. I was cold, bored and starting to get really frightened when, needless to say, the rescue team showed up, a little dot about the size of a fly far away in the distance. The sound of the engine grew louder and it wasn't long before the Air-Sea Rescue fellers were lowering a giant hook and winching me to safety, my every grimace captured on camera.

If you asked me if I enjoyed the experience, the honest answer would be no, I didn't. Even if it did make great telly.

When we arrived back on dry land, Bobby put his arms out but I didn't run into his embrace. The first thing I did was go down on my knees and kiss the ground.

~

Our home at Denham is a haven. It's my retreat. This is where I'm just a wife and mum, tucked away out of the limelight. At the beginning of May, we were curled up on the sofa there one evening, watching the Eurovision Song Contest. What we didn't know was that while we were in the sitting room downstairs, our bedroom upstairs was being ransacked by burglars. We must have overfed, over-cuddled and over-spoiled the Briards, because they didn't exactly do their job as guard dogs. They probably trotted up to the determined robbers as they came in through the bedroom window, and rolled over and waited for a tickle. The burglars stole about £250,000 worth of jewellery and furs and lots of stuff I'd accumulated from years of hard work, the endless tours and summer seasons, the pantomimes, records, television shows. Things are only things, I know, but our own things are precious to us. For me, they were tangible evidence of what I'd done, what I'd achieved.

Break-ins happen to loads of people, but that doesn't make you feel any better when it's your own home that's burgled. I felt sick that the thieves had actually been in my bedroom. I felt violated and dirty. I could not bear the thought that they'd rummaged through my underwear drawer, and I replaced everything in it.

According to the police, there had been numerous raids on the luxury homes in the area and it was a relief to know that we had not been singled out. The other thing that happens is that when lots of gear gets pinched, you don't even know things are gone until you look for them, and for months after you keep getting reminders when something isn't there. The one thing I missed immediately was the diamond engagement ring Bobby had bought, the ring I'd been terrified the alligator was going to swallow. I was so heartbroken, the BBC let me make an appeal for its return on *Breakfast Time*, not that it did any good.

~

During filming for *Surprise! Surprise!* I'd noticed for some time that I was bleeding unusually heavily every month, but I hadn't done anything about it. That Christmas, I was playing Dick Whittington in panto at Birmingham. During the show I had to walk up a flight of steps, singing 'You'll Never Walk Alone'. I'm not good with heights at the best of times, but this was something else: every time I got to the top I was dizzy with the effort, and the stage crew had to put in a pole that I could hold on to at the top just to keep my balance.

Back at Denham after the show ended, I was in the bedroom one day when everything suddenly started to spin. I collapsed in a heap and banged my head. When I came to, I called to Bobby and he drove me straight to St George's Hospital, Tooting, where Geoffrey Chamberlain now worked. When Geoffrey examined me, he discovered I was bleeding internally. It turned out I'd been walking around with several pints less blood in my body than I should have.

'I feel like a car with the needle in the red,' I joked, but Geoffrey wasn't laughing.

To make things worse, this was all happening on the Thursday before the very first *Surprise! Surprise!* – a live broadcast – was due to be transmitted. The doctors cleaned me up and pumped six pints of blood into me, and I came out to do the show. There was no way I was going to let the team – or the viewers – down.

So, with some kind donor's blood filling my veins, I made it to the studio for the big night. My knees were trembling and I felt as wobbly as a jelly, but Biggins was like the Rock of Gibraltar, the floor manager had his eyes on me, a nurse was standing by like an extra from a *Carry On* film, and there were all those young PAs with solemn faces rushing around like beetles in their black T-shirts. And, after nursing the show along for an eternity, Alan Boyd had the look of somebody on a sinking ship frantically pumping up a life-jacket. This was *live* TV, and his star, for all her bravado, was only just clinging on.

I did it, we all did it, and the next day, after the doctors had filled me up with more blood, I was told the examination had revealed a worrying growth. The only cure was to go under the knife and have a hysterectomy, which I did three weeks later.

The operation was a complete success, and the tumour was found to be non-malignant, but a bit of Cilla was missing. As I lay there in bed the next day, I felt as if I'd gone in one moment from the girl next door to the granny next door.

Then the door of my room opened and there stood Bobby with the biggest bouquet ever.

'They've taken away the nursery,' I said, sadly, 'and left the playpen.'

'Who wrote that?' he asked.

'I did.'

'You're getting too clever by half.'

He was smiling and I dredged up a smile, too. The show goes on. It's just not me to be depressed and I was back at LWT almost before they noticed I'd gone.

'Surprise, surprise!' I said to all the crew when I next walked on to the studio floor.

It wasn't really funny, but everyone laughed.

~

The reviews for *Surprise! Surprise!* were so-so, but shows need time to settle down.

'We're piloting an important new programme at peak time with no protection against the knockers,' Alan Boyd kept saying. 'It's like sailing a boat without a compass among the rocks.'

We all knew that certain strands of the show were wrong, but when you're going out live, as we often did, you don't have the luxury of an editing suite and the chance of switching stuff about. It was only as the show progressed that Biggins and I really worked out what we were supposed to be doing, but we could see that each show was better than the last. Many of the shows were recorded in advance, but when they were live, as we assembled to work, the air was charged with a very special excitement. To paraphrase Alan, it was rather like working without a safety net, just like it had been in my early days on the BBC, and I felt at my best when there was a sense of urgency, a bit of danger.

A lot of critics looked down their noses at *Surprise! Surprise!*, but the families who gathered around the box on a Saturday night liked it, and that's who we were doing it for. I'd always confused the critics. 'Why the hell do they like her?' they wanted to know. But this seemed to be a hallmark of my career; and it was just as bewildering for me when the marketing people, with their clipboards and consumer surveys, always seemed to be at odds with the viewers. My shows, they reported back, were faulty, downmarket, a chair with only three legs, but when the weekend came, ten million people tuned in.

There was one critic who always kept me on my toes, though – me mam. One of the strands in *Surprise! Surprise!* was reuniting families, which was often very emotional, and I had to psych myself up for these reunions, otherwise the show would fall to pieces with all of us sobbing into our hankies. After me mam had given me a mouthful years earlier for snivelling on TV, I'd trained myself to think of her if I was ever close to tears, and that would pull me together!

I also had the boys to worry about. I'd been an entertainer for donkey's years, had been famous before they were born, so they'd never known me not to be on TV – but I'd never forgotten the day when one of

Ben's little friends had grabbed me round the knees and said, 'I love you, Cilla Black.'

'No, this is my mummy,' Ben had said angrily. 'That's your mummy over there. You should go and love your mummy.'

Being a household name can have a deep effect on your children. Robert was thirteen now and he was upset when he saw the hatchets being plunged in. When I shared one review with him, however, even he had to laugh.

'Cilla's so bad, my daughter *likes* her,' one woman wrote.

'Her daughter's probably thirteen,' I giggled.

Robert looked thoughtful. 'Let's invite her to tea.'

'The critic?'

'No, the daughter.'

He was well on his way to getting interested in girls. I could hardly believe so many years had passed.

Ben, bless him, who was ten that year, brought this passing of time into even sharper focus.

'How old are you?' he asked me one day as he was sitting there in his school uniform, tie adrift, finishing his cornflakes.

'Thirty-five,' I lied.

'What age do people die?'

'Oh, when they're *old* – about seventy, or if you're really lucky older,' I said.

'Do you realise you're over half dead already!' he replied.

What adult would have the nerve to say that? But when a child says it, you have to laugh. I can honestly say that my children have done more to keep my feet on the ground than anyone else. They just have a way of reminding you of the realities of life, and keeping in focus what matters. They have been – and continue to be – a blessing to me.

Our 'secret' registry office wedding in London, 1969.

Downstairs at my best mate Billy Davis'
house for a party. This photo was taken
the first time Bobby and Billy met.

Happy Birthday to me!
Now I can never lie about my age!

Thank God for
Cathy McGowan –
Cathy introduced us
to the delights of
swinging London.

© CILLA BLACK

sexy new look for
968. The hair lasted
r about a week!

© CILLA BLACK

PLP 244E

With my new Bentley, outside my
new flat in Portland Place.

All sparkly in a new Biba dress for 'Sing A Rainbow'.

(*opposite*) Sher-oo! One of the photos that never made the final cut!

Jimmy Tarbuck (left), me, Bobby (right) and the only other
person Bobby could have married – the great Bill Shankly.

(*opposite*) 'Cooling' out on our first posh holiday in the Canaries.

Robert's first birthda
at our wonderful ne
house in Denha

(left) Frankie Howerd with me on my BBC show in 1978. We still miss him terribly.

(above) Me mam with Ben and Jack in 1983. It was a measure of the respect she was held in that everyone, even Bobby, always called her Mrs White.

Surprise! Surprise!

Our first Blind Date couple to be married – Alex and Sue.

Bobby and I on our last family holiday in Barbados
in January 1998. He was always so full of life.

(*opposite*) Bobby was a great thinker, a great listener, and his advice was
always sound and wise. But above all he loved his family and we loved him.

It's all about family. Ben, Robert, Fiona and Jack on Robert and Fiona's wedding day.

Still together after all these years. Jimmy Tarbuck (centre), Peter Brown (right), George Martin (left) and new recruit Paul O'Grady (far left).

A 'sextieth' birthday party to be proud of. Savage bangs on his tambourine.

Dale gives my old Liverpool mate Pat Davies a big hug.

Because I can!

24

Blind Date

The thing about live TV is that it's tight-rope TV – wonderful because you can ad-lib and be totally spontaneous, which I love, and awful because you can never be quite sure you won't be left with egg on your face. Towards the end of the first series of *Surprise! Surprise!* we did a piece with a young chap, not much more than twenty, who was so in love that he wanted to propose to his girlfriend live on telly. They'd been going out together for several years, and she'd even asked him to marry her several times. Obviously, this was a great human-interest idea, and we went for it.

We bought a gorgeous engagement ring for them and we arranged for him to take his fiancée off to a smart restaurant for a romantic meal on us after he'd proposed.

The feller came in to the studio, dressed up to the nines, and then a camera crew went to his girlfriend's house. When they got there, the girl slammed the door in their faces, but they persuaded her to open up again and explained that if she came to our studios there'd be a smashing surprise.

The young lady got to the studio and sat on the couch in front of the cameras, glancing at her feller, and clearly wondering what it was all about.

I did the interview, which went fine, and then it was the big moment:

time for the proposal. The young man knelt on one knee and, smiling up at his girl, asked: 'Will you marry me?'

'No,' she replied in a voice that brooked no argument.

I was flabbergasted. The audience gasped in disbelief and then, the normal after-shock, they laughed. This was a real live-TV moment.

'I can see it's a bit daunting to be live on television with millions of viewers watching,' I said. 'Would you rather your feller asked you in the privacy of your own home or over a romantic meal?'

'No,' she said again, even more emphatically this time. 'I don't want to marry him.'

'Calm down, luv,' I said. 'You've been going out with him for years. I'm sure in private …'

But, before I could finish the sentence, she butted in, saying, 'No, that won't help. I was thinking of chucking him anyway.'

My mouth was agape and my heart went out to him. The poor feller couldn't speak. The audience, realising this was not a send-up, had stopped laughing. We were dead on air, always horrible on a live programme, then I tried to fill the gap.

'It's been very traumatic,' I said, 'but whether this is going to be a make-up or break-up evening, at least go out to dinner on us.'

The girl shrugged. The boy looked mortified. And I looked straight into camera. 'Surprise! Surprise!' I said.

~

The show's viewers were so loyal, we got 300,000 letters during that first series and, even before that came to an end, I was under contract to start filming another series in October.

In free moments, I always used to enjoy looking through property columns in newspapers, and whenever I phoned to ask for more details I always tried to disguise my voice. After *Surprise! Surprise!*, however, people always twigged and said, 'Oh my God! It's Cilla Black.'

'No, it's not, luv,' I'd say lamely.

'Oh, yes it is! I'd recognise that voice anywhere. You going to find a long last auntie for me then?'

Even when I wanted an electrician or plumber to come, people at the end of the phone just burst out laughing and said, 'Surprise! Surprise!' This was funny at first, but it did get me down sometimes. Even worse was when I made a call and the person at the other end of the line thought it was someone pretending to be me. 'And I'm Cliff Richard,' they kept guffawing.

LWT were thrilled with the success of the show, however – and loved how I would really throw myself at a project. However hard the producers tried to get things organised, there was always an element of madness and risk for me, but because I'd been doing pantos for donkey's years, *Surprise! Surprise!* never really fazed me. Well aware of this, my bosses at LWT were eager to find something else for me to work on.

While they were thinking about this, 1985 rolled in, and Bobby and I did what we'd been doing for a decade now. We went to Australia – my tenth tour. It was while we were there that we just happened to catch a dating show called *Perfect Match* on our hotel TV. 'That's good!' we both said in unison.

From Australia, we went on to Florida, where we were due to meet the boys and Penny. While we were in Florida, we saw *The Dating Game*, the US version of *Perfect Match*. The kids loved it, and when Alan Boyd called to talk about *Surprise! Surprise!*, I said to him, 'Alan, we've just seen this great show – why haven't you got it for the UK?'

'I have,' he said. "I've had it for three years.'

When we got back, he told me a bit about the show. The concept had been dreamed up by Chuck Barris, an American who'd retired to the South of France after he'd made a fortune from inventing game shows. In the USA, the rights had been sold to the Fremantle Corporation, probably the world's biggest game-show production and distribution company.

Then Alan showed me the UK pilot he had made three years ago with the wonderful camp comedian Duncan Norvell. Alan's bosses – and

Mary Whitehouse and the TV watchdogs – had had reservations about this sort of show being made in the UK and considered it too sexy for a family audience.

That show, provisionally entitled *It's A Hoot*, was to become *Blind Date*! If there's anyone out there who hasn't seen *Blind Date*, the programme gets a feller to pick one of three gals, without being able to see them, just based on how they answer some fun (and sometimes fairly cheeky) questions. Then a different gal picks one of three fellers, and the two lucky couples get sent off on a date to exotic locations and come back on the show the next week to say how they got on. Simple – but great TV!

Having watched the pilot, I thought Duncan was phenomenal and the show was hilarious.

'What do you think?' Alan asked.

'It's fabulous,' I replied. 'Someone's got a hit on their hands.'

'That someone's *you*.'

'No way!' I laughed. 'I couldn't do anything like that, Alan. I could not even tell my oldest son where babies came from.'

'Leave it with me,' Alan said, a very decisive note in his voice.

Alan immediately rushed off to see John Birt, at that time LWT's Director of Programming, and John agreed with him: 'Cilla's the girl for *Blind Date*.'

'You're the only one for this show,' Alan told me.

'What you're really saying,' I retorted, 'is that I won't offend anyone because I'm the most sexless person on TV!'

'You said it, not me,' was his response.

Well, cheers, Alan!

I still had my doubts though. A woman had never hosted a game show in the UK before and each time I thought of all the brilliant, funny street-wise guys who'd gone before me, I felt really daunted. Bobby, on the other hand, was very keen.

The first pilot was lousy – very stiff and not at all funny. There were so many rules about the contestants not kissing or not holding hands that nobody could relax and it killed the atmosphere stone dead. I'd always hated failure and Bobby persuaded me to try again. 'Forget the dos and don'ts,' he said; 'just enjoy it and have fun.'

One of the things I'd noticed about the Australian and US programmes was that only one of the couples was invited back the following week, and I thought that was unfair. Likewise, given that people come in all shapes and sizes, I thought it was wrong to have only beautiful people on the show. Of course there was a 'Will they, won't they?' and 'Did they, didn't they?' sexy element to the programme, but the fun side was much more important to me. Like, for example, what the hell did that trainspotter from Birmingham have to say to the drama-queen hairdresser from Bath?

So we did the second pilot, and I had fun, and we made the changes, and it was terrific. This time, after John Birt, Alan Boyd and everyone at LWT had studied the pilot about a million times, the decision was 'go, go'.

~

The first showing of *Blind Date* hit the screens in November 1985, and it was an instant success. After the first seven programmes were aired, 80,000 people wrote in asking to be contestants on the next series.

The third series of *Surprise! Surprise!* was also running so, for all the people who'd been complaining that they didn't see enough of me on TV, I was now on telly more than anybody else, except for the newsreaders and weathergirls! It was also the second time in my career that I had had two shows on TV at the same time. The only difference now was that *Surprise! Surprise!* and *Blind Date* were both for the same network. Yet I still thought of myself as a recording artist who did a bit of television.

Like *Surprise! Surprise!*, there was always a lot of snobbery about *Blind Date*. Lots of people wouldn't own up that they watched it, but the ratings proved that many of them did. We even beat my own favourite soap, *Coronation Street*, from time to time, and once the show started, it seemed it would run forever.

For technical reasons, what with all the wires and radio mikes, I had to be very careful what I wore on *Blind Date*. 'Strap the battery pack to your inner thigh,' was one of the helpful suggestions, but this created a problem when I threw myself on to the sofa. My clip-on microphone was powered by this battery pack, and I didn't want the pack to show. In the end, I strapped it around my waist and wore long jackets to cover it at the back. All my outfits were designed by Stephen Adnitt, who was brilliant at hiding wires and making special allowances for clipping mikes to lapels and shirts.

I could always tell immediately if the couples would hit it off on the show. I saw it in their eyes when they came face to face for the first time behind the set; and many's the time that contestants whispered to me later, 'Oh, God, Cilla, I wish I'd picked the blonde instead', or 'Why did I choose the worst bloke of the three?'

I always made sure we edited out the really raunchy stuff, but inevitably some things did slip through and find their way into the tabloids the next day. Mostly, though, when the fellers made a really salty remark, my gut feeling told me if it was going to be considered too offensive and I tried to steer them towards good, clean, fun. And in spite of my 'sexless' crack, some of the guys even tried it on with me!

'Stop it,' I said. 'I've got tights older than you.'

My ad-lib went around town like a head cold and I was thrilled when I heard Max Bygraves plagiarising it on radio by saying: 'I've got a suit older than you.' When Max borrows a line, you know you've arrived.

And I certainly had arrived. I'd made it in a more mainstream way than ever before – and it was very novel to be in the papers almost every day and on the TV almost every night. I was dead chuffed to be reaching an audience that was the age I'd been when I started out – it really knocked me out that young people could relate to me.

The thing, though, about being everyone's 'Cilla' is that everyone thought they knew me – that I really was their girl next door. I was only too aware that when Bassey swept out of a theatre or into a room, everybody went all funny and almost swooned. But when they saw me, they put an arm around my shoulders, grabbed my hand or slapped me on the back!

After twenty-plus years in the entertainment industry, I decided to stop counting. I now had fans who hadn't been born when I started out, and my sixties contemporaries were now middle-aged mums and dads who brought their kids to my shows. Talk about scary. Though not as scary as my *Spitting Image* puppet, as if I needed any more proof that I had really arrived.

~

A somewhat more flattering way of knowing I was doing OK was having my photograph taken by Lord Snowdon. London Weekend had commissioned him to take my portrait, along with all the other LWT stars, and when I turned up at his studio, which was on the garden floor of the Kensington family home he shared with his second wife, Lucy, he insisted on taking me upstairs to the music room where his little daughter, Lady Frances, was having a piano lesson. Within seconds we were all singing 'Old McDonald Had A Farm'. It was completely surreal.

I'd turned up wearing white jeans, a shirt and Robert's old striped school blazer and tie, but I'd also come with so much gear for the session that Snowdon must have thought Bobby had kicked me out and I was moving in with him! Before I could get round to changing into something glam, however, he suddenly said, 'No, it's perfect.'

'What? Who?' I asked.

'You, my dear. I'll shoot you just as you are, in the shirt, blazer and tie.'

I'd always known photographers were a law unto themselves, and that they always looked as if they'd been disturbed in the middle of a crossword when they were still trying to work out seven down. That's exactly how Lord Snowdon was – and looked – and, click-click-click, he shot me just as I was.

He had a great eye – actually, neither of them was bad! – and a lovely, deep, plummy voice that reminded me of the newsreaders I'd listened to when I was a girl.

What's It All About?

Thanks to Lady Frances, I was so relaxed when he photographed me that the pics came out really well and John Birt stuck one of them in pride of place on the wall at the TV studios.

When I bumped into John in the corridor a couple of days later, he said: 'You know that crack about being the most sexless person in television?'

'Yes – thanks for reminding me, John.'

'Well, your picture's gone missing – been stolen off the wall. And it's the only one that's ever been taken.'

'There must be some pervert out there,' I grinned.

~

In March 1986, armed with a ton of storybooks, Bobby and I escaped with our kids to the Seychelles. Our task that holiday was to help Jack, aged five, with his reading. Robert and Ben had learned to read when they were only three and a bit. Jack had fooled us into thinking he could read by memorising books word for word. We found out later that he had moderate dyslexia – but I already had a mother's instinct that he might be having problems.

I started a new regime, promising Jack that I'd read his favourite story every night if he would also read one to me. At first he pulled his old trick, telling me a story he'd committed to memory, but I brought out new books and that stumped him. Once he faced the fact that he couldn't read, we went through the slow process of drawing A-B-Cs, and he began to make real progress. He also more than made up for his lack of reading skills by being a mechanical genius. If something was broken, he only had to look at it and it began working again. He also continued to be accident prone. Shortly after we got home from the Seychelles, he broke his collarbone when he was leaping like Batman from a wall.

While we were in the Seychelles, Robert, now fifteen, had discovered a new hobby: bird watching. There were hundreds of them – gorgeous topless girls – and he became the colour of mahogany lying on the beach and enjoying the view. For Ben, aged eleven, half-dressed dolly birds didn't hold quite the same fascination, not for longer than five minutes anyway, and he kept ruining his brother's cool and street cred by building sand-castles with elaborate moats and turrets.

~

The rules of *Blind Date* had now been clarified. Contestants had to be 'over eighteen, single and unattached, with no criminal convictions'. They also had to be 'lively and funny', but that was sometimes difficult to achieve!

We couldn't help noticing that some of the contestants were trying to use *Blind Date* to launch their own careers. I didn't blame them, but the truth is, you have to have something very special to make that happen, and that something is called talent. Now that the critics had got tired of writing bad reviews, it was the turn of the feature writers who were constantly stalking and following up the contestants and trying to dish the dirt. But the publicity – good or bad – only added to the show's popularity.

Fellers are always dead cheeky and a lot of middle-aged horny guys who applied were trying to get dates with girls half their age. We soon weeded them out, though, and sent them the standard 'Thank you ... but no thank you.' Then we started getting letters from senior citizens saying, 'Hey, what about us?'

'Right – all's fair in love and war,' I said – and the first of our Golden Oldies was seventy-year-old Gerald Scott from North Wales, who picked Evie Gillard, and they spent their date at the Ritz Hotel with an evening at the musical *Seven Brides for Seven Brothers*. They struck up a friendship that lasted for the rest of their lives and that made me feel as if we'd actually helped someone, not just given them a laugh.

Did many contestants find love? Some did. Mostly, though, the dates were a disaster, but then the show was probably at its best when the contestants were at each other's throats. I remember Sue Willis and Alastair Kennedy going off for a treasure hunt in Brighton, and when they came back I asked the usual question: 'Are you going to see each other again?'

'The only way I'd speak to him again,' Sue replied, hands on hips, 'would be through a medium.'

'I'm not grotesque, am I, Cilla?' the poor guy asked me after the show.

'No, of course you're not, luv.'

'I mean, I went out with Miss Wales last week.' he said, plaintively.

The girls on *Blind Date* were more powerful, more confident than I ever was, and they were so much better than the boys at speaking their minds and putting their partners down. In some circles *Blind Date* was even called *Women Behaving Badly*. At times, though, the boot was on the other foot. One feller came back into the studio, sat on the now-famous sofa and told the viewers: 'She's a pukka Sloane desperate to be an A-division yuppie.'

'I didn't know he despised me so much,' the girl gasped, fighting back tears.

Some weeks people were humiliated. Some weeks they were on the verge of tears, but it didn't stop the applications flooding in by the trainload and the viewing figures hitting fifteen million a week. When I was a young pop star I used to hold my breath as I scanned the charts in *NME* and *Melody Maker* to see if my new single had climbed another few places against Donovan and The Rolling Stones – now I was doing the same thing with the television charts, and I was thrilled out of my tights when we finally hit the number five spot with only the soaps ahead of us.

~

Like a pair of comfy slippers, *Surprise! Surprise!* was still filling all my spare moments and chasing *Blind Date* up the charts. The lovely Biggins had gone off to pursue his own career and Bob Carolgees had become my side-kick on the show.

As with *Blind Date*, there were some people who complained that *Surprise! Surprise!* exploited people's private moments by showing them in tears on screen, but the 'surprised' were so anxious to find their loved ones again, it really seemed they didn't mind. They were grateful and I genuinely believe we performed a valuable service. On the occasions when a reunion proved to be so emotional, so moving, that people asked us not to air the surprise, we never did.

In the eighties we were receiving about 170,000 letters a year from relatives and friends wanting to surprise or reunite their loved ones. One show that I will never forget featured a young girl searching for her twin brother. They'd been separated as toddlers when they were adopted – and, ever since then, she'd felt that half of her was missing.

We knew we were taking an incredible risk, but we decided to go ahead anyway and brought the girl on to the show.

We had a young floor manager bring her down to the studio floor; and he stood to one side wearing earphones.

'What would you say to your twin brother if you met him?' I asked her.

'I don't know,' she replied. 'I'd probably just fling my arms around him and give him a really big kiss.'

'Well,' I said, 'he's standing right next to you.'

'What?' she said stunned. 'Where?'

'You've already met him. He's the man with the earphones on.'

It was his turn to look stunned.

'Oh my God,' they both said in unison.

Then she did exactly what she'd said she'd do: she flung her arms around him and gave him a great big kiss.

Like his sister, he'd always felt that half of him was missing and I knew they would never lose touch with each other again.

~

To keep *Surprise! Surprise!* fresh, I did a lot of work on Cilla-ising the show and reinventing the style. That meant I was unable to use the autocue and had to remember *everything* – dates, places, names, something I can do on the floor, whereas off stage I can't even recall what I was doing yesterday. My head is usually a clutter, but there's magic on the set, and when I see the red light, another part of my brain switches on. I've never used an idiot board, which amazes me and everyone else.

Surprise! Surprise! may have been sixty minutes of fun and glamour, but making it was very demanding physically and emotionally. A two- or three-minute 'Cillagram' could take two days of filming, and I had to make sure the surprise really was a surprise when people were reunited. There were also disappointments. We might take on a man who said he was looking for his sister. My fabulous researchers would spend several months finding her, only to discover that she didn't want to see her brother. Sometimes the hurt ran so deep that the person was adamant that they wouldn't take part in the show.

'I wouldn't talk to that feller if he were the last person on earth,' one woman said to me. 'He's no brother of mine.' At times like that I felt so grateful for the warm, loving family that I had around me.

~

The trouble with working all the time, though, is that you don't get enough time to exercise. It was 1988 and I was forty-five years old, and I knew I was getting a bit overweight. My arms, legs and hips were still slim, but I'd put on the pounds on my bust (I'd never really had a bust before) and my waist. Nevertheless, when we arrived in Spain for a six-week holiday in June – the longest break Bobby and I had had in twenty years – I was carrying a chip pan in a plastic bag. When a customs guy started to eye this suspiciously, I mimed how we cooked chips in England. It was bizarre, there I was demonstrating cutting up potatoes and putting them in the pan, and there was Bobby, Robert, Ben and Jack all nodding away like the noddy dogs you see in cars. When we were eventually waved through, I knew the guy was thinking, 'Ah, ze Inglish, all crazy.'

Chip butties were a great favourite on that holiday and, not surprisingly, I weighed nine and a half stone when we returned to Denham. I didn't actually notice this until I put on one of my favourite dresses. I say put on, but actually I wriggled into it like a snake trying to climb back into its skin and the zip wouldn't budge. Bobby walked in just as I was struggling with it.

'I've got news for you, Bobby,' I said. 'We're going on a diet.'

'We?'

'Have you seen those spare tyres you're carrying?'

'I thought they made me look cuddly.'

'About as cuddly as a rubber raft,' I told him. 'Lemon chicken, veggies and no pudding from now on.'

'Maybe a glass of champagne occasionally?' Bobby replied, eyeing himself in the full-length mirror.

'*Very* occasionally,' I muttered.

As I'd just read about the Scarsdale Diet, I decided it was time to retire the chip pan. In all, I'd gained one and a half stone and I was determined to get back to eight stone, my weight in the sixties. By September 1988, when we started the fourth series of *Blind Date*, I was already able to pull up the zips on my dresses. True, I still had to take a deep breath, but the diet was working.

For the new series, we'd revamped the sets, bought a spanking new sofa and employed a video-cameraman to follow the winning contestants and capture their reactions on their dates. We always had to take our prime-time competitors into account, and that month, newsreader Sue Lawley's BBC chat show was being launched. I read in the paper that she'd signed 'a three-year contract worth £500,000' – making her the third highest paid woman on TV after Ester Rantzen and Cilla Black! 'Cor,' I thought, 'I've reached the top of the chart.'

Surprise! Surprise! was still rockin' on, but *Blind Date* had really won the nation's heart. When people continued to say, 'Oh, no, I never watch it', that was a sure guarantee they never missed it. Come coffee breaks on Monday, after the show had aired at the weekend, what were people talking about? *Blind Date*. 'Why did the guy from Norwich pick number three, that awful girl from Liverpool, when it was clear that number one was every woman's dream?' 'What did you think of Cilla's outfit? Skirt's a bit short. Nice legs, though. Hey, if you've got it, flaunt it.'

~

What's It All About?

In 1988, I'd been in show business for twenty-five years. My ever-loyal Circle of Fans decided there should be a special event for my 'silver jubilee', and on the afternoon of 17 September, they filled the Chelsfield Room in London's Royal Festival Hall. All the proceeds from the stalls, raffles and auctions went to Birthright, and I turned up in black trousers, a green top and a green jacket designed to show that I was the same girl I'd been twenty-five years ago – not quite an eight-stoner, but getting there. I'd lost nearly ten pounds, and Bobby had lost twelve. In the evening, I changed into a lemon mini-dress for a night-to-remember concert there. The BBC sent its sixty-five piece orchestra with musical director Ronnie Hazlehurst, and lots of people I'd worked with over the years joined the bill. For the second half I changed into a silver, full-length gown that showed every curve (yes, they were back) and the fans gave me some heart-warming cheers.

Not to be outdone, LWT spoiled me a week later with its own '25th Anniversary Reception' at the Savoy Hotel, and gave me a massive cake bearing the words 'LWT Says Congratulations for 25 Years on the Box, Cilla'. The cake had to be massive to get all that on. It was ten feet tall with twenty-five tiers, and I had to climb a ladder to cut it!

~

On 16 October, I found myself sitting in a dingy room at Broadcasting House, fielding eight of my then-favourite records for *Desert Island Discs*. It was the second time I'd been on the show; the first was with Roy Plomley in 1964, when I was just twenty-one and appearing at the Palladium with Frankie Vaughan. This time my choices were: 'Tobacco Being Discovered' (Bob Newhart), 'Everything I Own' (David Gates/ Bread), 'Why Do Fools Fall In Love?' (Frankie Lymon and The Teenagers), 'Stay With Me Baby' (Lorraine Ellison), 'You Send Me' (Sam Cooke), 'Long Tall Sally' (Little Richard), 'Land Of Hope And Glory' and 'The Long And Winding Road' by John, Paul, George and Ringo. For my book, I chose *Aesop's Fables,* which I'd won all those years ago for good atten-dance at St Anthony's, and for my luxury I decided on a manicure set and nail varnish. After all, even if you're on a desert island, you don't have to let yourself go.

The next year, 1989, a truly awful tragedy hit the headlines – a horror that Bobby and I could never get out of our minds. In April, during an FA Cup semi-final between Liverpool and Nottingham Forest, scores of football fans died from crush injuries at the Hillsborough Stadium, Sheffield. It was Britain's worst-ever sporting disaster and our city of Liverpool was in deep mourning. Six weeks later, I joined a host of Liverpudlian entertainers for a charity show at the Empire, Liverpool. With my heart breaking for the families, I sang 'Alfie' and 'Liverpool Lullaby', and then the entire cast and the audience stood to sing our Liverpool anthem, 'You'll Never Walk Alone'.

Hillsborough was an unbelievable tragedy – one that we Liverpudlians are still reeling from today. Yet even this terrible event could not change the fact that I had so much to celebrate in my own life. As 1990 hovered on the horizon, I was in a reflective mood: 'Can it really be over a quarter of a century since I was a guest singer on The Beatles' 1963 Christmas Show?' I kept thinking. Trembling like a leaf, I'd sung Paul's 'Love Of The Loved' and thought at the time it was the highlight of my life. Yet in 1989 alone there'd been so many highlights I'd almost lost count.

Our wonderful boys were eighteen, fourteen and eight years old. I was named 'Favourite Female Television Personality of 1988' at a *TV Times* 'do' in February, and IBA 'TV Personality of the Year' in April. And I'd had a racehorse and a rose named after me: the rose was a fragrant red bloom with yellow on its underside, and the racehorse, a sleek and beautiful mare, ended up costing me a fortune in fivers because she never won a race, at least not when I had money on her. Best of all, in January, while the sixth series of *Surprise! Surprise!* was being beamed into millions of homes, Bobby and I had celebrated our twentieth wedding anniversary with a glorious month in the tropical paradise of the Seychelles. As we relaxed in the luxury of our hotel and basked in the sunshine, I could think of no greater happiness than knowing that Bobby and I were each other's for ever.

partthree

25

Hanging On

It was a few days before Christmas of 1989, and we had just arrived in my dressing room at the Wimbledon Theatre, where I was enjoying being Aladdin in the panto. I was unpacking my things and unwrapping my costume when the telephone rang.

'I'll get it,' Bobby said.

It was Penny on the phone. After a moment I turned round to see Bobby, still holding the handset. His shoulders had sagged and all the colour had drained from his face. I knew that something terrible had happened.

'What's happened?' I asked urgently.

At the other end of the line, Penny was doing her best to break the news gently, but she was obviously distraught.

Jack, she was telling Bobby, had had a terrible accident on his bike. He was cycling along the lane when he hit a tree, fell off, and banged the side of his head, knocking himself unconscious. Fortunately, some dustbin men saw what happened, called an ambulance, and looked after him until it arrived.

Bobby grabbed his coat and ran from the theatre. I was in shock, but the show went on – even if it felt as though my whole being was with Bobby as he raced to the hospital.

When he arrived at Jack's bedside, it was even scarier than we had feared. Jack's eyes were open, but he didn't recognise Bobby. The fall, Bobby was told by a young registrar, was so bad that it had knocked one side of his brain and he was suffering from concussion.

'But what does that mean?' Bobby asked. 'Is he going to be OK? He's not going to die, is he?'

There was a bit of reassurance from the consultant who said he was in 'a stable condition', but of course they couldn't promise anything. I've hated that 'stable condition' phrase ever since. What does it mean? OK for now? Completely OK? All's well? When Bobby got back and told me what he'd been told, we began to fear the worst.

For over a week, Jack was never left alone. Day and night, one of us would sit by his bed. I went in the mornings, then, working in shifts, Bobby and Penny took over for the rest of the day and night – and Robert, now aged eighteen and Ben, fourteen, also made daily visits. We'd sit at the end of Jack's bed waiting for him to show a flicker of recognition, but it never came. We also brought in his drawings and paintings, but he showed no sign of recognising any of them.

It was terrifying – absolutely heartbreaking – and one of those times when being a performer made everything so much worse. I would be sitting there, holding his hand, willing him to get better, when a car would arrive, toot its horn and I would have to rush off to Wimbledon, slap on the greasepaint, and go on stage. Before every entrance – matinée and evening – I'd burst into floods of tears, convinced I couldn't go on, then I'd pull myself together.

My own little eight-year-old might be lying in a hospital bed, where he might never fully recover, but I could not let people down. Bobby always spurred me on. It was the way I had been brought up and trained and that's what I instinctively thought was the right thing to do.

Day after slow day we waited, then suddenly whatever it was that had slipped out of place inside Jack's head slipped back into place and he was on the mend.

Hanging On

The words, 'mum', 'dad', 'Robert', 'Ben' and 'I want to come home' had never sounded so sweet. He was finally allowed home on New Year's Eve, and needless to say, it was the best New Year ever!

After such a shock, it took all of us a while longer to accept that we had got him back, that he was not permanently brain-damaged, and that soon he would be his normal, mischievous self again – but slowly we began to trust that all was well.

Once he was back home after his ten days in hospital, clever little boy that he was, he immediately started putting the loss of his memory to good use, especially when it was his turn to do a chore, but we soon got wise to that!

I was so relieved when the panto closed at the end of January. Now I could spend all day every day with him, away from the tension of the hospital. The next series of *Surprise! Surprise!* was due on the screen in the middle of February but, thankfully, I'd finished all the work for that. The only danger now was that I would smother Jack to death with love!

It's not easy after such a terrible accident to let go – and each of us, including Robert and Ben, were over-protective for a time. My heart was in my mouth the first time he climbed back on his bike, but I knew I must not wrap him in cotton wool. I could only close my eyes and pray. After all, I hadn't been much older than him when I'd been hanging off the backs of lorries.

'Try not to worry, Cil,' Bobby kept saying, but I knew he was just as scared as I was; and Robert and Ben were forever shouting, 'Where are you, Jack?', 'What are you doing, Jack?'

Jack had never been so much in demand!

On the work front, apart from starting preparations for the next series of *Blind Date*, which was to be screened in late September, things were not too frantic throughout the early part of the year, and to take my mind off the accident – and the dreadful, haunting thoughts of what might have become of Jack – Bobby suggested that we should look for a flat, a pied-à-terre, in London that was within easy reach of the LWT studios.

We found a two-bedroomed penthouse in a handsome, red-brick Victorian building not far from the Houses of Parliament. The rooms were large, light and airy, not overlooked, and the flat had a lovely roof-terrace garden. We felt we'd be happy and secure there, especially as there was a huge Metropolitan Police headquarters just along the road. Linda Barker, who is now a star on *Changing Rooms* but who was then an unknown young designer, did the flat up for me – she even painted the walls herself. It also presented me with some lovely retail therapy – I had great fun diving in and out of Harrods buying lamps, curtains and rugs.

Having the flat in town meant that we now had the best of both worlds – a country house at the weekend and somewhere to use as an office and a place to stay when I was working or we were out with friends.

~

The first year of the new decade was going well. Jack had made a complete recovery and we thought our family troubles were behind us. We were all fine – all doing OK. But in truth we were in for another mega-shock, one that would scar everyone involved for the rest of their lives.

On 25 September, a couple of days before the sixth series of *Blind Date* was to be transmitted, I was returning home to Denham in a chauffeur-driven car. It was just after eight p.m. on a Tuesday when suddenly, only about half a mile from the house, we found there were cars pulled up all over the place. There'd obviously just been some kind of accident. My driver pulled over so that he could call 999 on the carphone. I got out of the car and as I did so, I saw a young man staggering around at the other side of the road.

'Oh, God!' I cried out. 'It's our Robert! What's happened?'

Suddenly terrified, I rushed to his side.

'Robert … Robert,' I kept saying, trying to get a hold on him, trying to get him to calm down.

Hanging On

At first, he was too shocked to say anything. He just kept reeling around, pointing behind him, before breaking down completely and sobbing in my arms. Slowly, I began to take in the scene. I realised that he had been involved somehow. Then, as I was trying to check my dazed son for injuries, the ambulance arrived and to my horror I saw the paramedics placing stretchers inside it.

As I began to piece all the details together it all started to make horrible sense. There'd been a terrible accident. Robert had been driving. Someone was very badly hurt.

It was, I learned later, a horror which had come from nowhere. Robert, who was at Oxford Brookes University at the time, was on his way back to his digs in Oxford. As he was turning his Renault 5 out of a side road on to the main road, his car had collided head-on with a Suzuki 750cc motorbike in the nearside lane, driven by a young man called Richard Potter, a twenty-five-year-old social worker. Richard and his pillion passenger, Mary Sholto-Douglas, were flung from the bike and badly injured, but Robert, who could have been decapitated by the impact and flying glass, was only dazed and suffering from minor cuts.

You can only imagine our horror when we learned from the police a little later that Richard, who had an eighteen-month-old daughter Ruby, and a partner, Joanna Thurston, who was three months' pregnant, had suffered brain damage and a fractured skull and had died in Mount Vernon Hospital, Northwood; and Mary, his pillion passenger, had suffered a serious leg injury.

Robert was breathalysed at the scene of the accident, of course, but the test proved negative. We were all shocked and traumatised, but we still had each other. Richard Potter's family had lost everything. We thought incessantly about what they must be going through. But I'm sure that nobody can understand that kind of loss unless it's happened to you.

Meanwhile, like any mother, my instinct was to comfort Robert as headlines appeared about 'Cilla's son'. Bobby and I had always done our best to protect our boys from any press intrusion into their lives. We wanted them to grow up as normally as possible. For this reason we'd always held press interviews in hotels, theatres or television studios. But once the news of the accident leaked out to the press, it was headlines in all the papers, and the boys experienced the worst side of what it meant to be my kids.

Whatever I said was going to sound wrong to Richard's grieving family – they had lost a husband, father and son, and I hadn't. And however much I wanted to talk to them, to try to let them know how desperately we wished this awful thing had not happened, the lawyers refused to allow us to make direct contact. For the first time in my life, I received hate mail. Publicly I had to deal with the cameras and privately I had to help my son through his dreadful experience. Within the walls of my home, though, I wept buckets for Richard's and Mary's families.

I know that Richard's father, Roy Potter, and his wife Noreen, and Richard's partner Joanna Thurston felt that we got most of the attention, understanding and condolences because of the way the press handled it. Still very raw from the tragedy, I mentioned Robert's accident and broke down in tears at a Variety Club pre-Christmas lunch at the London Hilton, where Frankie Howerd was the guest speaker. Richard's family were angry and offended.

People say that you know who your true friends are when calamities hit you, and this was certainly true of Frankie. He was absolutely wonderful. The boys loved him, and he came to our aid at the time of Robert's accident and gave us all wise counsel and support. Personally, I don't think we could have coped half so well without him

I was presented with a silver heart at that Variety Club lunch for my work in show business and for charity, and that really upset Roy Potter. Joanna, too, couldn't forgive me for breaking down at the Variety Club lunch.

'When you see Cilla Black on television and read the interviews,' she said, 'she seems so nice. I don't want to sound like some jealous whinger, but I hoped against hope she would make some effort to contact me. I don't want any admission of guilt, I just want to know she feels sorry for my loss. I don't want to believe that we are only the forgotten victims. Ruby hasn't forgotten. When she sees a motorbike in the street she still shouts "Daddy, Daddy!" '

As I read these words in the press I was even more heartbroken. I cried for hours at home, but I didn't make any general comments to the press about all the criticism, because I knew would only make the situation worse. As I had a regular column in the *Daily Star* at that time, though, I decided to write the following:

This morning my son Robert is going to Uxbridge Coroner's Court for the inquest into the tragic death of a young motorcyclist who was in collision with his car.

As a loving, caring, concerned mother, my place is at Robert's side, giving him comfort and support. But I won't be there today, although his father will. And no doubt some people will ask why, if we're such a close family, I can't take a morning off.

The truth is, that I shall be sitting indoors, listening to the ticking of the mantelpiece clock until he comes home. I desperately want to be at the inquest, but if I turn up it could become a circus. There will be photographers and sightseers, and the grieving family of the poor motorcyclist Richard Potter will have a lot of attention focused upon them at a time when they least want it. But by staying at home, I hope the way will be clear for the inquest to take place in a calm and dignified manner.

I'd hate to draw attention away from the investigation into the circumstances of Richard's death.

I have been publicly criticised by Richard's father for not sending a wreath to the funeral and for not getting in touch.

Richard's girlfriend, Joanna Thurston, has called me uncaring and selfish. She is expecting Richard's second child in March and they already had an eighteen-month old daughter, Ruby.

But I am not surprised at the fury directed at me by Richard's family. If my twenty-five-year-old son, or the father of my children had died as unexpectedly, I'd be angry, too.

The fact is that Bobby, Robert and I were advised that we should NOT attempt to get in touch with Richard's family. We were warned that in these harsh times even a message of regret could be misconstrued as an admission of liability or guilt.

That apart, we didn't know how Richard's family would react to an approach from us.

We're a very private family and in similar circumstances – please God forbid – we'd want to be left alone to mourn.

If there is one consolation it is that the comments are not being made about Robert, they are aimed at me.

After twenty-seven years as an entertainer, I'm used to criticism. I don't like it, of course, but I have to put up with it.

But it is our Robert, twenty years old and very much an independent young man, who has to live with the fact that Richard Potter was killed and his passenger, Mary Sholto-Douglas, was injured.

Since then we've all frequently wept real tears and not a day has gone by without us thinking of Richard.

If I could turn the clock back I would. But I can't. And because I'm Cilla Black I can't even exercise my right as a mother to be with my son today.

I'm not looking for sympathy. Please save all that for the family that Richard left behind.

Bobby and Robert were present at the two and a half hour hearing when the coroner, John Burton, ruled that Richard had died accidentally. Robert stood silently in the witness box as his statement saying he pulled out into a clear road 'then heard a crash' was read out.

The hurt and controversy, though, did not end with the inquest. The Crown Prosecution Service said it was considering a careless driving charge.

I cried myself to sleep that night, burying my head in the pillow so that Robert wouldn't hear me and be even more upset than he was already.

Roy Potter told the press he was going to sue for damages – no matter what the CPS decided.

'We will be seeking very considerable compensation,' he said. 'The money will be for the support of my son's child.'

When the case came up at the magistrates' court in Beaconsfield, Buckinghamshire, Robert pleaded guilty to careless driving. Once again, for the same reasons that I had had to avoid attending the inquest, I could not go with him. The magistrate said the sentence was only to be based on how the driving fell below what was to be expected of a 'reasonable and prudent driver'. Robert was fined £250 and given five penalty points.

The civil settlement was reached two years after the fatal crash, when Robert's insurance company and lawyers finalised a deal with Roy Potter's lawyers. It centred on compensation for Richard's partner and his daughter Ruby and Nathan, the son he never saw, and further costs were also met.

Throughout it all, my heart and Bobby's heart were torn between the tragic death of young Richard and the horror of this experience for our own son. There was no consoling Robert and, to this day, when we are together at Christmas, we are all haunted by the horror of Richard's death and the knowledge that his partner and children do not have him at their side. That's when we feel the worst.

You can't take pain away from your child. You can't always make it better. As a mother, you can never really get inside your child's head and know all the suffering that's going on, but I can see the shadow settling on his face and I know when he's thinking about it.

What's It All About?

He was only twenty at the time of the accident and he aged. He looked like an old man and had terrible rings under his eyes. But I say none of this to detract from the far greater grief that Richard's family suffered. Like so many people in this situation, I just wish I could turn the clocks back and kiss everything better. I'm haunted by the thought that if I'd arrived home just a few minutes earlier that night, Robert and I would have chatted in the drive, and Richard and Mary would have driven safely by.

26

Through The Years

The New Year – 1991 – came in with a bang – literally.

We were filming *Blind Date* at the Shepherd's Bush Theatre in January when the electrical current shot 350 volts through a circuit that could only cope with 240. As viewers in fifty homes nearby settled down to watch the programme, their televisions exploded and their sitting rooms were showered with glass and filled with smoke. Fax and answering machines were also affected. I know *Blind Date* was supposed to be about explosive passions, but that was taking things too far!

The autumn series of *Blind Date* drew in record audiences and, very important for commercial telly, proved it was still an advertiser's dream – a prime-time show with a massive audience to whom they could sell anything from champagne to washing-up liquid. During the weekend of 11 November, the programme was top of the ratings, with over fourteen million viewers. I was really chuffed. We had all put a lot of hard work into it and it was lovely to see the crew's faces when they heard the news.

From the start of the show, my dearest wish had been that one of the winning couples would find true romance.

'If that happens,' I said, 'I'll cry my eyes out.'

And, in February 1991, after six years of match-making, it finally happened. Bobby and I were on holiday in Barbados when LWT telephoned us to say that Sue Middleton and Alex Tatham, who had met two years earlier on the programme, had announced their engagement and were planning to marry in October. What's more, their news had pushed the Gulf War off the tabloids' front pages!

My first thought was, 'Oh, great. I can start looking for a really smashing hat.' But then I thought, 'No, I mustn't outdo the bride and bridegroom's mothers. They're the ones who should wear the most marvellous hats. I must keep a low profile!'

In early March, Bobby signed a new three-year contract with LWT, to run from 1992 to 1995, which made me the highest-paid woman on British television – the 'Queen of LWT'. That, I decided, was a moment to crack open a bottle or two of champagne.

'I've no intention of stopping work when the contract runs out,' I said to the journalists at a press gathering. 'I don't want to be like Frank Sinatra and keep making comebacks.'

Over the next few months, the newspapers kept coming up with names that the BBC was putting forward as competition. These included Bruce Forsyth, my mate Jimmy Tarbuck, and Lulu. Perhaps I should have shaken in my shoes, but I didn't!

When *Blind Date* returned to the screen for its seventh series in September, it seemed, horror of horrors, that Bruce Forsyth's *Generation Game* might be winning the battle of the ratings, but we came out top in the end with an audience of over fourteen million. I was very proud of that – and LWT celebrated the hundredth edition of *Blind Date* with a party at the Savoy. The cake, topped with one hundred candles, proved to be the star of the party. Having melted under the powerful heat of the cameras, it caught fire and I had to flee!

~

In the months leading up to Sue and Alex's October wedding, I'd given a lot of thought to the hat I was going to wear. I wanted one that was a bit different, but which at the same time allowed me to stay out of the spotlight. So I went to Philip Treacy, the 'British accessory designer of the year', and he created a cloche style that on the day – and afterwards – attracted the kind of attention I hadn't bargained for. Everyone hated it – and that hat, which the reporters just never stopped writing about, became almost as famous as *Blind Date* itself!

The wedding, however, was a truly wonderful occasion, which we filmed and screened the next day, drawing viewing figures of seventeen million. In fact, it was estimated that Sue and Alex's wedding was watched by more people than the wedding of the Duke and Duchess of York! It really was a Cinderella occasion. Alex came from a wealthy North Country family, and while Sue may not have been a pauper, she had a strong Brummy accent and wasn't out of the same drawer. But love truly conquered all obstacles, and although the wedding started with a certain amount of friction, the day ended beautifully. They have a fabulous marriage, and fabulous children who are an absolute delight. I am very proud of the whole family.

~

Christmas 1991 was extra special that year because me mam, whose eightieth birthday was in December, and my Auntie Nellie joined us at Denham. Earlier, we had had a conservatory built just off the dining room to give us an extra seating area, and it was finished just in time for the festivities. Bobby, bless him, had even arranged for the top windows to be made of stained glass featuring the 'Cilla Rose', the one that had been named after me at the Chelsea Flower Show in 1989.

Christmas has always been a big event for me ever since I was a child, and I've always loved going to town on the decorations. We had two large trees, one in the hall that I dressed, and the other in the living room which the boys did, using all the decorations which I had hoarded from when they'd made them as kids. It was hard for Bobby to enjoy it in quite the same way – his mother had died just after Christmas when he was eleven, and it was always a sad time for him – but he wanted me and the boys to be happy.

We always laid the table at least five days before Christmas, so that I could add more and more decorations to it and I always insisted that everything had to match. I'd plan the table setting well in advance so that I could be sure the colour scheme would be perfect. Bobby was in charge of the turkey and got up very early to do the stuffing, so that by eleven-thirty we could have a glass of champagne and open our presents. Me mam was difficult about presents – I always wanted to buy her extravagant things like jewellery, but she'd always ask for the receipt! She didn't approve of the opulence of our Christmas, but Auntie Nellie loved it, and really entered into the spirit of things.

I videoed everything – the table when it was beautifully laid and the table after the meal when it looked as if a bomb had hit it.

After lunch we played Trivial Pursuit with the boys, now aged twenty, sixteen and ten, watched the Queen's speech on TV, and then the video I had made. We also watched *Blind Date's Christmas Cracker*, which featured a visit to Lapland for eight of our contestants. The making of that was a scream! Although we'd been assured by the weatherman that there would be snow when the couples and camera crew landed at Rovaniemi, in Finnish Lapland, there was none to be seen! The group had to be bussed 150 miles north, inside the Arctic Circle, before snow could be found. In the studio, Frankie Howerd and I did a round-up of the last six years of *Blind Date*, featuring the most memorable moments, the hates, the loves, the perfect occasions and the times when everything went wrong.

It really was the most perfect Christmas Day.

~

The ninth series of *Surprise! Surprise!* began in April, but while I was doing the preparation work for this series, I was constantly worrying about Frankie. He'd been admitted to hospital in February with a viral infection and, although he'd been discharged after treatment and a short stay, he hadn't really been his old self since. By the end of March, he was readmitted to the Fitzroy Nuffield Hospital for more treatment. Then, when his condition suddenly deteriorated, he was rushed to the Harley Street Clinic. The news upset everybody who knew him.

Hoping that we would be able to avoid the press who had gathered outside the Harley Street Clinic, Bobby and I dashed there the moment Dennis Haymer, Frankie's partner and manager, phoned us.

Lying there in his bed, Frankie was very pale, tired and gaunt, but we sat there holding his hand and mopping his brow until he drifted into a deep sleep. I was shaken because, as well as him being obviously ill, it was the first time I'd ever seen Frankie without his wig on.

'He must be all right,' I told the waiting press as we left the clinic, 'because he tried to kiss me and he was smiling.'

But in my heart I knew he was feeling pretty grotty and that I'd better start praying for the friend I had first worked with in 1966.

At first my prayers seemed to be answered. Frankie was discharged from the Clinic on 19 April, but four days later he had a heart attack at his Kensington home and died in the ambulance on the way to hospital. He was seventy-two.

I was devastated. We had only just started to recover from the shock of Jack's bicycle accident and Robert's car accident, and now we had lost one of our dearest friends.

It was Frankie who had taught me about stage craft, how to be ready for every eventuality: a colleague who 'freezes', a camera that locks, an autocue that suddenly goes berserk and speeds up or slows down. He was, like most Pisces, a larger-than-life character, who had a habit of putting on a great show of bravado, but it was all an act. In reality, he was a rather shy, sensitive person who was easily hurt.

We had shared so much and, although he was always a very private man who kept most people at more than arm's length, he had trusted me enough to confide in me about being gay. We used to have really deep conversations about his life. He was very religious and he always felt very guilty about being homosexual.

'I envy you,' he once said to me. 'I *really* envy you.'

This upset me a lot at the time because I'd always thought envy was worse than jealousy. But Frankie was just trying to express how much he resented being gay at times and how much he would have loved to get married and have a family.

'Don't think I like being the way I am,' he once said. 'If there was a pill I could take that would change my nature, I'd take it.'

I thought that was very sad, as he'd been with Dennis for many years. Dennis was a very handsome guy with blond hair, and we used to go to the South of France for holidays with them both, although Frankie very rarely brought him to our Sunday dinners at Denham. I don't think he wanted to share those special moments, even with the lovely Dennis.

He was my father figure at that time. He would have hated me saying that, but it was true. He was the man I turned to when Bobby couldn't help me because he was going through the same problem himself.

In the early days of our friendship with Frankie, Bobby was a socialist, which drove Frankie mental.

'How can you call yourself a socialist,' he used to say, 'while you're sitting here in all this opulence? You're a champagne socialist, that's what you are, Bobby.'

I would try to keep out of it, but then he'd have a go at me.

'Look at this place, Cilla. Some socialist you are.'

In quieter moments, though, especially when the kids came in to say goodnight, he'd really let us see how much he cared for us all. The boys would give him a kiss and a hug and go off to bed. Frankie was always joking that he was the father of all my children. He'd known them since they were babies and he really loved them.

After he died, Robert was very upset, and one day, when he was missing Frankie like hell, he said: 'Do you think Betty [Frankie's sister] would mind if I had his old tweed coat?'

'I'm sure she wouldn't,' I said.

Betty was delighted; and Robert still wears it sometimes because it reminds him of Frankie.

~

The funeral on 29 April was held in the medieval church of St Gregory, near Frankie's country home in Weare, Somerset. Then a memorial service was held for him in July at St Martin-in-the-Fields Church, Trafalgar Square.

'I'm just very proud to have known him,' I said at the memorial. 'I could talk for a trillion years about dear Frankie's life and never get bored. He used to invite himself round for Sunday dinner with the subtlety of an avalanche – and, oh, how we loved him for that. I used to give him roast lamb, week after week, year in year out, because he kept saying how much he liked it. Then, one Sunday, he rang up and asked what we were having for lunch?

' "Roast lamb, of course," I replied.

' "Can't you cook anything else?" he asked wearily.'

In his will, he left instructions for June Whitfield and me to take some souvenirs from his personal belongings. June, he suggested, might like a marquetry table, which she did, and I selected some posters and pictures – in particular a framed poster from his 1973 film *The House in Nightmare Park*.

Whenever I look at this, I think of him. Our Sundays have never been the same since he said goodbye.

~

Robert, now at the end of his last year at college, had taken his finals, and we all had to be patient and await his results. Only a mother can know how proud I was when we learned that he had graduated. Out came the champagne for a very special toast. His plan now was to do a playwriting course at the Royal Court Theatre in London's Sloane Square, and then go on to write his own scripts and plays. Before that, he had got himself a job working for Bob Geldof's production company Planet 24, making the coffee, followed by some work in television. Bobby and I caught a glimpse of him on *The Big Breakfast* one day holding an umbrella over a presenter. All I was interested in was whether he was wearing a clean shirt and had combed his hair. Old habits are hard to break!

Ben, meanwhile, was tackling his A-levels.

In 1992, we were celebrating Elizabeth II's fortieth jubilee and there was a gala charity event in the presence of the Queen and HRH the Duke of Edinburgh at Earl's Court. Five hundred celebrities were there to mark the occasion – and my contribution was to sing my 1968 hit 'Step Inside Love'. It was that event that turned my thoughts to how I'd feel when I became fifty the following year. I was dreading it. I didn't like the thought of being so old because I didn't *feel* old. I still felt twenty, but I knew that life was running away from me, and I wasn't in control of it. Where had all the years gone? I only knew that I'd worked very hard and enjoyed nearly every minute of it.

I was also very aware that, now more than ever, I needed to keep as fit and healthy as I could. I loved food, but I had to be disciplined because my job called for it. 'On the day I retire, though,' I promised myself, 'the diet routine will stop.'

That wasn't made any easier by the fact that Bobby was a great cook. One of Bobby's best dishes was his Christmas stuffing for the turkey. I asked him once how he made it, and he just winked at me and said, 'I'm not telling – it's a trade secret!' I never did get the recipe. When I cooked, it was all plain stuff but, even before Frankie came into our life, I always did a really good Sunday roast. I love the taste of lamb, beef and roast pork – and crackling – and when I was in London on Fridays, I'd phone Penny and say: 'Can you get some pork for the weekend – and a couple of hearts.'

I love hearts – love all offal – but the kids used to go mental when they saw the hearts and all the little tubes leading from them on the work surface.

'How can you eat *that*?' one or other of them would ask, pulling a face.
'Just watch me,' I'd say.

They've never ever eaten offal and I'm sure that's because both Bobby and I were always tucking into liver and kidneys. Even today, Jack will say to me at weekends, 'How can you eat hearts?'

But that's the way I was brought up. It was considered natural in my Scottie Road home when I was a kid, and I never questioned it later when I had kids of my own. I don't know why they found it so strange, but they did. I think, although they do eat meat, they just tuned into a lot of vegetarian ideas when they were young.

We kept chickens at Denham and even I couldn't eat little Clover, because she gave us eggs. But I had no problems with eating a bought chicken with no personal associations.

Once we bought a suckling pig for the weekend roast, and when the kids saw it with its eyes closed, they were horrified.

'If you eat that, we'll have nightmares,' they said.

After it had been in the oven for a while, Bobby said to me, 'Have you checked the eyes?'

'They're closed,' I said.

He took it out of the oven and they were open!

'Aaaaaagh!' the boys all said in unison.

They wouldn't eat any of it. 'It looks like a baby,' they kept saying to each other, disgusted. Actually, even Bobby and I didn't much like the look of it. It was a bit like cooking – and eating – a human being!

When I started to moan about some of the girlfriends the boys were bringing home, Bobby always said, 'Don't interfere, Cil. The more you interfere, the more they'll do it.'

He thought we should let the boys live their own lives and make their own mistakes. I found this *very* hard, but I knew he was right and I tried to do as he did.

~

As part of the celebrations to mark my thirtieth year in show business, we released a definitive album for the 1990s, a video, a book and a TV special, all linked to the theme of 'Cilla Black Through the Years'. I began recording the songs, some of which were long-time favourites, while others were new ones specially written for the album, in March. As far as I was concerned, the bonus of this project was the chance to involve some of my friends. So we included duets with Cliff, Barry Manilow and Dusty. Cliff and I celebrated our long friendship by singing 'That's What Friends Are For', Barry and I did 'You'll Never Walk Alone' from the show *Carousel*, and Dusty and I opted for a totally new song, 'Heart and Soul'. Always tickled by the same sort of things, Dusty and I never stopped laughing at the recording session, and in the breaks we ate lots of her favourite Thai food.

Barry had neatly turned the tables on me during one of his concerts at the Royal Albert Hall. I'd had a mother and daughter on *Surprise! Surprise!*. The mother was in on the surprise for her daughter, but she'd far rather have gone to Barry Manilow's concert instead, so I surprised *her* by announcing I'd got them tickets for it – and I was coming too! Barry got the daughter up on stage to sing a duet, and then he totally took *me* by surprise by getting me up to sing 'You'll Never Walk Alone'.

'You've still got your voice,' he said to me after the concert. 'It hasn't gone away and it's not going to go away.' That was the best kind of reassurance he could have given me as I approached my fiftieth.

During this time, I also had to give some thought to my appearance. A photo session with John Swannell at Broughton Castle was being planned for the cover of the *Through the Years* album and video and for the book that was coming out at the same time. The image-makers at Sony suggested a new hairstyle, and they consulted my hairdresser Leslie about it. He suggested a shorter and more modern version of the layered look that he had created for me in the early seventies. I liked it once I was used to it, but it was a bugger to manage and I had to keep going back to Leslie to have it redone.

A poignant moment during these busy days was when June Whitfield and I unveiled a plaque to Frankie for the Dead Comics Society. This was placed on the Kensington house that had been Frankie's London home. I wept buckets that day. I was just so sad that Frankie wasn't around to share in my fiftieth birthday celebrations.

As it happened, I also shed tears on my birthday. A couple of days earlier, my brother John phoned to say that me mam had pneumonia and was in hospital. Fearing the worst, I cancelled my birthday party. I just couldn't get into the mood to celebrate while me mam was in hospital. Instead, I flew up to Liverpool and spent my birthday with her. She was really poorly, but she bucked up a bit that day. After I'd seen her and made sure she had everything she needed, I returned to Denham and we had a family meal with the boys. Bobby's very special birthday present to me was a painting by L. S. Lowry. I'd always loved Lowry's matchstick figures and I was over the moon to see it hanging in our living room.

I used to say to Bobby that I would jack it all in when I turned fifty, but he never really believed me. Casting his eyes up to heaven, he'd say, 'Come on, Cil. You'll be singing into a hairbrush in front of the mirror when you're seventy.'

He was right. In truth, I had no desire to give up, and the fact that I still had a very young mind helped, but I wasn't comfortable about being fifty – and I was honest about that. I couldn't stop the ageing process, couldn't not be fifty, but I was certainly not going to act it. 'I'm going to grow old disgracefully,' I told myself, 'and if people don't like me the way I am – *tough*!'

Being fifty didn't change me overnight and it wasn't restricting me in anything I did, but I just felt it was downhill from there on; and, although I kept joking about things dropping off and so on, I knew that – like it or not – things do start to happen to us at that age!

I must have been in a particularly reflective mood at that time, because I kept going up into the loft and sitting there looking at the overflow of my clothes – my Royal Command and Biba dresses – and some of the trophies I'd collected since the Cavern days. Word had obviously got around that I was a hoarder, because one of my early showbiz dresses (it was by Caroline Charles, and I'd worn it to sing 'You're My World' on *Ready, Steady, Go!*) was displayed in London's Victoria and Albert Museum, and Elton John had borrowed some of my Biba clothes for a video, so they did come in useful.

I've still got most of those clothes and hundreds of pair of shoes stuffed in every available space at Denham. Shoes have always been a special weakness of mine, and I have one pair that cost £900. They were set with pieces of diamanté, but at that price it should have been real diamonds!

As part of that year's celebrations, I appeared on *Top of the Pops*. Not having been on it for fifteen years, I found the prospect rather daunting, especially since Robert, Ben and Jack kept chortling at the idea. When I was on the programme, aged twenty-two, I'd said of a male singer who was also on, 'What's that old man doing on *Top of the Pops*'? Now that comment had come back to haunt me. Would the youngsters on the show say the same thing about me?

I needn't have worried. When I walked into the dressing room, it was full of flowers and there was a card which said, 'Welcome home from all at *Top of the Pops*.'

Once I was on the set, surrounded by all those brilliant spotlights, yards of cables, cameras and radiant faces, the years just dropped away. And when I was introduced as 'the person who holds the record for selling more singles in this country than any other British female singer', the young audience greeted me with the kind of cheer any performer would die for. I loved performing 'Through The Years' for them and it made me realise how much I had missed singing to a live audience.

Bobby knew me better than I knew myself – there was absolutely no way I was going to retire just yet.

27

You'll Never Walk Alone

I'd had my gold, if you can call your fiftieth birthday that, and now it was time for my silver. In January 1994, Bobby and I had been married for twenty-five years, and while planning the celebrations I often wondered, 'What would I have done without him?'

The truth is that if he hadn't been there to advise and guide me, I would have accepted all kinds of rubbish, done all the wrong things, and I would probably have had a very different career and found myself retiring early.

No one was a match for Bobby. He was a brilliant businessman who always got the best for me, yet no one resented him. In fact, I think the people at LWT liked him more than they liked me! At production meetings, he had an amazing talent for turning an idea around, so that the people who were against it in the beginning came to believe that they'd thought of it first!

I always felt that if I couldn't look across a room and see his face, I'd die inside. He really was the most selfless person – and the one whose judgement I trusted the most. Whenever anybody told me how terrific I'd been in a show, I always looked to Bobby for confirmation; and if he didn't give his seal of approval, I knew I could have done better. He was the only critic I really listened to, the only person who was really honest with me. We didn't even have to talk. It was all done by telepathy. He always stood at the back of the studio when I was recording *Surprise! Surprise!* and *Blind Date* and we had secret signals, like a tennis player and her coach. We were so close, we were almost joined at the hip.

I couldn't believe it when some journalists suggested that our marriage was 'a sham', that we had only 'stayed together for business reasons'. If that had been true, if we had been unhappy together, we'd have done something about it years before. But it wasn't true. We loved and trusted each other, and were even more in love when we celebrated our silver wedding anniversary than we were when we first married.

I honestly couldn't envisage life without Bobby. I always thought that if anything were to happen to him, I just couldn't go on. I'd have to retire not just from work but from life too.

But fortunately, when we celebrated our silver wedding in Mauritius that year, all was well. We stayed at the fabulous Le Touesserok Hotel, and they put us in a wonderful suite on the beach where Prince Andrew and Fergie had stayed for their honeymoon not long before. We thought it was great. I couldn't get over the fact that we were sitting in the chairs where they had sat – and that our bed was their honeymoon bed!

After Mauritius, we had a family celebration in Liverpool. Me mam, who hadn't been at all well since she had had a bout of pneumonia the previous year, was now in the Carnatic Court nursing home in south Liverpool.

'We might have a lovely surprise when we next come to see you,' I told her.

'Oh? What's that?' she asked intrigued.

'Wait and see,' I said, mysteriously

We knew that Pat Davies was coming over from LA, but we didn't tell Mam because Bobby wasn't sure that Pat would want to see her looking so frail and so ill. 'Perhaps,' he said, 'Pat would rather keep all her lovely memories intact – and remember your mam as she used to be.'

When Pat arrived, Bobby talked to her and said that we would completely understand if she didn't want to go to the nursing home.

'Bobby,' Pat replied firmly, 'of course I want to go. If anything happened to Mrs White and I hadn't seen her while I was in Liverpool, I would never forgive myself.'

My mam was an extremely strong woman and it was a measure of the respect she was held in that everyone, including Bobby, always addressed her as 'Mrs White'. So, Pat and I – and Bobby's brothers, Trevor and Bernard – all went to the nursing home. The staff knew that we were coming and had done Mam's hair and made her look as lovely as possible in the circumstances. Pat walked straight up to my mam and hugged and kissed her, and Mam was so thrilled to see her.

'How's my mother doing today?' I asked the nurse.

'Oh, Mrs White is very lively today,' she replied. 'When I was turning her over this morning, she said. "Do you like garlic, luv? I know you do, because I can smell it on your dress." She's just such a character! We all love looking after her.'

As we sat around the bed talking to Mam, Pat said, 'D'you remember all the times, Mrs White, when I used to stop off on my way home from work to have a cup of coffee with you, because you made the best coffee in Liverpool?'

'Ah,' Mam replied, 'it was Camp coffee, and I used to make it with half milk and half water.'

We all fell about giggling as we reminisced about this coffee, which came as a brown liquid in bottles – and I told them about an occasion when Robert, who had been brought up on Pat's story, went out and bought some.

'Pat keeps banging on about this coffee,' he had said, 'and Dad goes on about it, too, so I bought some and I think it's *awful*.'

'That's because you're not making it right,' I replied.

The next time he came home, I called him into the kitchen and said, 'This is the way Nana used to do it,' and I made it the way me mam used to. I put the steaming mug in front of him. He sipped it and put it down again.

'It's still awful!' he said.

~

At the beginning of February we went to another *Blind Date* wedding. The two contestants had met the previous October: David Fensom was seventy, and Lillian was seventy-one.

There was a lot of pre-wedding publicity in the papers and the *Sun*, recalling the fuss about the hat I'd worn for the Tathams' wedding in 1991, was determined that I shouldn't make another mistake. Having decided to run a 'hat poll', it invited its readers to ring in and nominate which hat, out of the thirteen shown from some of Britain's top milliners, would be the most suitable for me. I was very pleased when over four thousand people rang in to choose the one that I had already found myself in the Escada boutique in New Bond Street. It was made of nettle-green organza. But it still got the thumbs-down from the press and the public after the wedding!

Lillian and David had a civil ceremony, followed by a blessing at a small church in Devon. During the blessing, the rector said, 'And for the wedding of Lillian and David, we must thank God and Cilla.'

I couldn't resist a one-line response. 'That's the first time I've ever had second billing,' I called out, peeved – and everyone fell about laughing.

It was a wonderful day for Lillian and David. Over two thousand people lined the streets to the church, and there were many others leaning out of windows and even up in the trees along the way.

~

Once I'd turned fifty, there was a part of me that was amazed that people still wanted to employ me! But, with offers still coming in, I had to accept that I must have a certain talent beyond that of simply singing, and I began to feel better about my age. When the audience was there, the studio lights were on, and the camera was turning, I still lit up inside and everything started twinkling.

As far as my career was concerned, I realised I would never be completely free of self-doubt. Bobby could lay out twenty articles in which people had written nice things about me, but I would still find the one that criticised me and be crushed by it. I wanted *everybody* to love me, but I realised that there would always be some people who couldn't stand the sight of me. So I just had to look at the ratings and convince myself that the public in general wanted me around.

I certainly wasn't popular with some of the students at Liverpool John Moores University in 1994. The university was named after the man who founded Littlewoods Pools, which was based in Liverpool, and when I heard that the academic board had decided to present me with an honorary degree, I was chuffed. A group of students, however, had protested that I had done nothing to deserve it and that it made a mockery of their own qualifications. If the university went ahead with the presentation, the students planned to wreck the ceremony. I was really disconcerted by all the fuss and, although Bobby tried to smooth things out and protect me from the press fall-out, I turned down the degree.

While all this was going on, I had an opportunity to show just how important my Liverpool links were. I was asked to open the new Vauxhall Bridge that spanned the Leeds–Liverpool canal and linked two housing estates, and some local school kids came along to help me. Soon afterwards the Littlewoods organisation asked me if I would become vice-president of the Charities Trust which it had set up to allow workers to donate to charity directly from their pay packets. I was very happy to accept this invitation. I'd never forgotten my childhood in Liverpool, and the wonderful thing is that wherever I go in the world, I always meet people who have a connection with the city, and that always makes me feel that I'm part of a huge family.

~

What's It All About?

The eleventh series of *Surprise! Surprise!* was the first time that I had carried the show alone. Bob Carolgees had left in December and we had not appointed anyone to replace him. The researchers had to sift through 50,000 requests for that series – but one surprise turn of events left us all horrified.

Three sisters had written in to say that their sister Catherine and her nine-year-old daughter had not been seen since 1971. They wanted details of their sister and niece to be broadcast on our 'Searchline Appeal'. None of us working on the show could have imagined – even in our worst nightmares – that only weeks later detectives investigating the mass murderer Fred West would discover bodies – including that of his first wife, Catherine – at one of the houses where he had lived …

We inevitably heard many sad stories on *Surprise! Surprise!*, but this had to be one of the saddest and most shocking.

~

During the summer, David Liddiment asked Bobby if I could be persuaded to rejoin the BBC. Bobby told him that the offer had come too late. Negotiations had already been completed with LWT for another two-year contract. I was very flattered to be asked by the Beeb – and almost wished I'd been asked earlier – but, at the end of the day, it's not the company you work for that's important, it's the ideas for the shows.

'You're very highly regarded by ITV,' Bobby told me. 'They say that you're a star they can't afford to lose and you are worth every penny of your latest contract.'

Not long after this, David Liddiment left the BBC to move to LWT himself – but I'm sure that was pure coincidence!

~

Things to keep us on our toes were always happening on *Blind Date*, and that was a huge part of its appeal. That autumn we had an Italian count who kept saying things that I felt were a bit 'iffy' I had to keep shouting 'Edit!' Later on, he confessed he was gay! Two contestants then told us of their marriage plans, but not with the partners they had dated: one girl married the man who cut her hair for the show, and another married a South African fan who had seen her on the programme and got in touch.

'It's been my ambition to be on *Blind Date* since I started watching it when I was nine years old', one contestant told me.

This made me realise what a national institution we had become. People really had grown up with the show – and grown up with me.

~

Back home in Denham after a trip down under in January 1995, I learned that *Blind Date* had been nominated for a British Academy of Film and Television Award. Was I chuffed? You bet! I hadn't thought that the kind of programmes I made ever won BAFTAs. Now, invited to attend the BAFTA ceremony in Glasgow in March, I accepted the Lew Grade Award for 'The Most Significant and Popular Programme on Television'.

After the ceremony, feeling rather overwhelmed, I took my time back at the hotel getting ready before joining all the other guests for dinner. I had no idea I was keeping anyone waiting. Suddenly, the telephone rang.

'Where are you?' a desperate voice said. 'We can't sit down to dinner without you – and you're on the table with the Princess Royal.'

Can you imagine how I felt? I had no idea that Princess Anne was going to be at the dinner, nor that I was on the top table with her – and here I was keeping her and everyone waiting!

I knew HRH had a reputation for plain speaking, but I needn't have worried. When I reached the table, ready to receive a right royal reprimand, she was killing herself laughing. She was so natural and such fun to be with, and it was a lovely way to end a wonderful day.

The next day, though, was not so good.

I'd always had a great affection for all the contestants on *Blind Date*, always thought they were very brave to put themselves in the spotlight and cope with the publicity. So when I jokingly said at the BAFTA ceremony that I would like to say a very big thank you to 'all those idiots who appear on *Blind Date*,' I was being absolutely genuine, and not criticising them. I was really upset when the press accused me of slagging off the contestants with the word 'idiots'.

It was a joke! Of course I didn't think they were idiots. LWT then sprang to my defence and issued a statement: 'All the people who appear on the programme are renowned for their sense of humour. We are sure they would take Cilla's comments in the humorous sense they were intended.' The contestants may have done, but the press didn't.

As that tenth series of *Blind Date* came to an end, we found ourselves in yet more hot water, this time with the Independent Television Commission. Apparently, it had received eighteen complaints about 'sexual innuendos'. The ITC said that it had 'grave concerns about the increasingly obvious sexual innuendos' in the show and issued a ruling.

I thought this was all unnecessary fuss and bother, because the show really wasn't smutty. One day, for example, when I was watching Dale Winton on *Supermarket Sweep*, he was talking about a woman who had no knickers on. That was at 9.30 in the morning! – and I had never talked about no knickers on *Blind Date*. I had creative control over the show and I never wanted to be associated with anything offensive. Having three boys of my own helped me: the mother instinct came out in me when the contestants said something silly or needed to be put in their place. I did it with a twinkle in my eye, and I loved flirting with the lads, but I was also – thanks to working with the likes of Frankie Howerd – quite good at one-line put-downs, and I knew how to puncture their egos when I needed to.

The newspapers also had a wonderful time in September when two of the contestants had given details of certain aspects of their life on their application forms. One girl hadn't revealed that she was a porn model, and another, a drama student, didn't tell us she had been the star of a lesbian sex movie!

What kept me going through every storm, though, was that the public really enjoyed what I did on *Blind Date*. I loved the wealth – never knocked it – but I didn't do what I did for money, and never had done. I did it for fame, in a way. But mainly because that's who I am and that's what I am. I was Mrs Showbusiness, wasn't I? I did it for that.

~

When I learned that Linda McCartney had breast cancer, I wept buckets for her, Paul and their children. At times like that you remember all the occasions you have spent together, and I kept recalling a wonderful time when we were on holiday in Barbados, and Paul and Linda invited us to a meal at the fabulous beachside villa they had rented.

'It'll be a great evening,' Paul had said on the phone. 'Georgie Fame is gonna be there and Linda will cook us a meal.'

Later, after I'd accepted the invite, I remembered that Linda was a devout vegetarian and, as I was quite pernickety about food at that time and definitely into meat, I wasn't sure how I was going to cope with her cooking. I needn't have worried: it was some of the best grub I had ever tasted.

When I rang Linda the next day to thank her for such a lovely evening, she said: 'Could you be vegetarian, do you think, Cilla?'

'No,' I replied. 'I couldn't cook like you, Linda. Why don't you write a vegetarian cookbook and I'll think about it.'

Lo and behold, she did, and she sent me a copy. Sadly, though, even with her book to help me, my efforts never turned out like hers.

I really didn't know how to deal with the news about her cancer. I knew I should write to her, but I didn't know what to say. She and Paul had been part of our lives for so many years, it was as if they were part of our family. For work reasons, we didn't meet very often, but when we did it was as if there had been no lapse of time. I knew that it was important to remain positive about the outcome of her cancer and I could only pray that she would be OK. She was such a strong person and into such a healthy lifestyle, I couldn't believe that all would not be well.

Imagine my shock when, just after Linda's breast cancer was diagnosed, I discovered a lump in my own breast when I was having a shower.

Bobby and I were just about to leave for the South of France for a very short break between episodes of *Blind Date*, and my heart sank.

'You must go to the doctor,' Bobby said when I told him. 'I'll ring for an appointment now. She'll put your mind at rest.'

We didn't tell the boys or anyone else – and I certainly didn't want the press to get wind of it.

When I saw the doctor, she said that I should have it tested. That was shock enough, but I was glad that she was taking this route, because when Linda's lump was first discovered she had been prescribed antibiotics!

The specialist at the Nuffield in Oxford told me that I needed to have an operation, that I should stay overnight and that it could be done the next day. No one said or did anything to give me the impression that this was anything other than a routine course of action, but I was very frightened and worried.

On the next day as the stitches on my breast were being covered with a padded dressing, the sister said, in a tone usually used with someone seriously ill, 'Look after yourself.'

That really alarmed me.

'I've got a show on Monday,' I said, rattled.

'You're not going to work on Monday,' she said, firmly.

'Oh, yes, I am,' I said. 'And I don't want my dresser to know that I've had an operation. You'll have to do something about all this padding.'

After some discussion, I was given a cosmetic plaster that could be worn with a flesh-coloured bra and that couldn't be seen beneath a top garment.

When the specialist told me that he would telephone the following day with the result of the biopsy, I suddenly felt very uneasy. Why was it all happening so fast? Was it because I was Cilla Black? Or was this normal procedure? I didn't know what to believe, but Bobby was his usual positive, reassuring self.

'The specialist is one of the best,' he said. 'The top man. It's going to be all right, Cil.'

Thank God, he was right, and when the specialist rang the next day, it was good news.

'You got the all clear,' he said.

'What do you mean?' I replied. 'It was always all clear, wasn't it?'

'No,' he said, 'it wasn't. When I opened you up, it wasn't an ordinary lump and we had to do extensive tests. But congratulations, you're OK.'

Overjoyed, I sank into Bobby's arms, but then I felt very guilty that Linda had not been so lucky.

To this day, I regret that I didn't write to her while she was fighting the disease with typical courage, dignity and optimism. I still cry about that and I feel I failed her.

~

One problem about being a pop star and a television entertainer is that no matter how discreet you are about your life and how family-orientated you try to make it, the kind of publicity you attract can set you apart from other people. Me mam was forever telling me not to wash my dirty linen in public and never to try to be something I wasn't. I always tried to do that, and in general I think I succeeded. There were times, though, when people seemed to think I was from another planet, that I didn't feel things or think as they did. At worst, they saw me as standoffish, snobby, as somebody who didn't speak the same language. That was one reason why I liked being in Liverpool. People there still treated me as one of their own. It's also why I felt so much more at ease with showbiz friends.

On one occasion I read that someone in Denham had said to a reporter, 'She's done nothing for the community. She lives here, but she takes great pains to avoid mixing with the locals – it's as though she's frightened to get too close. We call her "Miss Havisham" because no one ever sees her.'

And another time, in 1996, when Bobby and I were developing an area at the front of our house into a small lake, we found ourselves in a heap of trouble with our neighbours and South Buckinghamshire District Council.

What's It All About?

Bobby was particularly keen on the lake idea because he thought the wildlife he so loved would enjoy it. So, as it was our land and we were not putting up a building, we honestly didn't give a thought to planning permission and went ahead and asked the builders to start excavating. After the work had started, though, we discovered that a neighbour had reported us to the local council. The media then got to hear about it and there was a huge fuss.

'Wouldn't it have been nice,' I said to Bobby, 'if someone had just knocked on our door and simply said, "You need to apply for permission."' As it was, we decided to shelve our plans, wait for all the fuss to die down, and then go through the proper channels.

After all that negative publicity, it was lovely to be able to bond with lots of other proud parents and brothers and sisters when Bobby and I and Robert and Jack went to the University of East Anglia in Norwich for Ben's graduation – a 2.1 degree in English and American Studies.

~

My mam, who was now eighty-four, had been in dreadful pain from her osteoporosis and critically ill for some time, and she kept saying she was ready to die. It was heartbreaking – I wouldn't have wished what she was going through on anybody – and sometimes I so wished the doctors *could* give her something to end her suffering. She was having great difficulty in swallowing, and it was only her still-strong heart that was keeping her going. My brothers usually tried to protect me by playing down just how ill she was, but there were other times when my brother John phoned to say that Mam really was very poorly – and we would hire a plane to fly up to Liverpool to be with her.

Despite all this, because she had pulled back from the brink so many times, I was totally unprepared when, just after filming the first episode of that series of *Blind Date*, the dreaded phone call came. Mam had died – and just like with my dad, I wasn't there.

I was inconsolable. The woman who had been so important to me was gone and I would never be able to talk or laugh with her again. As Bobby

330

held me in his arms, I cried and cried and thought I'd never be able to stop. My mother had been the driving force behind my life. With her lovely singing voice, she could so easily have been in show business herself, but she had poured all her ambition into me and my dad and brothers – and she had been a huge influence on my career. When I was growing up she never tired of me saying, 'I'm going to be a star', never told me to shut up, and always made me feel I could do anything. She brought us up, ran a business, always seemed to be there, and the house was always full of laughter. Nothing fazed her.

I'd heard friends describing how they'd felt when both their mother and father had died, and now it had happened to me. I was an orphan – and the sense of isolation was unbearable.

For weeks after me mam died, I was exhausted. I felt that the life force within me had drained away. Jack was at boarding school, Robert and Ben were settling in to their careers. There was work for me to get on with, but for the first time it held no interest and Bobby was having difficulty in motivating me.

When I was idly flipping through the pages of the *Daily Mail* one morning, I came across a news item about three puppies that had been abandoned in a cardboard box outside a Sainsbury's superstore in Thornhill, Cardiff. The staff had named the orphans Coffee, Tea and Sugar, and there was a large picture of them looking very sorry for themselves. They hadn't been cared for and had a skin disease.

Reaching for the scissors, I cut the picture out and put it on the kitchen floor. Then I said to Denver, our Briard dog, who was at my side: 'Which one shall we go for?'

His big, wet nose landed on Coffee, and I telephoned the National Canine Defence League rescue centre in Bridgend, Mid-Glamorgan.

When eleven-week-old Coffee arrived at Denham, she was tiny – only twelve inches long – but she had no difficulty in bossing Denver, who weighed nine stone.

What's It All About?

From then on, as I watched Denver and orphan Coffee waddling around the house and garden, I began to feel a little better.

A month later, at the 1996 British Comedy Awards, I received the Lifetime Achievement Award for Entertainment from my dear old friend, Jimmy Tarbuck. I think me mam would have been very proud to know about that. And who can tell – perhaps she did.

28

Love of the Loved

A few days before my fifty-fourth birthday on 27 May – and only six months after the British Comedy Awards – I received another gong, this time the Royal Television Society's 'Best Presenter' award at the Grosvenor House Hotel. I thought I'd got over not quite believing that all these wonderful things were happening to the girl from Scottie Road, but that feeling returned big time when I was awarded the OBE – the Order of the British Empire. I was delighted, and especially proud that it was awarded not for my charity work, but for 'services to stage and television'.

As Sod's law would have it, the Buckingham Palace ceremony was originally supposed to take place in March, but I wasn't free. There was something surreal about having to say that I was unable to attend because of television schedules and could I be given another date, please? 'No problem,' came back the answer – and I was given a date in July.

I went to Buck House along with Bobby and Jack and Penny. I was allowed three guests, and Robert and Ben both nobly stood back so as to allow Penny to go. I wore a lemon suit with matching hat designed by Stephen Adnitt. I wished me mam and dad could have seen me – they'd have been so proud. The ceremony was very theatrical, which I loved, and

it was great fun. I couldn't get over the fact that there was piped muzak –
when it was my turn, they were playing 'If I Were A Rich Man'! Afterwards
the four of us were whisked off by *OK!* magazine to a celebration lunch
with a hundred close friends and some of my relatives on the Thames
cruiser, the *Silver Sturgeon*. Jane Asher made me a special cake. It was
wonderful to celebrate my special day with so many of the people I loved,
and I enjoyed every moment of it.

I also received congratulatory telegrams, including ones from Princess
Diana and Sarah, Duchess of York. I was utterly gobsmacked by that – and,
of course, absolutely delighted. Those two telegrams are still treasured
mementoes in my home.

In late August, while Bobby and I were in our villa in Spain, it was
announced at the Edinburgh Television Festival that David Liddiment was
to be the new entertainment boss at ITV and that he would take up his
appointment in September. His plans, disclosed to the national papers,
made it clear he thought that *Surprise! Surprise!* had passed its sell-by date
and that another series would not be made. It was all news to me!
Inevitably, though, once David Liddiment's plans were made known to the
press, Bobby was constantly called to the telephone to deal with the fall-
out; and even though we were on holiday the subject kept cropping up
when we went out to dinner with friends.

Then, while we were still in Spain, we heard something that wiped
David's plans from our thoughts.

I was making coffee in the kitchen one Sunday morning. Bobby had
turned on the radio, but I was only half listening. The ten o'clock news was
saying something about Princess Diana, and the tone of the announcer's
voice caught my attention. I listened properly, then gasped, turned to
Bobby and said, 'Diana's dead.'

It was the most awful moment. Too stunned to speak, we stood rooted
to the spot, looking at each other, then we rushed into the sitting room
and turned on the television. Even as I watched the news and saw the

tangled wreckage of the car in the Paris underpass, I couldn't believe that such a beautiful woman could have died in such a tragic way.

'I can't bear it,' I kept thinking. 'How will her sons cope?'

Heartbroken, I set off to Gibraltar with our friends John and Alex to sign the book of remembrance there.

~

When it was time to go off to Barbados for the New Year, we decided to take the boys, now aged twenty-seven, twenty-three and seventeen, and their girl-friends with us. When Bobby rented one of the houses on the Sandy Lane estate, it cost £25,000 for the week, and Bobby said that if he was paying that amount of money for the pleasure, we should buy an apartment!

'What a good idea!' I said, resolving to keep him to that!

My current secret agenda, though, was to get a family photograph taken at the Sandy Lane Hotel's New Year's Eve party. It was going to be a memorable occasion in a magical setting, and I wanted to see – and be seen with – my four handsome fellers in their dinner jackets. The photo-graph would then take pride of place at Denham.

A few days before New Year's Eve, however, trouble arrived in the form of Michael Winner, who was also staying in the Sandy Lane, and who invited us to a private Sunday luncheon party in the hotel. We all loved Michael. A real character, he was such a sweetheart. I was delighted to accept the invitation, and on the day our large family party walked through the magnificent grounds for Sunday lunch.

As we took our places at a table in the dining room, Michael came over to greet us and said, 'What are you doing for New Year's Eve?'

'We're coming here, of course,' I said. 'So we'll see you.'

'Oh, no, darling,' Michael replied, 'I'm not coming here. I've hired the Carambola restaurant. I've got the Beluga caviar and Dom Perignon and everything else being flown in.'

'Why aren't you celebrating here?' I asked, shocked. 'You've paid a fortune to stay in this hotel.'

What's It All About?

'I won't wear a dinner jacket,' he replied.

At this point all my fellers' eyes lit up.

'Why don't you and the family come and join me?' Michael asked.

My heart sank. I so wanted to see my boys and my husband all together in their dinner jackets, just this once.

'Oh, we'd love to come, Michael,' they all said in unison.

So, because Michael likes to be comfortable in a shirt and shorts, that put the kibosh on my plans.

There were no regrets, though. He put on a spectacular dinner – and we had some fabulous photographs taken. The boys absolutely adored him; the girls fell in love with him, and he even invited us to join him for lunch the next day – and to see the carnival show. He is the most generous man and fabulous host – even if he did put a spanner in my motherly plans.

While we were in Barbados we followed up Bobby's idea to look for an apartment. On a previous occasion we'd seen an old hotel in St James that was up for sale and ready for conversion, and we'd been attracted to the idea of buying it. But Bobby had decided that we would need to spend a lot of time in Barbados overseeing it, which wasn't a practical proposition. This time, however, we were told that the hotel was now being converted into flats, and that if we went to the architect's office we could see the plans.

We loved what we saw and decided to buy a top-floor apartment, which would give us and the family – and our guests – plenty of privacy. We knew that it wouldn't be ready to live in for some time, but that was fine. It was something to look forward to.

After the holiday, I felt ready to face what was promising to be a busy 1998. In February I was booked to do my first-ever interview with Michael Parkinson. Michael and I had been friends for many years since meeting in Spain through Jimmy Tarbuck, but also on the show that night was someone I hadn't met before – Lily Savage, aka Paul O'Grady. The kids were all huge fans of his, and I had heard from various Liverpool friends that he had

336

said some very funny and wicked things on stage about me and *Surprise! Surprise!* I'd also heard from the same sources that he had a rather uncomplimentary opinion of me, so I was intrigued at the thought of meeting him.

This was the first show I had done for the BBC for a very long time and when I arrived at the television studios and went along to my dressing room, I was amazed at what I found. Paul Jackson, the then-Controller, had arranged for it to be filled with flowers, bowls of fruit and champagne.

'There's something weird going on, Bobby,' I said. 'I never got this kind of treatment from the BBC when I was working here.'

As there were no towels in the bathroom, I opened the dressing room door intending to get some from elsewhere.

There was a man posted outside. 'Is this for security?' I wondered, but I asked him for the towels.

In next to no time there was a knock on the door and I heard someone saying, 'Towels for Cilla Black.' I recognised the voice as that of Paul O'Grady.

'That's never you, Lily Savage, is it?' I called. Bobby, who'd opened the door, was taken aback. Out of drag Paul is a really handsome guy.

'It is, girl, it is,' and, as he came in, he said, 'I can't compete with this room, mine is f***ing hell.'

From his dressing room next door Paul had overheard what was being said about the towels and used it as an excuse to say hello. At that time he was working for the BBC and, looking at the flowers, he was cursing and cussing everywhere, saying, 'You don't even work f***ing here.'

By then Bobby and I were in fits and Paul stayed in my dressing room with me, even while I was being made up. The make-up artist was trying to do my eyes but, thanks to Paul, tears of laughter were rolling down my cheeks. Eventually I said to him, 'You'll have to go or I'll never be ready.'

I did Michael's interview and then Paul came on set to join us. The chatter flowed so quickly then between Paul and me that it left little room for Michael to get a word in edgeways!

'Can I have my show back, now, please?' he kept saying.

That meeting with Paul cemented an enduring friendship, which Bobby enjoyed as much as I did.

One day Paul phoned me up. 'Hi, Cilla, how are you?'

'I'm just cooling out,' I said.

There was a silence at the other end of the phone, then he said 'Cooling out?'

'Cooling out,' I repeated. 'I'm cool.'

He dined out on that one – and told me later that his friends were now using my expression and were saying 'cooling out' instead of 'chilling out'.

~

As Mothering Sunday approached that year, I found that at last I was able to talk about the loss of me mam. I hadn't really been able to deal with it before, and hadn't even had the strength to go through her things and sort them out. I was full of anger after she died because I couldn't bear the fact that she had been in so much pain for so long, and that all the money in the world couldn't help – or make her better. I was beginning to learn, though, that in talking about it I could pay tribute to her for all that she had taught me. The most important thing had been trust. I take people at face value, and I've rarely been betrayed. I'm dead straight, and she made me like that. I don't tell lies and I don't expect people to lie to me, either. Mam's attitude to life was that the glass is half-full not half-empty, and I inherited that outlook from her. Like her, I work hard, I'm career-minded and independent. We were more like friends than mother and daughter, but she was always the boss. I still can't believe I can't pick up the telephone and ring her.

As a little girl, I would buy her a box of chocolates for Mothering Sunday, but by the Saturday I would have peeled off the Cellophane and eaten the first layer. She never complained! On the Sunday, I would give her the second layer with a bunch of daffodils. On my own Mother's Day I'd have a lie-in and champagne and smoked salmon instead of tea and toast, but since my mam died, Mothering Sundays have always been bitter-sweet for me.

~

Soon after the Parkinson interview, LWT sent Bobby a proposal for a new game show they wanted me to host. Called *Moment of Truth*, this was based on a very successful Japanese show, *Happy Family Plan*. When the Japanese version was shown to me I was horrified. It seemed to centre on a bloke gabbling away twenty-to-the-dozen and taking great delight in snatching prizes away from people and depriving kids of bikes they thought they'd won.

'If ever there was "victim television",' I thought, 'this is *it*!'

'No way, chuck. I can't do that,' I said to Nigel Lythgoe, LWT's controller of entertainment. 'I'm not in the business of making people unhappy.'

So the powers-that-be went away and reworked the rules. Even so, I found the format a challenge. I'd never done a real game show before, and although I was happy to try something new, I didn't feel quite sure of this.

The basic idea was to feature three contestants who had the opportunity to win prizes worth £20,000. These were chosen in advance by their families from a Dream Directory. One family member then had to undertake a task – a luck or skill challenge set by me – before performing their challenge in front of a live studio audience. If they failed the challenge the whole family lost their fabulous prizes. Nigel Lythgoe had made it possible for children, if their family didn't win, to receive a consolation prize off camera after the show. I was much happier when I heard that, so we went ahead and did the pilot and waited to see what 'them upstairs' thought about it.

We got the go-ahead and set about filming the series, which was due to be screened on ITV from the beginning of September. Families' dreams of a lifetime were going to come true or be shattered in one 'moment of truth'. It was incredibly emotional and compelling, and, despite all my years on *Surprise! Surprise!*, I found I was not prepared for this roller-coaster.

Bobby, who knew that I would be mortified if it was not a success – that I would blame myself, and everyone else would blame me, too – thought that we should go to Spain while the first four weeks of the series were being aired. I was very glad he suggested this because there was a lot of controversy in the press. In fact, when the TV ratings came out we found that *Moment of Truth* was in the top ten and, by the time it came to an end in November 1998, it was the fourth most watched new programme of the year.

It was during that holiday in Spain that Bobby and I first properly met Dale Winton. He had telephoned my office to ask if I would appear on *GMTV* when he was sitting in for Lorraine Kelly for a week and, since he was in Spain at the same time as us, we invited him over to the villa. He came over with costume designer Lynda Wood for a drink and stayed the whole day. We're both Geminis (as is Pat Davies – she and Dale even share a birthday!) and we got on like a house on fire. We've been the best of friends since then – and Dale completed what the press likes to call 'Cilla's gay Mafia'. The other members, of course, are Savage and Biggins.

~

The fourteenth series of *Blind Date* was given an increased production budget, a new producer, Isobel Hatton, and a revamped format, and the series came up with some encounters that sent our temperatures and the ratings sky-high.

One girl, Jody Mutton, flew to Crete alone after her date, Jamie Hayden, was discovered phoning his real girlfriend and banned from the show; and there was drama galore when Sam, a female body-piercer and tattooist, picked Terry for a date in Mauritius, then threatened to head-butt him! Sitting on the sofa, she told Terry that he was 'a wimp, ego-tistical and a selfish bigot' and then ripped off her microphone and stormed off the set. Terry reacted by saying 'Good riddance' and added that the cushions on the sofa were more fun than she was! Sam was persuaded to return to the set, but when she did the bickering started again and she began swearing, a first for *Blind Date*. Somehow I wasn't surprised when a national newspaper followed up the story and found out that Sam was married and pregnant.

In the meantime, the *Blind Date* crew and I were wondering where Sam's thirty-two body piercings were. We could see the ones in her ears, tongue and nose, but when her boob popped out of the tight basque she was wearing, there was no pierced nipple. We never solved that mystery.

Bobby's only comment was, 'You could take her home on a curtain rail.'

In that series we also had our third wedding. Paul Pratt and Anna Azonwanna had met on the programme in 1993 and I'd been kept up to date with the couple's romance. In October 1998 they were married on the lawn of the Colony Club Hotel, one of the most expensive hotels in Barbados, which has a wonderfully romantic setting – deep blue sky, white sand, coconut palms swaying gently in the breeze.

LWT footed the bill for the couple's wedding and lavish champagne reception with seven-course meal. My special wedding present to the couple was three original watercolours of local Barbados scenes.

Anna wore a gold-tinged, figure-hugging wedding dress with a satin crepe bodice and looked absolutely gorgeous, and I wore a pale lilac chiffon suit and a lilac satin hat.

My thoughts during that time kept wandering to the possibility of a marriage within our own family. Robert and his girlfriend of seven years, Fiona Crane, were now engaged and were getting used to me asking them 'When are you going to get married?' Robert's Fiona always called me 'Mrs Willis', which I thought was very special because nearly everybody else called me Cilla.

I was so excited when Robert finally said, 'We're thinking of getting married next year.'

I kissed him and squealed a lot and then began bombarding him with enquiries like. 'What do you want from us as a wedding present?' Then, without giving them time to answer, I said, 'I know what, we'll buy you a house.'

I told them to take their time finding one, but I was surprised when, just a month later, they said they'd found one near Cambridge. The house was paid and wrapped before they had even set a date for the wedding.

'You've got the house,' I said, once they'd moved in. 'When's the date?'

'We're thinking about the year 2000,' Robert and Fiona said.

'You cheeky so and sos,' I wailed, happily. 'You've gone back on the deal!' But I didn't mind, really. They were so happy together.

When they moved into the house it was the first time they had lived together and I was quivering with the thought that there might be a possibility of grandchildren. I also knew that it would be very wrong of me to force the issue. What I wanted was not necessarily what they wanted. So, with Bobby's help, I had to learn to bite my bottom lip and be patient. In truth, though, I couldn't wait to be a granny. Whenever I saw all those baby adverts on the telly, I got all broody.

'I'll make a much better granny than I did a mum,' I kept telling myself. I had a rosy vision of Bobby and me growing old at Denham and taking joy together in our countless grandchildren, as the garden and the house echoed with their laughter and shouts. I couldn't think of a better way for the future to go.

29

Bobby

I was only seventeen when I met Bobby, but nearly forty years later, when we were celebrating our pearl wedding in Barbados in 1999, we still sat on the sofa holding hands, watching the telly and having a hug. For me, there was nothing better at the end of each day than cuddling up to Bobby. He was so warm, so patient – a real Prince Charming. We were like two pieces of a jigsaw, the same side of two coins. Bobby finished my sentences and I started his. We'd always believed that home is where the heart is, and we'd been totally faithful to each other, never even tempted to have an affair.

Of course we argued – like all married couples. But we never took our rows to bed. We had a rule that no matter how fierce an argument, there'd be no dragging of pillows and blankets into the sitting room to sleep on the sofa. Once we got between the sheets, that was it. I couldn't envisage a time when things would be different, when we would stop loving and being there for each other. Our home and our boys were the greatest things in our lives. Robert, Ben and Jack were what we worked for and, if we hadn't been able to be together as a family, we'd have thought, 'What's it all about – what's the point?' Once those electronic gates closed behind us it was just Mr and Mrs Willis. Our marriage had gone from strength to strength and the time in Barbados in our newly acquired apartment, celebrating our pearl wedding, was very special.

When we got back, we had a hectic work schedule: a *Surprise! Surprise!* special, a *Blind Date* spoof with Elle Macpherson, Lenny Henry, Helena Bonham-Carter and Twiggy for *Comic Relief*, and a big NSPCC fundraiser at the Theatre Royal, as well as schedules to work out for the second series of *Moment of Truth*. In March, I was devastated when Dusty Springfield, who had been diagnosed with breast cancer in 1994, died, and I was very upset that work commitments meant I couldn't go to her funeral.

The moment we finished filming *Moment of Truth*, Bobby and I planned to go back to Barbados for a holiday.

Bobby had had a ticklish cough for some weeks and, although he was taking all sorts of things for it from the chemist, it was no better. He was also feeling unusually tired. I insisted that he went to see the doctor, and he had a check-up, but as the doctor said he was absolutely fine we went off to Barbados.

I was hoping that the holiday would sort things out, but when we got there, Bobby, who was usually a very fit man, was still very tired. He'd always taken a nap on the couch after lunch on Sundays, but he was now taking afternoon naps every day. He really wasn't well and I said to him, 'This is not like you, Bobby. We have to go home.'

'No, no,' he protested. 'We're here to organise things for the apartment and that's what we're going to do. Everything's fine.'

So we went shopping for lamps and things, but, unusually, he always sat in the car and waited for me and never came into the store. Even so, he insisted on taking me to the shops one last time to buy a lamp on the day we were due to leave Barbados, and he carried my bags into the airport.

When we got back to Denham at six in the morning, he was clearly feeling unwell and said that he had a pain in his ribs.

'Phone the doctor,' I said.

'I'll do it tomorrow,' he replied.

Bobby

Then, tired and very anxious, I snapped, 'You could be dead by tomorrow, Bobby. *Do it now.*'

But he wouldn't call his GP until the following day, and the next time I saw him he was in the Nuffield Hospital in Oxford, having loads of tests.

Things could not have been worse. A scan revealed that he had a tumour on the liver.

We were both shocked and stunned, but the specialist immediately raised our hopes by saying that he thought the tumour was operable and that he wanted to refer Bobby to an oncologist at the Royal Free Hospital, London. After further tests at the Royal Free, though, the oncologist told Bobby that the tumour was more extensive than had been thought and that it was in a rapid state of growth. It would not be possible to operate on it after all, but it could be treated with chemotherapy. And if the worst came to the worst, Bobby could have a liver transplant.

When the consultant told me this in his consulting room, Robert was with me and, as I glanced at him, I could see that he was about to burst into tears. I gave him the kind of look that Bobby would have given me, as if to say, 'Do *not* make a show of me. Let's keep this all together.' That's a very Liverpool expression.

My next reaction was to be annoyed with Bobby, because I realised that he already knew and hadn't told me himself. I couldn't believe it at first, but then I understood that he was putting on a brave face and trying to look after me.

There was nothing for it but to try and keep going. Deal with the practicalities. But at home that evening, I went into a state of shock. I became icy all over and began to shake. All I could think was that Bobby was only fifty-seven and, apart from the ticklish cough and tiredness, there had been no symptoms when we went away. But what we had thought was 'a bit of a tummy' on our return was caused by fluid leaking from his liver into his stomach.

Everything in me was saying, 'Not my Bobby, *please not my Bobby*,' but I had to face the facts. He had cancer.

There he was, lying in hospital, and home alone, I didn't even know the routine for walking the dogs. I knew *when* this happened, because the dogs used to come in from the hall when they heard the signature tune for *News At Ten* and say, in dog-speak, 'Bedtime now, guys, but take us for our walkies first.' In a daze, I phoned Bobby at the hospital, burst into tears, and said, 'Where do I walk the dogs?'

'It's all right, Cil, it's not a problem,' he said calmly. 'They know where they go. They'll take you.'

They did, but, as I followed them, I thought, distraught, 'What have you done to me, Bobby? Is this how it's going to be?'

It was awful – my mind had drifted into a strange mixture of anger, resentment, denial and grief.

~

After the initial shock, Robert, Ben and Jack were absolutely wonderful and immediately initiated a rota system so that there would always be someone with Bobby at the Royal Free while he was undergoing treatment. Bobby and I were so proud of the way they handled themselves. Robert moved back into Denham to be with me and the other two boys, and Jack, who was finishing his A-levels, still managed to get on with his studies and do well in his exams.

That first weekend, on the Sunday, Pat called me from LA.

'What's up?' she asked. 'Something's wrong.'

'Who told you?' I said.

'Nobody's told me anything, luv,' she replied. 'I just know something's wrong. What's the matter?'

'Bobby's in hospital,' I said, realising that we had somehow communicated telepathically. 'It's serious, Pat. We haven't told his family yet.'

'I'll come tomorrow,' she said at once, 'and be there for you when you tell them.'

Bobby, meanwhile, was absolutely determined to put up a fight. He also insisted that I should film the next series of *Blind Date*. He knew that

346

work was a fixed, stable point in my life and that if I continued with it, I would have some respite from worrying about him all the time. I did carry on with the filming, but at times I found it an almost impossible struggle.

~

During her visit, Pat told me that her mother-in-law had had lung cancer, but had now been in the clear for six years. So when she returned to LA, she called her mother-in-law's oncologist and asked him for the name of the best liver oncologist. But when she spoke to the New York consultant whose name she was given, he said he did not think we should put Bobby through the trauma of flying over there for further treatment. We also discussed this with the specialist at the Royal Free.

'Shall I tell you straight?' he said.

'Yes, that's what we came to you for.'

'If this was my father, I would not put him through such an ordeal.'

Then any hopes we still had were dashed when we were told that the cancer had spread to Bobby's lungs.

By then the press were aware that we making daily trips to the hospital and LWT was forced to make an announcement explaining the situation and asking the media to respect our privacy. The press, however, staked out the hospital, which was very upsetting because even though we used the back entrance, we couldn't slip in and out without being photographed. It was also upsetting for Bobby. He had to have his name changed on the door to his room, so that he couldn't be identified by the more unscrupulous journalists.

When friends heard about Bobby, they kept ringing to console me. Some friends, like Paul McCartney and Cliff, were a great comfort when they phoned, but others struggled to find something to say, and I would have to go off on a tangent to put them at their ease. I'm sure people thought I was a little crazy during this time. Many people kept saying that Bobby must have known that he was seriously ill before the cancer was diagnosed, but he didn't.

What's It All About?

We were overwhelmed by the warmth and the support shown to us from well-wishers. Cards, letters, flowers – including some from the Duchess of York – flowed in, and there were messages of comfort and encouragement from people who had been through a similar experience. People all over the world, it seemed, were praying for Bobby, and we even had holy oil sent to us from Jerusalem. Judging from the amount of holy water we received, we felt that Lourdes had been emptied.

One day, in one of my many telephone calls to Pat in LA, she told me about a conversation she had had with Bobby some years back about her much-loved dog. The dog had become incontinent and she had put it into nappies.

'What's wrong with you?' Bobby had said to her. 'Would you like to be in nappies? Have him put down.'

'I can't do that, Bobby,' Pat had said.

'You're being cruel to the animal, keeping him alive,' Bobby had replied.

Pat's point was that if Bobby wouldn't keep a desperately sick animal alive, he wouldn't want to be kept alive himself if the quality of his life had gone.

Bobby's determination, though, throughout the programme of chemotherapy at the Royal Free was absolutely amazing. I looked worse than he did! It was my hair that fell out, me who lost about two stone in weight, and me who had grey circles under my eyes from lack of sleep. On 11 August, the eclipse of the sun took place. The boys and I were all with Bobby at the hospital. The boys went outside to watch, but I stayed beside Bobby's bed. I somehow didn't want to see the sun being blotted out.

It sounds selfish, but I just kept thinking, 'What on earth will I do without him?' and whenever I was in the garden that summer, I used to think, 'Perhaps he won't be here to see the winter.'

It was the most god-awful feeling. I was in such a state of shock and despair that I couldn't take it all in at once, and I seemed to be absorbing what was happening in a series of short bursts. I also kept remembering strange things, like when my favourite cherry tree had died.

'Oh, God,' I'd thought then, 'this house will never be the same again.'

But everything in the house had remained exactly the same.

How could anything be the same, though, if anything happened to Bobby?

All through this time Bobby refused to be negative and wanted everything to be as normal as possible. It was me, Robert, Ben and Jack who were freaking out. It was a long time since I'd asked God for anything because I considered myself such a lucky person, but I prayed and prayed for Bobby to be OK.

'Tomorrow's the unknown,' Bobby had always said, 'something to look forward to,' and I tried to look forward to the future with some degree of optimism. I'd always known our partnership couldn't go on forever, but I felt that if Bobby left me, I couldn't go on living and I certainly couldn't go on working. I would have to retire. I'd hate the idea of giving everything up and abandoning everything we had worked for, but I would have no choice.

Most of the time I didn't even dare think about the future or what would happen to me if Bobby wasn't there to share things with. He always monitored my shows on a closed-circuit screen. If anything was wrong, he would be down on the studio floor before anyone could count ten. If there was a fracas behind the scenes, he protected me from it. If he wasn't there, who would protect me, tell me what was right or wrong, or say I was being too flash? If I couldn't look across a room and see his reassuring face, I would want to die. My life, as I knew it, would end.

I passed those summer months in a trance, as if I was trying to find my way out of a maze.

One day, Biggins said to me, 'You have got to have a break, Cilla. Let me take you to lunch one day at Daphne's.'

'I can't do that,' I said. 'Whatever day we did it might be Bobby's last day.'

'But you look awful, love,' he said.

'Thanks a bunch,' I replied.

'Come out to Daphne's.'

So I did, but everything was too much. In the middle of the lunch I began to choke and had to go to the ladies. Then, with typical Cilla black humour, I even managed to make Biggins laugh about that.

'Bobby could be all right,' I said, 'and I could have choked to death in there.'

~

On the last Tuesday in September, we received news that, against all odds, Bobby's tumour had shrunk. A scan had revealed that there were just three microscopic bits in his lungs. It was the first positive news we had had – and we were told that the long-term prognosis was good.

We were overjoyed. We loved him so much – and he had every reason to beat the cancer and live. For the first time in weeks we dared to think ahead, and it was a great feeling. At the very least, we felt that we could now return to some kind of normality.

~

During all the weeks since his cancer had been diagnosed, Bobby had refused to feel sorry for himself, and once back home, he spent some time negotiating a new LWT contract for me. Robert and Ben carried him upstairs to bed every night because his legs were very weak; however, in the mornings he insisted on walking down the stairs himself, with Robert walking ahead of him, carrying a pillow to break any fall. But Bobby, who had kept his sense of humour, sometimes got away and went ahead of Robert into the garden, where he occupied himself designing a koi pond. The future looked brighter.

The problem with the chemotherapy, however, was that it had attacked the good organs as well as the cancer, and Bobby's kidneys began to pack up. He'd lost two stone and was very weak. He also developed ulcers in his mouth and his skin was very tender. To avoid hurting him when I cuddled him, I didn't wear any jewellery during this time.

Bobby

His treatment was now in tablet form for pain-management. Then one morning in late October he woke up with a chest infection and I was beside myself with anxiety.

Pat, back in LA, must have been sensitive to this, because when she telephoned, I said, 'Oh, Pat, I think this will be our last Christmas with Bobby.'

'Oh, God,' she replied, 'I'll see if we can come for Christmas.'

On the next day, though, I rang Pat to tell her that Bobby's chest infection had turned into pneumonia and he had been re-admitted to the Royal Free.

'I'll go straight to the airport now and get the first available plane to London,' Pat said.

~

On Friday, 22 October 1999, while Bobby was sleeping soundly in his hospital bed, I left the hospital at 10 p.m. and came back to Denham.

On the Saturday morning at about 8 a.m. Ben took a call from the hospital to say that Bobby was much worse. They told us to come as quickly as possible. We dropped everything, and Robert drove Jack and me, while Ben went on ahead. Bobby, who had not regained consciousness, had an oxygen mask placed over his face. In the afternoon, the boys were sitting there quietly, watching *Grandstand* on TV. I was sitting at the foot of the bed, massaging Bobby's feet. His breathing had been laboured for some time, but suddenly Robert noticed that the oxygen mask was no longer moving – was no longer going up and down.

Without opening his eyes one last time, Bobby had quietly slipped away from us and died.

And at that very moment, before we had had a chance to absorb what had happened, the room was suddenly flooded with sunlight.

30

Surround Yourself With Sorrow

I can't remember much about the rest of that day. I think I was on auto-pilot. It's hard to find words to express how you feel when your world falls apart. When someone you've loved and felt by your side for forty years is no longer there.

Back at Denham, I was totally numb, but there was some small comfort in following the usual, mundane routine of making cups of tea. I called Pat in LA to tell her Bobby had died, and fell into bed so drained and so exhausted that I went to sleep straight away. The next day, still on autopilot, I did all the things I would have done if Bobby were at home with me, including making the Sunday dinner for Robert, Ben and Jack – and Pat, who had astonished me by arriving on the doorstep that morning. She had dropped everything after my call and got straight on a plane.

The following day, Pat began to telephone some of our closest friends, and tributes began to arrive from the many people who had loved and respected Bobby.

As my numbness began to fade, the grief flooded in and I was inconsolable.

Later that day, I was so grateful when LWT came to our aid and, together with Pat and Michael Hurll, took over all the funeral arrangements.

Although I was anguished every time I realised I would never see Bobby again, I couldn't go to the chapel of rest to see him in his coffin. The boys did, his brothers did, but I couldn't. I didn't want to see him like that. I'm not proud of myself for this, but I was frightened and too distraught.

Bobby's funeral was held on the Feast of All Saints, 1 November, at the church of St Mary the Virgin, Denham. When we got to the church, the press, who had been given my permission to cover the funeral, were there.

Michael Hurll, who I had worked with for so many years, had planned the service. It began with Bobby's favourite hymn 'All Things Bright And Beautiful' – Biggins had suggested that. Then, sitting between Ben and Jack, I tried so hard to listen as Robert spoke very movingly about his dad.

'He was,' Robert said, 'a man who enjoyed and appreciated life and enriched the lives of everyone around him. A man who always saw the funny side of life. He was a great thinker, a great listener, and his advice was always sound and wise. But above all he loved his family, and we loved him.'

Then he read the Henry Scott Holland poem which begins, 'Death is nothing at all, I have only slipped away into the next room.'

When Jimmy Tarbuck spoke about Bobby, I laughed and cried at the same time. Bobby, Jimmy told the people gathered there, had confided in him once that the only person he could have married apart from me was the Liverpool manager Bill Shankly.

And George Martin spoke of Bobby as my 'guardian angel', and read the Joyce Grenfell poem, 'If I should go before the rest of you, break not a flower ...'

After the funeral, we had a private service at the crematorium, attended by the family and about twenty of our friends. And then, as well-meaning people kept saying to me, life had to move on.

LWT suggested that I might like to take the rest of the year off, but I said that I would be back at work within weeks. I had thought that if

Bobby died I wouldn't want to live, let alone work, but this was the only way I knew how to cope – and I wanted to continue, in Bobby's memory, the career that he and I had built together.

A week after the funeral, I returned to the studio for the filming of *Blind Date*. Work was a painkiller. It distracted me. It numbed the pain. The audience gave me a standing ovation that night, and I said, 'God bless you all. This is a *very* special night, so no long faces – just a *lorra, lorra* laughs.'

Then, dedicating the show to Bobby, I added, 'This is a very special show for me. I worked throughout Bobby's illness, and this one is for him.'

It wasn't easy going through my paces that night or any of the other nights, but I got through the recording without breaking down until I reached my dressing room.

During those early weeks, I often wanted to be alone. There were so many things at home to remind me of Bobby, so many good times to replay in my mind, so much to reflect upon, so many shared years and memories to thank him for. But, as I was only too aware, you can't put your arms around a memory and my heart was broken.

My chief solace was our sons, Robert, Ben and Jack, each in their different ways the living image of their father.

~

Just before Christmas, very much in need of a change of location and some new impressions, I forced myself to go to New York. I'd been invited by dear Peter Brown, with whom we'd stayed on many previous trips there for Christmas shopping. But this was the first trip I had ever made alone – the first of many things that I would have to learn to do by myself – and it was a very frightening, daunting prospect. I was so well cared for, though, when I arrived at Heathrow. Special services met me on the pavement as my car pulled up at departures, I didn't have to check in my luggage or deal with my tickets and passport, and a guy carried my hand luggage. Passing straight through security, I went into the first-class lounge, then got on to a trolley car that took me to the plane.

'Why was I so frightened?' I thought. 'It's so easy.'

It was the only time, though, that I used special services. It had attracted too much attention and, for the same reason, I never took a trolley car to or from an aeroplane again. I've now got flying alone down to a fine art and, since Bobby died, I'm not even afraid of flying any more, because I want to join him.

In New York, I stayed with Peter and he looked after me. On the Saturday afternoon, he took me to see Barry Humphries' show on Broadway and, once Dame Edna was in her stride, I forgot how unhappy I was for a few minutes and actually found myself laughing out loud.

'I knew you were in,' Barry said when I went backstage to say hello to him. 'I'd have recognised your laugh anywhere. I'm sorry about all the old gags. I know you've heard them all before.'

'You were brilliant, Barry,' I said. 'I never thought I would laugh again.'

~

The next 'first' was Christmas. I knew this would be a major hurdle, especially as it was leading up to the new millennium, but the arrival of the year 2000, which had promised to be such a big celebration, had to be got through somehow. It was just me and the boys and Fiona at Denham, and we did our best to support each other.

~

'If something makes you unhappy,' Bobby had been fond of saying to me, 'move on, turn the page'; and, after he died, Pat was the person who helped me to do that.

'Hey, girlfriend,' she would say, 'you can do this,' or 'D'you know what? This time is *your* time and you have got to be kind to yourself', or 'You and Bobby had a great life. Perfect. Now this is going to be another great part of your life. It's different, yes, but you can do it. We'll do it together.'

When Bobby was alive and we were not working we were couch-potatoes who didn't choose to go to that many functions, and after his death, I was determined not to be a burden to my friends. I didn't want them to think: 'What are we going to do about Cilla? We have to look after her – she's our friend.'

Paul O'Grady – who I call Savage – was wonderful. He was perfect company for me, and he just let me cry. Paul never sets out to be funny all the time, but he can't help it. It's a bit like my giggle, it just happens that way. It's certainly not because he's always cracking jokes, it's because he's a very angry man who hates nearly everybody and everything, which is terribly funny in itself. Fortunately, I seem to calm him down and make him laugh, and Biggins and Dale adore him. Sometimes – usually at my invitation – we all went out together.

When Bobby died, Dale lived only twenty minutes from Denham and he was a terrific support. When I'd had a really bad day and was feeling totally helpless, I'd ring him in distress and he'd say, 'Don't worry – I'll be with you in twenty minutes.'

'No,' I'd say. 'I feel fine now, Dale. I just needed to know you were there.'

But he often dropped everything and came straight over anyway.

The curious thing is when I walk down a street with Dale – in London or abroad – people descend upon us from all directions, become all touchy-feely and ask for autographs. But when I'm out with Savage, nobody comes near us. They may say 'hello', but they don't stop and they never become touchy-feely.

In the early days after Bobby died, I couldn't bear to go out with my married friends because it upset me so much. I would look around the table and there would be the friends who I had always seen when I was with Bobby, and there they were with their husbands, but Bobby was gone.

My unmarried friends, though, like Biggins, Savage and Dale, got together and forced me to go out because they didn't like me to do *Blind Date* and then go home. Slowly, I began to realise that there were lots of fabulous, new places I could go to with them and that I also had friends to visit all around the world. I decided then that I was going to make damn sure that I did it, even if it meant flying on my own.

Biggins – who is a great friend of Joan Collins – is a very sociable guy and, after Bobby died, he introduced me to so many nice people. He also made sure I was looked after, especially when I decided to brave going to Barbados alone for the very first time. Arriving there without Bobby was so painful, just awful, and, when the limousine was taking me to the apartment, I almost asked the driver to turn around and take me straight back to the airport so that I could get Concorde back to London in a couple of hours' time. It took every ounce of my strength to go into the apartment without Bobby but, even though it was very strange and totally heartbreaking, I managed it somehow.

Biggins had telephoned Sir Anthony Bamford and his wife, Lady Carol, who have the twenty-acre Heron's Bay estate on the island. Sir Anthony owns the well-known JCB business, and Bobby and I had met him and Lady Carol a couple of times in the past and had also been to their house there. The first thing Bobby, being Bobby, did whenever he visited a new house was to go to see the animals; and, when he heard that Sir Anthony had an aviary full of budgerigars, off he went.

'Why aren't they breeding?' Sir Anthony had asked Bobby.

'It's simple, really,' replied Bobby, who knew a thing or two about budgerigars, having kept them as a boy. 'They're all the same sex.'

After that, Sir Anthony told everyone that Bobby had sexed his budgies.

When I reached the apartment, Lady Carol was the first person to phone me.

'We're having a dinner party tonight, darling,' she said. 'There'll only be eighteen of us. I'll send my butler to collect you.'

To go to a dinner without Bobby – and without a friend as an escort – was another first for me, but Lady Carol wouldn't take no for an answer.

For me, it was like learning to walk all over again, but every baby step helped. In the event, I was fine that night and Lady Carol and I became close friends.

Jimmy and Pauline Tarbuck were a tremendous support too. I'd known Jimmy since my teens and he was one of the first people to come to Denham to be there for me after Bobby died. The four of us had had some great times together over the years and in February, when it was time for Jimmy's sixtieth birthday party – a dinner-jacket occasion at Coombe Hill Golf Club – I asked Ben to come with me. Although Ben didn't want to wear a dinner jacket, he did it just to please me, and he looked absolutely stunning. Bobby would have loved that party because some of his favourite sportsmen, including Ian St John and Kenny Dalglish, were there.

I was in a terrible state, desperately hoping that no one would come up to me and put their arms around me. I knew that if they did that I would wail like a banshee.

I'd so wanted to be there for Jimmy, to wish him happy birthday, but it was too much, too soon. After forty minutes or so, I was engulfed by a huge wave of grief and I had to leave.

I knew that my life had to go on without Bobby, but there were times when I couldn't bear the thought that he would never come through the door again. The mind plays strange tricks at such times and sometimes you hear footsteps, hear a voice calling, 'I'm home.' In better moments, I knew I owed it to the boys to remain sane and get through my grief somehow.

Some moments at home were unbearable, though. Surrounded by so many things that reminded me of Bobby, there were times when I just wanted to escape from the pain and sell the house and move, but Robert, Ben and Jack persuaded me not to do that. The house, they kept reminding me, was also a comfort. It reflected so many things that Bobby and I had done together – and so much of our life as a family. Gradually I began to see it this way and turned my attention to the London apartment. Having converted one of the rooms there into an office, I had the whole place redecorated from top to bottom. Any kind of displacement therapy helps at such times.

I was beginning to learn just how much Bobby had done for me. I'd never handled money or concerned myself with my financial matters, and when I started, I realised that I needed to delegate. Robert had been involved in my career and the family business for years, since 1994 when he had given up his job working as a producer for GMTV to become my agent. Now he stepped into his father's shoes, becoming my manager too, looking after television, charity and press-related matters. He also came to the TV studio in the same way that Bobby had when I was recording and, once a week, he came to Denham to organise my diary with me.

I was so proud of all our boys. Each, in his own way, had been wonderful. As well as coping with their own grief, they couldn't do enough for me – they wanted me to lean on them. But I resisted that. They were young men with their own lives to lead and their own work to do, Ben at Channel 5 and Jack with his studies at Westminster College. I had to learn to manage alone.

So it was, step by painful step – and with a lot of help from my sons and my friends – and knowing they were all there for me – that I found I could start to move forward.

~

When I received an award from the Television and Radio Industries Club (TRIC) in March 2000, it was my first official public appearance in seven months, and Robert and I went to the Grosvenor House Hotel together for the ceremony. It was a great feeling to get the award, really special, and it made me want to go on and get another – which is exactly what happened. The following month, I received a similar award from the Broadcasting Press Guild, and then in July I finally accepted an Honorary Fellowship from Liverpool John Moores University.

I donned a black cap and gown, edged in red and white, and the ceremony took place at the Anglican Cathedral in Liverpool. I was handed the scroll by the university's chancellor, Cherie Blair, and on it were the words 'Outstanding Contribution to the Arts'.

During this time, Savage and I used to go out for dinner, and one evening he dragged me off to a club called Heaven, one of London's most popular gay nightclubs, just off Trafalgar Square, where we stayed until four in the morning. There were several different rooms, all with loud 'banging' house music, full of thousands of men (and their female friends) all dancing and cavorting through to the early hours of the morning. It was hot and packed and sweaty – I'd never seen anything like it in all my life. I loved it! I hadn't done anything like this since my teenage years when I used to go to the Cavern, but when I go out with Savage, it's a case of 'fasten your seat belts, it's going to be a long night'. I always knew, though, that he would be very protective of me. If I'm with him, nobody gets near me.

On one occasion a guy sent over a bottle of champagne and the air immediately became blue with Savage's swear words. It was 'f***s' galore. But the salty vocabulary is such a natural part of his angry-man character that nobody takes offence.

'Just because you bought her a f***ing bottle of champagne,' he said to the guy, 'you haven't bought her f***ing time. So f*** off.'

The guy just thought Savage was a scream, laughed, and took it all in good heart.

~

The latest series of *Blind Date* was screened in November. I thought it was improving all the time and I said a personal thank you to LWT who had been my 'family' for the last sixteen years, and especially kind during the past few months.

People who had worried about my safety before Bobby died began to worry all the more when I continued to go shopping on my own or hailed an ordinary cab. But I had to live my life the way I wanted, and the last thing I wanted was a bodyguard. I was particularly keen to go Christmas shopping on my own, and I kept thinking, 'Why shouldn't I?'

It always annoys me when people fuss. 'Let's face it,' I would say to this or that fusspot, 'I don't have the kind of image or personality that encourages the wrong kind of attention. What's the worst that's going to happen to me? – "Hi, Cilla, can I have your autograph?" That's not a problem.'

It would only have been a problem if I made it a problem – and I had no problem walking the streets! When I trotted along Victoria Street, for example, which seems to attract odd bods, I quite enjoyed the sense of danger. But, having said that, New Scotland Yard was just along the road – and I was getting to know some of the plain-clothes officers quite well.

A great trick if I didn't want to be recognised, I found, was tunnel vision – I just looked straight ahead and didn't look at anybody, no matter how attractive they were! Interestingly, too, people who are used to seeing me on the telly don't expect Cilla Black to be as slim and as tall as I am, which is almost 5 ft 7 in – and with my high heels on I'm even taller.

For all my bravado, though, that first year after Bobby died was one hell of an ordeal and I often had to take to my bed for twenty-four hours, wishing, like Canute, that I could stop the next wave coming in. Many were the nights when I wouldn't have minded if the next day had not dawned. When you lose somebody who is as precious as Bobby was to me, the 'firsts' just keep on coming. The first wedding anniversary without your partner and the first birthdays – theirs, yours, your children's – are particularly painful. Then there's the first anniversary of their death when your mind keeps replaying scenes that you would much rather forget and hoped never to experience again.

Then the next wave of activity comes relentlessly in and you realise it's countdown to Christmas again – and all you can do is try to focus on that and set about making sure that everyone will have the best possible time opening their presents, listening to the Queen's speech and eating their Christmas dinner. Then it's another New Year that the person you loved most in all the world will not be there to see in.

The end of January 2001 proved to be a particularly poignant time. In recent years, Bobby and I had always gone to Barbados to celebrate his birthday and our wedding anniversary on 25 January. Now, just fifteen months after he died, I had to deal with this special date without him.

It was not an easy decision, but I decided to go to St James to wriggle my toes in the warm sand, and I asked Savage to come with me.

On the 25th, we were sitting sunning ourselves on the roof terrace of my Barbados apartment when a cloud of butterflies fluttered on to the balcony. I was thrilled. I hadn't seen a butterfly for ages and I turned to Savage and said: 'I bet Bobby sent them.'

Then, spying a pigeon with one leg, I added, 'And I bet that's Bobby over there.'

Savage was horrified.

'Cilla,' he said, 'that's a one-legged, ratty-looking thing with wings! And that's supposed to be the man you loved more than life itself. God help me if you have anything to do with my reincarnation. *Why* is that pigeon Bobby?'

'I don't know,' I said, 'but it is our wedding anniversary today and Bobby always loved waifs and strays so much, I can't look at one without thinking of him.'

'So I suppose,' said Savage, 'when I die, the first cat you see with one eye and the mange, you will say, "That's Lily over there."'

One way and another, it was a weird day, one on which I felt close to tears throughout, and I was so glad Savage was there.

At least, thanks to a trip I had made to LA during the autumn, I could see the butterflies clearly! In spite of wearing contact lenses, I'd been finding it increasingly difficult to read the autocue at work. So, biting the bullet, I'd gone to a clinic recommended by Pat to have some laser surgery to correct my eyesight. The procedure had altered the shape of the cornea, so that light entering my eye changed direction and corrected the defect. The press only found out about this when I was spotted wearing shades to protect my newly treated eyes!

On Valentine's Day – another big milestone for me – Savage decided to keep me busy. First, he took me to a student production of *Gypsy* at the Westminster Theatre, then to dinner at the Ivy restaurant, and then he took me to Heaven again. I really did have a great time – and we were the only couple still on the dance floor when the staff put the lights on at five-thirty in the morning. The press subsequently made out that I went clubbing in Heaven every night!

During this time well-meaning friends were busy trying to pair me off with guys at their dinner parties. Me! The queen of *Blind Date* – of matchmaking! When Mary Parkinson – Michael's wife – phoned, she said, 'You've got so much love to give, darling – you *ought* to be with somebody.'

But having had the great love of my life, I wasn't looking for another.

I knew a lot of women of my age would be happy to date thirty-something men, but I wasn't into toy boys – couldn't even go there. Joan Collins kept saying, 'Darling, you must never go out with a man with grey chest hair', but what would Robert, Ben and Jack have said if I brought young things home? Toy boys may have energy and stamina, but, for me, they don't have the intellectual staying power; and men of my own age just looked too old! This was brought into sharp focus one day when a very nice sixty-something man tried to chat me up on holiday.

'Your eyes,' he said, 'are as aquamarine as the ocean.'

'Oh, *please* release me,' I thought.

That compliment might have been acceptable – sweet even – if it had come from a thirty-something, but a man my own age – no way!

Despite all my friends' good intentions, though, meeting someone, dating again, was the last thing on my mind – and I couldn't imagine feeling differently about that for a very long time, if ever. It's not always easy, though, to deter friends.

When Pat rang me one day from LA, she said, 'I've met this doctor.'

By then I was going quietly mental with other people's attempts to sort out my love life, but I didn't want to tell Pat off on the phone, because I knew she'd be upset for a month.

'He's never been married,' Pat was carrying on.

'Pat,' I interrupted, 'that is *not* good news. He'll be set in his ways, for a start. Anyway,' I added laughing, 'no man can come anywhere near me unless he's got a Learjet – and those come very expensive. That's my yard-stick – my deterrent – Pat.'

Since that conversation, I've always said to everybody, 'If he hasn't got a Learjet and can't keep me in the way I'm accustomed to being kept, don't even think about it.'

These incidents reminded me of a conversation that Bobby and I had had with the boys some years earlier when we were discussing what should happen if either Bobby or I passed on – whether the remaining partner should remarry.

'I'd want your dad to remarry,' I said.

'And I'd want you to be happy if anything happened to me,' Bobby chipped in.

He then continued to say all sorts of lovely, fantastic, poetical things about me and what a wonderful wife I had been. Then turning to the boys, he added: 'I want you to know that if your mum does get another feller ...'

'No, Dad – no,' the boys were now chanting in unison, obviously thinking this deathly conversation had gone too far.

'I want you to know that *if* your mum does get another feller ...' Bobby repeated, ignoring the interruption. 'If she does get another feller, I want each and every one of you to knock seven kinds of crap out of him.'

I was glad he said that!

The Learjet deterrent didn't work! Couples still continued to invite me to matchmaking dinners, with no success.

Then, when they finally gave up doing this, they paired me off with my friend Pat Booth, whose husband Garth died almost two years after Bobby. We're now considered a couple! This is great. It means people are finally getting the message.

'If I do ever meet a really special feller,' I told my friends, 'you'll be the first to hear about it, but Bobby is still my last thought at night and my first thought in the morning.'

~

I was absolutely thrilled. Robert and Fiona had at last settled on a date for their wedding – 4 August 2001 – at our village church, St Mary the Virgin, Denham.

This was the same church where Bobby's funeral had taken place, but I wouldn't have wanted their wedding to be anywhere else, and I was determined that there would be no shadows cast over that day. It would be a joyous celebration, a day we would all remember for the rest of our lives.

'Right,' I thought, 'the time has come to get my figure really sorted out. I want to look my very best for the wedding.'

I'd always been interested in nutrition and fitness, but now I decided to get a personal trainer and begin regular workouts in the gym room at Denham.

I'd worn Escada clothes for some years, but as I slimmed down to a size eight again, I started to wear Ralph Lauren and Celine designs, and I thoroughly enjoyed going on shopping trips with Pat Booth and Patti Boyd in Paris – and with Savage in New York.

Now, aged fifty-six, I also found myself wearing skin-tight, leather trousers for the very first time. Jack was the first to give them the seal of approval.

'They're terrific,' he said.

'Cool,' Robert and Ben added when they saw me wafting around.

Knowing how common it is for kids to be embarrassed by their parents, I found my sons' reactions quite extraordinary and very comforting!

By the end of May – just after my fifty-seventh birthday, which was agony because I was missing Bobby so much – I was feeling very low and I decided to go back to Barbados. I had had a really bad bout of flu that had turned into bronchitis and I could hardly speak, but at least when I did I sounded very husky and sexy.

My apartment in Barbados is one of a block of fourteen, and all the neighbours know each other and are on first-name terms. We all muck in and have our barbecues on our part of the beach, where no one else walks at night, and it's a really relaxing, 'family'-type experience. When I went there for the first time after Bobby died, my neighbours were all very caring, but this time I just wanted to be on my own for a week before Robert and Fiona came out to join me.

I know some people think I'm a natural redhead, but of course I'm not; and one of the things I always do on holiday, because I find it very therapeutic, is to colour the roots of my hair.

After a few days in Barbados, the sun had really bleached my hair, so I put the rinse on. I must have been in a somewhat distracted mood because I left it on too long before rinsing it off. When I looked in the mirror and saw what had happened, I was horrified and burst into tears. The colour had gone very dark. I looked like Johnny Cash! I was already feeling low and rather vulnerable and this was the last straw.

At that moment the telephone rang and, pulling myself together, I answered it.

It was Lady Bamford, and when she asked me how I was, I burst into tears again, told her in a very croaky voice what had happened to my hair, and then added how poorly I was feeling.

'I look like Johnny Cash,' I kept wailing.

'I'm not going to take no for an answer,' she said again. 'We're all invited to a big NSPCC dinner party – and I'm sending the car for you. You were involved with the NSPCC launch in 1999 and you should be there. I'll send the chauffeur to pick you up.'

When I go on holiday I don't take dressy clothes with me, but at least I had a sparkly top and a pair of evening trousers in the wardrobe.

So, later that day, there I was at the house, my hair looking ridiculous, and still very hoarse from the worst bout of flu I had ever had. Suddenly, in comes her houseguest, Prince Andrew. I nearly died, my hand going instantly to my hair!

Dressed in his whites, he looked absolutely gorgeous. He came straight over to me, scooped me into his arms, and greeted me like a long-lost friend. If he was surprised at the colour of my hair, he was too much of a gentleman to say so!

Carol then sat me at the top table, next to Prince Andrew, who looked after me the whole evening. He told lots of jokes, and some of them very risqué too, but just like with Savage, you couldn't take offence.

On the phone to Carol the next day, I said: 'What were you thinking of? Why didn't you tell me Prince Andrew would be there?'

'If I'd told you when you were moaning and saying you were looking like Johnny Cash, and had nothing to wear, you wouldn't have come,' she replied.

It was a super evening, and I was glad that she hadn't told me.

By the time Robert and Fiona arrived in Barbados, I was feeling much better, and pleased that Dale, who was staying at the Colony Club in St James, was also able to spend some time with us. On the last day of Robert and Fiona's holiday, I hired a boat so that we could go and look at the turtles, and asked Dale to join us. We had no idea that there was an uninvited guest on that trip. A couple of days later, there was a double-page spread of pictures in a paper with the headline, 'Dale makes Cilla laugh again.'

I was shocked. I had no idea that the paparazzi were keeping such a close eye on me and, since then, I have kept a pair of binoculars at the apartment which I train on the boats bobbing about just offshore. My next purchase will probably be a telescope!

~

Back home at Denham, the plans for Robert and Fiona's wedding were gathering pace. Ever thoughtful, they had involved me in all their plans, and I was very touched when they asked if they could have the reception in a marquee in the garden. I really couldn't think of anything nicer.

Bobby and I had always known that Fiona was the right girl for Robert, and we had always looked upon her as the daughter we would have loved to have had. We felt they were like swans, that they would mate for life, just as we had done. In 2001, they had been together for ten years.

What's It All About?

For the big day, I chose a stone-coloured dress and jacket that I was going to wear with lilac slingback shoes designed by Jimmy Choo. As far as the hat was concerned, I'd decided that, after all my *Blind Date* experiences, I wasn't going to wear one. Instead, I wore tiny designer clip-on flowers in my hair. Robert had involved both his brothers in the ceremony. Ben was to be the best man and Jack was going to stand next to him and pass the ring.

The day of the wedding could not have been more perfect. Both families were there, and some of my closest friends, including George Martin, Dale, Savage, Biggins, Peter Brown, Jimmy Tarbuck and Michael Hurll and his wife Sandra. The sun shone and everybody – most of all the bride – looked gorgeous.

When the ceremony was taking place, I definitely felt Bobby's presence at my side.

'He's here,' I thought, fighting back my tears. 'I know he's here.'

It was an absolutely stunning day and the reception, held in a magnificent ruche-lined marquee in the garden, was a great success. People danced the night away and were still there dancing in the early hours of the morning!

Pat and her husband Jeff, who had come over from LA for the occasion, were staying with us at Denham. After the guests had gone, Pat and I curled up in the sitting room together to talk about the day.

'People kept on coming up to me,' she said, 'saying that you were too thin.'

'How did you deal with that?' I asked.

'I said, "Wait a minute, you're all Johnny Come Lately's. This is her natural size. You'se lot have got used to her being a little bigger than she used to be, that's all."'

I then told Pat that people were constantly worrying about me – and that, even in Barbados, they kept saying I was far too thin. This went right back to my childhood when neighbours in Scottie Road were always saying

368

to my mam that I was ever so thin and my mam was always retaliating by saying, 'Well, she eats like a horse and she's as fit as a fiddle.'

~

Three weeks after the wedding, the fourth – and last – series of *Moment of Truth* was screened at an earlier time to make way for ITV1's new football slot. That move lost the network at least 4.4 million viewers who didn't want to watch football and switched over to BBC1. There were also plans to move *Blind Date* to an earlier viewing time when it came back in November. I knew this was a big mistake. I had nothing against football – I loved the game – but I didn't think the changes were fair on the wives and mothers who looked after the kids during the week while the guys went out to watch their own teams playing. What was needed on a Saturday evening was light entertainment – and I felt that ITV was giving an unspoken message to the BBC: 'Do you want the whole of Saturday night? Here it is on a plate.'

'Who do I speak to about this?' I thought and I decided to go straight to the top, to Granada's boss, Charles Allen, and I rang his mobile, something I had never done before.

'You've got yourself thoroughly worked up,' I told myself, 'so now be brave.'

'Morning, Charles,' I said when he answered, 'you sound awful. Are you ill?'

'I've got this terrible flu,' he replied.

Brushing this aside, and going straight to the point, I said, 'About Saturday night, Charles … I'm totally upset. I will not be in the studio next week if you do not put *Blind Date* back into its original slot.' I could hardly believe what I was saying. But it seemed to work!

The football was moved to a late-night slot where it did very well and I got my prime-time slot back.

I know I wasn't the most popular kid on the block afterwards, and I don't think I was ever really forgiven for making my telephone call to

Charles, but I cared too much about the programming and the viewers to worry about that.

Bobby would have been proud of me.

~

One occasion when I missed Bobby desperately that year was on a Sunday evening when I was due to go to a charity 'do' to raise money for Westminster Cathedral's 'The Passage', a project to help homeless people. While dressing for this, I realised that the dress I had chosen to wear had a long zip down its back that I couldn't reach. After struggling this way and that for a long time, I sank down on the bed and, very frustrated and angry, began to rail at Bobby.

'Why aren't you here?' I kept sobbing. 'Why aren't you here? I *need* you.'

I knew it was irrational, but I just felt so angry that he had left me.

When I pulled myself together, I thought: 'I know, I'll ask my Paul, my chauffeur, to zip me up.'

But I was very reluctant to do this in case he interpreted it as a 'come-on'!

'Don't be daft,' I chastised myself. 'He's known you for years. He's a gentleman – that's the last thing he'd think.'

So, problem solved, I asked Paul to zip me up.

I really hate making solo entrances, so in the car I phoned Biggins to make sure he would be there to meet me as I stepped out of the car, which he did, ever the gentleman.

'Please don't let me forget to ask you to unzip my dress,' I added, 'when you drop me off at the flat at the end of the evening.'

Needless to say, both of us forgot.

Having escorted me back to my flat and seen me safely in, Biggins had waved goodbye. Now, there I was, alone again, unable to reach the zip and convinced I would have to sit up in a chair, stiff as a board, all night.

In despair, I was back to wailing at Bobby.

'Where are you? How could you leave me? I need you.'

'Perhaps,' I thought when I was all cried out, 'the dress will go up, rather than down, over my head!'

Taking a deep breath to make myself smaller, I twisted and turned and got myself into all manner of yoga-like contortions. It took an amazing twenty-five minutes of wriggling this way and that, but I finally got that dress over my head and fell exhausted on to the bed.

That was the night when I finally accepted that Bobby had died and would not be coming back. Up until then, I was still in denial and forever looking up from whatever I was doing and expecting him to walk through the door, saying, 'Hi, Cil – I'm home!'

Now, somehow, things were slightly different. In a very small way, I'd moved on.

~

I'd always loved the Royal Variety Performance, and in November 2001 it was being held at London's Dominion Theatre, with a wonderful cast of celebrities that included Elton John as 'top of the bill'. Raising money for charity is what showbiz people do best and we all have a wonderful time entertaining a fantastic audience. For that year's show, I got together with Barbara Windsor and Savage and, for a bit of light entertainment in what was going to a very long show, we decided to perform a dance routine from the musical *Gypsy*. We chose the basque sequence when three old strippers are teaching the young one that if you want to make it in this business, 'You've Got To Have A Gimmick' – and that was the song we sang.

There we were, dressed in fishnet tights and figure-hugging black basques, and when I turned around and bent over, the spotlight was strategically placed to reveal a heart, lit by fairy lights, on my bottom. That dance caused a furore and stole the show.

Later, when we were being presented, the Queen, with such a lovely smile on her face, said to me, 'You looked as if you were enjoying yourself', and then the Duke of Edinburgh said, 'We saw more of you tonight than we have ever seen before!'

The next day, the papers were full of our dance routine and it was even said that we'd upstaged the beautiful Jennifer Lopez, who had danced flamenco dressed in a beaded Versace evening dress seductively split up to her thigh and had been heralded as the sexiest woman of the year!

'Life is for living,' I said to the press, 'and I'm living it.'

A couple of days later the Queen visited various television locations, including the set of *EastEnders* and the ITN news studio, and then she hosted an evening reception for people in the radio and television industry at Buckingham Palace. I went to this with Charles Allen, and in contrast to my sexy basque, I wore a grey outfit and sensible shoes that made me look as if I had just stepped out of an office. It was a star-studded occasion during which other members of the royal family were walking around mingling with the guests.

When I was talking to Parky, Prince Andrew suddenly appeared at my side, scooped me up in his arms and kissed me on both cheeks.

'What's all this about?' Parky asked, surprised.

'Since doing that basque thing,' I replied, batting my eyelids, 'my street cred has gone up and up.'

A short time later, an equerry came up to me and said: 'The Queen and the Duke would like to see you in a private room here in a couple of minutes' time.'

I was amazed!

There were eight of us present in the ante-room, including Charles Allen, Greg Dyke and Michael Parkinson, and we all had to stand in a line as the Queen and the Duke entered. When the Queen saw me, she had a broad smile on her face, but I could feel mine getting redder and redder.

'Well,' she said as she came alongside me, 'this is a very different outfit from the one you were wearing the other night.' Then she continued to talk to me as if we had been friends for years.

31

Something's Gonna Happen Tonight...

They all thought I was absolutely crazy.

'Mum! Is this the Christmas champagne talking?' Robert asked.

'No,' I replied. 'It is not. I *want* to do it.'

When I mentioned my latest escapade to my mate Pat Booth, she gasped and said, 'You're crazy. But if you want to jump out of a plane it's your funeral!'

'*I'm* crazy?' I replied. 'What about *you*? You've just told me you're going trekking in Peru – and that's something I would never do, Pat. It makes me itch just thinking about the jungle.'

This drama had come about because we were making an experimental pilot for LWT.

One of the segments, which featured a girl who was married to a macho, sports-loving man, was about skydiving. The feller loved his wife to bits, and wanted her to join in his sporting activities. She kept saying she was not interested, but secretly she had written to LWT saying that she wanted to take private lessons and surprise him by making a tandem skydive.

What's It All About?

At the production meeting, just before Christmas 2002, she told me she was terrified of heights.

'I am, too,' I said, 'but I'll skydive with you.'

The day before the drop I had to have a medical for insurance purposes. I found myself being given a once over by a lady doctor who, it turned out, had done a parachute jump.

'How did it go?' I asked.

'Well, I'll give you a tip,' she replied. 'When you jump out of the plane, be very, very careful because the pressure will force you upwards. When I jumped, I went back up, banged my shoulder on the plane and blacked out.'

'You blacked out?' I said, horrified.

'Yes.'

'Oh, my God!' I exclaimed, and suddenly I found myself about to do a freefall while my feet were still on the ground! Steadying myself, I remembered that I would be jumping as one half of a tandem and, hopefully, we wouldn't both black out.

My tandem partner was also one of the cameramen and a trained skydiver, and when I mentioned what the doctor had told me, he said, 'Not a problem. If you black out, I'll look after you.'

'But what if *you* black out, too?' I pressed. 'What if it happens to both of us?'

'You're making me nervous now,' he replied. 'But if we both black out, we won't know anything about it, will we!'

I suppose that was meant to be reassuring!

We had half an hour's training for the dive, then we were given our instructions for the drop. The outfits we had to wear were awful. Everything had to be very tight-fitting because when you exit from the plane, the wind force is so strong that any loose garment would be ripped straight from your back.

The actual drop is made as you approach 12,000 feet. At the words

'Ready, steady, go!' you then exit from the plane, sitting on the tandem instructor's lap. The sportsman's wife went out before me. I realised I was very nervous because as I stood there, looking out of the plane, with thousands of feet of *nothing* beneath me, I became completely calm – almost comatose – and didn't say a word, which was most unlike me.

Then we exited from the plane. I hung on to my partner's belt for dear life while we played up to the cameras, somersaulting, waving and smiling. The best part was when the parachute opened. That was fabulous. It was a freezing cold day that left me feeling all my facial features had been erased, but I forgot all about that when I saw the scenery as I floated down to earth. It was dreamlike as we drifted down. Suddenly I hadn't a care in the world, and I thought this was what it must be like going to heaven – only I was going to earth. But would I do it again? Definitely not!

~

In April and May 2002, I was the surprise guest in *The Play What I Wrote* by Hamish McColl and Sean Foley at London's Wyndham Theatre. It was fun to be doing something by Eric and Ernie. Of the two, I'd always known Eric best. He and his wife had once had a villa opposite Mu Young's when we were staying with her in Portugal, and he was lovely with the boys. When Robert was small he used to call Eric 'Mr Tick-tock' because of being allowed to play with his watch. A naturally funny man, he always addressed me as 'kind sir'. This revival of their inspired comedy, directed by Kenneth Branagh, featured a different unannounced celebrity guest each night. As well as me, Ralph Fiennes, Richard Wilson, Richard E. Grant, Sue Johnston, Twiggy and Sting had all appeared in it.

For my appearances, I wore a long satin dressing gown which, when the belt was untied, revealed my legs in a black leotard with a diamanté belt. At the end of my scene, I had to do a quick change in the wings into an evening dress, to appear in the line-up at the end of the play with the rest of the cast, and sing 'Bring Me Sunshine' before our final bows.

There was no problem with any of that, except that I was not used to stripping down to my bra and pants in front of stagehands. I've always been a modest girl, so I asked the stage manager if I could have a quick-change tent. He looked at me in horror, then said, 'Sorry, we can't do that – but I'll tell the crew not to look.'

Satisfied with that, I did all my strips and thought no more about it.

Later, when I was telling Biggins about this, he started roaring.

'What's so funny?' I asked.

'Are you crazy?' he said. 'There would have been eyes everywhere! Of course they looked – and no doubt they've got the photographs to prove it.'

As it was 'art for art's sake', I was doing the show for a mere £500 a night and now I was having nightmares about those striptease pics doing the rounds! But when I told Biggins how worried I was, he said he was only sending me up – they were probably a great bunch of lads who'd done as they were told!

~

Still missing Bobby more than I could bear at times, I was throwing myself into a social life that was becoming increasingly busy. I now went to first nights and partied whenever I could, but I made sure that I left time for charity functions too. These included the *Daily Mirror*'s 'Pride of Britain Awards' and fundraising for the Alder Hey Hospital's 'Rocking Horse' appeal, and in April I agreed to become patron for Wellbeing (the new name for Birthright), a role previously held by Princess Diana.

Later in April, Robert phoned me in Barbados to tell me that Savage had had a heart attack and might need an emergency bypass operation. Savage and I were like brother and sister by now. I was so relieved when he made a good recovery and began to take more care of himself. As soon as he was well again, we went out for dinner. As we took a short cut through London's Soho, I looked at the many obvious prostitutes hovering on the pavements and street corners.

'You know, Savage,' I said, 'if I was a lady of the night, there's no way

I'd stand on a street corner. I'd go to the bank and ask for a business loan. Then, I'd book a room at Claridge's or the Ritz – and do it properly, in style. I wouldn't mind doing the dressing-up bit in leathers and high heels. I think I could persecute and punish men. I think I could do that quite easily! I could whip them.'

Paul's eyes were getting bigger and bigger.

'OK,' he replied. 'We'll do that! You can do the S&M and I'll do the nanny bit.'

'What's the nanny bit?' I asked, intrigued.

'Well, some guys like a nappy put on them.'

'Oh, my God, no,' I said, horrified. 'I couldn't put a nappy on a guy.'

'Oh,' Savage exclaimed, 'so you could beat the crap out of them, but you couldn't put a nappy on them!'

He had a point! But it was good to see him back on form.

~

A few days after I finished my appearances in *The Play What I Wrote*, I went out on a shopping spree with Lynda La Plante and Pat Booth. When we were planning the expedition, Pat suggested that we should have lunch at Gordon Ramsay's restaurant in Claridge's.

I'd first met Gordon at Le Caprice and after the introductions he had said petulantly, 'Cilla, you've never been to one of my restaurants.'

'You know why, Gordon?' I'd answered. 'Because you're always full.'

'Well, I will always make sure there's a table for you, Cilla,' he'd replied.

So now I told Pat, 'Remind Gordon what he said to me. Let's see if he's true to his word.'

He was – he reserved a table for us at two o'clock. When we arrived, he sent over 'a glass of champagne for the ladies', which was just what we needed to recover from the shock of spending thousands of pounds on clothes. As we sat there, giggling like schoolgirls, there was a tap on my shoulder. It was Cherie Blair.

'Hello, Cilla', she said. 'Sorry to interrupt you, but it's Tony's birthday today. We've got a table in the kitchen. You wouldn't come and wish him happy birthday, would you?'

It wasn't the first time I'd met him. Soon after Bobby died, Robert and I had been invited to Chequers, and Tony Blair said, 'Tell me where I'm going wrong, Cilla.' I'm sure he was pulling my leg, but I ploughed on anyway, and told him he ought to look after the middle-classes, women and pensioners. Not long after, he went to the Women's Institute and got slow-handclapped. That's how right I was! You underestimate the older woman at your peril!

I was delighted Cherie had come over now. 'Of course,' I said to her. 'Come on girls.'

We all rushed into the kitchen. And there we found the PM sitting at a specially arranged private table for his birthday lunch. Pat said to Tony, 'What did you get for your birthday?'

'This sweater and a new guitar,' he replied. Bless him.

'Aaah, it's lovely,' we all cooed, mothering him a bit. We wished him happy birthday and returned to our table, giggling at every little thing.

~

In summer 2002, I was invited to a charity polo match at Ashe Park, Hampshire, at which Prince Charles, Prince Harry and Prince William were all going to be playing. I'd met Prince Charles several times, once at St James's Palace when he hosted the fiftieth anniversary of Radio Four's *The Archers*, but mainly at other polo matches.

On this occasion, however, I made a faux pas. Having strolled into the refreshment tent to get a Pimms, I took myself off to the sidelines to watch the horses thundering past. I was aware that everybody was rushing off for the prize-giving, but I didn't pay any attention to the Tannoy. It was only later that I found out it had been saying, 'Would Miss Cilla Black please proceed to the ring?' I was meant to be presenting a prize!

'Where were you?' Prince Charles asked me at teatime

'I didn't hear the Tannoy,' I said. I was *so* embarrassed – and so sad to have missed seeing the two most beautiful boys in Britain – but at least I was able to apologise.

I made another faux pas when the Soil Association invited me to visit Highgrove. We try to be organic at Denham, growing our own organic vegetables and buying only organic meat, and I've been interested in 'green' issues for years, so I hadn't jumped on Prince Charles's bandwagon.

Patti Boyd and I went to Highgrove together and we bumped into Susan Hampshire, who was with a lady who looked so much like her.

'Is that your mother?' I asked.

'No,' Susan replied, 'it's my sister.'

Will I never learn!

Later, when Patti and I were walking through the grounds, we came upon the swimming pool. And who was swimming in it with not a care in the world? Prince William. I tried not to look! I should have said 'Hello', but I was so overcome, I scurried off.

~

Later that summer I went to my villa in Spain and was joined there by Pat who flew in from LA. While we were out there, a man invited me out who I had previously met several times in a group of friends. Not yet feeling ready to have dinner with a feller on my own, I suggested we should have lunch. I was worried about what I should do when he dropped me off at my villa after lunch. Should I invite him in for a coffee?

Pat couldn't understand what I was worrying about.

'In LA,' she said, 'I play mixed doubles five times a week with millionaires and I always invite them in for coffee.'

'In Britain,' I replied primly, 'inviting someone in for a coffee after a date *can* mean something else.'

I decided to ask Dale, who was staying with friends in Spain, what I should do. That night, Pat and I had dinner with him and, when he took us back to my villa, he said, 'I've been thinking about your lunch date.

What you say, doll, is, "I would *really, really* like you to come in for a cup of coffee, but ..." '

He paused, and Pat and I wondered what was coming next.

' "But I *really, really* don't want to shag you." '

'Dale!' I exploded. 'You want me to say *that*? Me, the girl next door? The family entertainer?'

I couldn't believe it. What sort of company was I keeping?

A couple of days later, I had a fabulous lunch with the guy, and he did come in for coffee, and everything was just fine.

Dale's advice was useful, though. Since then, when a feller asks me out, and I want to make it clear in the nicest possible way that I'm not into relationships, because I'm still in love with my husband, I tell them Dale's story. It breaks the ice, clears the air, and is imprinted on their brain.

One day during that holiday, Pat, Dale and I were shopping down at the port. Dale, quite rightly, likes to look his best when he is being photographed, but that day he didn't expect any photographs and he was dressed very casually in shorts and baseball cap and had a five o'clock shadow. But then two girls suddenly appeared and said very abruptly to Pat, 'Here, take a picture of us with Cilla and Dale.'

'Certainly,' she said, looking like butter wouldn't melt. But I knew that was *not* the way to talk to her.

While I was standing there thinking that, as I was out there, I was fair game, Dale was fussing around, whispering, 'Oh, my God, I'm really not looking my best.' The photograph taken, it was earache from Winton from the top of the road to the bottom as he wailed, 'Oh, my God, how can people do this to me?'

'Dale, are you crazy?' Pat eventually said. 'I was the one taking the picture. Do you think I was going to let those girls order me about like that? I can assure you neither of you is in that shot.'

~

As 2002 rolled on, it seemed to me that, despite Bobby's death, and despite me still missing him dreadfully, life was moving on. Somehow, without quite being able to put my finger on it, I was beginning to feel more in control – it seemed I could decide when and how things should happen without having them decided for me. Part of realising this was when I began to think the unthinkable – I began to think of leaving *Blind Date*.

When the first of the eighteenth series of *Blind Date* came back to our screens in October 2002, several changes had been made to the format. In the quest for more marriages on the show, the powers that be had introduced 'Date or Ditch?' – before deciding whether to date or ditch, the contestants now kept their eye on the audience's thumbs-up or down reaction. And the vocal introduction was now being done by a former contestant, DJ Tommy Sandhu, and the pickers were no longer aided and abetted by 'Our Graham' – Graham Skidmore. I was *very* upset about that change. Graham had always been there and the audience loved him, even though they never saw him.

Also, celebrities were occasionally going to take the place of contestants; and to keep up with the other major shows, behind-the-scenes footage and uncut interviews were to be transmitted on the same evening on ITV2. There was also going to be a Christmas Special and a live edition for the New Year of 2003.

I'd more than hinted in the run-up to this series that I was unhappy with the changes, especially 'Date or Ditch?', but Granada had taken over LWT and wanted to make its mark. In the end, although I'm a firm believer in 'if it ain't broke, don't fix it', I thought 'Maybe they're right, maybe they do know best', and I accepted the revamped formula.

Lots of things were still niggling away at me, though, and making me feel very miserable. There wasn't as much time for me to interact with the contestants, and I was missing chatting to the boys and girls. What had always excited me most about the show – and working with Joe Public – was not knowing what the contestants were going to say next. That might freak other artistes out, but I thrived on it, loved the unpredictability and the ad-libbing. Now I felt my job was becoming more and more like a presenter's job, and I am *not* a presenter. I am an entertainer.

All in all, it was becoming a different job from the one that I had known and loved, but I always made the best of it when I was on the set, because as that red light went on, a light went on in me, too.

Following the introduction of the revamp, though, there was a spectacular nose-dive in the ratings. A show that had commanded an audience of fourteen million plummeted to an all-time low of 4.6 million. Predictably, I was blamed for the fall in ratings – and the rumour factory went into overdrive. According to the press, I was going to be dethroned and the names of celebrities who were going to be asked to replace me were touted around. Graham Norton, Trish Goddard and Davina McCall – they were all apparently lining up to take over.

None of this was true.

What *was* true was that I wasn't as happy as I had been. I'd been doing the show for twenty-six weeks a year for eighteen years. I didn't like the changes, and I was stressed out. I love my food, but I couldn't eat for the anxiety of it all. What used to be fun was now becoming a hard slog. I knew it was time for some serious thinking when I realised that I'd lost so much weight, my size eight trousers were now too big for me. My dresser thought this was great, but I didn't; and, from the start of that last series, the idea of leaving was in my head.

Then, when Martyn Redman, my producer for the last three years, decided to leave halfway through making the series, I was even more unsettled and I had a really serious talk with myself.

'Cilla,' I said, 'eighteen years is a long time – maybe it is time to stop.'

When I told Robert about these thoughts, he agreed.

Around Christmas, when I was still in emotional turmoil and struggling with my decision to quit the show, I found myself asking what Bobby would have said – and I came to the conclusion that he would have told me to make the break.

This intuition was then backed up by a visit I made with Dale to the Belgravia home of his friend, Merril Thomas, to see Lynn, a psychic from the East End of London, who they were in the habit of consulting. I went along more out of curiosity than anything else. I was in for a shock.

I hadn't said a word to Lynn about what I was planning to do or why I wanted to see her, but the moment she clapped eyes on me, she said at once, 'Who's Rob?'

'My son,' I replied. (Robert is never referred to as 'Rob' in the newspapers.)

'Bobby is telling me,' she went on, 'that Rob's doing a very good job, but there are a couple of big decisions to be made and you are anxious and also excited.'

'I am anxious,' I confirmed, 'and very excited.'

'Be as excited as you like,' she said, 'but don't be anxious. Bobby is saying that everything will be all right. You're thinking of making a very big announcement, but you're dithering about it. Bobby says: "Go for it! It's OK. You're doing the right thing. Don't be scared. It will work out."'

I was stunned – and when she continued to tell me things about Bobby that no one could possibly have known and kept getting messages from him phrased in just the way that he used to talk, I was totally thrown and upset.

Bobby had never believed in psychics, so I said to her, 'You know, he doesn't believe in any of this.'

'Well, he does now!' she replied.

I wept buckets that night. I'd already made up my mind to resign before I saw Lynn, but it was still a terrible roller-coaster. I was shaking like a jelly on a plate, but it wasn't because I had decided to leave. It was because of how I was going to do it, and I was very worried that I would be accused of being unprofessional. That was the only thing that was bothering me.

Fortunately, I slept really well the night before the live show and on the Saturday, I woke up feeling incredibly calm.

What's It All About?

On the days when I did *Blind Date* I had to get to the studio at two o'clock, so that the team could do what is called the 'camera block' followed by the dress rehearsal at four o'clock.

'How are you feeling?' my executive producer, Chris O'Dell, asked me at one moment.

'I'm a bit worried,' I replied.

'It's a live show – you're bound to have butterflies,' he said.

'It's not that, Chris,' I answered. 'It's the opposite. I'm *too* calm. Let's hope I have a bad dress run because if I do the adrenaline will kick in and I'll do a great show!'

Then, as he went about his business, I thought, 'Stop worrying. Just go for it.' Suddenly, I felt excited, and I couldn't wait to get on and reveal the secret I had been hiding: I was going to tell the world, live on air, that I was leaving *Blind Date*. And no one at Granada or ITV knew a thing about it!

~

The reason I had decided to take everyone by surprise didn't have anything to do with sour grapes, or getting one over on ITV. It was because I didn't want to do a big press thing, and I knew that a live show would be the ideal opportunity to announce that I was leaving. Above all, I wanted the viewers to be the first to know. It was they, after all, who had made me and the show such a success. I realised I might be accused of being selfish and unprofessional for not telling the TV executives first and, on reflection, maybe I was. But it was about me – and my career – and I wanted to tell the viewers myself. They're the ones I owed – the ones I cared about most.

It really had been the best-kept secret. No one knew I was going to make the announcement that night except Robert and Fiona. It was very much an eleventh-hour decision and I didn't tell Ben and Jack or any of my friends because, after eighteen years, I might have changed my mind at the last moment.

Even, on the night, I said to Robert, 'If I don't do the announcement in the first ten minutes, you'll know I'm not going to do it tonight.'

Then, when I arrived on the studio floor, I turned to Lee Connelly, my producer, and said, 'Look, I might go off on a tangent, but don't worry if I do. It won't be because I've lost it. I'll come back – and I'll be solid.'

Those were the last words I said to him before the show started, and I only said that because I genuinely didn't want him to worry and think, 'It's live TV and Cilla's totally lost it!'

I was totally in control of my emotions, because I'm more in control in front of a camera than anywhere else. I took a deep breath, and turned to camera.

'This will be my last *Blind Date*,' I said.

And there was silence.

It seemed that everyone on the floor and in the studio did a double-take. It was eerie, like a movie. I could see everybody's reactions in slow motion. The technicians looked at each other, mouthing, '*What* did she say?' Everyone else was stunned as they tried to take it in, but for me it was over and done with – and I felt great. What I remember most, though, is looking up at Robert, who was sitting exactly where Bobby used to sit – and he gave me a thumbs-up, just as Bobby would have done. For a moment, it was as if he had morphed into Bobby.

As soon as I had said those magic words, I felt completely calm. It was a huge weight off my mind. Absolutely wonderful. The last time I had done anything so shocking on live TV was on my sixties BBC show *Cilla*, when I inadvertently announced the football results in advance of *Match of the Day*!

After the show, Paul Jackson, my boss, was terrific. He hadn't had an inkling of what I was going to do, but as the credits came up on the screen and we went off the air, he came rushing on to the set as I was saying my thank yous and goodnights to the studio audience. He said the most complimentary things about me and added that if he'd known it was to be my last night on *Blind Date*, there would have been flowers and champagne. Then, turning to the audience, he said, '*You* will have to be Cilla's present tonight, so please wish her well', and they all stood up and gave me a standing ovation. Until then I'd been perfectly calm and very happy, but you can imagine that seeing them all there, standing and clapping, I felt completely choked. I very nearly lost it at that moment.

Later that night, I went out with Dale for a fabulous dinner at Le Caprice to celebrate. He hadn't known that I was going to do it. I'd just said, 'Watch the show tonight!' – and he had watched the programme at home and been gobsmacked.

I had no regrets. I had had enough – and I didn't care tuppence that my resignation would lose me a £1.75 million-a-year contract. There were eight of us at Le Caprice and it was a really lovely way to end an extraordinary evening.

Ben heard about my decision that night, but Jack didn't know anything until he read about it in the papers when he got up on Sunday morning.

'I've just read the news,' he said when he rang me. 'You're not doing *Blind Date* any more. That's good.'

'Why?' I asked.

'I didn't like the changes they made,' he replied.

In some ways I was surprised that none of my friends had put two and two together. During the summer, when I was in Spain, I was forever saying, 'D'you know something? I could spend a lot of time here.'

It was obvious that I couldn't do that *and* do *Blind Date*, but nobody queried what I was saying or challenged me. After I'd made the announcement, though, John Hughes phoned me from Spain and said, 'I *knew* you had something up your sleeve, because in the summer you kept talking about taking a year out.' It seemed he was the only one who'd cottoned on. Perhaps some of the others had, but then again, perhaps they thought I was all talk and no action. If they did, I proved them wrong!

Although leaving *Blind Date* was a huge, life-changing decision for me, hand on heart I honestly didn't think my announcement would cause the fuss that it did in the papers and on the radio. It was even mentioned on the *Today* programme on Radio Four! Although I often made jokes on television about being a star, I never, ever think of myself as a star – and I was genuinely surprised by the furore.

All through the Sunday there were lots of photographers hovering behind the electronic gates of the house. I felt exhausted; and, after all the adrenaline, a huge black cloud came down.

I couldn't bear to look at the papers, because I don't like to read negative things about myself. Instead, I asked Robert if there were any negative comments and he simply said, 'No.'

Blind Date was my baby, but it had grown up, fled the nest and I went with it. One day I hope they will resurrect it. I've no desire to see it go down the tubes. People have short memories. If they rest it for a while, they could bring it back. It's a hit show and, if they did, I'd be the first to say 'good luck' to the new host.

In all, I had twenty fabulous years with LWT – and, of course, there were times later when I thought, 'Was that the most unprofessional thing I've done in my life?' and 'Was it the right thing to do?' But, that aside, I had absolutely no personal regrets. None at all.

Afterwards, when journalists kept asking me if I was going to carry on working in TV, I said: 'You know what? I'm only going to do stuff for fun or exciting things from now on.' And I meant it.

32

What's It All About?

On Tuesday, 27 May 2003, I was going to be sixty, and to celebrate this landmark I decided to do what Bobby would have done for me if he were still alive. I decided to indulge myself by hosting a lavish party at Denham and treating myself to a silver Ferrari and/or a pink diamond ring.

My new motto in life would be 'Because I Can'!

I got the idea for the ring when I was window-shopping in Bond Street. Spotting an absolute knock-out pink diamond (which I subsequently learned cost £1.4 million), I thought, 'Oh, God, I *love* it, but I want one with a marquise setting in exactly the right shade of pink.' I soon discovered, however, that this was easier said than done. There wasn't a pink diamond of that description to be found anywhere in London and I had to start making inquiries in Los Angeles, Amsterdam and Belgium. I'm still looking!

A million-plus pounds is a lot of money for a ring, which is why at one moment I thought maybe I should get a silver Ferrari instead. When I asked Robert how much this would cost, the price seemed so reasonable compared to the ring, I thought: 'Well, maybe I will have both!'

Why? *Because I can!*

I felt perfectly justified. I had, after all, spent more than forty years working my socks off – and I was in that kind of mood. What had driven me in the beginning was burning ambition. I was a docker's daughter who had big dreams. Our back yard in Scottie Road, Liverpool, was where we kept the coal and where our loo was situated; and when I saw my first Doris Day movie, which featured a 'back yard' that consisted of three acres of lawn, I'd thought, 'I want a bit of that. I wanna be famous.'

I'd also been a loyal, caring wife and mother, and I was now determined to spend the rest of my life pleasing myself.

Earlier in the year I'd been a bit down in the mouth at the thought of being sixty. I'd wanted to fight it! In an ideal world, I would have lied about my age, but I knew I couldn't get away with that. The press had known how old I was ever since I had a Number One hit record and celebrated my twenty-first birthday on the stage of the London Palladium.

When I was thinking about the party invitations, I didn't want to say how old I was going to be, but most of the people on my guest list knew it was my sixtieth. Jimmy Tarbuck didn't. He, charming man, phoned Robert and said, 'How old is the old cow going to be?'

One way and another, the thought of being sixty was a bit depressing, especially as I kept getting things through the post about hoists and stair-lifts, OAP bus passes and railcards! But then I had a change of heart and thought: 'Stuff it! I'm not sixty – I'm *sexty*. And even though I don't take so much as a vitamin pill, I've never felt fitter or been in better shape. I'm a picture of health, I'm a size eight and I can dress stylishly in tight-fitting, stone-washed jeans, shirts and ankle boots. What have I got to worry about? I don't have to dress for my age, I can dress to my size.'

For the first time in my life, I felt I could do exactly as I pleased. If I wanted to boogie on the dance floor with my mates, I could; if I wanted to wear orange and purple and drive a pink Cadillac, I could. I had nothing to prove any more and I was lucky enough to have sufficient money to indulge myself.

'Blow it,' I thought, 'I'm going to have fun. From now on, I'm not doing anything I don't want to do. I'm going to enjoy myself – big time.'

Robert, Ben and Jack were a bit concerned about the Ferrari. I am their mum after all – and they were worried about me getting carried away and driving too fast! It was a new experience for them to see their mum in that light, but it was also a new experience for me, and I was having a ball. In fact, one of the nicest thing about reaching *sexty* is that I felt I could take risks.

Robert did his best to reason with me: 'You wouldn't have let Dad have a Ferrari, would you?' he said. 'You'd have panicked every time he got behind the wheel.'

That was true!

'Anyway,' he added, 'Ferraris are so low down, you'll find it very uncomfortable getting in and out of one. Why don't you get an Aston Martin? They're much classier.'

Ever since then, I've been thinking about an Aston Martin, but the pink diamond remains my current priority. I can't kill myself with that.

'Hey, I'm gonna be *sexty*,' I kept telling myself. 'What have I got to lose? I don't care what people think. I don't know how much longer I've got on this earth, so I'm just going to go for it.'

I knew some people would say, 'Poor old Cilla, she's having her second childhood.' But whenever I worried about that, I thought about Joan Collins. She's an inspiration. She looks fabulous, is older than I am, and she can still do the splits!

Bobby had died when he was fifty-seven, so he would always be fifty-seven. It was very strange to think that I was now older than he would ever be. I couldn't get my head around that. But reaching sixty held no great fears for me. I had faced the worst thing that could have happened when he died. The coming birthday did make me think about my own mortality, though. I found myself wondering how long I had, even feeling as healthy as I did, but such thoughts made me all the more determined to go for it.

What's It All About?

The moment Bobby had become ill, God had gone right out the window – and, having been brought up as a Roman Catholic, I was left at sea spiritually. 'What kind of God would let that happen?' I kept saying to myself.

I still haven't been able to answer that question, but my faith is slowly returning and I'm very glad about that. I certainly believe Bobby's spirit is still with me, and that he will always be a part of my life. When he died, my grief was so overwhelming, I often drew the curtains and stayed in bed. But then I pulled myself together and began to spend more time with my single friends who taught me a different way of life.

I knew my birthday celebrations would be a bittersweet time, and that I would miss Bobby like hell, but I also knew he would be proud of me, and that he'd be up there, saying, 'Good on you, girl.'

Once I'd come to terms with being sixty, I was proud to be a senior citizen and I started to find all the discount stuff I was getting through the post very funny. I even decided to apply for a bus pass, so that I could frame it. When Savage phoned me one day, he said, 'They'll be asking you to do the adverts for those walk-in baths next.'

'I'll be delighted,' I replied, between fits of giggles. Then I added, 'My party's going to be a real northern knees-up.'

'Will there be a punch-up?' he asked.

'I wouldn't be at all surprised,' I replied.

Depression over, my party plans were well under way. I hired a black-and-silver marquee, which looked absolutely stunning, decided to serve Dom Perignon champagne, and chose to wear jeans and a psychedelic waistcoat.

When Saturday, 31 May came, it really was a star-studded bash with friends travelling to Denham from the four corners of the earth. I had two hundred guests, and the Scouse contingent was well represented by my brothers, Bobby's brothers, Billy Hatton, Joey Bower and Dave Lovelady of The Fourmost, Cyn Lennon and Mike McCartney. Paul and Heather were out of the country, but the next day when I was opening my presents,

What's It All About?

I found a really lovely letter from Paul. Other guests included Ronnie Corbett, Tim Rice, Jimmy Tarbuck, Joan Collins, Gloria Hunniford, Pat Booth, Patti Boyd, George and Judy Martin, Roger McGough, Ian Wright, Graeme Souness, the Prince of Jaipur (I know!), Jude Law (I know!!) – and, of course, my old muckers Biggins, Savage and Dale. There were also a lot of TV people, including Michael Hurll, Paul Jackson, David Liddiment and John Birt. Nasty Nigel Lythgoe, who produced the American *Pop Idol*, flew over from LA with his wife Bonnie, and, of course, Pat came in from LA as well.

The inside of the marquee was all decked out in white linen and on each table there was a top hat with silver streamers and balloons, and tambourines and maracas for anybody who wanted them. Which everybody did!

We started the evening with the Dom Perignon and canapés, but we also had an Art Deco bar for those who grew tired of drinking champagne! A disco band played all the sixties pop classics and Tommy Sandhu, who produced the club mix of 'Step Inside Love' as a present for me, DJed when the band was taking a break. As people arrived at seven-thirty, Tommy played a CD that Eddie Healey, a friend of mine in Barbados, had made of Nat King Cole, Ella Fitzgerald and Frank Sinatra classics.

Penny's sister Sue, who has her own catering business, did the food, which was absolutely sensational, with something to suit everybody's taste. There was baked salmon, coronation chicken, spicy lamb on the spit, and loads of delicious salads. For desserts there were lemon tarts and strawberry tarts. It was a help-yourself do, but to keep everything running smoothly, we had two members of waiting staff at each table.

Jimmy settled everybody down with a heart-warming speech about me and some really lovely reminiscences about Bobby. Another very nice moment was the cutting of the birthday cake that Jane Asher had made. It was in the shape of the basque that I had worn for the Royal Command, and it had a very discreet '60' in the corner.

When it came to the 'turns', Savage was the first one up. He sang 'I'm Evil', followed by a very naughty version of 'It Had To Be You' that could never have been played on radio! When he called me up, I sang 'Dancing In The Street' and Nat King Cole's 'Let There Be Love', then Jimmy sang 'Johnny Be Good', followed by Kenny Lynch and Tim Rice doing a whole medley of Mick Jagger songs, including '(I Can't Get No) Satisfaction'. They were brilliant turns.

Later, when I was having a lovely slow dance with Jude Law, he asked me who I would like to play me in the film about Brian Epstein that he is going to star in. I had absolutely no idea! 'That's one for your casting director,' I said. 'But whoever it is, Jude, she'll need to have a Scouse accent and an instantly recognisable laugh!'

At six a.m., ten and a half hours after the party started, the hard core was still there, having a singsong and playing the tambourines and maracas. Kenny Lynch was the last to leave.

And of course I had been enjoying one boogie after another with Cynthia Lennon and Patti Boyd, the same evening that the final programme of *Blind Date* was televised. The show had been a staple of the Saturday night schedules for eighteen years and a question mark was still hanging over its future. It seemed absolutely right, though, that the last show of that series – and my last *Blind Date* ever – should have coincided with my sixtieth birthday celebrations.

~

For about three years after Bobby died I couldn't imagine ever falling in love again, but in 2003 I found I could for the first time envisage finding a new man to share the future with. He would have to be handsome, solvent, not too young and above all acceptable to Robert, Ben and Jack. The problem is that all the good ones are married! So, as I will only settle for the best, there's no special man at my side as I finish writing this book – and I am honestly not at all sure I want one. I'm not lonely and I'm thoroughly enjoying being able to please myself.

'Do I *really* want to fight over the TV remote again?' I ask myself. 'Do I *really* want to be in a relationship?'

It would be a bonus to share all the fun I am having with someone, but I'm not at all sure I want to share my entire life. I'm only just discovering how enjoyable independence can be and, let's face it, there aren't many eligible men of my age who have kept themselves in good nick, while a toy boy wouldn't pass my 'Samantha Juste test'. In my view, if a feller doesn't know who Samantha is, then we won't have anything in common. (For anyone who missed the sixties, Samantha was a teenage model who landed a spot as 'disc girl' on *Top of the Pops*, then married Micky Dolenz of The Monkees.)

Meanwhile, I'm happy being in charge of the remote control. All that's changed for the moment is that while I used to say, 'No – I don't want another man in my life', now I say 'Perhaps.'

After nearly four years of grieving for Bobby, it's only in the last five months that I've not needed to take to my bed for twenty-four hours. For me that is an incredible achievement, but I'm in no rush, believe me, to meet a special man. I do get hit on, though. I don't think I've ever been out to lunch with my girlfriends when a guy hasn't sent over a bottle or a glass of champagne. I've met some men who have come on to me and I've had to say, 'Look, I'd rather sleep with your wife than you'! I compare everyone to Bobby and no one measures up to him. He was an awesome person. He had no O- or A-levels, but he was an intelligent, self-educated, successful entrepreneur and nothing fazed him.

To say that the past four years of my life have been fraught is an understatement. The two cornerstones of my life, Bobby and *Blind Date*, have gone, and it's only now that I realise how insulated I have been. My eyes have been opened big time and I can see that I took so much for granted. I've come to appreciate that the real world is very different from the protected one I knew.

Although I've been out on a string of dates in recent months, none of these has come close to romance. Some of my married friends still try to set me up with a guy but, when I meet some of them, I think, 'Mmmm, I know why *you* are single – or divorced!'

In any case, whoever I brought home would have to pass 'the committee'. Joan Collins is on it – and so are Biggins, Savage and Dale, and my three sons. I call them 'the committee' because they're always saying they know what is best for me. It would be a brave man to get through that lot – and I sometimes think there isn't a hope in hell of anyone making it. It's a bit like my quest for the flawless pink diamond. He would have to be just perfect.

~

In the same year that I cast off *Blind Date*, celebrated forty years in show-biz, qualified for my bus pass, and had my birthday bash, I was planning to take a big gamble and open a nightclub in the West End of London. That's been a lifelong ambition of mine – and one that Bobby never approved of. He always felt it was far too risky. But I'm beginning a new chapter in my life and I'm doing this for me.

I plan to become the new Regine, the legendary New York club hostess whose style I've always admired. The club will be open to all – I won't do the members-only thing. I hate that kind of snobbery. There will be a VIP area, but it won't be closed off. There will be a gi-normous bar – one that you can eat at – and we'll serve simple food like steak sandwiches with fine champagne. And there'll even be a private boudoir for me to change in if I feel like getting out on the floor and leading a sing-song. I want the club to be a place where people can have fun, not a poseur's paradise – and I plan to have the most fun of all.

I'm so excited about this. I've never found the perfect club for me and, when I quit *Blind Date*, I thought, 'Why don't I open one? There's nothing to stop me doing that now.'

My friends have been wonderful in recent times. I honestly don't know what I would have done without them.

What's It All About?

As well as my 'gay mafia', my best mates are my three Pats – LA Pat, Patti Boyd and Pat Booth, and Lynda La Plante. The girls are known collectively as 'The GirlsClub' or the 'Cindicate'!

Recently, we hooked up with Bassey for dinner at the swanky Annabel club. I won £500 on the roulette tables at the casino upstairs, then we decamped to Sketch, a notoriously expensive restaurant/bar, before ending up at the nightclub Chinawhite, where we stayed till the wee small hours. It was embarrassing because they turned the lights on and started sweeping up around us!

However much fun I have, though, Bobby is never far from my thoughts. I loved him so much. Not a day goes by when I don't think about him. He's with me every morning when I wake up and before I go to bed at night. But I have learned to appreciate my own space and I'm truly enjoying the life I have now. I have three wonderful sons whom I adore, each of them reminding me of Bobby in their own way. And meanwhile, I'm having a ball and I can do what I like. I may be a pensioner now, but I'm a pensioner who will soon have a flawless pink diamond on her finger, an Aston Martin in the drive, and a nightclub in central London.

At this point, some people might say 'enough', and settle down to a quiet retirement. Good luck to them, I say – but I can't help feeling that, strange as it may sound with sixty years behind me, life is beginning again.

I believe that life is for living. Every moment. That's what it's all about.

discography
1963–2003

Researched and Compiled by Stephen Munns www.cillablack.com

Singles

Release Date	A side b/w B side, Record Label & Catalogue Number	Highest Chart Pos.
27/09/1963	**LOVE OF THE LOVED** (Parlophone R5065)	35
	b/w Shy Of Love	
31/01/1964	**ANYONE WHO HAD A HEART** (Parlophone R5101)	1
	b/w Just For You	
01/05/1964	**YOU'RE MY WORLD** (Parlophone R5133)	1
	b/w Suffer Now I Must	
31/07/1964	**IT'S FOR YOU** (Parlophone R5162)	7
	b/w He Won't Ask Me	
1965	**IS IT LOVE ?** (Capitol, USA 5373) [US-only release]	133
	b/w One Little Voice	
08/01/1965	**YOU'VE LOST THAT LOVIN' FEELIN'** (Parlophone R5225)	2
	b/w Is It Love?	
15/04/1965	**I'VE BEEN WRONG BEFORE** (Parlophone R5265)	17
	b/w I Don't Want To Know	
07/01/1966	**LOVE'S JUST A BROKEN HEART** (Parlophone R5395)	5
	b/w Yesterday	
25/03/1966	**ALFIE** (Parlophone R5427)	9
	b/w Night Time Is Here	
03/06/1966	**DON'T ANSWER ME** (Parlophone R5463)	6
	b/w The Right One Is Left	
14/10/1966	**A FOOL AM I** (Parlophone R5515)	13
	b/w For No One	

Discography

02/06/1967   **WHAT GOOD AM I?** (Parlophone R5608)   24
b/w Over My Head

17/11/1967   **I ONLY LIVE TO LOVE YOU** (Parlophone R5652)   26
b/w From Now On

09/03/1968   **STEP INSIDE LOVE** (Parlophone R5674)   8
b/w I Couldn't Take My Eyes Off You

07/06/1968   **WHERE IS TOMORROW?** (Parlophone R5706)   9
b/w Work Is A Four-Letter Word

07/02/1969   **SURROUND YOURSELF WITH SORROW** (Parlophone R5759) 3
b/w London Bridge

27/06/1969   **CONVERSATIONS** (Parlophone R5785)   7
b/w Liverpool Lullaby

21/11/1969   **IF I THOUGHT YOU'D EVER CHANGE YOUR MIND**   20
(Parlophone R5820)
b/w It Feels So Good

04/12/1970   **CHILD OF MINE** (Parlophone R5879)   -
b/w That's Why I Love You

15/11/1971   **SOMETHING TELLS ME** (Parlophone R5924)   3
b/w La La La lu

11/02/1972   **THE WORLD I WISH FOR YOU** (Parlophone R5938)   -
b/w Down In The City

17/11/1972   **YOU YOU YOU** (Parlophone R5972)   -
b/w Silly Wasn't I?

04/01/1974   **BABY WE CAN'T GO WRONG** (EMI 2107)   36
b/w Someone

24/05/1974   **I'LL HAVE TO SAY I LOVE YOU IN A SONG** (EMI 2169) -
b/w Never Run Out

25/10/1974   **HE WAS A WRITER** (EMI 2227)   -
b/w Anything You Might Say

28/03/1975   **ALFIE DARLING** (EMI 2278)   -
b/w Little Bit Of Understanding

25/07/1975   **I'LL TAKE A TANGO** (EMI 2328)   -
b/w To Know Him Is To Love Him

12/03/1976   **LITTLE THINGS MEAN A LOT** (EMI 2438)   -
b/w It's Now

09/1976   **EASY IN YOUR COMPANY** (EMI 2532)   -
b/w I Believe (When I Fall In Love, It Will Be Forever)

15/07/1977   **I WANTED TO CALL IT OFF** (EMI 2658)   -
b/w Keep Your Mind On Love

12/05/1978   **SILLY BOY** (EMI 2791)   -
b/w I Couldn't Make My Mind Up

What's It All About?

22/09/1978	**THE OTHER WOMAN** (EMI 2840)	-
	b/w Opening Night	
09/1985	**THERE'S A NEED IN ME** (Towerbell TOW74)	-
	b/w You've Lost That Lovin' Feelin'	
12/1985	**SURPRISE, SURPRISE** (Towerbell TOW81)	-
	b/w Put Your Heart Where Your Love Is	
06/09/1993	**THROUGH THE YEARS** (Columbia CD6596982)	54
	b/w Through The Years (Orchestral Version),	
	The Feelings Just Get Stronger (Through The Years),	
	Through The Years (Do You Remember?)	
18/10/1993	**HEART AND SOUL with Dusty Springfield**	75
	(Columbia CD6598562)	
	b/w Heart And Soul (A Cappella Remix),	
	Heart And Soul (Instrumental), A Dream Come True	
06/12/1993	**YOU'LL NEVER WALK ALONE with Barry Manilow**	-
	(Columbia CD6600132)	
	b/w You'll Never Walk Alone (Hope In Your Heart Mix), Through The Years	

Specially Recorded International Singles

03/ 1968	**M'INNAMORO "STEP INSIDE LOVE"**	-
	(Dischi Ricordi S.P.A, Italy SIR20.080)	
	b/w Non c'e Domani 'Where Is Tomorrow?'	
1976	**FANTASY** (Private Stock, USA PVS45.077) *b/w It's Now*	-

Extended Plays

Release Date	*Title, Record Label, Catalogue Number & Track Listing*	*Highest Chart Pos.*
04/1964	**ANYONE WHO HAD A HEART** (Parlophone GEP8901)	5
	b/w Just For You, Love Of The Loved, Shy Of Love	
10/1964	**IT'S FOR YOU** (Parlophone GEP8916)	12
	b/w He Won't Ask Me, You're My World, Suffer Now I Must	
08/1966	**CILLA'S HITS** (Parlophone GEP8954)	6
	inc. Don't Answer Me, The Right One Is Left, Alfie, Night Time Is Here	
06/1967	**TIME FOR CILLA** (Parlophone GEP8967)	-
	inc. Abyssinian Secret, Trees And Loneliness, There I Go, Time	

Studio Albums

25/01/1965	**CILLA** (Parlophone PMC1243/PCS3063 (Mono/Stereo))	5
	Goin' Out Of My Head, Every Little Bit Hurts, Baby It's You,	
	Dancing In The Street, Come To Me, Ol' Man River, One Little Voice,	
	I'm Not Alone Anymore, Whatcha Gonna Do 'Bout It, Love Letters ,	
	This Empty Place, You'd Be So Nice To Come Home To	

Discography

18/04/1966   **CILLA SINGS A RAINBOW**   4
(Parlophone PMC/PCS 7004 (Mono/Stereo))
Love's Just A Broken Heart, Lover's Concerto,
Make It Easy On Yourself, One Two Three,
(There's) No Place To Hide, When I Fall In Love, Yesterday,
Sing A Rainbow, Baby I'm Yours, The Real Thing,
Everything I Touch Turns To Tears, In A Woman's Eyes,
My Love Come Home

06/04/1968   **SHER-OO!** (Parlophone PMC/PCS 7041 (Mono/Stereo))   7
What The World Needs Now Is Love, Suddenly You Love Me,
This Is The First Time, Follow The Path Of The Stars, Misty Roses,
Take Me In Your Arms And Love Me, Yo-Yo,
Something's Gotten Hold Of My Heart, Step Inside Love,
A Man And A Woman, I Couldn't Take My Eyes Off You, Follow me

23/05/1969   **SURROUND YOURSELF WITH CILLA** (Parlophone PCS7079)   -
Aquarius, Without Him, Only Forever Will Do,
You'll Never Get to Heaven, Forget Him, It'll Never Happen Again,
Think Of Me, I Am A Woman, Words, Red Rubber Ball,
Liverpool Lullaby, Surround Yourself With Sorrow

03/07/1970   **SWEET INSPIRATION** (Parlophone PCS7103)   42
Sweet Inspiration, Put A Little Love In Your Heart, The April Fool,
I Can't Go On Living Without You, From Both Sides Now,
Across The Universe, Black Paper Roses, Mysterious People,
Dear Madame, Oh Pleasure Man, Little Pleasure Acre,
For Once In My Life, Rule Britannia

05/1971   **IMAGES** (Parlophone PCS7128)   -
Faded Images, Junk, Your Song, Just Friends, It's Different Now,
First Of May, (They Long To Be) Close To You, Rainbow,
Make It With You, Our Brand New World, Sad Sad Song,
Bridge Over Troubled Water

01/1973   **DAY BY DAY WITH CILLA** (Parlophone PCS7155)   -
Without You, Thank Heavens I've Got You, Help Me Jesus,
The Long And Winding Road, I Hate Sunday,
I Don't Know How To Love Him, Day By Day,
I've Still Got My Heart Joe, Sleep Song,
Gypsies Tramps And Thieves, Winterwood, Oh My Love

07/06/1974   **IN MY LIFE** (EMI 3031)   -
Flashback, I'll Have To Say I Love You In A Song, Everything I Own,
Baby We Can't Go Wrong, Someone, Daydreamer, In My Life,
Never Run Out (Of You), Let Him In, The Air That I Breathe,
Like A Song, I Believed It All

What's It All About?

03/1976   **IT MAKES ME FEEL GOOD** (EMI 3108)
Something About You, I'll Take A Tango, September Love Affair,
Lay The Music Down, San Diego Serenade, Heartbeat,
Running Out Of World, To Know Him Is To Love Him,
It Makes Me Feel Good, Lay It All Down,
One Step From Your Arms, Lovin' Land

06/1978   **MODERN PRISCILLA** (EMI 3232)
Silly Boy, The Other Woman, Me And The Elephant,
Keep Your Mind On Love, Putting It Down To The Way I Feel,
Sugar Daddy, Opening Night, Brooklyn,
I Couldn't Make My Mind Up, Heart Get Ready For Love,
Love Lines, Platform Rocker

03/08/1980   **ESPECIALLY FOR YOU** (K-TEL ONE1085)
Baby Don't Change Your Mind, Sometimes When We Touch,
Just the Way You Are, Talking In Your Sleep, You Don't Bring Me Flowers,
How Deep Is Your Love, Bright Eyes, Don't Cry For Me Argentina,
When Will I See You Again, You Needed Me, If You Leave Me Now,
When I Need You, Knowing Me Knowing You , Still,
When A Child Is Born, Do That To Me One More Time

07/10/1985   **SURPRISINGLY CILLA** (Towerbell TOWLP14)
Surprise Surprise, I Know Him So Well,
You're My World (1985 Re-recording), One More Night,
There's A Need in Me, Conversations (1985 Re-recording),
Step Inside Love (1985 Re-recording), We're In This Love Together,
I See Forever In Your Eyes, Put Your Heart Where Your Love Is,
That's Already Taken, You've Lost That Lovin' Feelin' (1985 Re-recording)

12/11/1990   **CILLA'S WORLD** (Virgin, Australia CICHCD1)
The (Solar Powered, Practical, Combustible, Compatible,
Responsibly, Recyclable) Machine, Don't Argue With An Elephant,
A Little More Green, ABC Of The World, Penguin Strut, Rain,
Trees, Eggs, Panda, Personality, Weather Song/Sunshine Medley,
Please Don't Call Me A Koala Bear, Let's Hear It For Skin,
The End Of The Day, Goodnight

20/09/1993   **THROUGH THE YEARS** (Columbia 4746502)   41
Through The Years, That's What Friends Are For (with Cliff Richard),
Here, There And Everywhere, Heart And Soul (with Dusty Springfield),
Anyone Who Had A Heart (1993 Re-recording), A Dream Come True,
You'll Never Walk Alone (with Barry Manilow), Streets Of London,
You're My World (1993 Re-recording), From A Distance,
Will You Love Me Tomorrow?, Through The Years (Reprise)

Soundtrack Albums

02/1965   FERRY ACROSS THE MERSEY (Columbia/EMI SCX3544)   -
            'Is It Love' the song Cilla performed in the movie appears on the soundtrack
18/05/1999 EDGE OF SEVENTEEN (Razor & Tie, USA RE828472)   -
            American coming-of-age movie featuring 'You're My World'

Essential Reissue / Compilation Albums

1965   IS IT LOVE? (Capitol, USA ST2308)   -
            US-only repackaged version of Cilla's debut LP 'Cilla'
30/12/1968 THE BEST OF CILLA BLACK   21
            (Parlophone PMC/PCS 7065 (Mono/Stereo))

17/01/1983 THE VERY BEST OF CILLA BLACK   20
            (Parlophone/EMI EMITV38)
05/1987   LOVE SONGS (K-TEL ONCD5126)   -
            CD reissue of Cilla's 1980 'Especially For You' album,
            with different sleeve
15/09/1997 THE ABBEY ROAD DECADE 1963–73 (EMI CILLA1)   -
            65 track set of Cilla's A&B side singles and EP songs
            plus unreleased rarities
22/04/2002 CILLA/CILLA SINGS A RAINBOW (EMI 5388482)   -
            Mono CD issue of Cilla's 1965/66 studio albums
26/08/2002 THE BEST OF CILLA BLACK (EMI 5414442)   -
            CD issue of Cilla's 1968 compilation. Includes 11 bonus
            singles and rarities
26/05/2003 THE BEST OF 1963–78 (EMI 5841242)   -
            An epic 3CD, 80-track journey through 15 years of hit singles
            & albums featuring essential recordings all digitally remastered in
            STEREO. Comes with a comprehensive booklet and includes 7
            Previously Unreleased recordings

Unreleased Songs

circa 1970 TEA BREAK * (Produced by George Martin for EMI)
circa 1975 YOU'RE (TRULY) SENSATIONAL *
            (Produced by David Mackay for EMI)
circa 1976 BAD CASE OF ROCK 'N' ROLL (Produced by David Mackay for EMI)
circa 1978 SONGS (Produced by Mike Hurst for EMI)
circa 1985 NEEDLE IN A HAYSTACK *
            (Produced by David Mackay for Towerbell)

* Master tape for this song has not been located/verified as definitely being a Cilla Black
recording.

index

index